A Just Society for Ireland? 1964–1987

Also by Ciara Meehan

THE COSGRAVE PARTY: A History of Cumann na nGaedheal, 1923–33 (2010)

A Just Society for Ireland? 1964–1987

Ciara Meehan
University of Hertfordshire

© Ciara Meehan 2013

All rights reserved. No reproduction, copy or transmission of this publication may be made without written permission.

No portion of this publication may be reproduced, copied or transmitted save with written permission or in accordance with the provisions of the Copyright, Designs and Patents Act 1988, or under the terms of any licence permitting limited copying issued by the Copyright Licensing Agency, Saffron House, 6–10 Kirby Street, London EC1N 8TS.

Any person who does any unauthorized act in relation to this publication may be liable to criminal prosecution and civil claims for damages.

The author has asserted her right to be identified as the author of this work in accordance with the Copyright, Designs and Patents Act 1988.

First published 2013 by
PALGRAVE MACMILLAN

Palgrave Macmillan in the UK is an imprint of Macmillan Publishers Limited, registered in England, company number 785998, of Houndmills, Basingstoke, Hampshire RG21 6XS.

Palgrave Macmillan in the US is a division of St Martin's Press LLC, 175 Fifth Avenue, New York, NY 10010.

Palgrave Macmillan is the global academic imprint of the above companies and has companies and representatives throughout the world.

Palgrave® and Macmillan® are registered trademarks in the United States, the United Kingdom, Europe and other countries.

ISBN 978–1–137–02205–9

This book is printed on paper suitable for recycling and made from fully managed and sustained forest sources. Logging, pulping and manufacturing processes are expected to conform to the environmental regulations of the country of origin.

A catalogue record for this book is available from the British Library.

A catalog record for this book is available from the Library of Congress.

Typeset by MPS Limited, Chennai, India.

For Aisling, Cerrie, Pamela and Susan

Contents

List of Figures viii

Acknowledgements ix

Note on Terminology xi

Introduction 1
1 A New Ireland? 6
2 Winning the Party 20
3 1965: The First Failure 41
4 1969: The Second Failure 63
5 From Leader in Crisis to Leader in Government 83
6 National Coalition, 1973–77 105
7 1980s: New Leader, New Party 148
8 The Constitutional Crusade 162
9 A Liberal Ireland? 194

Notes 198

Bibliography 233

Index 244

List of Figures

1. Free State government meeting, January 1923. Reproduced by kind permission of UCD Archives — 100
2. James Dillon addressing Fine Gael Ard Fheis. Reproduced with kind permission of Fine Gael — 100
3. Declan Costello. Reproduced with kind permission of St Michael's House — 101
4. Declan Costello and Patrick Hillery. Reproduced with kind permission of St Michael's House — 101
5. Liam Cosgrave addressing Fine Gael Ard Fheis, c. 1969. Reproduced with kind permission of Fine Gael — 102
6. Fine Gael Ard Fheis under Garret FitzGerald's leadership. Reproduced with kind permission of Fine Gael — 102
7. Garret FitzGerald opening new party headquarters on Upper Mount Street. Reproduced with kind permission of Fine Gael — 103
8. First national conference of Young Fine Gael, November 1977. Reproduced with kind permission of Fine Gael — 103
9. Garret FitzGerald on the campaign trail with Tom Raftery for 1984 European Elections. Reproduced with kind permission of Fine Gael — 104
10. Leaflet from the 1987 general election. Reproduced with kind permission of both Alan Kinsella and Fine Gael — 104

Acknowledgements

This book owes much to many people. I am grateful to Jimmy Deenihan, who took such an interest in the early stages and organised a lunch with Declan Costello to discuss the project. Unfortunately, a planned series of interviews with Mr Costello could not be conducted due to a deterioration of his health and subsequent death as research for this book was being undertaken, but I am glad to have had the opportunity to discuss with him some of his recollections. I am grateful to Joan Gleeson and the Costello family for their continued interest in the book. Jim Dooge and Garret FitzGerald also passed away during the research stages; their generosity of time and willingness to discuss at length their political careers will be sorely missed by researchers.

Much of the research for this book was conducted during my time as an Irish Research Council for the Humanities and Social Sciences (IRCHSS) Postdoctoral Fellow at the UCD School of History and Archives. I gratefully acknowledge the IRCHSS for their generous funding. I had the good fortune at that time to share an office with Niamh Cullen, Patrick Walsh and Kevin O'Sullivan. I learned much from our discussions during those two invaluable years – and I am very thankful for their continued support and input into this book.

I owe debts of gratitude to a number of people who have been extremely generous with their time and feedback on most, or all, of the manuscript. John Bowman read drafts with great attention to detail and offered sharp insights. David McCullagh not only shared research but also cast a critical eye over chapters in a very timely manner. The support and advice of Paul Rouse was, as always, invaluable, and helped make completion of this book possible. Brian Girvin, Andrew Haworth, Jane Irwin, Justin Dolan Stover and Graham O'Neill also read various sections. I am particularly grateful to Paul O'Brien for his patience with my endless stream of technical questions. Thanks are also due to the anonymous readers for their helpful observations. Naturally, any errors or omissions are my own.

To the following people who assisted in a variety of different ways I extend my thanks: Margaret Ayres, Frank Barry, Niall Brophy, Brian Costello, Paschal Donohoe, Mark Duncan, Diarmaid Ferriter, Seán McKiernan, Ciaran McMahon, Gary Murphy, Alan Power, Kevin Rafter and Jillian van Turnhout. I must acknowledge in particular Claire McGing who has been unfailingly generous in sharing sources, ideas and her expertise on the position of women in Irish politics. The discussion of women's issues in Chapters 6 and 7 is partially based on research we carried out in preparation for papers we jointly delivered in 2012 at the Social History Society's conference in Brighton and for the 'BiblioFiles' series at the National Library of Ireland.

x Acknowledgements

I am indebted to the many politicians, journalists and participants in the events of the period who shared their recollections and, in some cases, also made available to me privately held papers: Vincent Browne, John Bruton, Stephen Collins, Liam Cosgrave, the late Declan Costello, Eamon Delaney, the late Jim Dooge, Jim Dorgan, Alan Dukes, the late Garret FitzGerald, Dónal Flynn, Paddy Harte, Gemma Hussey, Frank Kelly, Cormac Lucey, Maurice Manning, Gay Mitchell, Jim O'Keeffe, Mary O'Rourke, Maureen O'Sullivan, Ruairi Quinn, Barbara Sweetman-FitzGerald and Michael van Turnhout. Though not always quoted directly in the book, their recollections helped shape my writing.

I am grateful to the staff of the National Archives of Ireland, the National Library of Ireland, especially Mary Broderick, the Irish Labour History Museum and Archive and, in particular, Seamus Helferty and UCD Archives. Thanks are also due to Fianna Fáil and Fine Gael for permission to access the parties' respective papers at UCD Archives, and to the Costello family for access to the John A. Costello papers. I extend my appreciation to UCD Archives, Patsy Carton and Patricia Doherty at St Michael's House, Alan Kinsella of the Irish Election Literature Blog, and Jim Duffy at Fine Gael Headquarters for providing photographs and granting permission to reproduce them in this book.

At Palgrave Macmillan, I would like to sincerely thank Jenny McCall and Holly Tyler who have been patient, understanding and a pleasure to work with.

I can only express profound gratitude to the people who have lived through the ups and downs of this project alongside me. The support and patience of my parents, Patrick and Jennifer, continues unabated. I would be lost without the friendship of Cerrie Byrne, Pamela and Susan Casciani-Dawson and Aisling Corby: this book is dedicated to them in acknowledgment of that fact.

Note on Terminology

The terminology current at the time has been retained. For example, the description 'handicapped' rather than 'disabled' is used when citing the policies outlined in *Towards a Just Society*. Likewise, it would be anachronistic to substitute 'single parent' in the place of 'unmarried mother'.

Introduction

The 1960s were a period of change in Ireland. Political, economic and social thought was revised as a result of Vatican II, the arrival of television and the potential of EEC (European Economic Community) membership. That decade also marked the passing of the revolutionary generation from political power. This book examines the attempts made by a new generation of political thinkers and activists – the first to be born in an independent Ireland – to bring about transformative change in Irish politics and to reshape society. It focuses largely on the actions of Fine Gael, then Ireland's second largest political party, and, in particular, on two of its major figures: Declan Costello and Garret FitzGerald. It traces the continuities and discontinuities between Costello's Just Society policy document of 1964/65 and FitzGerald's Constitutional Crusade in the 1980s. In exploring the theme of transformation, the agents for external change are also considered: the legislature, judiciary, EEC and various lobby groups. In doing so, this book offers a new interpretation of Irish politics and society over a period of three decades, taking seriously the alternative vision offered by Costello in the 1960s, while also questioning some of the myths that have surrounded the Just Society's formulation, impact and legacy.

Fine Gael is a party with an identity crisis; this book traces its roots. The origins are typically attributed to Garret FitzGerald, his constitutional crusade and his efforts to recreate Fine Gael as a social democratic party in the 1980s. But it is necessary to take a longer view: one that stretches back to the 1960s, to Declan Costello and a growing socially minded wing of the party. In 1964 Costello put before Fine Gael a set of proposals designed to transform the party and which offered a blueprint for a new Ireland through greater state involvement. They represented a significant break with traditional Fine Gael policy – particularly in the area of private enterprise – and caused considerable unease within the party, especially with its rural members. Costello struggled to have his proposals accepted by the parliamentary party in 1964, and even when they were adopted as official policy for the 1965 general election, the leadership was not united behind the initiative.

Benefiting from access to the privately held minute books of the parliamentary party for the 1950s and 1960s, this book explores the internal workings of the party at a critical juncture in its history, and reconstructs the private debate surrounding Costello's proposals. Although the policy had faded away by the 1970s, with the Just Society merely serving as an inspiring slogan or a useful point of reference, the setbacks experienced in the 1960s should not be too strongly over-stated. For the first time, the central role played by Declan Costello in the longer-term transformation of Fine Gael is disclosed. Although he was never party leader and the Just Society effectively remained an un-tested document, he effected change by encouraging a new generation of politicians into the party, most notably Garret FitzGerald, who would go on to play a key role. Furthermore, it was his agenda for change that paved the way for FitzGerald. As Jim O'Keeffe, Fine Gael TD (Teachta Dála; Member of Parliament) for Cork South-West from 1977 until 2011, put it, Costello was a 'John the Baptist as far as Garret was concerned'.[1]

When Fine Gael formed the National Coalition with Labour in 1973, it was the first occasion on which the party found itself in government since adopting Costello's proposals. Costello had announced his retirement from politics in 1967, but was convinced to return because of the threat posed by the arms crisis. He was not given a seat at the cabinet table, however, and was instead appointed Attorney General. As a consequence, he did not contribute to policy formulation, although the coalition did implement a number of social progressive measures. The government's legislative agenda also attempted to address issues of private morality, most notably relating to the sale of contraceptives, which had been completely absent from Costello's Just Society document. This reflected a shift away from social justice towards pluralism that would become more significantly pronounced during Garret FitzGerald's time as Taoiseach in the 1980s.

The Constitutional Crusade and, in particular, the 1985 Anglo-Irish Agreement dominated profiles of Garret FitzGerald following his death in 2011. Reference was also made to his role as a supporter of the Just Society. FitzGerald was not yet a member of the party when Costello formulated his ideas; nonetheless, he had assisted in drafting *Towards a Just Society* for the 1965 election. He recalled of the original eight-point plan: 'They were very much his ideas and not mine; I would have done them a bit differently'.[2] An article in the *Irish Independent* after FitzGerald's death observed how he made the Just Society document 'mainstream party policy when he assumed the Fine Gael leadership from 1977'.[3] FitzGerald himself recorded in his autobiography how he enunciated the principles of Costello's document at the time of his accession to the leadership in 1977. This book challenges the notion that FitzGerald was heir to Costello's mantle in the area of policy. Influenced by his Belfast heritage on his mother's side and later by the tensions in Northern Ireland in the 1960s, FitzGerald was more concerned with creating a pluralist society, an interest articulated in a 1964 *Studies* article and in his 1972 book *Towards a New Ireland*.[4] FitzGerald thus had a very different agenda to his colleague, with the result that the Just Society document did not 'define the party for some 20 years', as one commentator suggested.[5]

Shortly after becoming Taoiseach for the first time, FitzGerald set the tone for his government in an interview with Gerald Barry on RTÉ Radio in November 1981. He spoke of how he wanted to 'lead a crusade, a Republican crusade to make this a genuine republic on the principals of Tone and Davis'.[6] His aim was to create a society acceptable to Northern Unionists, which would eventually lead to reunification. During that interview, the word 'sectarian' was repeated several times as FitzGerald spoke of past legislative developments in the Republic. The Constitutional Crusade was derailed almost immediately, however, when FitzGerald agreed to hold a referendum to insert a ban on abortion into the constitution following intense lobbying from pro-life groups. His agenda was dealt a further blow when, in 1986, his referendum to legalise divorce was defeated. On the occasion of FitzGerald's eightieth birthday, John Bowman asked him if he considered his Constitutional Crusade a success. 'In the long run, yes', was the reply, although he conceded that 'it turned out to be premature'.[7]

FitzGerald has been the focus of several biographies written by journalists, with analysis shaped by newspapers, his own writings and, sometimes, personal recollections. Though drawing on similar sources, this book also benefits from the recently released state papers at the National Archives of Ireland for 1981 and 1982, made available to researchers under the thirty-year rule. They offer historians the first opportunity to examine the official record of the inner-workings of FitzGerald's – and Charles Haughey's – time as Taoiseach. They cast important light on some of the major themes of FitzGerald's administration. Most notably, it becomes apparent that after he declared his Constitutional Crusade, he sought to pull back from his commitment to a pro-life referendum. Various inter-departmental correspondence and letters from the pro-life movement disclose much new information about how the Fianna Fáil government and Fine Gael-Labour coalition both grappled with the sensitive and divisive issue. They also offer an insight into the roots of the divergent opinions on the issue of abortion within Fine Gael that resurfaced in 2012/13.

FitzGerald is popularly recalled as a modernising, progressive figure. Paying tribute following his death, the then president Mary McAleese described him as a 'persuasive voice for progressive reform'.[8] Though often presented as a liberal politician, recently released state papers, combined with FitzGerald's own writings, reveal that many of his proposals were shaped by conservative thinking. His attitude in favour of legalising divorce, for example, was particularly telling. Divorce would allow the separated to marry again, rather than simply co-habit with their new partner, thus preserving the institution of marriage: a liberal measure conceived within a conservative framework. Drawing on newly available material, including FitzGerald's own papers shelved at University College Dublin (UCD) Archives, this book seeks to offer a re-assessment of the man considered Fine Gael's most popular leader.

The theme of continuity and change is one touched on in a number of recent publications, including Diarmaid Ferriter's *Transformation of Ireland* and, more particularly, his *Ambiguous Republic* (2012), an extensive and insightful exploration of 1970s Ireland. This book explores this theme over a broader time-frame, from the perspective of both the political elite and ordinary citizens. The manner in which the clash between conservative and liberal viewpoints manifested itself, and the implications this had for policy-making decisions, will be established. In his introduction to the 2008 special edition of *Irish Political Studies* that examines continuity, change and crisis in Ireland from the 1960s, Brian Girvin asked, 'How do we explain these changes, and what impact have they had on social, political and institutional norms and values in Ireland?'[9] The answers were sought in the actions of policy makers and political institutions. This book attempts to give an identity to 'society'. The transformation of Irish society was both exciting and disquieting. Opinions of the ordinary citizen were gleaned from newspapers and magazines, particularly the letters' pages where the intersection between government policy and everyday life can be identified. There is also extensive correspondence from the public contained in the files of the Department of the Taoiseach and the Fine Gael papers. These give an indication of the extent of approval or disapproval for various policy initiatives, while also offering a commentary on Irish society. They confirm the persistence of traditional values at a time of transformation, and reveal how a conservative generation – like the politicians who represented them – struggled to locate their place in and resisted a changing Ireland.

The internal politics of Fine Gael have scarcely been subject to the rigours of academic research. The only history of the party is Brian Maye's *Fine Gael*, which he acknowledges was written by drawing largely on secondary sources.[10] Declan Costello has been virtually overlooked by academic historians, occasionally mentioned briefly in survey histories.[11] This is despite the fact that his proposals represented a significant break with the traditional policy of a party that was inherently conservative, and that the debate he initiated ushered in a fascinating, if tumultuous, phase in Fine Gael's history. The near-silence on his contribution to Irish politics seems peculiar given the extent of the coverage that the Just Society – described by Deaglán de Bréadún as Costello's 'monument'[12] – received at the time of his death in 2011. Although the Just Society was an un-tested policy document produced by a member of the opposition, it is still worthy of consideration for what it reveals about Fine Gael, Irish politics and broader Irish society. While Garret FitzGerald has been the subject of several biographies, the narrative has been shaped largely by his own prolific writings and informed by contemporary newspapers. This book does not claim to be a complete biography of either Declan Costello or Garret FitzGerald, nor is it intended to be an in-depth history of Fine Gael. However, by examining modern Ireland through the lens of Costello's Just Society and FitzGerald's Constitutional Crusade, and drawing on interviews with key figures, recently released papers and privately held collections, a broader picture of Irish politics and society emerges. As such, this book seeks to supplement and add to the existing historiography.

1
A New Ireland?

'What was it all for? The whole thing was a cod'. Michael Moran – the principal male character of John McGahern's *Amongst Women* – found himself questioning the merits of what the independence struggle (1919–1921) had produced: 'some of our own jonnies in the top jobs instead of a few Englishmen. More than half of my own family work in England'.[1] Government spending had been hampered in the 1920s by the financial burden of reconstruction following the War of Independence and subsequent Civil War; the Great Depression stalked the 1930s, worsened by the Economic War with Britain, while frugality became the theme of the war years in the early 1940s, and rationing and strict controls remained in place after the world's theatres of war fell silent. The 1950s are often described as Ireland's 'lost decade',[2] characterised by high levels of emigration, unemployment and general poverty. These social ills were anathema to what the 1916/1919–21 period had *seemed* to promise and, like McGahern's Moran, many were left wondering about the value of independence. However, by the late 1950s, an air of confidence, already identifiable among international neighbours who had enjoyed more of the post-war boom, was noticeable as the economy began to show signs of improvement. It seemed that the Irish experience was, perhaps, not that different after all to Eric Hobsbawm's observation that 'for 80 per cent of humanity the Middle Ages ended suddenly in the 1950s; or perhaps better still, they were *felt* to end in the 1960s'[3] (italicised in text).

However, social development did not keep pace with economic modernisation. Social problems persisted. Roland Burke Savage, editor of *Studies*, laid down the challenge to decide Ireland's future, asking if the country would drift or if an attempt would be made to shape it according to its needs.[4] His article prompted several responses, and in following editions of the journal, a discussion about the nature of Irish society emerged. The contributions indicated a growing awareness of a responsibility by the state to enact social and economic change. David Thornley, an intellectual and future member of the Labour Party, advocated, for example, moving beyond debate to solid action. Parity of standards in education and social welfare with the rest of Western Europe, as he put it, was not a matter for 'ethical debate and budgetary calculation'.[5] It was in this context that Costello penned his proposals for a Just Society. He made his own contribution to the debate on Ireland's development through the formulation of an eight-point plan, which later developed into the policy document, *Towards a Just Society*. It was written at a time when international expectations about the role of the state were changing. This shift in thinking was confined not just to politicians and policymakers, but significantly it was also acknowledged by the Catholic Church. Such changes, both at an international level, but, more specifically, in Ireland, were made possible by economic transformation, technological advances and a major breakthrough in the hierarchy's thinking resulting from the Second Vatican Council.

Irish social policy: an overview

Irish policymakers were not typically concerned with social policy in the early years of the twentieth century. Political sovereignty was the dominant concern, followed by economic development. In 1919, before independence, the government of the revolutionary Dáil invited Labour Party leader Thomas Johnson to draft a Democratic Programme for economic and social reform. It was adopted at the inaugural meeting of Dáil Éireann on 21 January 1919. The young and the old – the most vulnerable in society – were addressed first. An emphasis was placed on the nation's duty to care for the welfare of children, including the provision of adequate food, clothing, shelter and education. The poor law system was to be substituted with a more sympathetic scheme. The focus then shifted to the utilisation of the country's resources – soil, peat and fisheries – for the benefit of the people. Although some of the radical elements survived, the finished product was stripped of much of the socialist content found in Johnson's original draft.[6] The interventionist approach certainly ran contrary to the church's view on the role of the state. Furthermore, it has been argued that Labour's socialist thinking might not have garnered sympathy in rural Ireland where a mix of peasant proprietorship and the high prices of the wartime agricultural economy had produced a sense of complacency about social issues.[7] Additionally, the invitation to draft the programme was widely seen as a sop for Labour standing aside at the 1918 general election, leaving the field open for Sinn Féin in the interest of national solidarity. Neither Sinn Féin nor its pro-Treaty successor in the Free State government, Cumann na nGaedheal, had either the means or the real desire to implement the programme. The cost of reconstruction following the war of independence and civil war had placed a considerable strain on the exchequer. Only after 1926/27 did compensation cease to rank among the top five heaviest charges on the state's expenditure.[8] As Margaret O'Callaghan succinctly put it, '[Pádraig]

Pearse's clarity of vision was a luxury the nation could no longer afford'.[9] Furthermore, in the early years of the Free State, the government was concerned with state and identity building and the achievement of democratic stability.[10] The Catholic Church also influenced policymakers. When viewed in the context of what these early statesmen were attempting to achieve, this was inevitable. As Ronan Fanning put it, with the island partitioned and a full republic unattainable, 'Catholicism, always central to so much of Irish nationalist ideology, took on an additional significance in the search for national identity'.[11] This meant that, in a state guided by the conservative principles of the pre-Vatican II Catholic Church, developments in social policy would be limited in scope.

Pope Pius XI expressed the view in his 1931 encyclical *Quadragesimo Anno* that, 'Of its very nature the true aim of all social activity should be to help individual members of the social body, but never to destroy or absorb them'.[12] This principal of subsidiarity favoured the individual or local community groups and opposed centralisation and state responsibility for the provision of social services. It was penned in the context of the growth of communism, the rise of fascism and the emergence of the totalitarian state in continental Europe,[13] and it proved very influential in Ireland. It meant that the 1930s saw little development in the area of social policy, although this had been the case in the 1920s, also. Both Cumann na nGaedheal and Fianna Fáil implemented housing policies, although the latter was considerably more active. De Valera's government also introduced the Unemployment Assistance Act in 1933, widows and orphans pensions in 1935 and children's allowance in 1944. His government prepared a Health Act in 1947, but lost power at the general election the following February and the responsibility for implementing it fell to the new Minister for Health in the first inter-party government, Dr Noel Browne. His scheme to introduce a comprehensive health service for mothers and children up to the age of sixteen never came to fruition, however, as it was blocked by the combined power of the Catholic hierarchy and the Irish Medical Association.[14] When Fianna Fáil returned to power, a scaled-back version was introduced in 1951. The episode offers an interesting commentary on social policy formulation: the spectacular failure of Browne's programme and the power of those who opposed it served as a strong warning to politicians who might otherwise have considered radical reform. Arguably, the most important development in social policy in the 1950s was the Social Welfare Act, 1952, introduced by Fianna Fáil's Dr James Ryan. The act gave birth to the social welfare system in Ireland. It consolidated and introduced benefits such as disability and maternity benefits, and it laid the foundation for future social welfare benefits.[15]

The 1960s, which saw the waning of the anti-interventionist ethos, witnessed an expansion of social policy, particularly in the area of education with the introduction of free post-primary education and the Local

Authority (Higher Education Grant) Act, 1968, which opened up third-level opportunities. Change was made possible by social and religious transformation and by the emergence of a new generation within the political establishment. However, as discussed in later chapters, the demand for change tended to come from society itself rather than from the political elite.

'An economic slum'

In addition to the multitude of localised factors, the West's recovery following the Second World War was largely stimulated by the Marshall Plan, outlined by US Secretary of State, George Marshall, in an address at Harvard University on 5 June 1947. By the time that the programme was wound up in 1952, the US had spent $13 billion, a figure that exceeded all of the country's previous overseas aid programmes combined.[16] Between 1948 and 1950, France, the Netherlands, Austria, Italy, Greece and West Germany recovered. In addition to the financial gain, there were also psychological benefits. As Tony Judt put it, 'one might almost say that the Marshall Plan helped Europeans feel better about themselves'.[17] Ireland's recovery between 1945 and 1950 was the weakest of all the European economies, except for Spain.[18] While Ireland initially experienced post-war prosperity, the boom was not sustained to the degree enjoyed by her western neighbours, and by the 1950s, the benefits had receded. The financial support received through the Marshall Plan was largely earmarked for agriculture in the belief that Ireland's future lay in farming.[19] Ireland had failed to maximise opportunities in the expanding European economy and was thus locked out of the affluence that accompanied it. The country went into relative decline compared to similar states in Western Europe,[20] prompting *The Irish Times* to report that Ireland was 'falling behind'.[21] In contrast to Britain's figure of twenty-one per cent and Continental Europe's of forty per cent, Irish national income grew by only eight per cent between 1949 and 1956.[22] 1956 was a year of economic crisis. Gerard Sweetman, Minister for Finance in the second inter-party government (1954–57), believed that Ireland's economic independence was at stake, such was the depth of the crisis.[23] He was not alone. As Tom Garvin has noted in his study of Irish newspaper coverage of the 1950s, papers such as the *Standard* also advocated launching the 'battle for economic freedom'.[24]

As Ireland struggled, British Prime Minister Harold Macmillan was telling his voters that they had 'never had it so good'. The 1950s in Britain was a period of affluence and increasing consumption.[25] Post-war reconstruction there created employment, and with few such opportunities in Ireland, the allure of a better life in the neighbouring country – relayed by relatives and friends who had already left – drew mainly young people away from their native land. By 1960, the average British worker earned at least forty per cent more than his Irish counterpart.[26] A Bank of England official who met with staff from the Irish Department of Finance while on a visit to Ireland in 1957 observed, 'the country gives the impression of being an economic slum from which there is a constant outflow of emigrants who have any initiative and any desire to better themselves'.[27] The stark reality of Ireland in the 1950s was captured in John B. Keane's *Many Young Men of Twenty*. The first act of the play shows brothers Kevin and Dinny preparing to leave for London, where they would join siblings already settled. Eighteen-year-old Dinny cried openly, admitting 'I don't want to go away at all'.[28] His tears reflected his frustration and the lack of choice available not just to him but also to those real emigrants whom his character represented. The fictional story of Kevin and Dinny was not far removed from the anguish of real emigrants captured in *The Vanishing Irish*.[29] Those who left in the 1950s and early 1960s were predominantly young, and they tended to be children of small farmers, unskilled or semi-skilled manual labourers.[30] Writing in *Studies* in 1951, R. C. Geary had wondered whether 'a large proportion of those born here are pre-destined to emigrate?'[31] Between 1951 and 1961, more than 400,000 people left the Republic of Ireland, a figure that accounts for almost one-sixth of the total population as recorded in 1951.[32] The 1961 census showed the population to be at an all-time low of 2,818,341.[33] Among those who left was Michael Sweetman, who went to Canada in 1957. As a future member of the Fine Gael policy committee and research staff who worked on the 1965 election campaign, he would do much to assist behind the scenes in the development of the Just Society ideas.[34]

The traditional government line on emigration had typically been one of denial. Eamon de Valera once claimed that 'there is no doubt that many of those who emigrate could find employment at home at as good, or better, wages – and with living conditions far better – than they find in Britain'.[35] The incentive to respond was diminished by the fact that emigration to Britain reduced the level of unemployment, the burden on the exchequer, and it alleviated potential social unrest.[36] However by the mid-1950s, when the Commission on Emigration and Other Population Problems filed its report, the problem could no longer be ignored. The failure of independent Ireland to support its own was thrown into stark relief by developments in Northern Ireland resulting from the 1946 commitment that the state would be granted parity of services with the UK outlined in the 1942 Beveridge Report. The contrast between services in Britain and Ireland was summed up in the account of one emigrant, Donál MacAmglaigh: 'the [Irish] people go in to the doctor as they used to go in to the aristocrats or the landlords long ago – shaking with humility. In England he'll give you to understand that you are a person and not a beggar'.[37]

Economic modernisation

Despite the problems of the 1950s, Irish policymakers were beginning to look to the future. By the end of that decade, the debate about the symbols of independence had been replaced with a discussion about how best to build a modern economy.[38] As Seán Ó Faoláin observed:

> Time was when common words on every lip in every Irish pub were Partition, The Civil War, The Republic, The Gun. The vocabulary of the mid-fifties and sixties was very different – the Common Market, Planning, Growth Rates, Strikes, Jobs, Educational Opportunities, or why this factory failed or that one flourished.[39]

Britain applied for membership of the European Economic Community in 1961. The decision to do so increased Ireland's dependency on her nearest neighbour (the country's application would be closely linked to the success of Britain). This opened Irish policy outwards, as policymakers began to look to Europe. It also resulted in a shift towards free trade and a more open economy.[40] The necessity for this outward-looking policy was something that British economist Charles Carter had advocated in his 'outsider perspective' when addressing the Irish Association in 1957: 'Economic prosperity is not beyond the reach of the Republic, but it is not to be found in self-satisfied isolation, nor in the narrow pride of economic nationalism'.[41] There was a gradual realisation that the old rhetoric had no place in a changing Ireland. The first programme for economic expansion – the work of T. K. Whitaker, secretary of the Department of Finance – was published in 1958. The document hailed a significant shift away from the economic nationalism of old Sinn Féin: the protectionist policies that Seán Lemass had put in place in the 1930s and which were maintained in the two decades that followed were to be stripped away and replaced with a more outward-looking policy. The removal of tariff barriers was an important preparation for an Irish application for membership of the European Economic Community. There had been earlier signs of this shift in Gerard Sweetman's budget in 1956 in which he suspended the Control of Manufacturers Act. Whitaker's document, with an emphasis on programming, set a number of targets to be achieved, thus allowing for economic growth. This interventionist approach ran contrary to the teaching of the Catholic Church, although, as Louise Fuller demonstrates, not all clerics in the 1950s took a dim view of state planning. In fact, Whitaker cited an article by the Bishop of Clonfert in *Studies* as having been a source of inspiration to him.[42]

Increased foreign investment and accompanying job opportunities resulted in a growing optimism as emigration figures declined, while there was also some increase in immigration, albeit at a much slower rate. The latter was further stimulated by Ireland's entry into the EEC, after which net immigration was recorded for the first time since the foundation of the State as returning emigrants arrived back in Ireland to avail of the new opportunities.[43] As a result, between 1971 and 1981, the population grew by 465,000.[44] This, of course, was reversed as a result of the downturn in the economy in the 1980s, and is discussed in Chapter 8.

Agents of change

Mobilisation of opinion on social policy was widespread outside political circles in the 1950s. New centres of social ideas had emerged. The People's College began to run lecture courses and summer schools in the early 1950s. In 1952, a Social Study Conference had been launched, while two years later, the Catholic Workers College was established. The Dublin Institute of Catholic Sociology also emerged in 1954. However, there was a clear disconnect between the themes discussed by these groups and the areas addressed by governments. Many of the issues raised were ignored in public policy.[45] Part of the problem for policymakers was the absence of forums that provided professional research into Irish society. As Joe Lee put it, a hidden Ireland awaited investigation.[46] The government of the day would benefit from the emergence in 1958 of An Foras Taluntais, which assisted with agricultural research, and the establishment in the 1960s of the Economic and Social Research Institute (ESRI) and the National Industrial and Economic Council (later the National Economic and Social Council or NESC). The appearance of publications such as *Crane Bag*, *Irish Economic and Social History* and *Irish Jurist* was also important in contributing to the debate on major issues. These developments helped create a decisive break with the past.[47]

A growing interest in social issues was also reflected in the socio-religious magazine programme *Radharc*, which explored Irish society extensively, while also looking beyond the island. Produced for RTÉ by Fr Joe Dunn, chaplain of UCD, the first programme was televised on 12 January 1962, and over a thirty-five year period, more than 400 films were shot in seventy-five different countries across five continents. From 'House Hunters' (28 February 1965), which told the story of Eamon Casey's Housing Aid Society that assisted Irish low-income earners in Britain with purchasing a home, to 'The Problems' (19 May 1966), which examined the work of missionaries in Kenya, the programmes connected the domestic audience to the diaspora, while also acting as a vista to the wider world.

The 1960s saw the emergence of a new mentality as the grips of Archbishop John Charles McQuaid and Eamon de Valera were loosened. That generation had a more pious, static image of what Ireland ought to be.[48] McQuaid, who had once wielded great power, appeared to recognise that his influence was waning. Among his papers at the Dublin Diocesan Archive are letters written to him by mothers concerned about the type of magazines that their daughters were reading. In the margins, he had written names of people to contact to pursue the subject. Previously, he would simply have had inappropriate literature banned or censored.[49] Seán Lemass succeeded de Valera as leader of Fianna Fáil in 1959. As Tom Garvin has pointed out, 'the idea of a virtuous Ireland surrounded by economic and ideational walls of tariffs and censorship was dying, but nothing much had yet taken its place'.[50]

The rise in Irish living standards in the 1960s meant that more people had disposable income and there were more options available. One of the negative implications was a surge in crime in the 1960s and 1970s.[51] From the mid-1960s, there were huge increases, for example, in housebreaking, robbery and indictable assaults.[52] That aside, an example of the psychological shift in Ireland is reflected in the replacement of the traditional céilí bands with showbands in dancehalls around Ireland. At the forefront of the new phenomena was future Taoiseach and Fianna Fáil leader, Albert Reynolds. As the owner of such establishments as Cloudland and Roseland, he was one of the most prominent organisers of such events. He twice booked 'The Beatles', but was forced to cancel because of the unavailability of a large enough space to cater for the inevitably large crowd that would attend. In his autobiography, he observed how Irish people at that time had more money in their pockets and their willingness to spend it on dances.[53] John McGahern recalled of the Ivy Leaf, run by Patsy Conboy, that 'people came by bus, by lorry, hackney car, horse trap, on bicycle and on foot to dance the night away'.[54] In addition to their own songs, the bands also played hits from the charts and imported foreign music. Brendan Bowyer of The Royal, one of the most important showbands of the era, scored a hit in 1965 with his cover of the 1949 American success, *The Hucklebuck*. The dancehalls, along with cinema and television, gave Irish people a different type of outlet, while exposing them to other cultures. As Father P. J. Brophy of St Patrick's Diocesan College in Carlow recalled, before such changes 'the mass house was the meeting house because there was nowhere else to go and nothing else to do'.[55]

It was technological advances that did most to open up a new world and present alternative lifestyles, helping to shape rising expectations and changing social attitudes. On 14 March 1958, the government announced the establishment of a television commission that would consider instituting a native television station; Irish citizens on the east coast were able to pick up transmission signals from Britain. The project was subsequently approved at a meeting of the cabinet on 31 July 1961. Eamon de Valera in his address for Telefís Éireann's inaugural broadcast on New Year's Eve 1961 commented that 'never before was there in the hands of men an instrument so powerful to influence the thoughts and actions of the multitude'. Although he was wary of the development, the arrival of television helped to lift Ireland from its isolation and insular attitude and to strip away the country's parochialism. Only one-in-three households in 1963 had television sets, but by the end of the decade, three-quarters of homes owned one.[56] There was a shift from a young John McGahern concentrating intently on the knob of the radio set, imagining the rough and tumble of the football game upon which the presenter was commentating,[57] to the young Gene Kerrigan who saw 'New York, London, Paris ... mountains and jungles and deserts and seas'. Television closed the distance between countries. As Kerrigan put it, television allowed those 'who had never set foot outside Ireland ... experience close up the look, the sound, the atmosphere of more foreign lands than the greatest travellers of the previous centuries'. He recalled that it was America about which they learned most.[58] This was due to a reliance on imported sit-coms and films, as the rights to American programming were considerably cheaper than the cost of home-produced programmes.[59] By 1985, Philip Nolan, writing in the pages of *Woman's Way* magazine, was lamenting the Americanisation of everyday language, which he attributed to '*Dallas, Dynasty, Falcon Crest* and their ilk'. He, perhaps facetiously, suggested that a bill might be introduced in the Dáil prohibiting the use of American phrases![60] How this was to be enforced, he did not explain.

The Late Late Show, a Friday night television chat-show hosted by Gay Byrne, has often been cited as an important vehicle for change. Although there have been often extravagant claims made about its impact, it provided audiences with access to free-flowing discussions and debates.[61] Two particular – and well-cited – incidents on the programme serve as examples of how certain topics had opened up. The first was a suggestion by one woman that she did not wear a nightgown on her wedding night, which caused Bishop Thomas Ryan of Clonfert to strongly protest at what was being inferred. The second was Brian Trevaskis's criticism of Bishop Michael Browne of Galway for allowing the construction of the county's new cathedral, which he described as a 'ghastly monstrosity'. Unsurprisingly, even before these incidents, the Church was concerned about the impact of television. *The Irish Ecclesiastical Record* had cautioned readers to give 'long and careful preparation before you admit the monster to your homes'.[62] In the rush to embrace modernism, there was a fear that traditional values were being abandoned. It is notable that a time when American lifestyles were entering Irish homes through the medium of television, censorship increased. Judge J. C. Conroy, chair of the Censorship of Publications Board, declared that 'there is a little bit of Adam in everybody. If we were all in paradise we wouldn't want it'.[63] Between 1946 and 1965, 8,000 books were banned, and in the twelve-month period between 1962 and 1963 alone, thirty-nine films were banned.[64]

From the perspective of policymakers, the impact of Vatican II was as important as the arrival of television. The Second Vatican Council opened under Pope John XXIII in October 1962 and closed just over three years later in December 1965 under Pope Paul VI. The resulting philosophical change resulted in 'a thorough-going reassessment by the people and the Council Fathers of the Church's role in the modern world'.[65] Although the Church did not change its policy on family-related issues such as contraceptives or abortion, the vision for the Church's mission changed from that of charitable activity to working for structural change to help deliver social justice.[66] There was also a fundamental shift in its thinking regarding the role of the state. The Church had previously been concerned with the redemption of the soul and strongly advocated the right of the family to support itself; this had been particularly evident during the Mother and Child controversy in the 1950s. But by the 1960s, notions about the role of the state had changed internationally, something that Pope John XXIII recognised. The Pontiff played the seemingly contradictory roles of traditionalist, pragmatist and reformer. He was sceptical of television and not only initially upheld the ban of Pope Pius XII on priests owning television sets but he was also acutely aware of how fast the world was changing and he did much in the last two years of his life to turn the Church in a new direction.[67]

His 1961 encyclical, *Mater et Magistra*, represented a major breakthrough in the hierarchy's thinking. It spoke of the necessity 'to remedy lack of balance, whether between different sectors in the economy, or between different parts of the same country, or even between the different peoples of the world'.[68] Moreover, he stated that 'governments have the care of the common good and in these conditions it is urgently necessary for them to intervene more frequently'. *Pacem in Terris*, 1963, which dealt with establishing universal peace in truth, justice, charity and liberty, placed a particular emphasis on social justice. Archbishop McQuaid treated the new developments in the Catholic Church with suspicion. However, key changes in personnel resulted in the spread of Vatican II thinking. The appointment of William Conway to the see of Armagh as the successor to Cardinal D'Alton was significant. Though cautious, his attitude to change was important. His leadership was instrumental in steering the Irish church towards change at a critical time.[69]

The aforementioned documents, as explained in the introduction to *Towards a Just Society*, 'informed and moulded' the social and economic arguments put forward in the document. Declan Costello framed his policies in the language of this new thinking and saw the church as a forum to help bring about change. As he put it, the church

> must act as a social conscience and speak out, not with a still quiet voice, but if necessary a large and strident one. If civil authority has failed to bring about social justice, it can, and I suggest, should, point out the failure.[70]

In this respect, Costello's policies diverged with those formulated by Garret FitzGerald, who advocated a more pluralist approach. Costello was certainly a committed Catholic, but there may also have been a further reason why he chose to frame his document within the context of Church teaching – that was to defend from the charge of dangerous socialism. This was important in the international context of the Cold War and the suspicion that surrounded socialism.

If television opened up the world and Vatican II contributed to a reassessment of the role of the state, the EEC was also an important agent for change. As already noted, from the late-1950s, membership had become a priority for the Irish government. While Lemass was keen to secure entry for economic benefits, Europe would come to have an important influence on the development of social policy in Ireland. As will be seen over the coming chapters, many of the changes that took place, such as the introduction of equal pay for women, came as a response to lobbying from pressure groups or to EEC directives.

Framing the Just Society

Fergal Tobin opened the preface to *The Best of Decades* by explaining what his book was not: a history of 1960s Ireland. Written in the early 1980s, before the relevant archives were available, it was, instead, 'a selective chronicle of public events, a somewhat nostalgic recollection of what is still remembered as the pivotal decade of change in modern Ireland'.[71] Once the state papers for those years were released at the National Archives of Ireland, a different story began to emerge. Despite Seán Lemass's well-recited observation that 'a rising tide lifts all boats', social development had not been all encompassing. Lemass himself had admitted to the national convention of the Junior Chambers of Commerce in 1963 that 'inequalities and distortions have emerged or widened'.[72] Behind the scenes, some Fianna Fáil deputies were also expressing concern. In January 1965, Kevin Boland, Minister for Social Welfare, wrote to James Ryan, the Minister for Finance, noting that there was a 'general feeling that we have not paid sufficient attention to the weaker sections of the community and that there has not been an equitable distribution of the increased prosperity to which we point as an achievement'. He also insisted that the existing social assistance schemes were inadequate. Boland's fears were expressed in the context of concerns that Fianna Fáil had become too associated with the middle and upper-middle classes,[73] but they nonetheless illustrate the problems with government policy.

Amidst depression and recession, the quest for economic recovery and stability had taken precedence over social planning. As David Rottman and Philip O'Connell pointed out, improvements in living standards were almost universally experienced, but the differentials between the top and bottom of the class structure remained. The knock-on effect of those with large-scale property holdings or professional qualifications in the 1950s meant that there was a level of advantage for children born to those families in the 1960s and 1970s. Those without such resources emigrated or remained in marginal positions. As the two authors concluded, 'Economic growth did not secure the promised social reform'.[74] This analysis invites comparisons with Italy. Italy had also sought to stimulate its economy by abandoning protection in the post-war period, which led to the country's so-called 'economic miracle'. But items of necessity to society, such as low-cost housing and schools, were not prioritised and the emphasis remained on the family unit.[75] Social reform in Italy followed a similar trajectory to Ireland, and it was not until the 1970s that both governments began to formulate social policies comparable to those introduced by other western countries in the 1960s.

The Dublin Housing Action Committee (DHAC) had done tremendous work in the early- and mid-1960s to expose the deprivation in housing. The

DHAC addressed issues not dissimilar from the appalling housing conditions that came to light during the 1913 strike and lock out, and, indeed, protests took place in many of the same streets.[76] The housing situation attracted Declan Costello's attention, and he attributed problems in that area to the policy choices made by the Fianna Fáil government. In 1961, owner-occupied housing accounted for only one-third of Dublin dwellings,[77] with the rest of the population resident in rented accommodation or social housing. The situation, particularly in Dublin's inner-city, was dire. The once splendid Georgian houses, former symbols of great wealth and decadence, had come to be equated with poverty and degradation. The often crumbling buildings – immortalised in the plays of Seán O'Casey – were routinely divided into one-room tenements and typically housed large families. In his memoirs, James Downey recalled visiting slums in the capital during the early years of his journalistic career, which began in 1951: 'Picture a woman with eleven children living in one room with no electricity, no running water, no sanitation, and rotten floorboards through which a careless person could easily put a foot'.[78] Little changed as the decade progressed. The matter came to a head when in one week in June 1963 the collapse of several tenement houses claimed the lives of four people and led to the evacuation of 155 families. One of those evacuated was Bridie Perry, a resident of number eight Hendrick Street, which had been designated unfit for habitation. She recalled how the ceiling had previously collapsed in on her and her two young children; there was one toilet for the entire three-story building, and the ground floor was infested with rats. Conditions were so appalling that the landlord had not called to collect rent since 1960.[79]

The Dáil debate on the incident was revealing. Statistics requested from the Minister for Local Government, Neil Blaney, provided a shocking snapshot of the depth of the problem. Of the seventy-five housing authorities that returned surveys on the number of problematic houses that were suitable for economic repair,[80] thirty-nine found that more than half of the unfit dwellings in their area would not qualify. Extremes cases could be found in Mayo County Council, where only thirty-eight of the 4,894 problematic dwellings were deemed suitable for repair, and in Kilkenny District and Borough Council where none of the 143 could be repaired at a viable cost. In only two areas – Castlebar District and Borough Council, and Granard Town Commissioners – was there a 100-per cent possibility of economic repair.[81] In his contribution, Costello placed the blame for the collapse of the tenement homes squarely at the feet of the government rather than at Dublin Corporation. As he put it, 'the Corporation have carried out the government's stated economic programme of cutting down on social investment, in favour of so-called productive investment'.[82] In the same year that Costello presented his proposals to the Fine Gael party, the Fianna Fáil government published the *Housing Progress and Prospects* white paper; it confirmed the existence of tens of thousands of homes unfit for human habitation. This prompted large-scale investment in public housing, resulting in the development of large housing estates in such areas as Tallaght, Clondalkin and Blanchardstown, and a high-rise development in Ballymun.[83] The language that pervaded Costello's Just Society proposals was particularly evident in his Dáil contribution on the housing crisis.

Declan Costello

Declan Costello was born on 1 August 1926, the second eldest in a family of five. He attended Xavier School in Donnybrook, and subsequently chose to study at UCD where he took a degree in law and economics, won the Swift-MacNeill scholarship and graduated in 1948 with first-class honours. During his time at university, he played a prominent role in the student Law Society, serving as auditor during the 1945/46 academic year.

It was perhaps inevitable that Costello would enter politics given the household in which he grew up. At the time of his birth, his father was a member of the Cumann na nGaedheal government and, remarkably, he held the portfolio – Attorney General – to which Declan Costello would later be appointed in the 1970s. John A. Costello would later go on to become Taoiseach of two inter-party governments (1948–51 and 1954–57). Costello recalled how his father had a 'very strong influence' on him in the areas of religion and politics, 'like most fathers have on their growing sons'.[84] Though born mid-way through Cumann na nGaedheal's ten years in power, Costello considered W. T. Cosgrave, President of the Executive Council, and his father's other colleagues 'great heroes of mine'.[85] But although Costello followed in his father's footsteps and entered Leinster House, politics was not his first choice.

After leaving UCD, Costello went to King's Inns to train as a barrister. His studies were interrupted, however, after he contracted an unusual form of tuberculosis that affects the kidneys. He initially spent ten months recuperating in Switzerland in 1946 and returned following a relapse at the end of 1947. He was still there when his father was chosen to become Taoiseach of the first inter-party government, and received a letter in which John A revealed that he had been reluctant to accept the position, fearing that he would be 'a flop as Taoiseach'.[86] Declan Costello was called to the bar in 1948, three years before he contested his first election, and subsequently to the inner bar in 1965.

Far more is known about Costello's distinguished, if at time controversial, legal career than the time he spent in politics. He was Attorney General in the Fine Gael-Labour coalition of 1973–77, went on to become a High Court judge and ultimately became president of that court. He was responsible for the establishment of the Law Reform Commission and the office of the Director of Public Prosecutions (DPP). He also presided over the inquiry into the Whiddy Island disaster in which fifty people were killed when an oil tanker exploded in West Cork in January 1979. Some of the more controversial cases in which he was involved appear to draw into question his commitment to social justice. Eileen Flynn, a teacher at a Catholic convent school, was dismissed from her post because she lived openly with a married man whose wife had left him and with whom she had had a child. Her case challenging the dismissal was heard in the High Court by Costello in March 1985; she had already lost appeals in the Employment Appeals Tribunal and in the Circuit Court. Costello also found that her dismissal was not unfair. Noting that Flynn was employed by a religious, not a lay, school, he remarked, 'I do not think that the respondents over-emphasised the power of example on the lives of the pupils in the school'.[87] More controversially, he was the High Court judge in the 1992 X-Case who granted the request of the Attorney General Harry Whelehan for a temporary injunction to prevent a fourteen-year-old girl, pregnant as a result of rape, from travelling to Britain for an abortion. Costello differentiated between the role of a TD and a judge, however, explaining that the latter is concerned with a different type of justice. 'He does justice between parties before him in the case and they are based on facts that he finds and the law which he applies. As a judge one isn't concerned with social justice as such, what one is concerned with is doing justice between the parties before one. It is a different task'.[88] It should also be remembered that his Just Society proposals did not touch on or recommend reform of matters of a moral nature.

He was first elected as a TD in 1951 at the age of twenty-four, making him the youngest member of the fourteenth Dáil. Widely considered a candidate for a cabinet position when his father formed a second inter-party government in 1954, he was overlooked for fear of prompting accusations of nepotism. As a representative of the working-class constituency of Dublin North-West, he witnessed the effects of poverty, unemployment and emigration, problems that were widespread and from which he had been largely shielded during his privileged upbringing. Looking back, he recalled that during this period he was developing 'very strong feelings about what was happening in Irish society, and the poverty in Irish society, particularly about the housing situation and the decline and how this could be improved'.[89] He also read widely and was particularly interested in French post-war reconstruction and the British Labour Party's policy of economic planning.[90] His eight-point plan grew from observations on the need for similar reform in Ireland. He revealed in one interview that he would like to 'get into office in a government for about three or four years' to bring about 'a number of considerable social and economic reforms' in various areas. At the end of that period, he wanted to see if they were 'acceptable to the electorate for a further period'. He wanted the opportunity to test if the ideas that had been considered over a number of years could be put into operation to bring about the changes it was believed they could. It was something he regarded as 'well worthwhile doing'.[91] However, before Costello's ideas could even have their first public test, he needed to convince Fine Gael to adopt a set of proposals that did not sit comfortably with the party's traditional policies.

2
Winning the Party

John A. Costello expressed the fear in 1960 that the 'label of conservatism or Toryism' would be affixed to Fine Gael.[1] An image of the party as one dominated by an older generation of politicians, who were either unwilling or unable to change, had emerged, prompting his concern. Languishing on the opposition benches, most deputies had become despondent, although it did not stop some optimists contemplating a single party Fine Gael government. This was despite the peculiar advice that candidates should not be too forceful in presenting themselves as alternatives![2] They were, as journalist John Healy once sarcastically described them, 'the gentlemen of politics'.[3] Minutes of parliamentary party meetings for the period are dominated by criticisms of a lack of activity and persistent appeals for TDs to attend the house, partake in proceedings and vote in divisions. Even the big set-piece occasions like the Ard Fheis were poorly attended. Photographs of those events show 'small numbers of delegates, well wrapped up in coats, sitting glumly ... in what appear to be cold and largely empty halls'.[4] In a written exchange with James Dillon, John A. Costello encouraged a nurturing of the younger elements of the party and a more dynamic approach to Irish political life. He warned against cultivating, through inaction, the impression that Fine Gael was stagnant or devoid of ideas.[5] Four years later, his son put before the party a proposal that provided an opportunity to challenge these perceptions.

When Declan Costello circulated his ideas to Fine Gael in 1964, the party had been in government for only six of the previous thirty-two years. In a circular to all members of the parliamentary party on 27 April, he appealed to his colleagues on two grounds: firstly, that his proposals were the 'right ones for the country' – which would address the problems examined in Chapter 1 – and secondly, that they offered Fine Gael an opportunity to define its role in Irish politics. Costello argued that, if adopted as official policy, his proposals would have a dramatically favourable effect on the party's fortunes.[6] Effectively, his proposal offered Fine Gael an opportunity to reinvent itself against the backdrop of a changing social and economic climate and to claim its place in the party system by clearly defining itself as a party concerned with social justice. The lack of ideology in the Irish party system at the time offered the potential for a party to claim such a niche for itself. Periodically since its political metamorphosis into Fine Gael in 1933 – the consequence of a merger of Cumann na nGaedheal, the National Centre Party and the Army Comrades Association, more commonly known as the Blueshirts[7] – the party's demise has been predicted. In 1943, for example, Clann na Talmhan's Joseph Blowick concluded that 'Fine Gael are virtually dead and any attempt on their part to give that party a few extra years is doomed to failure'.[8] Although Fine Gael became the senior party in the first inter-party government formed in 1948, the performance in that election was actually catastrophic. Clann na Poblachta, a republican party that had emerged in 1946, had shaken the party system and, as Cornelius O'Leary put it, the new party had a 'snowball effect', attracting attention and support rapidly.[9] Although it principally challenged Fianna Fáil on its traditional territory, Clann na Poblachta's energy also provided a counter-point to the ageing profile of Fine Gael. Fine Gael's share of the vote dipped below twenty per cent for the first time – its worst performance since the party's emergence in 1933 and also if the Cumann na nGaedheal era (1923–33) is included. Participation in the government, followed by another term in power between 1954 and 1957, reignited the party to an extent, but fundamental organisational problems persisted. Patrick Lindsay recalled the selection convention for the 1952 by-election in Mayo North. Joe Leneghan had traditionally contested the constituency on the Fine Gael ticket, but, on arriving at the convention, he is alleged to have commented 'this place is packed' and left. 'To say that it was "packed" would be to seriously over-estimate our organisational ability at that time', according to Lindsay.[10] The minute books of the parliamentary party reveal a constant problem with attendance at meetings but more particularly at Dáil Éireann. Repeatedly the need for action was stressed, with disciplinary proceedings regularly threatened as punishment for repeat offenders. However, warning rarely translated into action (expulsion would have been damaging to the party), and the problems inevitably persisted. As the party returned to the opposition benches after 1957, apathy, born of disillusionment, set in. For many backbench TDs, as well as those on the frontbench, the workings of the Dáil were combined with other forms of livelihood, resulting in them leading – to borrow the title of former Laois-Offaly TD Tom O'Higgins's aptly-named memoir – 'a double life'. This was not necessarily surprising, particularly for those with a family to support. As Lindsay, first elected in 1954, recalled:

> Our salary was £624 per annum. We paid for our own post. Local calls were free (a lot of use to a TD from North Mayo!). There were no secretaries, and if you wanted one you paid out of your own salary. We did have

a travel allowance which helped to keep the car on the road – but not much more and did not cover travel within a constituency.[11]

Double-jobbing was not a feature unique to Fine Gael. Frank Dunlop – one-time Fianna Fáil head of research – recalled that when Fianna Fáil moved to the opposition benches in 1973 after sixteen years in government, former ministers found it difficult to operate on a TD's salary and many returned to former professions. 'Politics – at constituency level and at national level, for those who were members of the front bench – took second place'.[12] Law was one of the dominant 'other' professions among the Fine Gael TDs. John A. Costello returned to the bar the day after the second inter-party government, which he led, left office.[13] That the legal profession took precedence over public service was reflected in the fact that a whip was placed at the law library in 1959 to ensure the attendance of Fine Gael deputies at divisions![14] In the 1950s and 1960s, only about one-quarter of branches actually registered with headquarters.[15] In his foreword to Brian Maye's 1993 history of Fine Gael, John Bruton – the then party leader and a future Taoiseach who joined in 1965 – joked that it was twenty-eight years since he had become a member and twenty-seven since he attended his first meeting, 'a commentary on the frequency of meetings in those days'.[16]

When Richard Mulcahy announced his resignation as party leader in 1959, it was felt that a full-time politician ought to be selected as his successor.[17] As David McCullagh has pointed out, John A. Costello's part-time leadership in the Dáil had been causing concern: 'He generally attended the Dáil after court had risen for the day; and if the High Court was in Cork, he didn't attend at all'.[18] Thus Costello, despite his interest in the position, was dissuaded from putting his name forward. Members were given the choice of James Dillon or Liam Cosgrave, then only thirty-nine. Mulcahy alone counted the ballots and the outcome – in a tradition since retained by Fine Gael – was not publicly announced. However, when approached by Dillon, Mulcahy is said to have revealed that he received sixty votes, Costello (despite not being an official candidate) twenty-six and Cosgrave six.[19]

There was change at the top of the two main political parties in 1959, and the contrast between the two new leaders at that time was striking. Fianna Fáil's Seán Lemass, who turned sixty shortly afterwards, succeeded Eamon de Valera. Although Fine Gael's new leader was a few years younger than his Fianna Fáil counterpart – who was described by Todd Andrews as being 'spun out' by that stage[20] – Lemass was seen as the more dynamic of the two, particularly due to the role that he had played in the Department of Industry and Commerce. Dillon, in contrast, was a conservative politician, wedded to the principles of the Fine Gael party that he had been instrumental in shaping in 1933. Lemass, impatient to break with de Valera's era and to promote younger talent, transfused new blood into Fianna Fáil. This was despite resentment from some party stalwarts, although the old guard, as

Bryce Evans has pointed out, was not totally cast aside.[21] Furthermore, the newcomers did not always represent a break with the past: the 'violence of language' that occurred during the 1963 debate on the turnover tax – the young Brian Lenihan being especially guilty – harked back to the 1930s.[22] An anonymous article in the Fine Gael journal, the *National Observer*, called on Dillon to encourage talent and provide the 'necessary space for growth and development'.[23] But the party's young tigers were not afforded the same opportunities as their Fianna Fáil counterparts. Lemass sided with youth, Dillon with the traditionalists.

Under Dillon's leadership, little changed and he had no great interest in formulating fresh policies. Fine Gael typically did not think of its frontbench as a shadow cabinet; this robbed the party of the propaganda value of calling its members 'shadow ministers' and presenting them to the public as credible alternatives to the government.[24] This unwillingness to think in terms of and project itself as a shadow cabinet had problematic implications for how the frontbench functioned. Incredibly at a party meeting in 1963, one deputy actually had to ask for members of the frontbench to be identified and suggested that they hold regular meetings.[25] A circular from the then leader Richard Mulcahy in 1957 had instructed frontbench members to meet more frequently,[26] but evidently little notice had been taken of the order. A clearly defined and structured frontbench is imperative for an effective or, at the very least, informed opposition. Furthermore, 'shadow ministers' typically drive the parliamentary party and shape the direction of policy. In the absence of such a structure, it was hardly surprising that Dillon observed that 'performances in the Dáil were not up to standard',[27] and that there was no active discussion of policy. There was a touch of irony to his complaint. The issue of the frontbench resurfaced at the 1964 Ard Fheis when a request for the publication of their names was placed on the agenda.[28] In an age before television, it was not unusual for frontbench members to be unfamiliar to the ordinary voter, but that members of the parliamentary party did not know the identity of those figures was telling. Jostling for frontbench positions is to be expected in healthy parties, but there was an obvious lack of interest or activity within Fine Gael. This was symptomatic of a dying party.

On several occasions, John A. Costello had made clear his views on the role of non-government parties. He declared that opposition was an opportunity to develop 'a national policy adequate and suitable to the ever-changing conditions of a complex world',[29] while on another occasion, he asserted that a party in opposition 'should be preparing to be the next government' and, as such, should offer voters a broad outline of alternative proposals.[30] But despite such views, there appeared to be a damaging lack of interest in developing policy documents within the party, and, indeed, Costello himself at times appeared to be more interested in his legal career. Gerard Sweetman – who would be a significant figure in the Just Society debate – argued in

1958 that a 'distinctive policy was not so important when we were so far from a general election' and cited changing political circumstances as an impediment.[31] Shifts in electoral dynamics, and not policy, had previously propelled Fine Gael into office. Between 1948 and 1957, the government had changed every three years largely due to the economic difficulties facing Ireland. Each government had been forced to take drastic action, which subsequently eroded the party's popularity at the polls.[32] Fatigue or dissatisfaction with a Fianna Fáil government was an electoral asset to Fine Gael, and the party was thus cautious of setting out its ideas too clearly at the risk of alienating floating voters or those disaffected by the incumbent government. Nonetheless in July 1958 and again in September 1959, contributors to meetings of the parliamentary party had emphasised the need to formulate policy. Although Sweetman offered a valid argument against such activity in a non-election year, ruling out any sort of policy statement seems premature, and it left the politically curious unsure of where the party stood. In late-1959, Sweetman announced that the front bench had been discussing policy for the previous few weeks, but there were no major initiative launches and the party's broader programme, beyond its commitment to the agricultural sector, remained unclear.

In outlining Fine Gael's plans for the future in 1960, James Dillon identified six urgent areas for attention: the first five were directly concerned with agriculture, while point six – which called for a reciprocal Trade Area Agreement with Great Britain – also came under that heading. At a time when agriculture was Ireland's major export to the UK, the latter point was particularly important. If weighted in order of priority, then Fine Gael's main concern was to 'complete the job of eradicating bovine TB'.[33] This was an understandable priority given the threat posed by the disease to the livestock industry.[34] Dillon's emphasis on agriculture was unsurprising. Aside from the strong farming profile of many Fine Gael voters, Dillon had been Minister for Agriculture between 1948 and 1951 and again between 1954 and 1957, and he was most comfortable with that subject. In fact, he claimed it was the only ministry in which he was interested.[35] Nonetheless, during the course of his speech, he also acknowledged the urgent necessity to expand opportunities for industrial employment; he affirmed his party's preference for doing so through private enterprise. This preference would later be at odds with the methods advocated in *Towards a Just Society*. However, there were areas where Costello's proposals did not represent a complete break. Dillon also mentioned education, foreshadowing the criticism in *Towards a Just Society* of the compulsory nature of the Irish language in schools. The party advocated reforming the manner in which the language was taught, which he claimed contributed to the 'dislike' of the subject.[36]

Fine Gael's stated aspiration approaching the 1961 election was to form a single-party government; though over-optimistic, it was also the product of Labour's aversion to coalition. Consequently, the party fielded ninety-six candidates, an increase of fourteen on the 1957 figure. The objective had been decided at a meeting of the special committee on organisation in July 1960,[37] and Dillon subsequently reiterated the intention in a circular to members of the parliamentary party.[38] In the absence of opinion polling at this time, parties had to rely on local activists to gauge support levels in the constituencies. Fine Gael suffered from two problems: it was not sufficiently organised nationally to get an accurate read and there was also an element of delusion within the party about its prospects. William Murphy had criticised the Dublin organisation at one meeting of the parliamentary party in 1959, only to be admonished by Michael O'Higgins who expressed the view that Fine Gael had once been the largest party in Dublin City and County and could return to that position.[39] The state of the organisation that prompted Murphy's remarks was not discussed. In a letter to Dillon in 1960, John A. Costello had expressed his view that the concept of an overall majority was 'illusory' and that the efforts by the party organisation to work towards such would 'not be successful, may do damage and cause such disappointment as to break the spirit of Fine Gael supporters'.[40]

The 1961 general election was the first test for Fianna Fáil without de Valera as leader. Although the government's majority was 'virtually shattered',[41] a minority Fianna Fáil administration was formed under Seán Lemass's leadership. Expectations for the life of the government were not high, and before counting came to a close, predictions were already being made that another election could be held as early as the following summer.[42] But, as Maurice Manning has pointed out, by 1962 'the belief that the minority government could easily be displaced had given way to a feeling that it could go quite a distance'.[43] Fine Gael, having failed to come anywhere close to an overall majority, would not simply displace the incumbent government.

Fine Gael's reluctance to consider coalition was understandable as it was still a reasonably new concept in Ireland. Indeed, as David McCullagh has noted, when the first one was formed in 1948 there had been no real tradition of coalition government in the English-speaking world (a consequence of the first-past-the-post electoral system).[44] The fact that the governing partners in 1948 and again in 1954 insisted on referring to their arrangements as 'inter-party' governments was testament to the abnormality of the situation.[45] In both governments, Fine Gael had been forced to compromise on its core values, and fear that its identity would be further eroded was natural. John Grattan Esmonde had this in mind when he considered if Fine Gael should 'go it alone' in a 1959 article for the *National Observer*. His conclusion was that the party should forget about 'being one of many' and instead adopt 'the role of leader in political thought and action'.[46] The concept of the party playing a leading role was one easily reconciled with Declan Costello's intentions, and so it is hardly surprising that such opinions were found among the pages of Costello's and Alexis FitzGerald's

National Observer. What Costello subsequently outlined in 1964 provided Fine Gael with an opportunity to seize that leadership role. Despite the aversion to the concept of coalition, the reality was that Fine Gael was incapable of holding government on its own. Fianna Fáil had held a referendum in 1959 to abolish the voting system of proportional representation (PR) by means of the single transferable vote (PR-STV). PR-STV benefits smaller parties as the multi-member constituencies allow them to win seats they would not achieve under the first-past-the-post system. The electorate rejected what was, correctly, perceived as an attempt to bolster Fianna Fáil's position. The corollary of that decision, however, was that the prospect of Fine Gael achieving an overall majority was also unlikely. An exchange in the minute books of the parliamentary party from 1964 indicated that Declan Costello, aware of this reality, had advocated an alignment with Labour.[47] His father had made a similar point in a correspondence with James Dillon four years previously.[48] The Just Society had the potential to cause a re-alignment of the party system, or at least to make Fine Gael candidates more transfer friendly for Labour voters. In this respect, the Just Society should not be seen just as a document designed to change Fine Gael and Irish society but also as a tool for inter-party co-operation. Although, as the following chapters show, Labour maintained an anti-coalition stance in the 1960s, by the time of the 1973 general election, it was prepared to stand on a joint platform with Fine Gael. This was partially not only due to the disappointment of its own strategy to grow the party, but it was also made possible by Fine Gael's gradual shift to the left during this period.

By the 1960s, there was a general perception that the main political parties had little to separate them, except for their length of time in office. Michael Mills – former political correspondent with the *Irish Press*, reflecting on the situation in 1964 when he began writing about politics– recalled, 'I felt that if half of the members of any of the parties were transferred across the Dáil to another party they would be there for six months at least before they would recognise any change'.[49] Fine Gael had done little to create a distinct role for itself. John A. Costello, when asked in 1950 to contrast the nature of the governing parties and Fianna Fáil, had suggested to a gathering of diplomats in Rome that there was 'really no essential differences between the two'.[50] An article from 1958 in *Fine Gael Digest* observed that there was a lack of knowledge about what the party was doing.[51] The following year, John Grattan Esmonde, a future TD for Wexford, writing in the *National Observer*, argued that deputies were not doing enough to communicate party policies to the public, with the result that there was an air of indifference towards Fine Gael.[52]

By early 1964, Declan Costello was becoming increasingly uneasy. By-elections in Cork Borough and Kildare – both held on 19 February and prompted by the deaths of Fianna Fáil's John Galvin and Labour's long-sitting deputy and former leader, William Norton, respectively – resulted in

Fianna Fáil retaining a seat and gaining a new one. The results shattered the optimism with which Fine Gael had approached the campaigns. The party's confidence was the product of a positive experience at an earlier by-election in Dublin North-East that had been held in the immediate aftermath of the 1963 budget. The two-and-a-half per cent turnover tax, designed to stabilise prices and income, introduced in that budget was one of the most 'unpopular and controversial' of Lemass's fiscal initiatives.[53] At the by-election, the Fianna Fáil candidate Stan O'Brien was out-polled by his Fine Gael rival, Paddy Belton. However, the degree to which the unpopular turnover tax contributed to the result should not be overstated. Belton was contesting a seat vacated by Fine Gael through the death of his brother, Jack. Despite this and buoyed by its success, the party attempted to make the turnover tax the main focus of the aforementioned by-elections of February 1964; the sub-headings of the party's *Points for Speakers and Canvassers* show a heavy emphasis on the subject.[54] James Dillon had previously explained that his party was opposed to the turnover tax because 'no matter what the government says, it operates to put a growing burden on every household in this country'.[55] However, by the time of the 1964 by-elections, the tax had been begrudgingly accepted. Moreover, workers had been placated by a new wage agreement negotiated by Lemass that gave them a twelve per cent pay increase. Fine Gael's great problem was that there was little evidence that any other part of its policy, as much as one existed, had seeped through.[56] Significantly, the party had failed to capitalise on the momentum of the May 1963 by-election victory by not outlining a programme of its own. There was, as an *Irish Times* editorial suggested, a sense that history was passing the party by and that it would 'fade away' if 'something radical' were not done.[57]

Dillon felt that Fine Gael should not be discouraged by the outcome, pointing out that the party had not lost a seat. Declan Costello, in contrast, took a more dim view. In a candid appraisal of the results, he pointed out that the electorate had endorsed Fianna Fáil in two very different constituencies. It was no longer enough to simply denounce Fianna Fáil – a viable alternative had to be offered, and Fine Gael had failed to do so. Echoing the observations of various newspapers, he attributed this to the lack of an alternative or clearly-defined programme. He challenged the party to specify the nature of its programme for government, if it were put to the test. The seventeenth Dáil had a minority government, and there had been speculation that adverse by-election results would lead to an early election. Had that happened, Fine Gael clearly would not have been in a position to offer voters a clear programme. (By gaining an extra seat, Lemass's government was in a more secure position, now reliant on the support of only one Independent, and any plans to call an early election were temporarily shelved.) Costello's concerns were repeated by Paddy Byrne and Gerard Sweetman, both of whom felt that a failure to communicate ideas, combined with a lack of activity in the Dáil, had impeded their prospects.[58] It was at this time that Costello began to draft his proposals to transform Fine Gael into a social reform party. The aim was not just to tackle society's ills but also to end the inertia within Fine Gael. By giving the party a definite policy that firmly located its place on the political spectrum, he sought to give Fine Gael a sense of purpose, thus allowing it to define itself as something other than Fianna Fáil's opposition.

There is a general perception that Costello's proposals led to the setting up of a policy committee. However, as minutes of the parliamentary party show, on 4 March 1964 – one month before Costello circulated the proposals – the formation of an organisation and propaganda committee and of a policy committee was announced. Recognition of a need for change appeared to be gaining momentum. Fine Gael's failure to communicate its ideas to a wider audience had previously been a fatal flaw. Telefís Éireann was keen to engage with politics, but politicians in general had been wary about interacting with this new medium, conscious, as John Bowman explains, that television had the 'reputation of being both powerful and fickle'.[59] Arrangements were now being put in place to communicate the party's work to the television network to ensure coverage of its plans. However, there were limits to the extent to which Fine Gael would embrace change. The left-leaning *National Observer* journal, which Costello had been instrumental in creating, had attracted some criticism, while the internal Research and Information Centre that he had helped to establish had been wound up. In discussing the remit for the policy committee, Liam Cosgrave, who was to serve as chairman, favoured 'examining existing policy, re-drafting and expanding'.[60] The group, judging by Cosgrave's description, was thus not intended to function primarily as a forum to debate and develop new ideas but rather to build on existing policies. With such an obvious lack of interest in change, Costello began to question his place in Fine Gael. FitzGerald recalled a lunch with Costello in Dublin's Unicorn restaurant at this time in which he expressed his interest in standing for election, to which Costello replied: 'For God's sake, don't join Fine Gael at the moment, I may be leaving it'.[61] Defecting to the Labour Party would have been the obvious choice. Commentators have pointed out that Labour was not overtly socialist at that time, refraining from describing itself as such until June 1964. The political scientist Basil Chubb had observed in a 1959 publication that 'there is no radical or socialist party in Ireland', while Noel Browne claimed that it was only in the late sixties and early seventies that 'talk of liberal, even socialist thought in the Republic' emerged. Nonetheless, Labour would almost certainly have been more receptive to Costello. Indeed, when Brendan Halligan became political director of the Labour Party, he was given a series of tasks by Brendan Corish, one of which was to recruit Declan Costello and Garret FitzGerald.[62] When *Towards a Just Society* was later published, the party criticised it publicly as a late conversion to Labour's policies. But, as Michael

Gallagher has pointed out, 'some senior members were privately impressed by Costello's efforts'.[63] It is unclear who prompted Costello, if indeed anyone did, to place his ideas before the party. He once recalled that 'my father didn't interfere with me except on that occasion. He said to me, "Look, I know, Declan, how you are feeling, but give them a chance". So I did'.[64] Subsequently, during the course of an interview for the RTÉ television series *One-to-One*, he told David McCullagh that his father never discussed the situation with him. Rather Michael O'Higgins – possibly at the prompting of Costello Senior – made an approach and urged him to give the Fine Gael members an opportunity to examine his proposal in detail before making any decisions about the future.[65] The identity of the person responsible is a moot point as Costello did ultimately place his proposal before Fine Gael. Vincent Browne has raised the possibility that Costello may have even anticipated the rejection of the document, leaving him free to join Labour.[66] As the son of John A. Costello, Declan Costello's choice of Fine Gael as the party to join was unquestioned, and to leave would have been an extremely difficult decision to make. Halligan was convinced that 'he would have joined the Labour Party had it not been for his father. It's as simple as that'.[67] Given the strong dynastic complexion to Irish politics, it has been a rarity – though not unheard of – for politically-active relations of high-profile party members to switch allegiances.

Aware that the views he had held for some time were not 'shared by the majority' of his colleagues on the front bench, Costello took the extraordinary step of breaching protocol. He by-passed the front bench and instead sent a circular to all members of the parliamentary party on 27 April 1964. It was a bold but decisive move that ensured his proposals were discussed. It also revealed his political astuteness. Had the proposal been formally placed before the front bench and rejected by it, the wider parliamentary party would never have had the opportunity to examine the document's content. Costello explained how he wanted to gauge the reception of the party in general, asking for a formal vote on his proposals if necessary. As will be discussed more fully in the coming chapters, work on advancing the Just Society lapsed between the 1965 and 1969 elections; one of the criticisms made of the failure to progress the concept was directed at Declan Costello himself, who was accused of lacking ambition. To deliver on his aims, it was felt by some that he should have challenged the leadership. However, it would have been inadvisable for him to have done so in 1964, and the fact that he approached the party as a whole, rather than building up support within and creating a cohort of supporters, helped his case. In doing so, he protected himself from the charge of acting out of personal ambition, and it meant that the debate focussed largely on policy rather than personalities (although the divide between himself and Gerard Sweetman could not be avoided).

The document was the subject of discussion at four meetings of the parliamentary party, beginning on 29 April. Costello proposed that the policy be based upon eight principles:

1. Sufficient Economic Progress cannot be achieved by economic 'programming'. Full scale economic planning is necessary.
2. Economic planning will involve not only detailed targets for the public sector, but for the private sector as well. The government must take the necessary legislative power to ensure that the targets are realised.
3. A new Ministry for Economic Affairs should be established which would, with the assistance of a Planning Board, draw up the detailed Plan and ensure its implementation.
4. No effective economic planning and no effective economic progress are possible unless the credit policies of the commercial banks are brought under government control.
5. The government must undertake direct investment in the industrial field.
6. The declared policy of the present government cutting down social capital investment is wrong and must be reversed.
7. The declared preference of the present government for indirect as against direct taxation is wrong and must be reversed.
8. Full and effective price control must be introduced.

The Dublin correspondent of the *Connacht Tribune* observed that 'the youth of the party' had 'taken up the challenge' to transform Fine Gael.[68] The debate, in which nearly every deputy participated, was depicted by many at the time, and has been since, as a struggle between two generations within Fine Gael: the so-called 'young tigers' led by Declan Costello and the establishment represented by James Dillon and Gerard Sweetman. However, the divide was not so clear-cut. Costello was thirty-seven, making him twenty-four years James Dillon's junior. But Patrick McGilligan – whose intervention was crucial for the policy's acceptance – was seventy-five, while opponent Paddy Belton, at thirty-seven, was the same age as Costello.

The initial reaction of the parliamentary party was one of wariness. Several colleagues, including Richie Ryan, Michael O'Higgins and Tom O'Donnell, all of whom would have been on the conservative side of the party, favoured a fuller discussion of the content and proposed sending the document to the newly instituted policy committee for further consideration. Maurice Dockrell – first elected to the Dáil in 1943 and from a strong Fine Gael family – was the only deputy to voice his opposition at that first meeting. Although he later showed himself to be a liberal on social issues during the debate on family planning in the 1970s, he was 'categorically' opposed to the views expressed in the document. At that meeting, Gerard Sweetman expressed the view that the country needed 'alternative governments rather than alternative policies'.[69] Although this was not the clear-cut rejection made by Dockrell, there could have been little doubt about where he stood.

Gerard Sweetman first came to prominence through his involvement with the Blueshirt movement. A member of the League of Youth (one of the movement's many incarnations), he was elected to its national council at the Second Annual Blueshirt Congress in August 1935.[70] He entered active political life as a candidate for Carlow-Kildare in 1937, but on the two occasions which he contested that constituency – in 1937 and again in 1943 – he was unsuccessful. The composition of the constituency did not favour a candidate with a base in north Kildare. However, in 1943 he was elected to the Seanad for the agricultural panel and remained a senator until 1948. At that year's general election, he contested the newly created three-seat constituency of Kildare and was successful, holding his seat at every subsequent election until his death in January 1970. Though spending much of his career on the opposition benches, he held the position of Minister for Finance in the second inter-party government. He is probably best remembered for appointing the then thirty-nine-year-old T.K. Whitaker as secretary of the department in May 1956. It was an extraordinary move to appoint such a young man to the head of the civil service above his more senior colleagues. It was a particularly difficult time to hold that portfolio due to financial uncertainty, and Sweetman's popularity plummeted. His 1956 budget was largely blamed for the government's defeat the following year.

His first experience as a TD had coincided with Fine Gael taking office in 1948 and he was appointed party whip (Liam Cosgrave was government chief whip). It was not only a challenging role given the diversity of that government and the conflicting ideologies of the various parties but it also gave him an opportunity to establish himself within the parliamentary party. When Fine Gael returned to the opposition benches in 1951, he retained the position. Such were his organisational skills that he became national director of organisation in 1957. This post gave him an extensive knowledge and understanding of the party across the country. Oliver Flanagan later described him as the 'most energetic and able political organiser in Europe',[71] while a profile in *Nusight* claimed 'he commanded a widespread respect, if not the loyalty, of the Fine Gael rank and file'.[72] Furthermore, as a trustee of the party, he had an intimate knowledge of the profile of those who gave crucial financial support.

There was more to his opposition to the Just Society than him simply being a member of the old guard, unable to change. As Garret FitzGerald put it, 'he was not an ideological right-winger, but rather a politician with a business orientation and a practical interest in winning power for his party ... In what he conceived to be the interests of the party he could be quite ruthless'.[73] It is conceivable that his opposition to the Just Society was driven less by own his personal views and more by his concern for the implications that the proposed policy shift might have on the party, both electorally and financially. It was a period before opinion polling was regularly used to measure political sentiment and support, but, more than most of the deputies, he had a working knowledge of Fine Gael's support base and of the profile of the party's financial backers. And when it became apparent that the proposal could not be defeated, as discussed below, he fought to have the interests of the farmers and those who favoured private enterprise – Fine Gael's traditional supporters – represented in the compromise document that emerged.

By the time of the next meeting on 5 May, deputies had had an opportunity to consider and discuss Costello's proposals among themselves. The nature of the contributions varied between those of Seán Collins, deputy for Cork South-West who favoured new methods, and of Louth's Paddy Donegan, who preferred the maintenance of Fine Gael's traditional role as a private enterprise party. Both in their forties, their contrasting views serve as a further reminder that the Just Society debate was not a generational clash. By then the battle lines had also been drawn between Costello and Sweetman, with the former imploring his colleagues to 'avoid any spurious compromises'.[74] The gap between the two men widened as the debate progressed.

Patrick McGilligan's was the dominant voice at that second meeting. First elected to the Dáil in 1923 as a representative of the then National University constituency, he was invited to the cabinet table as Minister for Industry and Commerce only three months later and brought great energy and creativity to the portfolio. He held that ministry – along with External Affairs from October 1927 – until the government's defeat in 1932. When Fine Gael returned to power as part of the first inter-party government sixteen years later, he became Minister for Finance and was subsequently Attorney General by his own request in the second such government (1954–57). He was identified as one of the three most influential people at the cabinet table; the other two being John A. Costello and Gerard Sweetman.[75]

When taken in the context of one of his most popularly recalled speeches of the 1920s, McGilligan's endorsement of Costello's proposal seems peculiar. During the course of a debate on unemployment in 1924 he had made the extraordinary admission that people might have to die of starvation. Far less reported is his remark that such an occurrence would not be a type of solution he desired.[76] However, he proved himself capable of radical thinking by initiating the great Shannon electrification scheme during those years. The project was widely criticised at the time, largely because of the scale envisioned. The River Liffey, considered more reasonable in size, was proposed as an alternative. Reflecting this, four private bills were put before a Dáil committee in 1924. However, McGilligan stood firm, arguing that the Liffey was too small and would supply Dublin only. The Shannon scheme was completed on 29 October 1929 and by 1937 the power station at Ardnacrusha supplied eighty-seven per cent of the demand across the Free

State.[77] His support for the Just Society reflected this ability and willingness to think broadly. In what the *Connaught Telegraph* described 'as one of the best [speeches] of his career',[78] McGilligan argued that securing full employment and increasing the standard of living should be the party's objectives. Echoing Costello's own concerns, he asked his colleagues to consider the policies upon which they would have based their programme for government had they formed an administration after the 1961 election.[79] As one of the most respected senior members of the party, McGilligan's decision to associate himself with the document was central to having it accepted. In 1955, John O'Donovan, TD for Dublin South-East, had suggested that McGilligan had 'the power of persuasion' over Dillon.[80] Indeed, the party leader – though not necessarily agreeing with the content – considered the intervention to have been of 'priceless value'.[81]

The next scheduled meeting, due to take place on 13 May, was cancelled as a mark of respect following the death of their colleague and TD for Roscommon, James Burke. This meant that before the parliamentary party could reassemble to continue the debate, delegates would gather for the annual Ard Fheis, occurring on the weekend of 19 and 20 May. Costello had asked that his document be kept confidential, but by then, the media was well aware of the discussions due to a leak, and the Fine Gael politicians were closely watched for indications of how the party had reacted to the proposals. When later asked if he was responsible for releasing the content, Costello replied that he was 'absolutely innocent'.[82] *Nusight* reported in 1970 that 'it is now widely believed that [Gerard] Sweetman was the person who leaked this document to the papers in the hope of nipping it in the bud'.[83] Paddy Harte, then a first-time TD for Donegal North-East, has since claimed responsibility in his autobiography, *Young Tigers and Mongrel Foxes*. If indeed he was responsible, the circumstances were innocent. He missed the first two meetings at which the document was discussed due to his attendance at a conference in Hamburg for young European politicians. On his return to Leinster House, he found an envelope marked 'confidential' waiting for him. When he met fellow Donegal-man and journalist Seamus Brady in the corridor, Brady asked to see the envelope, which Harte duly handed over, later claiming that he had not noticed the 'confidential' classification. When Brady returned the content, he promised that he would not use it. Although he kept his promise, the story appeared in print in other publications the following day.[84] Regardless of the identity of the person responsible, the leak was hardly surprising. Moreover, it forced the issue: with the eyes of the media on Fine Gael, the parliamentary party had to reach a conclusion. Costello later reflected that had he known the effect that leaking the document would have, he might have considered taking that course of action himself.[85] *The Irish Times* broadly welcomed Costello's initiative, recognising it as having the potential to 'end the present "purgatory" of the party' and suggested that it could have far-reaching consequences for the other two main parties.[86] In contrast, the *Irish Independent* adopted something of a respectful curiosity, preferring to wait to see how the policy developed.[87]

The Just Society proposal did not feature specifically on the agenda for the Ard Fheis. An *Irish Independent* editorial suggested that if the two-day meeting did not clarify Fine Gael's position, the country would be left without a clear understanding of where the party stood: 'The nation's interest requires that Fine Gael declare itself'.[88] However, the Ard Fheis is not a policy-making forum. Furthermore, as the document was not fully discussed and the parliamentary party had yet to vote, it could not have appeared officially on the agenda. Nonetheless, Costello's philosophy was represented in other ways. The political correspondent of *The Irish Times* observed that of the seventy-six motions on the agenda, 'almost all of them could be described as socially radical'.[89] Among the motions was a resolution from M. Reidy of the Dublin Central branch advocating the establishment of a Ministry for Economic Planning, a central tenet of Costello's proposals. Clearly Costello's thinking, while at odds with his front bench colleagues, captured the views of a wider section of the party. A special correspondent from *The Irish Times* noted that there were 'some reports ... [of] a big volume of support for most of the eight points',[90] and Costello himself later recalled that there was a lot of support forthcoming from ordinary members of the party.[91] Jim Dorgan of the John Marcus O'Sullivan branch described the plan during the Ard Fheis as 'a very bold one' and said that 'it was in the interests of the Fine Gael party that bold and imaginative plans should be put forward'.[92] He recalled that there was 'dead silence' from the platform.[93] Although the document was not directly dealt with during the two-day event at the Mansion House, interest in the proposal was considered by one commentator to have been an important factor in the success of that year's gathering and 'the vitality with which most questions were tackled'.[94] It also suggested that the leadership's reservations (although a reflection of their desire to maintain traditional policies) were out of touch with the party, and, perhaps, the wider community also.

The full extent to which Costello's views represented those of the grassroots is hard to gauge. Although records for the party's branches are held at UCD Archives, they do not pre-date 1964, making it difficult to draw conclusions about the level of debate and new thinking that might have emerged. Additionally, the available collections vary in content from branch to branch, with the emphasis mostly on membership records. The Central Branch, which was by far the most active and was home to some of the more progressive elements of the party, was the exception. That branch appeared to welcome Costello's proposals, and he was later the guest speaker at a branch-organised meeting on the subject of economic planning.[95] The executive of Costello's own constituency of Dublin North-West 'enthusiastically' supported his efforts and unanimously passed a resolution of congratulations after the parliamentary party adopted the policy.[96]

There were indirect references to the behind-the-scenes discussion at the Ard Fheis, particularly evident in unscripted remarks by Dillon. Although he did not refer directly to Costello's proposal, he spoke of how Fine Gael would always encourage free discussion, but then remarked that 'Young men could dream dreams and have visions, but there were no short cuts'.[97] If this were not wounding enough, in his leader's address he also 'denigrated young men in a hurry', while praising Gerard Sweetman.[98] Observers were left in little doubt as to where he stood. While the *Irish Independent* refrained from speculation,[99] the political correspondent of *The Irish Times* reported that 'the principals had taken up their positions' at the Ard Fheis. There were no real surprises: James Dillon and Gerard Sweetman were named as favouring the party's existing policy, while Liam Cosgrave was deemed a supporter of Costello.[100] On initial inspection, the latter might appear a surprising designation. But although Cosgrave was not an ardent supporter of Costello's ideas, he took a pragmatic approach. Patrick Lindsay described him as having a 'great "nose" for changing circumstances, a "nose" and an instinct that would help him go in the right direction and make the right decisions'.[101] Though only forty-four, he was one of the longest serving members of Fine Gael. Having been in Leinster House for twenty-one years, he had sat on the government benches for a total of only six years during that time. He saw in the document an opportunity to challenge the dominance of Fianna Fáil.[102] As he put it to those assembled at the Ard Fheis, 'if we are content merely to be critics of Fianna Fáil we will accept a negative role which may be a self-satisfying ordinance but is, in fact, frustrating and unrewarding'.[103] The Just Society provided the scope to offer a credible alternative. He also viewed the document as an opportunity to 'still forever the haunting spectre of a Tory ghost' – of which John A. Costello had warned – sometimes attributed to the party.[104]

Cosgrave's Ard Fheis speech is likely to have been a pivotal factor in the policy's acceptance; he had the ability to appeal to both groups. Although not making explicit reference to the document at the Ard Fheis, he referred to the necessity of keeping 'slightly to the left'[105] – a clear indication that he supported the direction in which Costello was attempting to shift the party. But because he had not moved openly to the left himself, he could retain the support of the traditionalists, and by acknowledging the potential of Costello's proposals, his views were palatable to the more progressive elements. Essentially, he took up a centrist position. Potentially this was a carefully calculated approach, with an eye to future leadership. His pronouncements, according to the political correspondent of *The Irish Times*, seemed to have 'impressed a lot of the more senior members of the party who already had been shaken in their beliefs by the brilliant analysis' provided by McGilligan.[106] When the parliamentary party next met on 20 May, Cosgrave – confirming his belief that the party should 'appear to be progressive and to be moving with the times' – endorsed Costello's proposal, albeit with some reservations. Tom O'Higgins also announced his '100%' support. But despite the admissions of the Fine Gael heavyweights, some lingering doubts remained. Anthony Esmonde, whose family had represented the party in Wexford since 1923, declared that he could not accept the proposal in full, while Stephen Barrett of Cork Borough wanted certain unspecified technical difficulties clarified.[107]

The final discussion took place on 26 May. Dillon made reference to talks over the weekend that had involved Deputies Liam Cosgrave, Michael O'Higgins, Declan Costello, Gerard Sweetman and Senator Michael Hayes.[108] It is believed that a compromise was ultimately reached when Costello and Sweetman met in a pub in either Clonskeagh or Churchtown on the evening of the 25 May.[109] The outcome of the ninety-minute meeting was a revised nine-point document, put before the parliamentary party the following day. Points one (the need for economic planning), three (Ministry for Economic Planning) and six (reversal of government's policy on reducing social capital investment) either remained unchanged or were reworded only slightly. But with the inclusion of such expressions as 'where necessary', 'as far as possible' and 'in so far as possible', the remaining document offered far less commitment than Costello's original proposals. For example, the second point in both documents related to targets for the public and private sectors. Costello declared that the government 'must take the necessary legislative power to ensure that the targets are realised'. Though essentially similar in content, the compromise document included the suitably vague expression 'where necessary'. The subtle difference in language was important; it allowed Sweetman to allay the concerns of those who favoured Fine Gael's traditional role as a private enterprise party. As he explained, he would not have assented to 'any coercion of private enterprise'.[110] Similarly, 'where desirable in the public interest' was added to number five in which Costello had originally stated that the government 'must undertake direct investment in the industrial field dealt with direct government investment in industry'.

In addition to providing loopholes that would allow room for manoeuvre on certain commitments, the compromise document contained some substantial changes from the original. Point number four had proposed bringing the commercial banks directly under government control; instead, it was suggested that that responsibility be given to the Central Bank, with practice in line with government policy. The focus also shifted in point seven, in which Costello had suggested that the Fianna Fáil government's preference for indirect as against direct taxation should be reversed. This was modified to propose that the taxation system, which weighed most heavily on the poorest sections of the community, should be reversed, bringing the proposal into line with traditional Fine Gael policy.

Significantly, a new ninth point was added. This related to improving the standard of living in the agricultural sector to equate with non-agricultural occupations.[111] As Dillon's biographer points out, some saw this as a sop to the party leader.[112] Dillon's commitment to the agricultural sector is unquestionable, but to dismiss the inclusion of that sector as merely a concession is unfair to what was arguably a strategic and shrewd inclusion by Sweetman. It also further suggests that Sweetman's opposition to Costello's proposals was not based purely on ideological grounds, but that he was being guided by his concern for the party's electoral health. An earlier article in *The Kerryman* had complained that Costello 'had no message for agriculture'.[113] Though Sweetman's own family was of the landed-class and the Kildare constituency was hardly representative of the wider electorate, he would have been mindful of the party's membership profile, a large component of which was composed of the agricultural community. By the late 1950s, the National Farmers Association (NFA) was 'deeply disturbed' at what it perceived as a growing imbalance between agricultural and industrial incomes.[114] By introducing this extra point, which reflected the main plank of past Fine Gael policy, Sweetman sought to reassure traditional supporters that their interests would still be represented, despite changes in the party's outlook. Additionally, it gave the Just Society proposals a rural dimension and reassured those who were struggling that Fine Gael was aware of their difficulties. As many farmers were suspicious of Lemass's commitment to agriculture, this was an important statement.[115] Intriguingly, as discussed more fully in Chapter 3, when the points were developed into a complete policy document, agriculture did not receive a dedicated section. This reflects the fact that it was predominantly the work of Costello, and it left the document open to the criticism of a Dublin, urban-bias.

Costello described the nine-point plan as a 'milestone in the history of Fine Gael' and deemed it a 'fair consensus of views' – a description echoed by Gerard Sweetman. Behind the scenes, however, Sweetman remained opposed. Michael McWey assisted Sweetman on many campaigns before joining him on the party ticket in Kildare for the 1969 election. He recalled a tirade against Costello and the Just Society from Sweetman during a particular car journey to Roscommon to canvass for a by-election there in July 1964.[116] It is reasonable to surmise that Costello would have left Fine Gael had the proposal been rejected and, perhaps, motivated by fear of the consequences of his departure, Fine Gael unanimously, but tentatively, endorsed the nine-point programme, requesting that its content be developed into something more substantial. John A. Costello is reputed to have told his Garda driver that had it been rejected, 'he would nearly have felt he would have to resign'.[117] However, despite Sweetman's utterances of support – and those of James Dillon – when put to the test at the 1965 general election, the leaderships' commitment seemed to not only waiver but also collapse. This was arguably due to an unyielding belief in Fine Gael's core values, reinforced by the opinions of traditional supporters expressed during the canvass.

Throughout the talks, and despite what would transpire during the election campaign, there was an apparent consciousness of the need to modernise Fine Gael and to carve out a definite place for the party in the political system. The need to display a united front was particularly emphasised at the last meeting. In the longer-term, a unified appearance would be essential to selling the policy to the media and ultimately to the electorate. There was also a more immediate requirement: the party was facing a by-election in Roscommon following the earlier-mentioned death of James Burke in May. His widow, Joan, contested the seat on the Fine Gael ticket and was elected on the second count. Although the party was in the stronger position of defending its seat, the experience of Cork Borough and Kildare had clearly shown that Fine Gael urgently needed to define itself as something other than a party opposed to Fianna Fáil.

Liam Cosgrave's policy committee was to provide the forum for the process of developing the nine-point policy into a comprehensive programme. Costello invited Garret FitzGerald – a future leader of the party who was wrestling with the idea of joining Fine Gael 'in its current incarnation'[118] at that time – to contribute to the formulation of the policy document. FitzGerald recalled in his *All in a life* how 'the following nine months were a busy period as our somewhat heterogeneous group, which was bound together by one common factor – admiration for Declan Costello and for his effort to give a new, contemporary relevance to Irish politics – struggled to produce a set of coherent policy documents covering a wide range of issues'.[119] An initial draft covering national, economic and social policy was submitted to Cosgrave's committee by July 1964.

Cosgrave described his involvement as that of filling the role of 'chairman until agreement was reached on an agreed document';[120] he never participated in the actual drafting. This was typical of how the committees worked. For example, Dónal Flynn recalled that the social policy committee, chaired by Paddy Belton, met only twice.[121] The drafting was conducted mostly at Costello's home, and although assistance was available during the process, Costello authored the majority of what was produced. As FitzGerald explained, this was because Costello had worked hard on and thought out his ideas over a longer period of time; the others were coming to theirs much later and as a result their policies were not as well advanced.[122] FitzGerald's own contribution came in the form of a wealth tax to replace death duties, but this was not included in the final document. He later succeeded in having it incorporated into the programme for government outlined by the Fine Gael-Labour coalition that came to power in 1973, although its implementation proved unsuccessful. Richie Ryan was the secretary of Cosgrave's committee. When the document reached them, he argued against the use of language typically associated with those ideologically committed to the left. *Towards a Just Society* – the party's 1965 election manifesto – was consequently edited to remove any such terminology. As he explained, its inclusion would have led people to believe that Fine Gael had swung to the extreme left, which was never the intention.[123] Protecting itself from the charge of dangerous socialism or even communism, the manifesto was framed within the context of 'the social doctrines contained in the Papal Encyclicals'.[124]

In late 1964, hints were offered of what the Costello group was producing before the finalised product was officially unveiled in March the following year. Addressing an audience on the eve of polling day for the Galway East by-election in December, Dillon spoke of the need for a ministry for economic planning, the provision of an extensive housing programme, equal opportunities in education across all three levels, free health service and a choice of doctor for all. Effectively Dillon outlined a policy that had at its core the guiding principles of what would become the party's manifesto in 1965. He followed this up by affirming that his party – acting out of the conviction that 'any nation which cannot look after its poor cannot long protect its rich' – was committed to creating a just society.[125] With an increase of almost twenty-eight per cent on the 1961 figure,[126] Fine Gael secured an impressive victory in the constituency, but it would be incorrect to interpret the result as a resounding endorsement of the party's new direction. The vacancy had been created by the tragic death of Clann na Talmhan's Michael Donnellan during the all-Ireland football final in which the Galway team was captained by his son, John. Sweetman secured a political coup when he succeeded in convincing John Donnellan to contest the seat; the emotional nature of his candidacy 'transcended all traditional allegiances' in a constituency that was a Fianna Fáil strong-hold.[127] This was emphasised by *The Irish Times* in the days after the contest. An article appeared in its pages enquiring about the existence of the policy committee, which had disappeared from the public eye, and warning Fine Gael against resting on its laurels. Failure to deliver on the promised policy, coupled with an overoptimism based on the recent result, it was suggested, could result in East Galway being the 'mirage that finally led the party to destruction'.[128]

The decision was ultimately taken to postpone publication of *Towards a Just Society* until after the forthcoming mid-Cork by-election, scheduled for 10 March 1965. It was generally accepted that an adverse result for the government would finally lead to the much-anticipated general election. Moreover, although the document would not have impacted on the result, Costello's opponents could have depicted an adverse result as a rejection of his policies. Labour's Eileen Desmond retained the seat of her late husband, Dan, but before she could even take her seat, Lemass visited President de Valera at Áras an Uachtaráin to request a dissolution of the Dáil. Lemass's decision to call an election earlier than was necessary was perceived by Fine Gael as an attempt to pre-empt the publication of a fully-fledged proposal. A letter from Costello to Dillon on 6 February 1965 would seem to indicate that his Fine Gael colleagues had caused a delay preventing completion.

Costello bemoaned the fact that much of the work had been completed – including reference to economic experts – but that a final decision had yet to be made by the parliamentary party. He also feared that the document would be presented to the wider party via the front bench, whose members would take the opportunity to revise contentious content. Although Dillon responded that such would not be the case, Costello expressed further concern on 13 February that the lingering debate would only result in a hardening of opinion, particularly since those opposed had not offered any alternatives.[129] Indeed, during the year in which the manifesto was being drafted, no other policy initiatives had been forthcoming. Garret FitzGerald recalled that, although Costello was happy that his proposal had been accepted, he was sceptical of the party's true support. When FitzGerald was approached to stand for Fine Gael in Dublin South-East, he initially agreed but withdrew his name thirty-six hours before the deadline. Though his actions were guided largely by his wife's unhappiness about his entry into parliamentary politics, on reflection, he suggested that his decision was also 'influenced perhaps by Declan's doubts'.[130]

The 1965 general election would be the first real test of the Just Society: an opportunity for the party to step out from Fianna Fáil's shadow and to convince the electorate that it had created a document not only reflective of a changing Ireland but one that also addressed those areas that had not benefited from Lemass's rising tide. But the document's reception by certain members of the Fine Gael parliamentary party– in particular, the leadership – did not bode well for its prospects among the party's traditional supporters. Furthermore, although the parliamentary party had unanimously endorsed sending Costello's proposal to the policy committee, the decision was not comparable to unanimously supporting the policy itself. And even though the document formed the foundation of the 1965 election manifesto, as the campaign clearly showed, Fine Gael was not yet ready to fully embrace change.

3
1965: The First Failure

The 1965 general election was the first public test for the Just Society. In the year between Fine Gael's adoption of the nine-point plan and the unveiling of the manifesto, *Towards a Just Society*, work had been on-going to develop Costello's proposals. In the resulting document, the outlined economic policies were largely in-line with the thinking of the day, influenced particularly by the French planning model, while the social policies reflected emerging thinking that challenged traditional practices and methods. The document was finalised only after the election was announced. Although there had been unease among certain elements of the party, no alternative policies had emerged during the course of the year. The Just Society, therefore, became official Fine Gael policy for the election almost by default. As a campaign tool, it would prove ineffective. *Towards a Just Society* was a statement of the problems in Ireland at the time and, though Costello offered some solutions, they were not the type of appealing promises that would be seen in the type of documents produced after Fianna Fáil's give-away manifesto of 1977. Essentially, what Fine Gael published was a policy document, not an election manifesto in the accepted sense. It made little impact on the voters. With limited time to publicise the document, hampered also by restricted circulation, voters never had the opportunity to familiarise themselves with the content. At national level, the impact was further undermined by the leadership's lacklustre endorsement, while, at constituency level, candidates opted instead to focus on local issues.

That Lemass called the election early was not surprising. Anxious to win an overall majority, he no doubt recalled how his former party leader had previously used snap elections to consolidate power. In 1933, 1938 and again in 1944, Eamon de Valera had called a general election within a year of the previous one. On each occasion, the outcome strengthened Fianna Fáil's position. Observers suggested that an anxiety to hold the election before the next budget had to be unveiled was among the motivating factors. A more cynical reason, advanced by Fine Gael, was supported by some commentators. Garret FitzGerald – not yet a member of the party, but who was assisting

Costello in expanding the Just Society proposals – later maintained that Lemass had called the election in an attempt to pre-empt the publication of a fully-fledged policy document.[1] It was a view that Costello himself expressed during the campaign.[2] A similar suggestion was made by Joseph Foyle, who wrote a current affairs column for the *Tipperary Star*, while an editorial in *The Irish Times* had previously suggested that the Taoiseach might go to the polls early if the opportunity to 'break Fine Gael completely' arose.[3]

As discussed in Chapter 2, the public received a glimpse of the type of proposals on offer at the Galway East by-election in December 1964. However, by January 1965, *The Irish Times* reported that people were becoming 'impatient to see some signs of Fine Gael's ability to produce the policy to which the party pledged itself'.[4] The process was slow-moving, but rushed in the end. Garret FitzGerald recalled a meeting in his house the night after the general election was called to assemble the documents for presentation to the party the following morning.[5] These were approved by the front bench in the first few days of the campaign and were presented with the title *Towards a Just Society* as the party's official election manifesto. The majority of the document contained new policy initiatives, and it was hardly surprising that it thus ran to almost 40,000 words. While Costello's original eight-point plan had focussed heavily on economics, the developed document gave equal attention to social policies. The proposals outlined ranged from greater state involvement in the economy through planning, to reforms of the health system, to a national programme for youth.

In the introduction, Costello summed up society's social ills:

> Too many are unemployed and are forced to emigrate; too many ... are employed at miserably low wages and salaries; too many have only a small income or pension; many survive on a bare subsistence from a small farm; many are kept just above starvation level (but nothing more) by the inadequate social welfare payments they receive; many live in squalor and appallingly overcrowded conditions.[6]

The document argued that equality of social and economic opportunities did not exist in Ireland, as the nurturing of productive investment to stimulate the economy had taken precedence over social reform. While acknowledging that 'no government can abolish all the hardships and difficulties of life', Costello argued that 'many avoidable ones exist in present day Ireland'. This could only be rectified by a 'bold and vigorous programme of economic and social reform'.

Towards a Just Society: economic reform

Costello's social policies, as discussed below, were very much informed by an emerging debate in Ireland about the needs of society and the government's responsibility for providing for those needs. His economic policies were influenced by trends abroad – by the success of French post-war reconstruction and by those policies advocated by British Labour leader, Hugh Gaitskell.[7] Fine Gael had traditionally been a party of private enterprise. It was Costello's rejection of that attitude that caused most unease within the party, prompting Sweetman to reassure supporters that he would not have assented to any compromise that would have threatened that position. However, *Towards a Just Society* did advocate greater state involvement.

Having succeeded Clement Attlee as Labour Party leader in 1955, Gaitskell had attempted to change the party's approach to meet new social and economic conditions. Much of what Costello later proposed would have fit comfortably with Gaitskell's programme, which, not unlike the Just Society, divided his party. Gaitskell, as Costello would, coupled social justice with economic efficiency, to be achieved through economic planning. During his leadership (1955–63), the party was split between the Gaitskellite social democratic right and the socialist left, grouped around Aneurin Bevan, who had also contested the leadership. Speaking at the party's 1959 conference, Gaitskell defined socialism as 'first of all equality and social justice'. His aims included, co-operation, accountability, planning for full employment and higher productivity.[8] The divisions within Labour, which his policies exasperated, signalled to the electorate that the party was divided. Moreover, the Conservative Party, which claimed the post-war prosperity to be a product of their governance, exploited the disagreements over Gaitskell's strategy at the 1961 election with the slogan, 'Conservative prosperity works, don't let Labour ruin it!'.[9] Like the Just Society, Gaitskell's policies remained untested as Labour stayed on the opposition benches during his leadership.

The economic section of *Towards a Just Society* drew heavily on the French planning model. Costello identified a number of parallels between the two countries, including 'considerable regional disparities in development' – a theme he reiterated in a 1965 article for *Hibernia*.[10] In late 1945, Jean Monnet had communicated to Charles de Gaulle a series of proposals that included developing national production and foreign trade, increasing productivity, ensuring the full employment of manpower and increasing the standard of living.[11] This led to the establishment in January 1946 of the new Commissariat Général au Plan, of which Monnet was the head. The body, which initially co-ordinated the government's economic policy and subsequently drafted and implemented the economic plan, was explained in great detail in Costello's document. He maintained that the French model of economic planning, rather than the Irish government's favoured policy of programming, would be a more effective method for the Irish situation. The extent to which the dynamic change experienced in France after the war was the product of planning has since been the subject of debate. As Maurice Larkin has noted, the example of the West German miracle, achieved without planning, is often used to suggest that the contribution of planning to France's resurgence has been greatly exaggerated. But, as he further points out, this contention fails to take into consideration well-established German entrepreneurial attitudes and the advantages of rich mineral and demographic resources. The aim in France was to create a mind-set similar to that which already existed in Germany.[12]

Costello, as he explained in *Towards a Just Society*, did not simply propose transposing French planning onto the Irish situation without modification. But he felt that there were lessons to be learnt from their experience, ones that offered Ireland a better structure for economic growth than the approach favoured by the Fianna Fáil government. He was particularly critical of the programme for economic expansion, which he felt was a statement of what would happen in order to obtain growth, but that it did not offer any explanation as to how that could be achieved.[13] 'One of the central arguments running through' *Towards a Just Society* was that:

[M]erely to talk about economic growth and forecast economic growth without planning for it, is a serious abdication of responsibility. Faith in economic progress is a desirable virtue, but unaccompanied by the necessary activity to ensure it, it becomes a dangerous delusion; it is as wrong to presume salvation in the sphere of economics as it is in the realm of theology.

Doubt has since been cast over the alleged success of the first programme: 'another view posits that the economy which was emerging from recession in any case would have performed just as well in the absence of the programme'.[14] Costello certainly maintained that the government's programme benefited from fortunate timing and changing circumstances,[15] a claim not undisputed by economists. As Cormac Ó Gráda has suggested, the growth of 1958/59 probably had much more to do with the end of the recession in the UK than such factors as economic planning or Seán Lemass's accession as Taoiseach.[16]

Towards a Just Society: social justice

In many ways, *Towards a Just Society* was a document reflective of its time. Many of the social policies proposed were part of an emerging international discourse that re-evaluated the role of the state and its duty towards its citizens. According to the party's election handbook, Fine Gael was 'dedicated to wage war on poverty in this country'.[17] It was language reminiscent of American president Lyndon Johnson who had announced a similar mission the previous year: 'This administration today, here and now, declares unconditional war on poverty in America'. His state of the union address led to a poverty bill, at the centre of which was community action.[18] Garret FitzGerald later commented that, although there was a certain level of consciousness about reforms in America, Costello and his supporters were not influenced by such developments.[19] Nonetheless, Ireland, perhaps unconsciously, was taking part in a broader reinterpretation of the role of the state. As already discussed in Chapter 1, this change was not confined to politicians and policymakers; the Catholic Church was also beginning to reconsider the responsibilities of government. The shift in thinking was apparent in Costello's proposals on the health service, mental disabilities, the care of children in institutions and the treatment of young offenders.

Criticism was made of 'totally inadequate health [services]'. Extension of services and a choice of doctor for all were advocated in place of the dispensary service. Previously, Fianna Fáil's Seán MacEntee, in his role as Minister for Health, had considered introducing a choice of doctor, but within the dispensary system.[20] A proposal, similar to Costello's to cease with the system altogether, was later outlined in the 1966 White Paper on Health. It too proposed that the dispensary service be replaced throughout the country by a system that would allow for a choice of doctor, and it was estimated that the majority of the population would have access to a range of at least two doctors.[21] The old dispensary system was in line with the Catholic Church's principle of subsidiarity: providing health care for the poor through the system was considered acceptable when the poor could not provide for themselves.[22] The shift away from the dispensary system reflected the Church's changing attitude towards the role of the state, contrasting with the controversy over the Mother and Child scheme. Costello argued that, in addition to high administrative costs, access to a dispensary doctor could be problematic for those not living in close proximity. Additionally, if a patient lost confidence in their doctor, there was no alternative. Costello also pointed out that the lack of financial assistance for middle earners had resulted in over-crowding in hospitals. It has been estimated that approximately thirty per cent of the population was entitled to free dispensary treatment, a figure roughly unchanged since the 1920s. However, the 1953 Health Act had provided for free or heavily-subsidised hospital treatment for the majority of the population.[23] As the average charge in 1963 for a visit to a doctor was 10 shillings and a house-call cost 15 shillings,[24] it was hardly surprising that patients not covered by the free dispensary service by-passed their doctor in favour of the free-of-charge service at a hospital.

Costello estimated that his health policies would cost the state ten or eleven million pounds. The service would be based on insurance, financed through a one-third contribution from the state, and two-thirds by employers, employees and the self-employed. This approach was broadly in line with recent Fine Gael proposals. Dr T. F. O'Higgins, the party's then spokesperson on health, had proposed a scheme from the opposition benches in 1961 that he urged Minister MacEntee to accept. Based on proposals outlined by Fine Gael during that year's general election campaign, O'Higgins outlined a comprehensive health service based on the principle of insurance, extended to eighty-five per cent of the population. It was to include free choice of doctor and hospital and specialist and diagnostic services. Those within the scheme would be taken out of the medical card bracket.[25]

In addition to general health, 'mental handicap' was given a specially-dedicated section in the manifesto. Costello was particularly active in this area. Addressing the annual conference of the Rehabilitation Institution in April 1964, he had advocated state assistance in expanding services for the mentally handicapped.[26] Speaking at his party's Ard Fheis the following month, he asserted that 'mentally handicapped children constituted one of the gravest social problems existing in this country'. He argued for the establishment of a board which would have statutory authority and function to provide institutional service and, where necessary, day centres and special schools.[27] There was a personal dimension to Costello's concerns. His eldest brother Wilfrid had been left with a mild mental disability after suffering a cerebral haemorrhage during birth,[28] while one of his own children was handicapped. At an Association of Parents and Friends of Mentally Handicapped Children event in 1957, he had spoken about the 'constant anxiety' of caring for a child who was physically handicapped.[29] Probably the least publicised of Declan Costello's undertakings is the one of which he was proudest: 'Of all the things that I did with my life, being associated with St Michael's [House] was the one I regard as the most important of all'.[30] St Michael's House today offers support and provides services to people with intellectual disabilities and their families in the greater Dublin area. The voluntary organisation had its genesis in an advertisement in *The Irish Times* in June 1955. Patricia Farrell, whose son Brian had Down's Syndrome, was seeking people interested in forming an 'Association for Parents of Mentally Backward Children'. She had been prompted to place the advertisement after discovering that institutionalised residential care was the only service available to children who had intellectual disabilities. Costello chaired the first public meeting that resulted from her appeal, and St Michael's House subsequently grew out of that meeting. He later became president, taking over that position from his mother. In a letter to *The Irish Times* after Costello's death, Maurice Bracken, chairman of St Michael's, outlined the central and active role that Costello had played in helping the organisation 'grow to become one of Ireland's largest providers of community-based day and residential services'.[31]

Towards a Just Society, in highlighting the lack of adequate services, was also critical of the fact that not only was the number of mentally handicapped persons in the state unknown but also 'no organised effort' had even been made to ascertain the figures. Perhaps even more damning than the absence of any data was the manner in which such people were treated. Paddy Harte, then a councillor in Donegal, recalled that the mental hospitals made no distinction between slight, mild and severe handicap.[32] A 1958 memorandum prepared for John Brady, the assistant secretary at the Department of Health, claimed, 'we are keeping patients at a low level of animal existence and actively destroying any little bit of individuality, confidence or self-respect they may have left'.[33] Many children with mental disabilities had simply been placed in adult mental hospitals, which were entirely the wrong environment for them, or they were sent to industrial schools; this was the situation with which Patricia Farrell had found herself confronted. Her experience was not unique. Annie Ryan's eldest son was born in 1964. At the age of four, Tom was diagnosed with autism. What followed was years of frustration and rejection as the Ryan family, living in Sligo, searched for a service that could assist. From Sligo to Dublin and eventually across the border to Belfast, it was impossible to find adequate care – while in Belfast, Tom developed epilepsy. As a last resort, his parents took the decision to send him, now twelve, to St Ita's mental hospital in Portrane. It was there that they met other parents in a similar situation and discovered that large numbers of people with mental handicap had nowhere to go except to such a facility. Given Tom's age, he was kept in the children's ward in the main hospital, but up to 200 people with mental handicap were resident in six wooden huts in the grounds. These had originally housed the workmen who had built the hospital in the late nineteenth century. Not until 1982 was the practice finally ended and the huts dismantled.[34]

Costello's arguments reflected an emerging new approach to the treatment of the mentally disabled. As Dermot Walsh and Antoinette Daly have pointed out, by the 1960s, the practice of institutionalising was being reversed and this was reflected in policy; the new philosophy was later articulated in the 1966 report by the Commission of Inquiry on Mental Illness.[35] The Commission had been set up in 1961 to investigate the number of people being institutionalised as the Irish figures were considerably higher than those of European neighbours. The treatment of children was one of the areas criticised in the findings. Like Costello, the authors of the report pointed to the absence of statistical data on children suffering from mental illness, although they pointed out that this was not unique to Ireland. The recommendations included the provision of child psychiatrists and the use of foster care and family group homes as alternatives to institutions. Where the latter was necessary, units were recommended that would cater specifically for short- or long-term treatment, and for those children with psychosomatic disorders.[36]

The one area of the health policies outlined above that attracted the most attention was the future plan for the dispensary service; mental health issues were mentioned only in passing in those letters retained within the Fine Gael archives. The dismantling of the dispensary service was the most controversial of the health proposals, and party headquarters received much correspondence from relevant doctors concerned for their future. Compensation, naturally, appears to have been the main concern. The disestablishment of the dispensary service would have led directly to a significant loss of earnings. Noel Reilly, the medical secretary of the Irish Medical Association, wrote for clarification as to the amount and form the compensation would take.[37] His letter was echoed by Dr Seaghán Ua Conchubhair, a dispensary doctor from Oranmore in County Galway. He wanted to know how the compensation would be financed. The response, he explained, would influence his decision and that of his friends and colleagues when casting their vote. Fine Gael's general secretary, Colonel P. F. Dineen, replied that persons made redundant would be compensated out of general taxation, pointing to the Transport Act, 1958 and Great Northern Railway Act, 1958 as examples of precedent.[38] Ua Conchubhair replied with a hard-hitting deconstruction of the health section. Though he affirmed that he would once more cast his vote for Fine Gael, it was not for the reasons the party might have wished. In fact, the doctor felt that is was safe to continue his support because he felt that Fine Gael 'had no real plan thought out in detail'. He accused the authors of having a local view of Ireland, one that was confined to Foxrock, Killiney, Portmarnock and Lucan – all upper middle-class suburbs of Dublin. As an example, he cited the reference to the 'blue card system', which ignored the fact that each health authority had its own colour for medical cards. He feared that there would be no joined-up thinking between the proposed child welfare clinics and the family doctor, and envisaged a possible scenario where the family doctor would not be informed of a treatment prescribed at one of the clinics. Ua Conchubhair also dismissed the welfare clinics, of which the mental health out-patient service for pre-school and school children would be part, as 'a lot of pretentious nonsense'. He recalled that of his near sixteen years' experience, he had seen only two school children with mental issues. He did, however, commend the abolition of the school medical examination system, voicing instead the profession's preference for review by local doctors, already familiar with many of the children. And though he felt that the proposals for dealing with mental defect were good, he felt they did not go far enough, pointing to those institutions that did not provide even basic education.[39] Dineen also engaged in extensive correspondence with Noel Reilly. When Reilly enquired if existing pensions for retired local authority officers could be adjusted in line with the increase in the cost of living, Dineen replied that Fine Gael would be amenable to such a proposal, adding 'Fine Gael always has been, is, and I can assure you will be, on the side of salary and wage earning classes and pensioners'.[40] It was a comment very revealing of the Fine Gael mind-set that Costello sought to challenge.

Towards a Just Society could further be seen as part of an emerging discourse in the area of youth policy; this subject received greater attention by policymakers in the 1960s. During that decade, the National Federation of Youth Clubs, a co-ordinating body, and the National Youth Council were established in 1961 and 1967 respectively. Significantly, from 1963 onwards, the state became more involved in youth provision. This was partially a response to Ireland's expanding young population. As previously discussed, the high levels of emigration that occurred in the 1950s had greatly affected Ireland's younger generation. With that process reversed in the early 1960s, population composition shifted. Between 1961 and 1971, census figures showed a growth in the fifteen to twenty-four age category from 391,839 to 482,978, or an increase of just over twenty-three per cent.[41] The government of the day could not ignore this expanding demographic. The publication of the Albermale Report in Britain in 1960 also proved influential.[42] That Ministry of Education White Paper– officially called *The Youth Service in England and Wales* – investigated the lack of development in youth services and made forty-four recommendations, with a specific emphasis on training, expanding the number of professional leaders and providing a funding programme for buildings and facilities. This trend towards youth provisions was reflected in the section outlining 'a national programme for youth' in *Towards a Just Society*. Quoting from the 1960 White Paper stressing the need 'to offer individual young people in their leisure time opportunities of various kinds', Costello was critical of the paucity of trained professional youth leaders. It has been estimated that there were no more than fifteen fulltime personnel involved in youth work in Ireland in the mid-1960s.[43] Echoing the Albermale report's recommendations, Costello advocated 'more trained professional leaders to supplement and assist the work of voluntary workers, and more money to finance suitable premises and equipment'. He anticipated the public authorities working alongside existing youth organisations, including Macra na Tuaithe and Comhairle le Leas Oige. However, Ireland was slow to catch up with its European neighbours in the provision of state support for youth work; it was 1969 before such aid was made available. Moreover, the first serious attempt to frame youth work within the broader educational and community structure and to outline an overall development strategy came almost a decade later when, in May 1977, John Bruton, the then parliamentary secretary to the Minister for Education in the National Coalition, published 'Youth and Sport'.[44] As discussed more fully in Chapter 6, this too had its difficulties in reaching the public sphere.

The section on youth also contained some particularly prescient observations. Costello identified a problematic area that in the fullness of time would come to be one of the most damning indictments of modern Ireland. The housing of children in institutions has had a long and troubled history. Industrial schools had their origins in the second-half of the nineteenth century, when Ireland was under British rule. They were thus inherited by independent Ireland, but the new Free State did not follow suit when the system was abolished in England in 1933. By 1950, 6,000 children were under detention in industrial schools, although the figure had dropped below 4,000 by 1960.[45] Many myths surrounded these religious-run institutions. There was a misconception, cultivated by the religious orders which oversaw them, that the industrial schools were orphanages or reformatories for children who had been found guilty of criminal offences.[46] The truth was somewhat different. As Mary Raftery and Eoin O'Sullivan point out in *Suffer the Little Children* – their devastating study of Irish industrial schools – only about eight per cent of all children committed came under the category 'lack of proper guardianship', which included children of unmarried mothers not eligible for adoption, those who had lost one or both parents, those whose parent was incapacitated through illness, or those whose families had broken up through desertion or imprisonment of a parent. Around ten per cent were committed for non-attendance at schools, while less than one per cent of girls and eleven per cent of boys were guilty of criminal offences.[47] Destitution was, in fact, the single largest contributing factor in the retention of children. To an extent, Costello gave expression to this reality in *Towards a Just Society*. He observed that of the 3,405 children in institutions in 1964, 'very few of these were criminal offenders and the majority are those who have been committed to industrial schools because their parents are dead or because they are destitute, or because they are non-school attenders'. The orphan myth had been cultivated by the religious orders to elicit sympathy, and it also meant that there was no public discussion about the state providing financial assistance for poorer families to care for their children at home. The state's policy was not reversed until 1970.[48] Costello did not argue for the closure of the institutions or for providing state funding for troubled families. Rather, he advocated the availability of 'adequate substitutes' in cases 'where the family fails'. There was a progressive dimension to his policies, though, that were shared in later official reports. He outlined five proposals to affect change: that the institutions be re-accommodated in new buildings with sufficient facilities; that the existing grant of £2.15.0 per child be increased (the amount was unspecified); that psychiatric care be made available; that small family group homes be established and that an adequate after-care and follow-up service be put in place. The provision of psychiatric and after-care services was part of Costello's wider concerns about mental health. The report of the Commission of Inquiry on Mental Illness made similar recommendations in 1966. The authors observed that children in industrial schools constituted a 'group whose emotional needs are far greater than those of normal children' and advocated the provision of psychiatric and psychological services in all such institutions.[49]

Costello also outlined serious deficiencies in the response to juvenile delinquency and reformatories. In particular, Marlborough House in Glasnevin and St Patrick's Institution, both in Dublin, were highlighted as problematic. The former was a detention centre for boys established in 1944, which was included in the May 2009 report of the Commission to Inquire into Child Abuse. Costello argued in favour of shifting the focus at St Patrick's away from being a detention centre to being a training and rehabilitation unit. He also proposed an after-care system. The Kennedy Report, discussed below, would later identify the almost non-existence of such after-care.

The arguments made in *Towards a Just Society* were part of a broader series of narratives. In 1964, Michael Viney published an eight-part series on the young offender in *The Irish Times*. The following year, the London branch of Tuairim – a forum for young Irish people to challenge prevailing orthodoxies that they considered inadequate[50] – produced the *Some of Our Children* report. Collectively these reports, articles and observations provided the backdrop to the decision by the Minister for Education, Donogh O'Malley, to appoint the Kennedy committee that produced the *Reformatory and Industrial Schools Systems Report* in 1970.[51] More commonly known as the Kennedy Report, it has been described as a 'watershed in terms of childcare policy'. Significantly, it focused on supporting families in the communities, rather than removing children to institutions.[52] The Kennedy Report, taken with the reports issued by the Commissions of Inquiry on Mental Illness and Mental Handicap, finally signalled a move away from the state policy of institutionalisation.

Public test

1965 was one of the last old-style campaigns: political marketing was on the margins and campaign organisation was still largely decentralised. The election was, of course, the first in which television played any role, although there was no coverage of the campaign itself. The regular RTÉ television schedule was suspended on the day of the count for results coverage, which was anchored by John O'Donoghue. *Irish Times* columnists John Healy and Garret FitzGerald, John O'Sullivan of the *Cork Examiner* and political scientist Basil Chubb joined him in studio. A state-of-the-art computer was borrowed from Bord na Mona to process the results.[53] An election special also ran on RTÉ radio from 3 pm onwards that day. Although radio pre-dated television, Radio Eireann had previously made no attempt at rolling coverage.[54]

There were some efforts on the part of Fine Gael to shake its amateur appearance. At the suggestion of Conal Gogan, a temporary press bureau and information centre was set up at Powers Hotel on Kildare Street in Dublin City Centre for the duration of the three-week campaign. The function of that centre was to maintain election propaganda and organise publicity releases to foster a certain image of the party. According to a circular sent to all candidates and party workers, the centre was 'staffed by skilled professional writers, publicity and advertising men'.[55] One of the volunteers was Michael Sweetman, who had previously worked as an advertising executive. A note from Colonel Dineen after the election thanking him for his efforts, commented on his usefulness in 'helping us with advertisements, slogans and aspects of publicity that were apt and attractive'.[56] A strong supporter of the Just Society, he would later replace Declan Costello on the Fine Gael ticket for Dublin North-West at the 1969 general election following Costello's retirement from politics. Other notable names included Joe Jennings, who went on to become the head of the Government Information

Service in the 1980s. But, contrary, to the claims of the circular, not all those who contributed were 'professionals'. Maurice Manning, then only twenty-one, recalled the appeal of being involved for the social side, and how he and others turned out speeches on all aspects of the campaign, without always being fully informed on the topic.[57] Of the other workers at the centre, at least two were students.[58]

Rumours of an early election in 1963 had prompted James Dillon to advise that Fine Gael constituency committees be established to examine the situation in each area and to arrange for selection conventions.[59] Members of the party's central branch raised the issue again in early 1964.[60] However, the Fine Gael campaign was slow to respond. When the election was announced, despite instructions from headquarters, only fourteen of the constituencies had selected their candidates. The delay in holding conventions had the negative knock-on effect that the printing of posters and literature was then held up. The campaign was also hindered by a 'long delay' in putting the election machine in place, a problem that headquarters later attributed to 'poor organisation and slothful, negligent officials'.[61] In what was a particularly short lead-in time to polling day – there were only twenty days for the actual campaign – any delay in addressing the voters was damaging. And even when everything was in place, Colonel Dineen recalled after the election how 'we have found from experience that many of our followers are reluctant to canvass, that is to request votes from voters'.[62] They may well have been, to recall John Healy's description, too gentlemanly to ask for a first preference. Such was the extent of the problem that the party's Central Branch later organised a training weekend in 1969 that included 'canvass coaching'.[63] This lack of professionalism and enthusiasm reinforced the perception that Fine Gael was an amateur party.

Towards a Just Society was officially unveiled on 18 March. The press launch was a disaster. To the assembled journalists, party leader James Dillon declared: 'we shall rely on private enterprise. We are a private enterprise party'. In two short sentences, he appeared to contradict the content of a manifesto that advocated greater state involvement. Dillon and Costello had categorically denied on the eve of the 1964 Ard Fheis that there was a serious breach within the party ranks,[64] but the terms 'crisis' and 'rift' had crept into various newspaper headlines.[65] Dillon's speech gave further credence to the widely spread rumours that Fine Gael was divided on the party's new direction. Naturally, Fianna Fáil made much of this. A handbill addressed to the voters of Dublin South-East, for example, described Fine Gael as a 'house divided against itself' and asked 'how then can it aspire to govern the nation?'[66] Candidates spent the remainder of the campaign defending the official line, and literature, including an article submitted by party headquarters to *The Kerryman*, emphasised that the proposals were being 'put forward by the united Fine Gael party'.[67] In its post-election analysis, headquarters acknowledged that reports of splits militated against the party, but described the dissension as 'imaginary' and the creation of political correspondents.[68] Though Fine Gael had always been a coalition of interests, the media was correct to be sceptical. For many politicians, support had been given based on the absence of any alternative.

The press launch was also a disaster in organisational terms. Limited copies of the manifesto had been hurriedly typed-up, and requests for copies far exceeded those that were made available. As a result, several journalists returned to their offices without a copy, which was only supplied at a later stage. In fact, the manifesto was only widely distributed towards the end of the campaign. John Healy, *The Irish Times* columnist who wrote under the penname of 'Backbencher', caustically wondered how a party seemingly incapable of organising its own press conference could possibly run a country.[69] Though a known supporter of Fianna Fáil, his observation had merit. The reach of the manifesto is difficult to measure. The party's election records show that each constituency received a minimum of fifty copies; the exceptions were Galway East and West, which were sent thirty each.[70] The date on which these were distributed is not stated, but given reports that the document was circulated late in the campaign, it can be assumed that there was little time to read and recirculate them. Furthermore, it is likely that they were received by party workers and supporters, rather than by the key, undecided voter. In one of its election advertisements, Fianna Fáil observed Fine Gael to be a 'party which is all at sixes and sevens producing a patchwork document which is neither available to the general public nor acceptable to their own party'.[71] The document could, in fact, be obtained by 'applying' to headquarters at a cost of one shilling and three pence, but Fianna Fáil's observation about its circulation was not unfair. *The Irish Times* reportedly learnt from a party spokesman that only a 'limited number of copies' was available.[72] One commentator suggested that by polling day, 'it is most unlikely that one per cent of the voters ... will have read the Fine Gael documents'.[73] Party headquarters later concurred with such views, and in its observations on the results noted the failure of the document 'to make any real impact on the electorate'.[74] Given its length, few but the politically interested were likely to have read *Towards a Just Society* in its entirety. The content would thus have had to reach the voters indirectly. As such, the key to selling the proposals would have been to hone in on a number of key areas, which would be emphasised through a carefully co-ordinated campaign. A series of such advertisements, prepared by Padbury Advertising, appeared in *The Irish Times* and *Irish Independent*, but, as discussed in more detail below, these were not extended to the provincial newspapers.

Irish election manifestos had had a 'shadowy existence' and were often little more than reproduced statements or speeches.[75] At eighty pages, *Towards a Just Society* was, therefore, something of a new departure. Noting that 'the old enthusiasms have little appeal and the national ideals of half a century ago no longer seem relevant', the document looked to the future.

While Gerard Sweetman might have previously argued that the country needed 'alternative governments rather than alternative policies',[76] Costello considered it 'an obligation on every political party who seeks power to tell the people how it will use it'. But although *Towards a Just Society* set out the party's economic and social policies, Donal Flynn, a member of the Central Branch, recalled that it was 'useless as an instrument for political campaigning', a point reiterated by Jim Dorgan, president of the UCD branch who canvassed in Meath in 1965.[77] In contrast to the manifestos that followed – particularly Fianna Fáil's 1977 document – *Towards a Just Society* contained very few specific promises with tangible results that could be raised on the doorsteps. The document did not propose, for example, as Fianna Fáil would in 1977, to spend £30 million on construction to create 5,000 new jobs, to subsidise telephone charges for old age pensioners living alone or to give a grant of £1,000 to first-time house buyers.[78] But if the content did not lend itself to useful canvassing pledges, the title of Costello's proposal certainly offered a ready-made slogan. As Jim O'Keeffe, a future member of Fine Gael who admired Costello, colourfully put it, 'the Just Society was like milk and apple pie. Who could possibly be against [it]?'[79] Commentators could have expected to see a cohesive canvass, with the theme of building a just society interwoven through Fine Gael's campaign. Yet, the party did not build its campaign around that theme. Fine Gael was certainly hampered by the short lead-in time to the election, and the fact that the document was finalised only after the election was called. Nonetheless, the drafting had been underway for months and, given the awareness that an early election was probable, the party could have been expected to have basic preparations in place. However, as an internal post-election assessment observed, it was not 'sufficiently realised' within Fine Gael that general elections were not won 'by an intensive last-minute campaign'.[80] Costello himself later pointed out, 'parties don't win elections by the policy put out three weeks before the election. Parties win elections over months and months of work and the image they create to the electorate before the election'.[81] There was no opportunity to build momentum behind the Just Society, and Fine Gael was also faced with a lack of interest or a Fianna Fáil bias among elements of the provincial press. One of the aims of the party's temporary press bureau was to ensure maximum publicity both in daily and local newspapers, but in the case of the latter, the workers struggled. Regional papers such as the *Leitrim Observer* were not always politically interested and gave few column inches to the election in general, while the editorials in others, including the *Roscommon Champion* and *Donegal Democrat*, openly proclaimed their confidence in Lemass's abilities. An editorial in the *Roscommon Champion*, for example, informed readers that their choice was between 'a stable, progressive and virile Fianna Fáil government, or an incompetent and bungling coalition'.[82]

Fine Gael further undermined the force and impact of the document through the individualism of the campaign in the various constituencies.

As already mentioned, Padbury Advertising had created advertisements for the national newspapers that made clear reference to the Just Society. In contrast, this theme was largely absent from the provincial papers. A notable exception was the *Tipperary Star*, in which the party ran an advertisement with the message, 'Fine Gael invite you to participate in a Just Society'.[83] Generally, however, the party's advertisements gave the name of the local candidates and asked readers to cast their votes in order of preference. In his analysis of how manifestos were prepared for the 2007 general election, Thomas Däubler suggested that one way to increase campaign discourse on policy issues would be to reduce the personalisation of politics.[84] His inferred observation that Irish politics is largely personality driven is particularly true of earlier periods. As Jim Dooge put it, the constituencies in the 1960s were 'run by a cabal. The only thing they [the local TD] were interested in was being returned at the next election. They weren't interested in the party'.[85] Given the nature of multi-seat PR, intra-party rivalry is endemic in the constituencies, with candidates competing against members of their own party for a seat. Fine Gael incumbents regularly resisted running mates. An interesting example of this can be found in an exchange between Sean McKenna, Kilkenny county secretary, and Dineen. McKenna had examined the constituencies with a view to maximising the Fine Gael vote to oust Fianna Fáil at the 1965 election. Tipperary South was identified as one of the constituencies where the party had the potential to take an extra seat, if there was a strong contender. A ready-made candidate was available: John Doyle, captain of the Tipperary hurling team that had won the all-Ireland, already had a public profile and was interested in standing. Dineen replied, however, that he 'might do some harm to the sitting deputy, Surgeon Hogan', if he were added to the ticket, and if he contested North Tipperary, 'he would certainly do harm to Tom Dunne who lives in Thurles, right beside him'.[86] Fine Gael's line-up in both constituencies remained unchanged at the general election, as did the party's seat numbers. Campaigns focussed on the individual, rather than on the party's message, were thus inevitable. It was not until 1964 that permission was granted to print the name of a political party next to that of the candidate's on the ballot paper. This emphasis on individuals was reflected in the publication of the aforementioned candidate-focussed advertisements, and it hampered the dissemination of the Just Society.

Occasionally, the electorate was asked to 'vote Fine Gael for a better and more secure future for Ireland'[87]; other advertisements listed some of the main strands of the party's policies, but never actually used the term 'Just Society'.[88] And in one case, the advertisement invited voters to 'read paragraph 3' of the statement on banking and monetary policy for more information on agricultural credit facilities, but without giving any indication as to how or where the relevant document could be acquired.[89] The contrast between advertising in the national and provincial newspapers gave the impression that Fine Gael was running two campaigns. There was, of course, a culture of decentralisation and a lack of standardisation in campaigning during what David Farrell terms the 'pre-modern' era – those elections that preceded 1977.[90] This generally extended across the political spectrum. Fine Gael's campaign could potentially be explained in this context. However, the effect of a disjointed campaign contributed to the impression that the party was reluctant to fully embrace the Just Society. It also contrasted with the well-coordinated campaign run by Fianna Fáil. That party's use of repetitive language – identifiable in speeches, leaflets and advertisements – emphasised the same core message: a Fianna Fáil government under Lemass meant progress; the alternative would lead to opposite results.

Effectively, the 1965 election was driven by the Fianna Fáil message that the outcome had already been decided. A Fianna Fáil government, it was argued, could not only be expected to continue making progress but it was also the only viable government. Honing in on Fine Gael's inability to form a single-party administration, Fianna Fáil candidates repeatedly argued that the only alternative was a coalition and pointed to the shortcomings of the second inter-party government (1954–57). That administration had been plagued with difficult choices amidst financial uncertainty and ultimately failed to provide stimulus for growth. During the crisis of 1956, Gerard Sweetman, Minister for Finance, introduced a special import levy, followed by a proper budget that increased taxation, and subsequently what was effectively a third budget that brought cuts in spending.[91] By the middle of the year, Taoiseach John A. Costello had acknowledged that the country was facing a 'trinity of problems': emigration, unemployment and a balance of payments deficit. 'Any one of these problems would be formidable by itself', he observed, 'taken together, they are both a warning and a challenge to the country'.[92] During those years, unemployment reached its peak, despite emigration being at its highest level since the famine of the mid-nineteenth century.

Essentially Fianna Fáil ran a negative campaign in 1965, focussed on attacking its rivals' previous shortcomings in government. The party's candidates and speakers rarely engaged directly with the content of *Towards a Just Society*, but when they did, it was almost invariably in the context of the second inter-party's performance. Handbills were produced, such as that issued by Frank Aiken and Padraig Faulkner in Louth, comparing the effects of the inter-party government – 'mess and near hopeless depression' – with that of the outgoing Fianna Fáil administration.[93] An emphasis in particular was placed on the coalition's record in the areas of social welfare, employment and housing – all themes central to Fine Gael's and Labour's 1965 campaigns. Fianna Fáil's 'You and the General Election' leaflet issued on 18 March stressed the coalition's alleged shortcomings in those areas. Referring to the peak in unemployment in 1957, the leaflet also pointed out that state financial assistance was never increased for those who found themselves out of work. Moreover, it argued that every new social welfare scheme introduced had been instituted under a Fianna Fáil government.[94]

The theme of the campaign was, thus, not simply 'Let Lemass lead on' and 'Keep moving ahead with Fianna Fáil', but also, 'Don't put the clock back on April 7'.[95] By framing the campaign in the language of time, Fianna Fáil sought to emphasise that progress would continue and the country would keep moving forward under Lemass's leadership, but that a vote for Fine Gael and Labour would represent a step backwards. Members of the Fine Gael backroom predicted that 'if the campaign continues to be fought on the present lines of Fianna Fáil versus some sort of unstable government, Mr Lemass will win'.[96] The party subsequently sought to counter Fianna Fáil's argument by using similar language and produced an advertisement with the slogan 'Put on the clocks'.[97] The response was less effective than its rival's, which had the advantage of being part of a broader, co-ordinated campaign that reinforced the main message. Costello made the point in *Towards a Just Society* that Fine Gael was 'a party which has not grown complacent from too many years in office'. Peculiarly, Fianna Fáil's long stay on the government benches was not emphasised on the canvass. Fine Gael sought, however, to highlight a contradiction in Fianna Fáil's case by pointing to the fact that Lemass had led a minority government, dependant, as Patrick Lindsay in a radio broadcast put it, 'on the support of a few so-called independents whose votes were exercised solely for their own parliamentary preservation'.[98] There was a validity to Fine Gael's argument that a minority government, subject to the whims of independents concerned with their own agendas, hardly offered greater stability than a formal coalition. Fine Gael's message was undermined by Labour's attitude. Brendan Corish's party never entered into any formal agreement, and, therefore, had no reason to be mindful of Fine Gael. But from the point of view of Fine Gael, Labour's response to Fianna Fáil's strategy was particularly damaging, both for the prospect of government formation and because of the message that it sent to floating voters.

Speaking at a rally in Tullamore for the Laois-Offaly candidate Harry Byrne, Corish told his audience that 'whatever the result of this election, Labour will pursue an independent policy in the next Dáil and will not take part in a government. I want to make it clear again that after this election, Labour will not enter a coalition with any party'.[99] This anti-coalition stance was the product of Labour's involvement in the two inter-party governments (1948–51, 1954–57) in which it felt that its identity, as well as some of its core values, had been compromised. As Michael Gallagher put it, 'Labour was probably more relieved than disappointed to leave office' in 1957.[100] At the party's first conference after returning to the opposition benches, members voted against any future coalitions. Corish's announcement, to quote the *Irish Farmers Journal*, 'crystallised the position'.[101] The election ceased to be a Lemass government versus a coalition. From the Fine Gael perspective, by opting out of government, Labour automatically blocked the possibility of Dillon's party vacating the opposition benches. Fianna Fáil's position as the incumbent was thus never seriously challenged. A private Fine Gael survey carried out at the mid-way point in the campaign had found that among those voters who had no traditional loyalty to any particular party, of those surveyed, more than ninety per cent felt that Corish's Tullamore speech and the Labour party campaign in general had strengthened the government's position.[102] If Fine Gael was incapable of forming a government alone and Labour was not willing to join the party in government, then for the undecided voter there was little benefit in giving a first preference to candidates from either party.

Results

The outcome of the 1965 general election represented both continuity and change: the results had little effect on the parliamentary arithmetic of the Dáil, but the profile of its members was noticeably different. With seventy-two seats, Fianna Fáil had gained one since the dissolution of the Dáil (or two since the 1961 election), thus improving Lemass's position only marginally. Labour performed best, winning twenty-two seats. The party had succeeded in broadening the basis of its support, making a break-through in the Dublin constituencies. This was largely due to a concerted effort to improve branch structure, notably through the establishment of the Dublin City Organisation Committee.[103] Nonetheless, with its face firmly set against coalition, the party was destined for the opposition benches. Fine Gael increased its share of the vote by just over two per cent, which was not enough to deliver any increase in seats and it remained unchanged with forty-seven. But if the seat numbers varied only slightly, the nature of the deputies changed significantly. Nine outgoing deputies did not seek re-election, including the former revolutionaries and long-serving TDs Robert Briscoe, who had joined his Fianna Fáil colleagues in ending their policy of abstention in August 1927, and Dan Breen, who had broken the policy at the start of that year. The defeat of Fine Gael's Seán MacEoin – Irish Republican Army (IRA) commander in North Longford during the independence struggle, a former chief of staff of the Irish army, a member of parliament since the 1920s and Minister for Defence between 1954 and 1957 – further confirmed the passing of the revolutionary generation. Other senior members of the Dáil, including Fine Gael's Patrick McGilligan and Fianna Fáil's James Ryan, who had been a member of the first Dáil formed in 1919, also departed. In 1961, twenty-eight of the 144 deputies were under the age of forty; after the 1965 election that number increased to thirty-seven.[104] The eighteenth Dáil represented something of a generational shift.

While focus groups now play an important role in shaping policy considerations, the absence of such a tool in the 1960s meant that a political party like Fine Gael, which was not particularly active on the ground, often had difficulties gauging public opinion. *Towards a Just Society* certainly did not appeal to certain elements of Fine Gael's traditional voters. A small sample of letters retained at the party's election archive reveal unease about the direction in which the party appeared to be moving. Most received variations of a standard reply with the message that Fine Gael sought to work for a better, fairer Ireland.[105] That the leadership was concerned that the Just Society might impact negatively on the party's electoral health was understandable, but ultimately misguided. The position invites comparison with the British Conservative Party. The Conservatives had begun the process of moving towards the left as a consequence of their defeat in 1945, which as R. A. Butler has pointed out, led them to 'accommodate themselves to a social revolution'. Government spending was increased, and commitments to achieving full employment and maintaining house-building targets were made.[106] Garret FitzGerald, writing in his *Irish Times* column shortly before he joined Fine Gael, noted that the Conservatives 'have lost no support by moving to the left ... because their right-wing supporters have nobody more attractive to vote for, and it is on the cards that the much less ideologically-minded right wing supporters of Fine Gael will also for the most part remain faithful'.[107] (FitzGerald's article was written almost five months in advance of the Conservative defeat at the 1964 general election. However, it is worth noting that Alec Douglas-Home's government fell principally over the downturn in the economy in 1961 and not by the shift in his party's ideological outlook.) There was no immediate threat to Fine Gael's share of the vote. By the mid-1960s, the composition of the party system had altered significantly. Clann na Poblachta was a spent force and Clann na Talmhan had ceased to contest elections, thus limiting voters' choices to the three principle parties of Fianna Fáil, Fine Gael and Labour. Moreover, Fine Gael did not face a challenge from the right that could fill any potential vacuum caused by a slight shift to the left in the way that the newly emerged Progressive Democrats would attract Fine Gael voters in the late-1980s.

The Just Society had the potential to broaden the party's voter base – a prospect welcomed by some ordinary members who wrote to headquarters to express their support.[108] Had the document been convincingly sold to the electorate, the Just Society had had the potential to mark the party out as having a clear policy and as offering a credible alternative to Fianna Fáil. As Richard Sinnott has noted, Fine Gael and Fianna Fáil (and indeed Labour) started out with a corporatist ideology, but the adoption of social democratic ideology via Costello's proposals as expressed in the 1965 document, resulted in a shift of the party's location on the political spectrum. For the first time, a clear contrast emerged between Fianna Fáil and Fine Gael.[109] In the aftermath of the 1964 Ard Fheis, Seán McKenna, county secretary for Kilkenny, had expressed the view to Colonel Dineen that with 'give and take, the "new approach" will broaden the foundation and base of the party'.[110] Though the Just Society indicated a degree of vitality within Fine Gael, what impact did it actually have on the electorate?

The party sustained its heaviest losses in urban areas, in particular, in Dun Laoghaire, Dublin South-Central, Dublin South-East, Cork Borough and Limerick West.[111] Seats were lost in Cork Borough, Dublin South-West and Dublin County. This was despite the seemingly urban or even Dublin-bias in *Towards a Just Society* pointed out by its critics. Commenting on the loss of support from the urban middle-class – 'consistently ... our strongest supporters' – headquarters partly blamed the new programme. 'There is no place in Fine Gael's Just Society for the middle class man'.[112] The party's strongest showing came in Connacht-Ulster, where its share of the vote rose by just over eleven per cent, despite any real appeal in the document to the more rural voter. Fine Gael recorded its best performances in Mayo North, Mayo South, Galway East, Roscommon and Monaghan.

Even with limited circulation, had members of the farming community, for example, received the lengthy document and flicked through its eighty pages, there was no clearly identifiable section on agriculture. Fianna Fáil's Brian Lenihan drew attention to this at election rallies in various parts of the largely agricultural constituency of Roscommon. He described *Towards a Just Society* as having a 'purely urban appeal, and in which neither agriculture nor the problems of the West of Ireland were examined'.[113] Though Sweetman had pushed for a ninth point relating to agriculture in 1964, when the nine-point plan was developed into a full policy document, agriculture was mentioned only in passing. Not until 1969 when *Winning through to a Just Society* was produced did agriculture receive its own section. There appears to be no correlation between the document and Fine Gael's performance. Rather, it was a case that the party benefited in rural and less prosperous areas – as it had done with the demise of previous farmers' parties – from Clann na Talmhan's departure from the political stage, combined with local candidates exploiting parish pump politics and running personalised campaigns. Clann na Talmhan, formed in 1939, catered mostly for smaller farmers and was based largely in the West of Ireland. Securing thirteen seats at the 1943 election, the party performed well in its first electoral test. Its strongest showing was in Connacht, where both Fianna Fáil and Fine Gael suffered.[114] The West remained its heartland as the party went into a slow decline, and only in those constituencies where TDs were elected did its organisation survive.[115] By the time of the 1965 election, Joseph Blowick was the party's only remaining deputy. Michael Donnellan – the only other candidate to secure election in 1961 – had died the previous year. As already discussed, his son John had successfully defended the seat at the resulting by-election, but on the Fine Gael ticket. He retained the seat at the 1965 election, giving the party a second seat in the constituency, thus improving on the 1961 result. Fine Gael also gained seats in Mayo North and Mayo South. In Mayo North, Thomas O'Hara, who had previously contested the constituency unsuccessfully for Clann na Talmhan, stood under the Fine Gael banner and secured a second seat for the party. Fine Gael's share of the vote increased by just over twenty per cent. Similarly, the party gained a second seat in Mayo South after the Clann's Joseph Blowick had decided to retire, while Thomas Thornton, his 1961 running mate, also declined to contest the election. The beneficiary was Michael Dalgan Lyons, himself a farmer. With the field narrowed, Fine Gael's share of the vote rose by almost fifteen per cent.

Headquarters acknowledged the 'late arrival' of the policy and its consequent 'failure to make any real impact on the electorate'.[116] The Just Society might have had little to offer the middle-class voters, but Fine Gael's support base had been noticeably changing since 1961, before Costello ever approached the party with his ideas. As Michael Gallagher has pointed out, although falling slightly in wealthier constituencies, the party lost no ground in the intermediate ones and gained more than ten per cent in most agricultural areas.[117] As already discussed, the absence of Clann na Talmhan bolstered Fine Gael's position. Elements of the farming community were also suspicious of Lemass's commitment to developing an export-led industrialisation policy. As Bryce Evans, one of his biographers, has observed, one of Lemass's weaknesses was the 'perception that he held a dismissive attitude towards agriculture in general'. This was despite the fact that, as Taoiseach, he was actually more attentive to the area of agriculture than he had previously been.[118] Members of his own party shared the farming community's view. Paddy Smith, the Minister for Agriculture, resigned from his position on 7 October 1964. Ostensibly over Lemass's intervention in a dispute between employers and building workers, his decision was largely influenced by the urban/rural conflict in the party. Describing himself as 'a countryman', he had grown up on a twenty-acre farm in Cavan. Lemass, in contrast, was a 'Dublin politician' whom, he felt, failed to appreciate how men had to work on the land in frost and rain 'with bloody bad equipment or just their hands' to earn a living.[119] Beyond general suspicion, Lemass also faced unrest from the agricultural community due to their standard of living. Disappointed by the failure of the Anglo-Irish Trade Agreement to deal with agriculture, the NFA had actively encouraged Ireland's application to join the European Economic Community, membership of which would have provided access to the Common Agricultural Policy (CAP) and the guarantee of high prices and greater trading opportunities. European integration would be, Juan Greene, President of the NFA, suggested, 'our salvation, if we wish it so'.[120] However, the decision of French president Charles de Gaulle to veto Britain's application in January 1963 effectively derailed Ireland's also. Agricultural prices fell as Ireland remained on the edges of Europe. It was this reality that had prompted Gerard Sweetman to push for a clause pledging parity of wages for those in the agricultural sector with those working in industry.

Arguably the defining moment in the campaign was Corish's Tullamore speech. It clearly signalled that the only viable government was a Fianna Fáil government. Fine Gael would have needed a breakthrough on a major scale to achieve single-party government, but, organisational problems aside, there was no momentum for such an occurrence. Fianna Fáil was not so unpopular as to face collapse; in fact, the residual effect of the ninth-round wage increase was still being felt.[121] Fine Gael was outmanoeuvred by Fianna Fáil's negative campaign and undermined by Labour's anti-coalition stance. The extent to which any of the party's gains could be directly attributed to the Just Society is questionable.

Fine Gael's true commitment to the Just Society would be tested in the aftermath of the general election. The party had adopted the concept in 1965 because the document was already under preparation and there was no alternative on which to fight the campaign. As discussed in more detail in Chapter 4, there were some signs of activity. For some of the more conservative elements, though, there was a sense that adopting the policy was sufficient and that no further discussion was necessary. Fine Gael did not completely shelve the concept. Rather it conducted its campaign for the 1969 general election under the banner of *Winning through to a Just Society*. However, there was a sense of disillusion among Declan Costello's supporters that the party had not done more to develop the ideas laid out in 1965. By the time of the next election, Costello had retired from politics. The question remained, should he have challenged the leadership?

4
1969: The Second Failure

In the aftermath of the 1965 general election, James Dillon announced that he was stepping down as leader of Fine Gael. There were two obvious contenders to succeed him: Liam Cosgrave and Declan Costello. Dillon was replaced by Cosgrave at the same meeting where he announced his resignation. That day's events raised a number of questions: how committed was Fine Gael to the Just Society? Had there been a private arrangement to ensure that the leadership did not pass to Declan Costello? And did Costello even want to be leader?

Dillon cited his age – he was then sixty-two – as a deterrent from him continuing in his role at a meeting of the parliamentary party on the evening of 21 April 1965. Earlier that day, Liam Cosgrave had nominated him for the office of Taoiseach when the new Dáil assembled. Although he was expected to retire, few predicted that the announcement would come at the first meeting after the general election. Rather than reconvening at a later date to select a successor, at the same meeting of the parliamentary party, Cosgrave was proposed by Gerard Sweetman and seconded by Michael O'Higgins. The identity of Sweetman's nominee came as a surprise to many. In his memoirs, Paddy Harte recalled that when Sweetman 'had been speaking for four or five minutes without yet mentioning a name, many of the older members, who were aware of the strained relationship between himself and Liam Cosgrave, wondered what was going on'.[1] Jim Dooge, who was very close to Cosgrave, was one of those who found himself speculating as to whom the former minister for finance was about to propose. He remembered thinking that it might be the Wexford TD Anthony Esmonde, 'possibly the only person as right wing' as Sweetman. The reality 'vastly surprised' him.[2] Relations had deteriorated between Sweetman and Cosgrave. Two stories are offered: Cosgrave blamed Sweetman for the 1957 budget that made the inter-party government unpopular, and that as Minister for Finance Sweetman had, in Cosgrave's opinion, slighted his father by making him call to the Department to make a request on behalf of the Racing Board that he chaired, when all other ministers who had business called to W.T.'s house.[3]

However, Cosgrave has clarified that the tense relationship was a product of hostility between W.T. and Sweetman over the latter's decision to reduce funding to the Racing Board.[4] Aside from his disagreement with Declan Costello's policies, Sweetman would have been opposed to his leadership on the same grounds that he had opposed the original Just Society proposal in 1964: the alienation of the party's conservative vote. Consequently, as Cosgrave was more trusted by the traditionalists, Sweetman was prepared to rise above their personal animosity for the sake of the party. Costello's election would have sent a clear message and confirmed the party's commitment to the Just Society. Reporting on his election, the political correspondent of *The Irish Times* observed Cosgrave to be 'a strong believer in the policy of the Just Society'.[5] However, Cosgrave had supported the policy as a tool to oust Fianna Fáil. With him at the helm, the party was non-committal to any ideological transformation. While there were some new policy developments, Cosgrave was more concerned with winning power.

The pace – described by Maurice Manning as 'uncharacteristic haste'[6] – at which the leadership change occurred also caused surprise. Manning, Dillon's biographer, has suggested that the swiftness of events does not seem designed to have prevented an alternative candidate, namely Costello, from emerging.[7] However, a number of Costello's supporters saw in Dillon's resignation and the settling of the succession question all in the space of one meeting as a deliberate attempt to stop Costello becoming leader. As Dooge put it, the aim was to 'keep Declan out'. He recalled that Costello's name was proposed by newcomer John Donnellan of Galway East, although Cosgrave has suggested that it was, in fact, Thomas O'Hara of Mayo North.[8] Regardless to the identity of his proposer, Costello withdrew his name from consideration. This is not recorded in the very brief official minutes, nor is there any indication of the reasons Sweetman gave in commending Cosgrave as the next party leader. They simply state: 'Mr Liam Cosgrave was proposed by Deputy Sweetman and seconded by Deputy Michael O'Higgins for election as leader of the Oireachtas party and he was elected unanimously'.[9]

In September 2006, Maurice Manning and Brendan Halligan pondered the question 'What if Declan Costello had become leader of Fine Gael?' as part of Diarmaid Ferriter's *What If?* series on RTÉ radio. Halligan suggested that, if Costello had succeeded, there was a very real possibility that there would have been a realignment in Irish politics. A new social democratic party, similar to the SDLP in Northern Ireland, would have emerged. There was a fleeting moment in the late 1960s, discussed below, when such an occurrence seemed a possibility, but it never progressed beyond the idea stage. Halligan also suggested that if Costello had become Taoiseach, he would have been responsible for creating a more urban, modern and meritocratic society. That Costello had potential to think big and to think in terms of reforming society was undeniable – it was clearly written across the pages of *Towards a Just Society*. However, as Manning interjected, there would always be the question mark over Costello's interest in canvassing across the country and engaging in the 'glad-handling' associated with leadership.

Michael McInerney of *The Irish Times* would later describe Costello as a man 'who possibly could, some time in the future, be a Taoiseach'.[10] But did Costello even want the leadership of Fine Gael? Did he withdraw his name because he was not interested, or because he was unprepared and had not anticipated that the leadership change would happen so quickly? His ambition, Vincent Browne suggests, has been underestimated.[11] 'He wanted it'.[12] Manning is less convinced: 'there is no reason to believe Costello was interested in the leadership, or would have been temperamentally suited to it'. His shy disposition may have precluded him from leading the party.[13] That 'shy disposition' was a character trait frequently recalled by those who were acquainted with him.[14] Many considered him a gentleman. Jim O'Keeffe, a practising lawyer before entering politics as a Fine Gael TD for Cork South-West, briefed both John A and Declan Costello on occasion. He recalled John A as being a 'much more outgoing and ebullient figure', while his son was 'more reserved'.[15] John Healy, though generally critical of Fine Gael, had shown quite a degree of support for Costello in his *Irish Times* 'Backbencher' column; he had previously questioned if Costello lacked a 'talent for gut politics'.[16]

There was another factor that should not be underestimated, and it came into play when Costello later announced his retirement, albeit temporarily, from politics in 1967: he also had a successful legal career. He once admitted, 'I can never remember wanting to be anything else [except to be a barrister]'.[17] He had been called to the bar in 1948, and would later be called to the inner bar in 1965. He always maintained, according to Stephen Collins's study of the Cosgrave legacy, that he was not interested in the leadership and that relations between himself and Liam Cosgrave were never strained.[18] The nature of that relationship was tellingly revealed in a reply to a question about the extent to which Costello and FitzGerald (with whom it was widely known relations had soured) had created an identity crisis within Fine Gael. Cosgrave commented that 'Declan Costello never created an identity problem. He was loyal to the end'. FitzGerald was never mentioned.[19] Donal Flynn posits a view that potentially comes closest to the truth. Costello did challenge the leadership, but not in the conventional sense: his support for Garret FitzGerald was the challenge.[20] His view is echoed by John Bruton.[21] There is merit to this interpretation. As Ronan Fanning has noted, 'given Declan Costello's progressive disenchantment with politics, [FitzGerald] was becoming more and more the standard-bearer'.[22] There is no doubt that FitzGerald, as discussed in greater detail in Chapter 6, was a leader-in-waiting and that he was a better fit than Costello. Moreover, FitzGerald, unlike Costello, was a single-career politician. By the time he entered politics, he had left his job at Aer Lingus and had given up his part-time lecturing position at UCD; his only remaining distraction was his weekly *Irish Times* column. Moreover, as Fanning further observed, 'he was passionate about changing Irish society, an objective he knew he could best achieve through political leadership and his becoming Taoiseach'.[23]

At forty-five, Liam Cosgrave was the party's youngest leader, and remained such until Alan Dukes became leader in 1987 at the age of forty-one. He had a strong Fine Gael pedigree. His father, W. T. Cosgrave, had been President of the Executive Council between 1923 and 1932 and, apart from a brief interlude in 1933–34, was leader of Cumann na nGaedheal and subsequently Fine Gael until his retirement in 1944. He considers his father's administration 'easily the best government of the State'.[24] Although Liam Cosgrave initially joined the army, where he rose through the ranks, he subsequently followed his father into politics. Elected at the age of twenty-three at the 1943 general election by the voters of Dublin County, he became the fourth generation of Cosgraves to enter political life and briefly joined his father in Dáil Éireann. He served that constituency until the 1948 election at which he was elected for Dún Laoghaire and Rathdown (which became Dún Laoghaire for the 1977 election).When the first inter-party government was formed after that election, Cosgrave was appointed parliamentary secretary to the Taoiseach and to the Minister for Industry and Commerce. He also served as government chief whip. When the second such government was formed in 1954, Cosgrave was elevated to the position of Minister for External Affairs. Though only thirty-four, by that stage he had been in the Dáil for eleven years. He retained his seat at every general election until his retirement in 1981. Loyalty was considered his greatest quality,[25] and this extended not only to his friends and colleagues but also to the memory of his father's legacy. The influence of that legacy on his decision-making – particularly in the area of law and order – almost cost him the leadership in 1972.

Cosgrave's frontbench appointments were interesting, and they surprised many political commentators.[26] Despite the support he received from Gerard Sweetman, he was not inclined to give him a position and was only persuaded to do so by Michael O'Higgins who argued that the omission would significantly weaken the front bench.[27] Though finally assenting to include him, Cosgrave made Sweetman spokesman on agriculture, rather than returning him to his traditional role in finance. Clearly, the enmity between the two men had not been fully healed. However, there might also have been a more pragmatic reason. Labour's antipathy to Sweetman after the second inter-party government was such that he was a potential barrier to any further arrangement between the two parties. By keeping Sweetman out of a position of power, Cosgrave, who clearly wanted to take Fine Gael into government, potentially sought to downplay his importance in the party.

The progressive wing of the party was given prominent positions. Finance went to Tom O'Higgins, a strong advocate of the Just Society, while Health and Social Welfare were merged and made the responsibility of Declan

Costello. The presence of these leading figures in key positions prompted John Healy, writing in the *Irish Farmers Journal*, to declare that 'Fine Gael now seems to be left-of-centre',[28] the position that Cosgrave had advocated for the party at the 1964 Ard Fheis. His appointments also included other enthusiastic supporters of the Just Society: Mark Clinton became spokesman on Local Government and Paddy Harte on Board of Works. This was part of Cosgrave's strategy to balance both groups – his frontbench also included Paddy Donegan, Maurice Dockrell and Patrick Lindsay, who had all opposed Costello's proposals – but it is also plausible to interpret it in the same manner as Sweetman's appointment: that is, an effort to present Fine Gael in a light that would make coalition attractive to Labour. An unsigned document among Michael Sweetman's papers certainly places Cosgrave's choice of spokesmen in the context of coalition: 'it remains to be seen whether this alliance between Cosgrave and the left wing can in fact put enough real life back into the party to enable a Fine Gael/Labour coalition to beat Fianna Fáil … But the prospects are now more promising than they have been for many years'.[29] Cosgrave would later become uneasy with the advancement of that group, particularly amidst rumours that there were intentions to replace him as leader. In an unscripted remark during his address to the Ard Fheis of May 1972, he likened the group to 'mongrel foxes'.[30]

1966 Presidential election

In 1966, Fine Gael came remarkably close to electing their first head of state. The presidential election was important for the party for a number of reasons. The impressive showing injected new life into the party, enthusing supporters and attracting new members, many of whom had already been impressed by Declan Costello. 'It is hard to exaggerate the morale-boosting effect of the success of this campaign on Fine Gael', John Bruton, who had joined the party the previous year, later suggested.[31] It also saw the party place a greater emphasis on pluralism. As Garret FitzGerald put it, this 'added to Declan Costello's social democracy a liberal element that was to remain an enduring factor within the party thenceforward'.[32] It was a concept, more so than social democracy, that strongly shaped FitzGerald's own thinking.

As Eamon de Valera's term as president was coming to a close, it was widely expected that he would seek a second term. When Seán T. O'Kelly sought re-election in 1952; Fine Gael did not oppose him. Liam Cosgrave had initially intended to adopt the same attitude in 1966. However, the party, and in particular the grassroots, was not happy at the prospect, feeling that Fine Gael was failing to offer any strenuous opposition to Fianna Fáil. A letter sent to Tom O'Higgins from the Kilkenny County Executive regarded this attitude as 'the last straw in the weak and impotent history of opposition by Fine Gael to Fianna Fáil in recent months'. It was felt that 'serious damage' had already been done among party workers and supporters who, in the main, were 'disgusted with the whole business'.[33] Once Fine Gael officially decided to run a candidate, several names were mentioned, including party elders John A Costello's and James Dillon's.

That election, however, marked the emergence of a new type of candidate. By 1966, the presidency was seen as something of a distant office, a place of retirement for elder statesmen. It was an understandable perception. The first president, Douglas Hyde, was almost eighty-five on his departure; O'Kelly was seventy-five by the end of his two seven-year terms and de Valera was eighty-four contesting the office for the second time.[34] It was decided at a meeting of the Fine Gael parliamentary party that their candidate should represent a 'younger and more positive approach', combined with experience in public office.[35] A more engaged role in which, for example, the President would promote the country's trading relations – a feature commonly associated with more recent presidencies – was also envisaged and emphasised during the campaign.[36] At forty-nine, O'Higgins was the youngest candidate yet to stand. His age was very much emphasised as a point of contrast with the eighty-three-year-old Eamon de Valera. O'Higgins's letter to the voters, printed in his election leaflet, encapsulated the idea of a more active president. He argued that the presidency:

> must be progressive, and able to personify a nation fit to take its part in the fast-moving world of tomorrow. As a small country, we need a president pledged to the projection of this image – someone of whom we can say, 'This is Ireland, today and tomorrow'.[37]

Despite their ideological differences, Gerard Sweetman was O'Higgins's director of elections. Peter Prendergast, a marketing consultant, acted as the unofficial campaign manager, while a group of speechwriters, which included Alexis FitzGerald, Garret FitzGerald, Patrick Dillon-Malone, John Kelly and Michael Sweetman, completed the campaign team. Sweetman was, perhaps, the most important of the speechwriters. A supporter of Declan Costello and the Just Society, he was one of the intellectual heavyweights within the party. He also advocated a pluralist society, and he sought to centre the campaign around that concept.[38] Speaking at Tullamore, for example, O'Higgins said that if a truly Just Society was to be created, it would require equality of opportunity for all people, regardless of their class or creed or vocation in life.[39] This theme of multi-culturalism was to the forefront of O'Higgins's campaign. Michael Sweetman expressed similar views in speeches he penned for Liam Cosgrave. In a draft speech on Northern Ireland, he argued that:

> [T]he achieving of a just society should be the priority of politicians on both sides of the border. That means making it possible for every Irish

person whether in the North or in the South to have decent secure employment, decent living conditions and fair impartial democratic government.[40]

After the presidential election, Cosgrave asserted that the support for O'Higgins represented 'recognition of the positive value of this party's progressive concept of a Just Society which had not sufficient time to make an impact upon the electorate in the 1965 general election'. It is more likely, however, that Fine Gael's appeal in that election – explaining why the party came so close to defeating a senior commander of 1916 in the year of the golden jubilee – was the emphasis that was placed on youth and energy, and the alternative offered.[41]

Over the course of the five-week campaign, O'Higgins travelled an estimated 22,000 miles and addressed over 130 meetings.[42] De Valera chose not to canvass, although his position as the incumbent required his attendance at such State events as the fifty-anniversary commemoration of 1916, thus giving him exposure. But although the 1960s celebrated a signature date in Ireland's history, they were also a decade of change. O'Higgins's theme of youth and energy captured that spirit. In thirteen of the thirty-eight constituencies, he out-polled de Valera, while in a further five, de Valera's margin of victory was less than one thousand votes. In the case of Wexford, there were as little as sixty-five between them. When the vote was concluded, only 10,717 votes separated the two men, which remains the smallest margin to date in an Irish presidential election. The result seemed to be as much of a shock to Fine Gael as it was to Fianna Fáil. In a circular to party members, Colonel Dineen suggested, 'we narrowed the gap so drastically as to astonish many of our own supporters and confound the opposition'.[43] Jim Ryan writing in *The Citizen* – a party newspaper with the stated aim of supporting Fine Gael only as long as it was committed to the Just Society – projected that 'by 1968 Fine Gael will have become the throbbing, restless, dynamic force for social justice and the inspiration and motivation for the realisation in Ireland of a Just Society'.[44] Though Ryan could not possibly have known it, 1968 proved to be an unfortunate year to suggest that Fine Gael would, by then, be a dynamic force for creating a Just Society. As discussed below, at that year's Ard Fheis, it seemed that the party was as divided as ever on the subject.

Progress?

To what extent did Fine Gael pursue the Just Society in the aftermath of its first public test? The first indication that the party would retain the policies it outlined at the 1965 election came two months after the general election. Fianna Fáil's Jack Lynch delivered his first budget speech as Minister for Finance on 11 May 1965. Describing it as a 'social services budget',[45]

Lynch announced increases in the maximum rate of non-contributory old age, blind and widows' pension, disabled persons' maintenance allowance, unemployment benefit and maternity allowance. In response, Fine Gael's new spokesman on finance, Tom O'Higgins, welcomed the Minister's budget statement as 'merely a first step on the road towards a Just Society'. He reminded the Dáil that his party had campaigned on these issues at the recent general election, and concluded that the government's social relief efforts were 'due in a large degree to the efforts of the Fine Gael party'.[46] Concluding his speech, O'Higgins confirmed that Fine Gael would continue to advocate economic planning to achieve equitable social reform. Someone like Tom O'Higgins, one of the Just Society's leading supporters, could be expected to make such a speech heavily laced with the language of the document. Generally, though, policy was unsettled. Garret FitzGerald recalled in his memoirs that after his election to the Seanad in 1965 he asked Jim Dooge as to how he could be certain he was not straying from the official party line. Dooge replied, half-humorously, 'make it up'.[47]

It would be a mistake to suggest, however, that the Just Society – used again as the theme for Fine Gael's 1969 election campaign – was allowed lapse entirely between the two general elections. Speaking in the aftermath of the presidential campaign, Cosgrave explained that a committee had been formed within the party to re-examine the Just Society document in the belief that there were other aspects of policy that required attention.[48]

Fine Gael published a policy document on the Irish language on 23 June 1966. It was the culmination of nine month's work by the party's policy committee, chaired by Michael O'Higgins. Entitled *Fine Gael Policy for a Just Society: Irish Language*, it represented a broadening of *Towards a Just Society*, which had not dealt with the language question. The specific attention now being paid to the language question reflected growing activity in the area of language policy. In 1958, Fianna Fáil had established the Commission on the Restoration of the Irish Language, which delivered a 500-page report in 1963. The government then published a White Paper, *The Restoration of the Irish Language*, in 1965. The proposals contained within the Fine Gael document had much in common with the Commission's report, excerpts from which were quoted throughout the twenty-three page bilingual document. Fine Gael's aim was 'the preservation of the language by means of realistic policies designed to secure the support of the people'. Those policies were intended to minimise hostility to the language, which Fine Gael attributed to the compulsory nature of the subject for educational and employment purposes. Irish had been a compulsory subject for all students undertaking state examinations since 1933, with the awarding of the Leaving Certificate dependent on a pass-mark in the subject. From 1949 onwards, the requirement that Irish be an essential subject for state examinations had been a live political issue,[49] dividing Fine Gael and Fianna Fáil. Fine Gael's 1966 policy document proposed that the 'pass' requirement be abolished. This was not a new departure for the party.

When James Dillon was elected leader in 1959, *The Irish Times* speculated that the party's position on the Irish language would change: though he was a lover of the language, he did not favour compulsory teaching.[50] Although Fine Gael remained in favour of the language being taught in schools, under its new leader, it did revise its attitude on the compulsory pass grade required to achieve the Leaving Certificate. This new departure divided Fine Gael's policy from that of Fianna Fáil's, making the two distinguishable for the first time. Dillon had broached the subject in the Dáil in 1961, but his suggestion was dismissed by Fianna Fáil's Michael Hilliard as 'an act of national treachery which brought Ireland back a century in the national advance'.[51] The party's attitude was also criticised at the time in the annual report of the Gaelic League.[52] However, party members felt that the electorate had reacted favourably to Tom O'Higgins's early speeches during the presidential campaign on the need for a reappraisal of policy,[53] convincing policy advisers of the necessity to clearly include a review of the language as part of the process of updating the Just Society policies. Fine Gael favoured the continued teaching of Irish in national and post-primary schools, but the party proposed in its document that the subject be taught as part of a broader Irish studies course that would also explore folklore, tradition and literature, giving students a better grounding in the country's cultural heritage.

In the area of employment, the language test for entry to or promotion within the public service would be discontinued, although public servants working in the Gaeltacht areas would still be expected to be proficient in the language. In terms of the broader community, Fine Gael felt that Irish language programmes on television could and should be improved, while acknowledging that Irish language programming could not be imposed on audiences.[54] Although the term pluralism was not used, by removing the compulsory aspect of the language, the party recognised the rights of non-Irish speakers and broadened the scope of opportunity for them. As explained in the questions and answers section of the policy document, 'This recognition of a bi-lingual situation, deriving from our mixed heritage, should entitle any suitably qualified Irishman, to serve his country in its public service'.[55] Irish as an essential subject for the Leaving Certificate and the language qualification for the Civil Service was eventually dropped in 1973.

By 1966, the recorded population of the Gaeltacht had declined to under 70,000, a figure less than twenty per cent of what it had been at the foundation of the state in 1922.[56] Despite stating that priority would be given to the problem of the Gaeltacht over any other aspect of the language question, the document is peculiarly quiet on the subject. The fate of the Irish-speaking regions is discussed in a twelve-line section, four of which actually refer to non-Gaeltacht areas. The document asserted that 'more could be done than has been done to assist these areas to become economically viable'.[57] The Commission on the Restoration of the Irish Language considered the Gaeltacht the victim of apathy because of the absence of any coordinated policy.[58] However Fine Gael's document offered no indication that such an integrated social and economic strategy might be implemented, or of how economic performance might be improved.

Language enthusiasts did not welcome many of the party's proposals. CARA, the Irish language organisation, was particularly critical, as was Na Teaghlaigh Ghaelacha. The committee of the latter issued a statement claiming that the implementation of the party's policies would result in the early disappearance of the Gaeltacht. By abandoning, as they put it, the Irish language in several areas, Irish-speaking families would be reduced to the status of foreigners in their own land.[59] Similarly, Comhar na Meán mhúinteoirí, the organisation of secondary school teachers specialising in Irish, called on Fine Gael to reconsider a policy it felt would lead to the eventual extinction of the language.[60]

The Irish language policy document was followed by a wider examination of education, representing a further development in the range of policies under the 'Just Society' umbrella. Education had been dealt with only briefly in *Towards a Just Society*, and had not been the subject of a standalone section. *Fine Gael Policy for a Just Society: Education*, was launched on 28 November 1966. The introduction explained that the party was now giving priority to education over other important policy matters. Fine Gael's observation that the education system had changed little since the birth of independence was not unfounded. With the exception of the Vocational Education Act, 1930, there had been no noteworthy change. This was in contrast to other European countries where, in the late 1940s, there was a general aspiration of equality of educational opportunities. Many countries lowered the financial barriers to educational participation, granting access to low-income families.[61] Free universal education for all up to the age of fifteen was introduced in England and Wales, for example, under the Education (or Butler) Act, 1944. The Irish Department of Education did not appear, however, to recognise the importance of an educated workforce for economic development, and the principally German and American idea of investing in human capital took time to take root in Ireland.[62] This view was eventually articulated in the 1965 OECD-sponsored report, *Investment in Education*.

Fine Gael's proposals covered re-organisation of the Department of Education to improve its policymaking machinery, the establishment of an educational planning committee to assist the Minister for Education with curriculum development, an acceleration of the school-building programme, training and re-training of teachers and grants for educational research, amongst others. Perhaps most significantly, the party proposed 'as one step towards securing greater participation in post-primary education', a scheme that would enable almost all secondary schools to offer free education, without incurring financial loss, to all children in the school system. Fine Gael intended to publish the document as a White Paper, if the party acceded to government. Similar proposals had emerged from the policy committee of the Labour Party, which had been established in the early 1960s, and it included Barry Desmond, Catherine McGuinness, Dan Desmond, Seamus Pattison, Seán Treacy, Tim McAuliffe, Denis Larkin and Donal Nevin. Their 1963 report, *Challenge and Change in Education*, was scathing of the class distinction in the Irish education system, and they proposed free post-primary education.[63] This increased interest in education coincided with a more interventionist approach to the area by policymakers in the 1960s. Prior to Seán Lemass's appointment of reforming ministers – Patrick Hillery, George Colley and subsequently Donogh O'Malley – to the Department of Education, previous office holders had held the conservative view that the direction of education was the domain of private interests, effectively the Protestant and Catholic churches. As an article in *The Irish Times* put it in 1944, the Department was a 'sleeping partner'.[64] The nomination of Hillery as minister in 1959 initiated a period of expansion that would overhaul the system and open up opportunities beyond the privileged few. Both Lemass and Hillery were increasingly influenced by policy ideas promoted by the OECD, which advocated coherent planning for educational needs.[65]

Towards a Just Society had highlighted the paltry thirty-six per cent of the fifteen- to nineteen-year-olds in the country who were continuing in further education. Costello was not alone in arguing that a child's future was determined by his/her father's position in society. Education, with the exception of the 'very able and the very energetic', was reserved for the wealthy. John Bruton has argued that the concept of equality contained in *Towards a Just Society* 'led directly to the introduction of free secondary education two years later'.[66] At the time, Liam Cosgrave claimed that only when Fine Gael published its comprehensive policy in 1966 was the government 'stampeded into taking some action after many years of complete neglect'.[67] However, the policy of free post-primary education had been under consideration by the Department of Education since 1962, two years before Declan Costello ever approached Fine Gael with his proposals, and four years before Donogh O'Malley, who announced it, became minister. O'Malley thus inherited a coherent policy, although, in making the surprise announcement, he took the initiative and was responsible for the timing of the introduction. The Department had recommended a timetable of 1970, to coincide with raising the school-leaving age to fifteen. O'Malley was anxious to introduce the scheme sooner, and it is here that Fine Gael's influence is apparent. He wrote to Lemass seeking support from the cabinet on 7 September 1966: Fine Gael 'are evidently panicking at the fact that in their publication *The Just Society*, they have no proposals whatsoever on education'.[68] O'Malley warned that Fine Gael was preparing to unveil its own education policy. The policy to which O'Malley was referring was, of course, the aforementioned document, which included a proposal for free education. The proposals had been drafted, it was claimed in the introduction, to fill a void left by the Fianna

Fáil government that had been in power since 1957, which had begun to make promises about educational reform but had not delivered a comprehensive policy. O'Malley recommended pre-empting their main opposition. In that respect, Bruton was correct: the Just Society certainly impacted on the timing of the scheme's introduction. The policies were not greatly publicised, however, and at the party's Ard Fheis in May 1967, Maurice O'Connell lamented that 'although Fine Gael had a good education policy, no one knew anything about it'. Patrick Lindsay, the party's spokesperson on education, thus urged all delegates to read the document.[69]

Exit Costello

On 8 February 1967, Declan Costello announced he would not seek re-election at the next general election. The official explanation stated that there were great demands on a politician's time, which he had to couple with being a practising lawyer. As his doctor had advised him that he could not continue in both roles, he had chosen to withdraw from political life. He also explained that his decision was guided by 'family and personal responsibilities'.[70] Added to these reasons must surely have been a sense of disillusionment. The response was one of shock and agreement that the decision was a blow to Fine Gael. Labour's Michael O'Leary paid tribute to the Dublin North-West TD, describing him as having 'summed up the best aspirations of Irish youth, understanding the spirit of the age we live in'.[71] Even the pro-Fianna Fáil *Irish Press* willingly conceded that Costello was 'one of the most able and most popular members of the Dáil'.[72] There was no by-election, however, as he did not formally resign his seat. He continued to vote in divisions from the backbenches, but did not make any further speeches in the Dáil after his announcement. While Cosgrave initially assumed his responsibilities, his place on the frontbench was later filled by the forty-five-year-old Roscommon TD Patrick J. Reynolds, who came from a minor Fine Gael dynasty. His father, Patrick, had been a Cumann na nGaedheal deputy for Sligo-Leitrim from 1927 until his death in 1932, when his mother, Mary, subsequently defended the seat and held it until 1961. Reynolds was as a businessman and large farmer with fifty-five acres.

Costello's decision, John Healy later claimed, was seen as a 'silent public protest' over his party's treatment of the Just Society.[73] Development of his policy had stalled – a disappointment highlighted in a critical article published in *The Citizen* the same month that he signalled his intentions. Branch meetings, it was argued, were taken up with trivial issues, such as the selling of raffle tickets, while at a national level deputies were more concerned with 'baiting "Charlie" [Haughey], than with describing the Ireland Fine Gael hopes to build on the basis of the Just Society'. The paper advocated a more complete examination and debate of the policy within the parliamentary party and at grassroots level.[74] Although new policy documents had been produced, the level of debate that the contributors to *The Citizen* sought never occurred.

With the exception of expressing the hope that he might continue to contribute to the framing of party policy, Costello made no specific reference to economic or social affairs. When he reaffirmed his decision in 1969, the *Irish Independent* reproduced the statement and letter side-by-side. There was a noticeable difference in content. While health and family considerations had been stressed in 1967, these issues were not mentioned in his letter to Liam Cosgrave on 7 January 1969. That is not to imply that Costello did not have health problems in 1967, but rather by emphasising those concerns then, he saved the party some embarrassment. By 1969, it was apparent that Fine Gael was not ideologically committed to the Just Society, but rather saw it as an electioneering tool to challenge Fianna Fáil. He noted, 'recently ... I learnt that the front bench was considering the appointment of a research officer for the party'. He had considered making himself available and taking up a full-time career in politics. 'I am now quite satisfied that this way does not afford a solution to the personal problem with which I am faced'.[75] Though the overall tone was friendly and Costello offered his assistance at the 1969 election, there was a sense that he had bided his time since 1967 but there had been little to convince him to remain in political life. The publication of these letters only added to the interest surrounding Costello's departure. Was it due to the demands of carrying out two full-time jobs? Or was it a disagreement over policy?

Costello's decision to quit politics was interpreted by some, particularly Cosgrave's critics, as a vote of no confidence in the leadership. Cosgrave's supporters were quick to dismiss that this was the case. Renegade Maurice O'Connell, who had already been censured by the party for implying that a leadership change was possible, broke his agreement not to publicly raise the issue again when he suggested that Costello might have been made to reconsider if the party had 'a more vigorous and dynamic leadership'.[76] However, speaking at a meeting of the Mespil branch of the party in Ballsbridge, Garret FitzGerald sought to dismiss the rumours and categorically stated that his colleague had not withdrawn over policy disagreements.[77] It seems more likely that FitzGerald was supplying the official party line, designed to counter any sense of splits or divisions.

With so much discussion of the spirit of youth in the 1960s, there was speculation that Fine Gael should pass the leadership to a younger member, namely Declan Costello.[78] In fact, the age difference between Costello and Cosgrave was quite small (only six years), yet there was a tendency to think of Cosgrave as being older than forty-nine – probably because he had been on the political scene for so long. The difference between the two men, of course, was that while Cosgrave read from scripted speeches about the Just Society, Costello knew the content by heart. Moreover, Costello had already decided not to contest the 1969 election. With the pending general election,

Fine Gael began to work on updating the Just Society. There was no direct input from Costello, who did not publicly comment on the revised version of his policy document. In January 1969, Liam Cosgrave visited Costello in an attempt to convince him to contest that year's general election, but Costello was adamant. A statement, signed by thirty-four members of various units of the party, was issued urging him to return to active political life and 'help towards the realisation of that idea of a Just Society which he has done so much to inspire'. Among the signatories were John Bruton, Jim Dorgan, Donal Flynn, John Maguire, Enda Marren and Michael Sweetman.[79] Garret FitzGerald, Jim Dooge and Paddy Harte also called to the Costello home. According to Harte's memoirs, the discussion lasted around four hours and they left at two o'clock in the morning, confident that they had persuaded him to change his mind. He was thus shocked to hear a statement from Costello on radio the following morning in which he thanked people for their support, but affirmed that he was withdrawing from political life.[80] Jim Dooge's recollection of the discussion was somewhat different, speculating that 'maybe Paddy was more optimistic' and recalling that, in contrast, he had walked away feeling uncertain.[81] Either way, Declan Costello did not contest the 1969 general election. It was not an easy decision, and he confided in John Kelly that he had been 'going through a rather minor political dark night of the soul'.[82] His place on the ticket was taken by Michael Sweetman, a man described by Tom O'Higgins as 'liberal in outlook, with a burning zeal for social justice and an intellectual capacity to indicate achievable reforms'.[83] Although Costello was not actively involved in supporting Fine Gael, he offered his personal support to John Kelly.[84] He later wrote, regretting 'I am letting you down', that he had been 'gravely disturbed' by the Maurice O'Connell affair. 'I could not see my way to approach anyone to sign' a letter of support: 'I would just feel too much of a hypocrite'.[85]

Commentators of the day suggested that the Just Society might have stood a better chance if Costello had been in a stronger position, one that could only have been achieved by successfully challenging Liam Cosgrave's leadership. Once at the helm of Fine Gael, he would then have been able to direct party opinion. It remains to be seen, however, how the conservative elements of the party would have responded to or, indeed, accepted his leadership. But, as earlier established, Costello was not a leader in waiting. However, if the Just Society was to be developed, it had to be driven from the top. Though Costello had had help formulating the *Towards a Just Society* document, it was essentially the work of his hand. Without its author, the concept was like a ship without its captain.

1968 Ard Fheis

If there had been scope in 1967 to convince Costello to reverse his decision, it was greatly undermined by the 1968 Ard Fheis. An effort was made at the party's annual gathering that year to formalise the new direction in which Costello and his supporters had been attempting to shift Fine Gael. Resolution number twenty-two was tabled in one of the morning sessions: 'That this Ard Fheis proposes that the name of our party shall henceforth be Fine Gael: the Social Democratic Party'. The new tag would replace 'the United Ireland Party', adopted in 1933. Sponsored by nine branches, it was significant that the idea originated with the party's youth group. Vincent Browne, who proposed it at the Mansion House gathering, writing ahead of the event for *The Irish Times*, commented on the 'impatience and irritation' of Fine Gael's younger elements with the 'lethargy, equivocation and torpor of the Oireachtas party'.[86]

There was no opposition to the proposal that morning. However, Jim Dooge, who was on the platform, recalled 'there was a great silence' when the resolution was read out. He subsequently spoke from the stage and supported the motion, arguing that it was 'proper to call Fine Gael a social democratic party because it sought social reform through democratic action'.[87] Tom O'Higgins also voiced his support, as did a number of student members of the party. A decision, as was the case with the morning's other motions, was deferred until the afternoon. That session proved to be stormy, with the political correspondent of *The Irish Times* even suggesting that the events made for 'the liveliest political conference seen in Dublin for thirty years'.[88] Two councillors, Maurice O'Connell and P. T. Shanloy, had requested a suspension of standing orders to allow for a card vote. However, Sweetman argued from the chair that the decision would have to be put to a postal vote of all members. While Sweetman advanced procedural reasons, his response also registered his position on the measure and was intended to kill off the proposal. Arguing that the adoption of 'Social Democratic Party' would reflect terminology used in other European countries, he urged the party to project itself in a uniquely Irish manner. He was supported by Michael O'Higgins, who also favoured a postal ballot, pointing to the fact that some delegates had gone home. Indeed, Dooge and Tom O'Higgins were no longer present by the afternoon, while FitzGerald and Costello were also absent. Agitated student delegates chanted 'debate', and one was reputedly heard to shout 'fascist' and 'dictatorship'.[89] Sweetman is reported to have interjected: 'Fine Gael and the Blueshirts fought and won before the battle for freedom of speech and we are not going to be defeated today by a rabble-rousing young mob'.[90] Sweetman stamped his authority on the proceedings, and though the majority of those who were in attendance was said to favour the name change, the decision was put to a postal vote.

All branches received a circular in January 1969 requesting them to hold a meeting and to submit the branch vote. A second circular was sent at the end of February on the instruction of the party's standing committee; this broadened the ballot to include all other people who had been entitled to vote at the Ard Fheis. The postal ballot resulted in an overwhelming rejection by 653 votes to 81. The Michael Collins Youth Group passed the motion,[91] while the Cork North-East branch, though rejecting the official wording, offered an amendment of 'Fine Gael: the Democratic Party'.[92] However, the official records of the branches are patchy and, as few recorded their decision, it is almost impossible to build a profile of where support lay. Nonetheless, the event was an interesting microcosm of the struggle between the party's two wings. It also revealed that Sweetman still exercised considerable power, while confirming that the slight shift to the left had divided the party.

1969 General election: *Winning through to a Just Society*

Although Costello had departed the political stage, Fine Gael returned nonetheless to the concept of a Just Society for the 1969 general election and published *Winning through to a Just Society*. However, this was not simply a rebranding of the 1965 document. The party evaluated the existing materials and edited where necessary. Where *Towards a Just Society* had been divided between economic and social policies, *Winning through to a Just Society* included a third major heading: government and administration. This was concerned with public administration, local government and state enterprise. At twenty-eight pages, it was considerably shorter than the extensive eighty-page document produced in 1965, but it nonetheless contained fresh material. Elements of the first document were certainly reproduced, as discussed below, but new topics were also covered for the first time. Significantly, the economic development section contained subheadings on both industry and agriculture. Though passing reference had been made to them in 1965, they had been incorporated into a broader discussion of economic planning. Interestingly, the discussion on social welfare was expanded to include emigrant welfare. Reflecting the work that had been on-going between the two elections, the main points from the policy documents on the Irish language and education were also incorporated. The reduced scale may have been intended to encourage more people to read and engage with the document.

It was significant that agricultural policies were included in the document. By the time of the 1969 election, the power of the farmers could not be ignored. On 7 October 1966, Rickard Deasy, President of the NFA, had started a twelve-day walk to the Department of Agriculture in Dublin from Bantry in West Cork, gaining 30,000 supporters along the way. The protest was prompted by growing anger and frustration that farmers had not benefited from the growing prosperity of the 1960s, and the perception that the bureaucrats in Dublin did not understand or care about their problems. Denied access to the Minister, they camped for twenty days and nights outside the offices. As Maurice Manning has pointed out, the events of 1966/67 demonstrated the arrival of farmer power, which all future governments would have to take into account.[93] Gerard Sweetman had been sensitive to farmers' concerns, and, as discussed in Chapter 2, the compromise reached between Costello and Sweetman in 1964 had resulted in the inclusion of a new ninth point that dealt with the standard of living of agricultural workers. Given that Fine Gael had strong support among big farmers, it was important to signal that a shift in policy would not be damaging to their interests. However, *Towards a Just Society* had not included any specific policies on agriculture, other than to say, for example, that farmers with holdings valued at less than £25 would be exempt from the payment of rates and valuations under £15 would not have to contribute to the compulsory health insurance scheme. The omission was peculiar, but arguably was a consequence of a blinkered Dublin view. *Winning through to a Just Society*, reflecting the demands of farmers at the time, outlined as the party's aims in agricultural policy: 'To maintain on the land at an acceptable standard of living, the maximum possible number of farmers' and 'to develop and foster a healthy and expanding rural community'. The proposals for assured outlets for production and guaranteed economic prices, to be achieved through long-term government planning, would have been popular with the rural farmers in particular.

In contrast to the 1969 election, Fine Gael's leadership presented a more committed front to the voters. Although Gerard Sweetman tended to make only indirect references and generally refrained from using the term 'Just Society', Liam Cosgrave regularly incorporated the title of the 1969 manifesto in his speeches, often saving it for the last line for ultimate effect. His closing words at the final Fine Gael rally at the GPO advised that 'by not wasting your vote on any other party you, the voters, will ensure that Fine Gael gets a decisive mandate to implement progressive reforms and wins through to a "Just Society"'.[94] And in Costello's former constituency of Dublin North-West, the concept was ably and enthusiastically communicated by thirty-three-year-old Michael Sweetman who was attempting to make the transition from the Fine Gael backroom to Dáil deputy. Costello was very supportive of the candidacy. Mary Maher, writing in *The Irish Times*, described Sweetman as the obvious successor to Costello's mantle. Although she was suggesting that he might win Costello's old seat, she was clearly implying that he was also an heir to Costello's policies. Sweetman was certainly not only a strong advocate of the Just Society but he also favoured building a pluralist society and, as such, had much in common with Garret FitzGerald. In Cabra, Finglas, Ballymun, Phibsboro and other parts of the constituency, Sweetman spoke on the subject of rates, community work, social reform, the Irish language and local government. A statistic of emigration himself in the 1950s, he believed in seeing beyond numbers to real people. 'The community is ... not a set of statistics', he told one audience. In Cabra, he spoke of the need for recreational facilities – including playgrounds, youth clubs and community centres – for young people. In

Finglas, he argued that the system of rates, which he deemed 'antiquated and unjust', should be abolished as soon as possible. With a first preference count of 2,180 votes, he was the second strongest performer of the four Fine Gael candidates in the constituency. However, Dublin North-West did not traditionally yield more than one seat for the party, and, with only 165 votes between him and his running mate, Hugh Byrne, he was eliminated after the seventh count. The bulk of his transfers subsequently went to Byrne who took the only Fine Gael seat.[95] Sweetman later died tragically, along with eleven other captains of Irish industry, in the 1972 Staines air disaster. During his young life, he made an important contribution to the transformation of Fine Gael through his support for the Just Society and the development of pluralist thinking.

By the time of the 1969 general election, Fianna Fáil – dismissed by Cosgrave as 'stale, divided, weakened, dwindled'[96] – had been in power continuously for fifteen years. Fine Gael questioned the party's capacity to oversee a further administration, and also raised questions about the future of democracy if Irish politics were to turn into a one-party system. The party's pamphlet, *The Time for a Change has Come*, emphasised that Fianna Fáil had been in power for thirty-one of the past thirty-seven years.[97] The government was repeatedly portrayed as a coercive one, and its method of decision-making was continuously questioned. Fine Gael promised, as a contrast, more accessible decision-making processes. Essentially, in government, the party wanted to build a more inclusive political system. When the National Coalition was formed in 1973, Fine Gael and Labour attempted to create this and had a much more open relationship with the press than had been the case with the outgoing Fianna Fáil government.

One element of the Fine Gael campaign that was peculiar was the use of nationalist rhetoric. Although 1969 marked the fiftieth anniversary of the first meeting of the Dáil, the 1960s were also a decade of change. The 1965 election had seen the passing of the revolutionary generation within electoral politics; this was confirmed by Lemass's retirement and his replacement by Jack Lynch who had no association with Easter Week or the fighting which followed in the years after. Although there were some concerns that Irish membership of the European Community would degrade sovereignty, Cosgrave and his candidates spoke more in the context of 1916 and 1919–21. Fine Gael's attempt to make nationalism such an issue in the 1969 campaign seemed redundant. It was also contrary to the spirit of the Just Society. As discussed in Chapter 3, the introduction to *Towards a Just Society* noted that the old struggles were no longer of interest; that document was concerned only with Ireland's future development. Fine Gael attempted to suggest that if the people returned Fianna Fáil to power, they would simply be replacing one ascendancy with another, arguing that the party was interested only in power and money. This was linked to the suspicions regarding the manner in which Charles Haughey had attained his wealth. The party aimed to project this implied greed within Fianna Fáil as the antipathy of the type of Just Society that Fine Gael was promising to build.

As the 1960s progressed, Fine Gael had made considerable efforts to convince Labour to reconsider its anti-coalition stance. On 31 May 1968, Michael O'Higgins, speaking in Arklow, called for dialogue on the possible formation of another inter-party government. The following month, speaking on RTÉ's current affairs programme *7 Days*, he made what David Thornley described as 'by far the clearest public appeal for coalition made by a front bench TD in the last 10 years'. As O'Higgins put it:

> It is of course not enough simply to put a government out, another government must replace it. Surely it's reasonable to assume that an electorate as intelligent as the Irish is alive to so basic a political fact, and will recognise as the logical corollary to combined effort in putting one government out, the necessary measure of co-operative effort, to put another government in.[98]

The party's Central Branch had intended to follow up on O'Higgins's appeal with a symposium on 5 July 1968. However, Liam Cosgrave intervened and, in a letter on his behalf to Donal Flynn, J. W. Sanfey, the party's new general secretary, explained that 'for reasons which I would prefer to discuss with you in person, Mr Cosgrave feels that you should not go ahead with the symposium'.[99] Flynn later explained that Cosgrave was attempting to preserve the unity of the party, and was concerned about potentially divisive discussions.[100] Rather than a symposium, a party meeting was held instead, although the theme was still 'Fine Gael and Labour: an alliance for reform'. Prominent Labour supporters were reported as having been in attendance.[101] Despite the party's efforts, Labour remained committed to its long-term (and ultimately unrealistic) strategy of developing the party into one capable of forming government on its own. 'The seventies will be socialist', Brendan Corish had declared, opening his speech at the party's conference in Dublin's Liberty Hall in 1968. Encouraged by the findings of private polling, the party approached the 1969 election with confidence – only to be severely disappointed. Though the party's share of the vote increased by almost two per cent, it was not sufficient to deliver the type of breakthrough that party members had been, not only predicting but also expecting.

From Fine Gael's perspective, the path to power had yet again been blocked by Labour's stance, prompting Tom O'Higgins to charge that Frank Cluskey and his colleagues were the 'greatest friend' that Fianna Fáil had in the Dáil.[102] Fine Gael's share of the vote rose by less than one per cent (from 34.08 to 34.10 per cent), giving the party a total of fifty seats, three more than had been won in 1965. Nonetheless, Fianna Fáil still had a twenty-five-seat majority. The Just Society had failed its second public test. In the aftermath of the election, an editorial in the *Irish Press* observed that, despite Fine Gael's propaganda of inaugurating a Just Society, the party 'found the people, by and large, satisfied with what they have' and asked, 'Where does it go next?'[103] That question went unanswered until Garret FitzGerald became leader in 1977. Although Liam Cosgrave would take Fine Gael into government in 1973, the party had not launched a new, major policy initiative, but rather it benefited from Labour's decision to end its opposition to coalition. Furthermore, Cosgrave had a much bigger, personal question to answer – and that related to his leadership. Doubts about his future had been expressed before a single vote was even cast in the 1969 election, and by 1972, his position as Fine Gael leader seemed untenable. That he would be elected Taoiseach less than one year later was, at the time, unimaginable.

5
From Leader in Crisis to Leader in Government

In 1969, *Nusight* seriously underestimated Garret FitzGerald. He was described as being 'totally devoid of political savvy or "gut" [and] wouldn't know how to go about becoming leader'.[1] FitzGerald, however, had set himself that task. 'For that to happen', Conor Cruise O'Brien suggested, 'the skids had to be greased under Liam Cosgrave, and they were'. Cosgrave himself contributed.[2] If Liam Cosgrave had a major decision to make, he would ask himself what his father would have done.[3] Cumann na nGaedheal – Fine Gael's antecedent led by W. T. Cosgrave – was born in the midst of the Civil War and, as the government party, was charged with the task of building the new state. Facing down challenges from both within and outside the political system, it presented itself as the party of law and order. It was a legacy of which Liam Cosgrave was proud and one on which he placed a great premium. Speaking at the final rally for the 1969 election, he told his audience 'it is well to remember that the institutions of this State were set up by this party, and defended by this party before Fianna Fáil ever was heard of'.[4] Cosgrave saw himself in the same 'defender of the state' mould as his father. Such was his commitment that he risked his leadership of Fine Gael to support Fianna Fáil's emergency security legislation in late 1972. Had bombs, planted by Loyalist extremists, not exploded in Dublin, Cosgrave may well have become the first Fine Gael leader to be ousted by the party.

Cosgrave's position, however, was under pressure long before Des O'Malley introduced his amendment to the Offences Against the State Act. Various elements within the party were growing increasingly dissatisfied with what they perceived as a failure to convincingly challenge Jack Lynch. His leadership was undermined by his response to the referendum on PR in October 1968. For the second time, Fianna Fáil attempted to amend the voting system, arguing, as Charles Haughey put it, that democracy never died in a country that used the straight vote system, but that PR had paved the way for a dictatorship of the left or right.[5] Cosgrave also favoured the abolition of PR, believing that, in the longer term, it offered Fine Gael the best opportunity to form a single-party government. His opposition was not popularly shared by his party colleagues, however, although some elements of the grassroots supported his view. The Carlow organising committee, for example, communicated a resolution calling on the party to agree a pro-straight vote stance and to secure an agreement with Fianna Fáil.[6] Cosgrave's position created an uncomfortable situation for the parliamentary party. Ultimately, he put aside his personal preference and supported Fine Gael's campaign against the referendum, but his views did not go unnoticed. When asked about his party leader's attitude on *7 Days*, Fine Gael councillor Maurice O'Connell replied that Cosgrave would not be leader forever.[7] He was censured for the remark, which almost led to his expulsion from the party. O'Connell remained Cosgrave's most outspoken and consistent opponent. As late as 1971, he referred to the 'idiocies and inadequacies of the present management'.[8] By so publicly criticising the leadership, he found himself in the peculiar position of being expelled multiple times from the party. But O'Connell was not alone in suggesting that a leadership change was possible, if not needed. Writing in the aftermath of the unsuccessful PR referendum, Michael McInerney was critical of the failing leadership of both Lynch and Cosgrave, and he suggested 'these are the days of decision for Lynch, Colley, Hillery, [Declan] Costello, Garret FitzGerald, Dooge'.[9] The internal struggle between Colley and Haughey to succeed Lynch that convulsed Fianna Fáil is well documented elsewhere.[10]

By 1969, Fine Gael was polarised between two groups: one led by Cosgrave and supported by party stalwarts like Gerard Sweetman, Richie Ryan and Oliver J Flanagan, and a second group consisting of Garret FitzGerald, Alexis FitzGerald, Jim Dooge, Tom O'Higgins and Michael Sweetman. From the late 1960s, this group met regularly at Alexis FitzGerald's home on Nutley Road.[11] These men were at the core of the 'mongrel foxes' group. At one particular meeting in Alexis FitzGerald's home in 1969, the idea that the liberal elements in Fine Gael might leave to form a new social democratic party was raised. The plan, Vincent Browne has suggested, was to cause a sensation, thereby giving the new party much publicity, with the aim of securing fourteen to sixteen seats at a general election. Although Labour was opposed to an alliance, it was felt this option would be attractive to Brendan Corish and his party, as the conservative elements within Fine Gael would not play any role in the new party.[12] It was hoped that a left-wing government would be formed. It is likely that there were tentative approaches made to the Labour Party, and Costello is believed to have been in touch with Brendan Halligan. However, the idea never developed as Garret FitzGerald – who had inherited John A Costello's constituency – felt that he could not leave his constituency organisation.[13] This conversation came shortly after a discussion between elements of the Fine Gael and Labour parties about a merger, which was considered a more plausible option than coalition. Brendan Corish and Mark Clinton had raised the possibility separately, and there was strong support within the two parties. There were, of course, also reservations on both sides. In particular, Gerard Sweetman and Maurice Dockrell were opposed.[14] This was hardly surprising, as both men had been opposed to Costello's Just Society and were, thus, unlikely to favour merging with a party sympathetic to his views. Nothing came of the discussions. Corish put the proposal to his frontbench, but, according to FitzGerald's memoirs, he reported that there was 'nothing doing'.[15] The issue was not pursued further.

In the aftermath of the 1969 election, Liam Cosgrave urged members not to be distracted by 'unnecessary controversy among ourselves', and to instead focus on strengthening the organisation and winning support for the party's policies.[16] But concern about Cosgrave's position was not confined to his colleagues. A survey for *Nusight* conducted by Gallup found that a relatively high proportion of the party's supporters were not satisfied with Cosgrave's leadership. A separate article in that edition of the current affairs magazine suggested that nothing had been done because 'no good excuse has presented itself to provoke the leadership crisis'.[17] The matter came to a head in 1972.

On 22 November, Des O'Malley, the Minister for Justice, sought leave to introduce a bill to amend the Offences Against the State Acts, 1939 and 1940, to deal with an ever-growing IRA threat. The Fine Gael parliamentary party convened the day before the second reading. Liam Cosgrave and Paddy Cooney offered differing opinions, with the majority of the party supporting Cooney's view that the bill should be opposed. It was a peculiar stance. Having always modelled itself as the party of law and order and the defenders of the institutions of state, the position smacked of political opportunism. Speculation was rife that the party would use the issue to defeat the government. That some members saw the possibility of breaking Fianna Fáil's seemingly unending rule as alluring cannot be rejected, and it would later fuel Fianna Fáil propaganda in the 1973 election. Brian Lenihan, for example, labelled them 'the power-hungry majority'.[18] But a close reading of the speeches later delivered in the Dáil also indicate that, in public at least, members were articulating the same concerns as their colleagues in the Labour Party and those outside the political system who were also voicing opposition: that is, that the Bill undermined fundamental citizens' rights.

In response to the Minister's opening speech on the second stage, Fine Gael tabled an amendment proposing that the Dáil did not give a second reading to the Bill, deeming the legislation 'unnecessary and excessive' and 'repugnant to the basic principles of justice and liberty and the long-established fundamental rights of citizens'.[19] In a show of party solidarity, the amendment was proposed by Paddy Cooney and seconded by Liam Cosgrave. However, Cosgrave's speech subtly indicated that his support for his party's spokesperson on justice was not unequivocal. Cosgrave restated his party's resolute opposition to 'irregular and illegal organisations' and pledged support for 'any proposals necessary for the preservation and defence of the institutions of State'. He wondered, however, if the existing legislation was inadequate, and sought assurance that any amendments made would be 'both necessary and justified'.[20] Paddy Harte recalled that many deputies who served with Cosgrave 'formed the opinion that he was reliving the role of his later father'.[21] That Cosgrave was willing to break with his party on the issue offered those who were plotting against him the perfect opportunity to change the leadership. O'Malley's bill, in the ever colourful words of John Healy, offered them 'the coffin in which they'd bury Liam'.[22]

In outlining the reasons for the Labour Party's opposition, Frank Cluskey expressed the view that the bill was attempting to 'deprive Irish men and women of their basic human right'.[23] That question of human rights was the major issue discussed outside Leinster House also as an array of groups and individuals came out to voice their concerns. Members of the SDLP urgently sought a meeting with the Taoiseach to register their opposition to what a party statement described as a serious infringement of 'accepted standards of civil liberties'.[24] The Irish Transport and General Workers Union (ITGWU) labelled the amendment 'hideous', while the Irish Federation of Trade Unions went as far as to suggest that the Bill was 'designed to recreate the iniquitous conditions of Nazi Germany'.[25] Around 200 students from St Patrick's College, Maynooth, marched to Leinster House to present a petition against O'Malley's Bill.[26] And the letters pages of the daily newspapers were filled with criticisms from ordinary citizens, such as William Sweetman of Dundrum in Dublin, who felt that membership of an illegal organisation could be too easily accused, but not as readily disproved.[27]

Following the debate on the second stage, Tom O'Higgins recalled that 'telephone calls, letters and messages of all kinds were received [from party supporters] ... expressing disappointment and displeasure, and most of them renouncing further support'. This prompted Cosgrave to summon a party meeting for Thursday morning, 31 November 1972, where he appealed to deputies to withdraw their opposition. However, the objections to the bill were repeated with 'force and conviction'.[28] The final stage was due before the Dáil on Friday 1 December. The Fine Gael members convened again in the morning to discuss a proposition from Tom O'Higgins. With the members' agreement, that afternoon O'Higgins and Cooney met with O'Malley in an effort to persuade him to amend the legislation in exchange for Fine Gael withdrawing its opposition to the second reading of the Bill.[29] O'Higgins later explained to the Dáil that they had requested that subsection 2 of section 3 be amended so that the accused could swear an oath declaring that he was not a member of an unlawful organisation; that section 4 be amended to exclude an innocent bystander and that the lifespan of the Act's application be limited to six months.[30] O'Malley was not in a position to comment without first consulting with the cabinet. O'Higgins recalled coming away from the meeting 'somewhat optimistic', but a phone call from Patrick Hillery, who had also been present, came through before five o'clock to inform him that the government would not accept the amendments.[31] 'Unless something unforeseen occurs', Michael Mills, unaware, of course, of the behind-the-scenes wrangling, had surmised in his *Irish Press* column that day, 'the government will be defeated by 71 votes to 70; the Taoiseach will seek the dissolution of the Dáil and a general election will be held as soon as possible'.[32]

But the unforeseen did occur. As the debate was underway that night in the Dáil, a car bomb exploded in Eden Quay at 7.58 pm, followed by another explosion at Sackville Place at 8.16 pm. Two people were killed and 127 others injured. The bombs had been planted by the UVF. The loyalist paramilitary organisation had a history of not always claiming responsibility for acts of violence, sometimes in the hope that blame would be apportioned to Republicans.[33] Indeed, initial speculation believed the IRA to be responsible and forced some to reconsider what the press had dubbed the 'anti-IRA Bill'. O'Higgins had been speaking in the chamber when he was made aware of the explosions. He continued, nonetheless, to press his party's concerns about aspects of the legislation, while still stressing that Fine Gael remained committed to upholding law and order.[34] His own account of what happened next places himself at the centre of the decision-making process in Fine Gael. As Cosgrave was unavailable, O'Higgins, in his capacity as deputy leader, gathered his colleagues and proposed that Cooney be authorised to withdraw the amendment. After the meeting, he was informed that Cosgrave was in the Dáil restaurant with some visitors; he encouraged his party leader to join Cooney in the chamber.[35]

Stephen Collins gives a dramatic account of the events as they unfolded within the Fine Gael corridor of Leinster House that night:

> Liam Cosgrave's enemies ... had him cornered. He was almost completely isolated with only Paddy Donegan ready to stand by him whatever the consequences. Virtually all his TDs and senators were in the process of walking out of the Fine Gael party room in disgust ... Suddenly a loud thud was heard and the windows of Leinster House vibrated. The first Loyalist bombs had gone off in Dublin. They killed two people and saved Cosgrave's political life.[36]

Joe MacAnthony, writing in the *Sunday Independent*, judged that 'the thunder of the two explosions ... proved a louder argument in favour of the new Bill than anything that had gone before'.[37] But there was not a complete conversion to Fianna Fáil's legislation. Labour remained opposed. Brendan Corish reaffirmed his party's view that the bill was 'unnecessary, unwarranted and unjustifiable' and his TDs would not be 'stampeded' into voting for it because of the atrocities.[38] Nonetheless, even with four former Fianna Fáil members voting against, the legislation was passed comfortably by seventy votes to twenty-three. But just as the bombs had not convinced some politicians of the need for the legislation, opposition continued outside Leinster House. The Citizens for Civil Liberties group, for example, issued a statement criticising the government for exploiting the bombings and creating a siege mentality. A public meeting was to be held, addressed by such leading public figures as Mary Robinson, Ivan Cooper and Maynooth Professor Enda McDonagh.[39] The Seanad passed all stages without divisions by 1.30 am, and the Bill was taken to President de Valera to be signed into law.

'Fine Gael caves in at the last moment', *The Irish Times* reported.[40] Seán Sherwin – a former Fianna Fáil TD for Dublin South-West who had left the party after the arms crisis and who voted against the Bill – commented, 'If the dastardly act that happened last night had not occurred we would not be here now discussing the Bill, and we would not have this Bill passed, as it is likely to be, because Fine Gael would not have the way out they have got so conveniently through the UVF bombs'.[41] The atrocity allowed Fine Gael pull back from an untenable position. Liam Cosgrave might have been guided not only by his father's legacy, but there was also a practical dimension to his approach that many of his colleagues appeared to overlook. Had the Bill been rejected and an election called, the campaign would have been fought on law and order. Fianna Fáil would have been able to take the high moral ground and to outflank Fine Gael on one of the party's core values. ('Law and order' is still listed under the 'values' section of the Fine Gael website).[42]

It was widely accepted that the defeat of the Bill would result in an early election, but that was no longer expected following the change in circumstances. Lynch, however, took the opportunity over the Christmas recess to reflect on the situation. Though Fine Gael had ultimately united behind their leader at the last moment, the party was 'so obviously divided and demoralised' that, as Tom O'Higgins suggested, its viability as a political force was under question.[43] On 5 February, two days before the Dáil would resume as scheduled, Lynch requested a dissolution, wrongfooting the opposition. Labour and Fine Gael had not yet reached an agreement on a joint platform for the election. Lynch claimed that he was calling the election early to 'remove any feeling of uncertainty'. The announcement was met with widespread criticism, not least because the timing disfranchised 140,000 eighteen- to twenty-one-year-olds who had been given the right to vote in December, but whose names would not appear on the electoral register until April 1973. Twenty-year-old Trinity College student David Reynolds went as far as to take a case to the High Court to secure the right to vote, but was unsuccessful.

Negotiating a joint platform

Two days after the dissolution was announced, members of the Fine Gael and Labour parliamentary parties met at Leinster House to formally approve the coalition agreement, the first of its kind in the history of independent Ireland. It marked a massive policy reversal for Labour. As already discussed, that party had approached the 1969 general election in a buoyant mood. A bruising experience at the polls, however, caused some members to rethink their strategy. The party increased its share of the vote nationally by just over 1.5 per cent, but the figure of 17.02 per cent was bitterly disappointing. As Niamh Puirséil has pointed out, disappointment with the results is best understood when they are considered in light of the inflated expectations that had preceded them. A poll commissioned by the party and conducted by Gallup had put Labour on twenty-nine per cent in Dublin and eighteen per cent outside the capital.[44] The party came in at just over twenty-eight per cent in Dublin, but only achieved thirteen per cent in the rest of the country. The predicted breakthrough did not materialise, and Labour actually lost four seats. Labour was reluctant to join a coalition after earlier experiences, but the alternative of single-party government was out of the question. Fianna Fáil's conversion to coalition in 1989 under the leadership of Albert Reynolds lay, unimagined, in the future. The only alternative to a Fine Gael–Labour coalition was for the party to continue on the opposition benches. Thus, there was no bargaining chip for Labour, as a junior partner, to make demands.

As the leadership acknowledged the failure of the strategy, a special delegate conference was called for 13 December 1969.[45] The desire for power cannot be underestimated. Like Fine Gael, Labour had spent the past sixteen years on the opposition benches and, as the results of the general election had shown, a major breakthrough, even after much internal reflection and a concerted effort, was unlikely. The feeling was growing that Labour was destined to be a party of permanent opposition unless it reassessed its attitude towards coalition. The party could spend hours formulating policies, but without the power to implement them, such documents would simply be confined, unfulfilled, to the archives for future historians to analyse. A document submitted to the Cork conference captured this realisation:

> Labour's policies were not designed for permanent opposition but for implementation. To be a socialist is not to be condemned to perpetual opposition, but rather is to be committed to achievement, where the opportunity arises to do so with honour.[46]

The timing was also important. The government had been plunged into crisis by the arms plot. As Stephen Collins details, Cosgrave received a tip-off about a plot to import arms allegedly involving Ministers Haughey and Blaney. When Jack Lynch announced in the Dáil on 5 May 1970 that Michael Moran, his Minister for Justice, had resigned (for reasons unconnected to the arms crisis), Cosgrave asked if that was the only ministerial resignation that could be expected. Lynch, at that stage, was unaware of the information that Cosgrave possessed, but later that night Cosgrave spoke personally to the Taoiseach, who confirmed the validity of the allegations. Lynch subsequently asked both men to resign, and when they refused, he issued a statement that they had been fired. Peter Berry was the civil servant who initially learnt of the plan to bring arms and ammunition into Dublin airport. His diaries reveal that Lynch, having been informed, had decided to bury the issue. He was only prompted to act after Cosgrave pressed him on the matter.[47] The arms crisis had convinced the opposition that the troubled Fianna Fáil government had to be removed from office. This could only be achieved by a significant change in Labour policy. Recognising this, Corish told delegates attending the conference, 'I see Fianna Fáil in action every day. I see the threat to our democracy as long as they remained unchallenged'.[48] It was a view shared, of course, by Liam Cosgrave.

The conditions necessary for change complemented this momentum. As Barry Desmond recalled, by 1973 'nobody doubted that we were entering a period in which no single party could preserve its hegemony alone in government'.[49] The changes that had taken place within Fine Gael made the possibility of coalition, to an extent, more attractive than had previously been the case. The efforts to redirect the party's policy outlook at the instigation of Declan Costello brought Fine Gael closer to Labour ideologically. Personnel changes also made the process more straightforward. Gerard Sweetman had died in a car crash on 28 January 1970, and, recalling his political outlook, *The Irish Times* suggested that his economic policies had had the ability to make Labour 'wince'.[50] On leaving the second inter-party government, Brendan Corish swore that he would never serve in government again with Sweetman.[51] Brendan Halligan later suggested that had Sweetman still been in active in politics in 1973, any arrangement between Labour and Fine Gael would have been unthinkable.[52] However, sixteen years on the opposition benches can have a sobering effect, and had Sweetman still been alive in 1973, given the other factors that motivated the coalition, it is unlikely that his presence would have been a major impediment. His absence, though, arguably allowed for smoother negotiations.

1973 general election

For the first time in sixteen years, voters were offered a genuine alternative at the 1973 general election. The coming together of Fine Gael and Labour ended the dominance of Fianna Fáil. Moreover, the actual option of a coalition was a healthy development for what could be seen as the stagnation of the Irish party system. The change of government, resulting from the choice available to voters, should not be seen as inevitable, however. A memorandum on campaign strategy for the Labour Party noted in early December that the message of an alternative had not yet been received by the public, and that a 'herculean effort' would be needed to communicate the message in the space of a three-week campaign.[53] In the end, the election was very close, with the results from every constituency counting.

Fine Gael and Labour ran a co-ordinated campaign at constituency level, although this did not extend to joint advertising. But while the two parties did not print requests asking supporters to continue their preferences for the other party, advertisements did carry the slogan, 'support the national coalition'. The future coalition partners released a statement of intent. With a promise to reduce the cost of living, it was an attractive package for an election that was dominated by the economy. The fourteen-point programme included economic and social reform, a new housing strategy, amendments to rates and taxes, a reassessment of education policy and an end to discrimination against women. The implementation of these proposals, it was argued, would transform Ireland into a 'modern progressive society based on social justice'.[54] Jack Lynch dismissed the fourteen-point programme as a 'collection of pious aspirations and platitudes',[55] but in government the coalition did much to deliver on its election promises.

Writing in *Fortnight*, Dennis Kennedy surmised that after the votes had been cast, regardless to which party won the election, 'Fianna Fáil lost the campaign'.[56] Fianna Fáil attempted to drive a wedge between the potential coalition partners on the issue of law and order, pointing to the parties' contrasting approaches to the Offences Against the State (Amendment) Act. In conjunction with the 'weakness of coalition' line, the party also attempted to make the North the major theme of the election. The party's campaign was initially framed in the context of the pending publication of a British White Paper on Northern Ireland. In a television broadcast, Lynch explained that a strong government would be needed to 'deal effectively with the crucial issues' ahead, and that in considering the White Paper, the government would need 'the firm and unequivocal support of the people'.[57] The importance of the Northern dimension, unsurprisingly, was echoed by the *Irish Press*, an editorial in which it was argued that the question facing voters was simple. Framing it in the context of the troubles, the paper asked if the people wanted change from a 'leader and governmental team, tested and known through the years of tension and toil'.[58] On the surface, emphasising Northern Ireland and the security question seemed like an obvious strategy with the election coming so soon after the Dublin bombings and with emotions still raw. William Craig, leader of the United Loyalist Council, suggested that 'the Dublin people will now have a better understanding of the horror that has been endured for so long here in Ulster', implying that there would be a greater sense of empathy. But although the bombings had visited the reality of the Northern troubles to Dublin doorsteps, the security question was not a dominant concern as voters faced into the election. Furthermore, the potential coalition partners refused to be distracted from social issues. At the launch of the coalition's 'statement of intent', Labour's Brendan Corish rebuffed Lynch's efforts, stating 'we will not play politics with the North', while Richie Ryan – Fine Gael's spokesperson on Northern Ireland – explained at a meeting in Carlow that his party regarded the North as a 'question above party'.[59]

Fianna Fáil had made a grave miscalculation. Partially acknowledging this, but still emphasising the security question, the party began to attack the statement of intent. By doing so, the focus of the campaign shifted, and it meant that it was being fought on the coalition's issues, rather than Fianna Fáil's. Lynch's first detailed response to the coalition's proposals came on 15 February. He criticised the removal of VAT, arguing that it favoured the wealthy, giving them a saving of £1.50 per week, compared to a saving only of 25 pence for poorer families. The problem for Fianna Fáil was that the party's willingness to criticise the alleged shortcomings of the coalition's proposals was not balanced with a detailed policy statement of their own. Though Lynch promised reform, he explained, 'I do not propose to indulge in the coalition game of extravagant promises by attempting to spell these out at this stage'. Such vague statements were criticised more than once in the newspapers, with *The Irish Times*' Dick Walsh summarising the Fianna Fáil message as 'the party is the policy and the policy is the party'.[60]

'Prices may sink Lynch. North seen as less vital issue', was the front-page headline of the *Irish Independent* on 26 February. An Irish Marketing Surveys poll published in the newspaper that day confirmed that the outgoing government had made a 'major blunder', as voters were more troubled by the cost of living, rising prices being the dominant concern. The North was ranked only fourth in order of priority, while internal security came second-last in the nine-issue questionnaire.[61] Fianna Fáil had gradually come to realise this, and just four days before the poll was published, Lynch announced the abolition of domestic rates. It had every appearance of a political stroke. Only the previous year, the government's White Paper had concluded that the removal of rates would be impossible.[62] But more destructive to the Fianna Fáil campaign was the publication in the *Limerick Leader* of a half-page advertisement. The copy read:

> Jack Lynch has not tried to ensure re-election by trading on the innocence of some of the people. He does not dangle rosy promises of no VAT on food, no rates, etc. The plain people of Ireland know only too well that remission of these taxes will only result in drastic increases in taxes on other essentials, such as electricity, fuel, clothing, household goods, and indeed on drink, cigarettes and, yes, income tax.

The advertisement had been placed by Fianna Fáil's Gerry Collins, clearly unaware that his party was about to announce what was a significant policy reversal. It provided much propaganda for the opposition, and it allowed Garret FitzGerald to deliver a devastating blow during a televised debate with George Colley. An 'almost speechless' Colley looked on as FitzGerald read out the text. It dominated the last days of the campaign.[63] At the final Fine Gael rally in the Mansion House, Cosgrave denounced Fianna Fáil's 'switcheroo' on rates.[64]

Although not as prominent as the economy, women's rights were an important issue at the 1973 election. Second wave feminism emerged in America in the early 1960s and spread internationally. It was apparent in

Ireland from the 1970s and the reason why was aptly captured by *Bread and Roses*. That magazine was produced by women in UCD in the mid-1970s. A pencil-sketched picture of a young woman on the front-cover of the second issue was set against a pink background. The caption read: 'Girls! Looking for a career? Become a wife!!!' The sarcastic 'job-description' reflected a growing sense of frustration about the limitations imposed on women:

- Free room and board
- Lifelong unbreakable contract
- All materials provided
- Work at home – in your spare time
- Steady hours – 99.6 per week
- Work during maternity leave
- Plus, the constant reminder that a part of you is needed.

The description is rounded off with the reassurance that training was not necessary: 'it's all been taken care of by the time you're fourteen'.[65]

When the 1970s arrived, contraception was illegal, women had to leave the public service on marriage, deserted wives and unmarried mothers were not supported by the state, female jurors were unheard of and women were paid less money than men for the same work. Female TDs were also conspicuously absent from the Dáil, a problem that dated to the foundation of the State in 1922. Those women who had been to the forefront of the revolutionary movement had opposed the Anglo-Irish Treaty the previous year and, by refusing to recognise the new, independent parliament, they effectively removed themselves from active constitutional politics. In the early years of the new State, between 1922 and 1937, only seven women were elected to the Dáil.[66] Further factors prevented women from participating more fully in the political system. As Fiona Buckey and Claire McGing have pointed out, Article 41.2 of the 1937 Constitution fuses womanhood and motherhood, and firmly locates women in the home. 'This constitutional declaration, coupled with the prominence of the Catholic Church in Irish society, which viewed the role of women as being childbearers, carers and nurturers, meant that Irishwomen were met with strong cultural, societal and legal barriers in their attempts to enter public life'. By 1973, there were fewer women in parliament than there had been fifty years earlier (four women were elected in 1973, one less than the number elected in 1923).[67] Fine Gael's Joan Burke, addressing a meeting of the National Federation of Business and Professional Women's Clubs in 1971, contended that 'it would be a big help if there were more women in parliament to bring pressure on the government to do something about the many blatant injustices which Irish women were expected to accept'.[68]

Various women's groups, most notably the Irish Women's Liberation Movement (IWLM) and Irish Women United, appeared at this time. The

IWLM had emerged in the summer of 1970 from a meeting of five women of different backgrounds in Bewley's café in Dublin. That many of its members were journalists gave the women direct access to the media, which allowed them spread their message beyond Dublin.[69] They published *Irishwomen: Chains or Change?* in 1972. A charter of demands, it outlined the various areas in which women's rights were compromised, including employment, education and taxation. It also dealt with the difficulties facing unmarried mothers, deserted wives, widows and single women. Irish Women United grew out of an informal gathering of women in April 1975 to discuss a possible charter. A conference was subsequently held on 8 June, attended by approximately 100 women, at which the organisation was officially inaugurated. They also launched *Banshee*, a short-lived magazine that was designed to counter a perceived media-bias towards men. It was intended to 'detail, monthly and minutely, the oppression of women and the means of removing that oppression'.[70] But rather than engaging directly with politics through the party system, these women's groups chose instead to take on the role of activists and lobbyists. They campaigned for change for women from the outside. Other interest groups, such as Action, Information and Motivation (AIM) and Cherish, also emerged, and although they were not specifically women's movements, they dealt with issues of concern to women.

Women's rights thus became an area that political parties could not afford to ignore when it came to the 1973 general election. A questionnaire was submitted by the women's editor of *The Irish Times* to the party leaders, asking for their opinions on equal pay, financial support for unmarried mothers and contraception, for example. These were key issues on which the various groups lobbied the political parties. All generally responded favourably, recognising that female voters would become a key demographic. The National Coalition pledged to end all forms of discrimination against women in the fourteen point programme. It did much in government to improve the status of women, but initiative for change came from the women's groups who continued to lobby after the election was over.

Results

Though it was predicted that the 1973 election would be close run, Fine Gael had not expected to win. On the morning of the count, Jim Dooge received a phone call from Garret FitzGerald to say that the Dublin constituencies were not performing as well as they had hoped. He phoned again at 12.30 pm requesting guidance as to what he should say on the one o'clock news. Dooge advised him to avoid giving any opinion until all results from the west had come in. He described the next few hours as 'touch and go'. However, by the time that Liam Cosgrave phoned him just after 11 pm that night, he felt confident enough to suggest, 'go to bed, Taoiseach, and get a good night's sleep'. However, every seat counted in the 1973 election, and the potential for a Fine Gael–Labour coalition was almost undermined. Counting had been suspended in the Laois-Offaly constituency where Oliver Flanagan's surplus had 'scattered disastrously' after the first count.[71] After an anxious wait the following day, Thomas Enright retained his seat on the tenth count, while, crucially, Charles McDonald ousted Fianna Fáil's Bernard Cowen, to take a third seat for Fine Gael on the eleventh and last count.

With counting in the constituencies concluded – and recounts conducted in Mayo East, Galway West and Dublin South-East – the final results gave Fianna Fáil sixty-nine seats, Fine Gael fifty-four and Labour nineteen. Two Independents had also been elected: Joseph Sheridan in Longford-Westmeath and Neil Blaney in Donegal North-East. Sheridan had stood unsuccessfully for the Dáil as a Fine Gael candidate in 1951, 1954 and 1957. Following a disagreement with the party – although he retained a personal friendship with many of its members, including Liam Cosgrave[72] – he successfully contested the 1961 election as an Independent and held the seat for the next twenty years. Despite his Fine Gael background, he supported Lemass's minority government, and it was reported that Jack Lynch could also rely on his support.[73] Blaney had been dismissed from cabinet in May 1970. Lynch had cited Blaney's disagreement with government policy on the North, and no mention was made of his role in the arms crisis, although this was widely seen as the real reason for his removal. He was expelled from the party two years later. Addressing the Dáil in 1970, Blaney had affirmed that his allegiance would continue to lie with Fianna Fáil, believing the party and its continuance was 'synonymous with the advancement of this country and the ultimate brining about of unity and the betterment of all our people'.[74] Campaigning in 1973 under the banner of 'Independent Fianna Fáil' – although this title did not appear on the ballot paper as it was not an officially registered party – he successfully defended his seat. The coalition partners had a combined total of seventy-three seats. If Blaney's seat was added to the official Fianna Fáil total and Sheridan gave his support again, Lynch's party would have had seventy-one seats. The loss of Bernard Cowen's seat in Laois-Offaly to Fine Gael arguably decided the election. Had he retained it, the result would have been a hung Dáil with both Fianna Fáil, supported by the Independents, and a coalition of Fine Gael and Labour holding seventy-two seats. Victory was thus won by a tight margin and, as Maurice Manning observed, 'a thousand votes nationally in a few key constituencies could have seen Fianna Fáil back in office'.[75]

Despite finding itself on the opposition benches, Fianna Fáil's share of the vote had increased by 0.58 per cent and it won new seats in three constituencies (off-set, though, by losses in nine others). Fine Gael also saw its share of first preferences rise, by 0.98 per cent, but Labour's vote actually dropped by 3.31 per cent, giving the two parties a combined vote that was less than their 1969 figure. However, the breakdown of votes cast reveals a steady transfer pattern between Fine Gael and Labour that was absent at the previous general election. Labour received just over seventy per cent of Fine Gael's transfers where there was no Fine Gael candidate left in the running, and almost seventy-two per cent of Labour's transfers went to Fine Gael when there was no Labour candidate available.[76] This was a significant increase on the 1969 transfer figures of just over thirty-three and thirty-four per cent respectively.[77] There were obvious benefits in certain constituencies where the coalition partners gained seats at the expense of Fianna Fáil. For example, it has been observed that if only ten per cent of Labour's non-transferable votes in Laois-Offaly had gone to Fine Gael in 1969, Fine Gael would have won a third seat. With the pact in place for the 1973 election, a much larger proportion of Labour votes transferred to Fine Gael with the result that Charles McDonald, who narrowly missed out in 1969, took a seat. Similarly, Labour's and Fine Gael's combined share of first preference votes in Roscommon-Leitrim exceeded fifty per cent in 1969, but as Labour voters did not continue their preferences for Fine Gael candidates, Fianna Fáil took two of the three available seats. Transfers to Fine Gael were substantial, however, in 1973, allowing the party to reverse the results of the previous election and to take a second seat.[78] Overall, Fine Gael won Fianna Fáil-held seats in Laois-Offaly, Longford-Westmeath, Roscommon-Leitrim and Sligo-Leitrim. In the case of the party's fifth seat gain at Fianna Fáil's expense, Mayo West, the outcome was unaffected by transfer pacts as there were only Fianna Fáil and Fine Gael candidates in the field. Labour won seats previously held by Fianna Fáil in Kildare, Tipperary-North and Waterford. At times, the two parties gained seats at the expense of their potential coalition partners. In Cork Mid, Labour took a Fine Gael seat, while Fine Gael won seats at Labour's expense in the Dublin constituencies of South-Central, South-East and South-West. Fine Gael also sustained losses to Fianna Fáil in Cavan, Mayo East and Monaghan, cancelling out some of the party's seat gains elsewhere.

The national coalition

The twentieth Dáil assembled on 14 March 1973. Liam Cosgrave was proposed for Taoiseach by Labour leader Brenan Corish and seconded by Fine Gael's Maurice Dockrell. With Erskine Childer's motion that Jack Lynch be elected to the office defeated by seventy-three votes to sixty-nine, Cosgrave made history by becoming the only son to follow his father into the highest office in Ireland. That afternoon, the new Taoiseach unveiled his cabinet. In a briefing document for Corish before the coalition negotiations had started, Brendan Halligan had identified the allocation of cabinet seats as 'an obvious flashpoint' between the partners.[79] The process, however, proved very straightforward. Corish, not fully expecting to get all of the portfolios he requested, asked for Industry and Commerce, Posts and Telegraphs, Labour, Local Government and Health and Social Welfare. Much to Corish's surprise, Cosgrave offered six seats, including Finance, but only if the Labour leader took that portfolio himself.[80] Although Corish declined to do so, that still left his party with five seats at the cabinet table, more than the party was proportionally due. Such was the line-up of those available – intellectuals like Conor Cruise O'Brien, long-serving deputies like Mark Clinton and upcoming talent like Garret FitzGerald – that the press had commented on the embarrassment of talent. There was a glimpse of Cosgrave's wit as he responded to such observations. 'I need hardly say that I am glad to have got a place on it',[81] he quipped after naming his team.

In his memoirs, Garret FitzGerald noted that the ability of the 'dissidents' to submerge their previous unhappiness with Cosgrave depended on him demonstrating a new trust and confidence in them. 'He did so, and it worked'.[82] There has been speculation, however, that Cosgrave purposely side-lined his rivals when choosing his cabinet colleagues. Declan Costello had been persuaded to return to politics because of the arms crisis, and he successfully contested the Dublin South-West constituency. Nell McCafferty in her *Irish Times* column had observed that those who spoke of coalition during the campaign, referred to Costello as a minister.[83] Much to the surprise of his supporters, however, he was not given a ministry, but rather he was appointed Attorney General – the position held by his father under W. T. Cosgrave in the 1920s. Unusually, he was given permission by Corish to fully participate in all debates in the cabinet. Previous Attorneys General had been silent participants, giving legal advice only when asked. Donal Flynn has argued, however, that Costello was not side-lined because Cosgrave did not have to side-line him: he did not have leadership aspirations.[84] It does seem unlikely that Costello wanted to be leader, but Cosgrave may have by-passed him for a different reason. As was potentially the case with FitzGerald also, keeping Costello out of an economic or health and social welfare portfolio – those to which he was best suited – moderated the more progressive views at the cabinet table. But there is also the possibility that had Costello contested the 1969 election, he might have stood a better chance at becoming a full, senior minister. As leader of a coalition, Cosgrave had only a limited number of seats available to him, and a large pool of talented politicians from which to choose. Costello maintained, perhaps magnanimously, that he was 'very glad' to be given the opportunity to be involved in the work of the government.[85] Cosgrave later insisted that he had made the correct decision, describing Costello as a constitutional lawyer of 'great distinction'. 'In retrospect, I think people would agree that Attorney General was the correct appointment for Declan Costello, where he was first class'.[86] Once retired, Cosgrave refrained from commenting on politics. However, in a rare public appearance, he used the occasion of his speech at a book launch in October 2010 to publicly address the criticism, reaffirming his opinion.[87]

FitzGerald's appointment to the Department of Foreign Affairs could also be seen as the side-lining of a rival. He had been the party's spokesperson on

Finance in opposition, yet that portfolio was given to Richie Ryan, who had little experience of the area. On a special RTÉ Radio 1 programme following the first meeting of the Twentieth Dáil, John Bowman put it to FitzGerald that his appointment was one of the most surprising. FitzGerald, no doubt diplomatically, dismissed the suggestion, explaining that there was no certainty as to what post any politician would receive.[88] But as Joe Lee put it, 'it might not be too speculative to surmise that from Cosgrave's viewpoint, Foreign Affairs might do a Seán MacBride on FitzGerald'.[89] The responsibilities of that Ministry require extensive travel. As Minister for External Affairs in the first inter-party government, MacBride spent much time out of the country and quickly lost touch with both his party's executive and the grassroots.[90] FitzGerald himself considered this interpretation unlikely, although he did not refute the notion that he had been moved from Finance, which he had shadowed since 1971, because of the possible impact of his perceived radicalism on that portfolio.[91] Ryan had shadowed Foreign Affairs in opposition, but by appointing him to Finance, Cosgrave was able to reduce the social democratic influence in the party. With the benefit of hindsight, the appointment boosted FitzGerald's career in the long term, while ultimately destroying Richie Ryan's leadership ambitions (although Cosgrave could not have foreseen this nor would it have been his intention). FitzGerald's engagement on the international stage further improved his growing profile, and he was not directly associated with the tough decisions that Ryan was faced with at the Department of Finance after the oil crisis.

Cosgrave's other appointments included Mark Clinton to Agriculture and Fisheries, Paddy Donegan to Defence, Tom O'Donnell to the Gaeltacht, Paddy Cooney to Justice, Peter Barry to Transport and Power and Tom Fitzpatrick to Lands. The group represented both wings of the party. Of those who had been TDs at the time of the Just Society debate, Clinton had supported Costello's initiatives, while Donegan and O'Donnell had been opposed. Of the other Ministers, Cooney was initially considered a liberal TD, but this appearance was revised in the 1980s when he strongly opposed divorce and abortion. Peter Barry was conservative. Fitzpatrick has been described as a 'healer of divisions in a time of difficulty', and he had done much to keep harmony between the party's two wings.[92]

Brendan Corish, in addition to being Tánaiste, also took the Health and Social Welfare portfolio. The other Labour ministers included Justin Keating in Industry and Commerce, Michael O'Leary in Labour, James Tully in Local Government and Conor Cruise O'Brien in Posts and Telegraphs. In cabinet, FitzGerald was closer to his Labour colleagues – a relationship that would be repeated when he became Taoiseach in the 1980s, often to the frustration of his more conservative colleagues.

Taoiseach Liam Cosgrave and Tánaiste Brendan Corish had a good working relationship. Conor Cruise O'Brien later recalled, 'it was a coalition which on the whole worked remarkably smoothly because there grew up a relation of confidence between Cosgrave and Corish, personally'.[93] The coalition viewed itself and acted as a homogenous unit. As Cosgrave put it, 'the legislation on all matters was approved by the government'.[94] Similarly, when asked how much of the socially progressive legislation that emerged was due to Fine Gael and how much was due to Labour, Richie Ryan replied, 'it was due to the government'.[95] Furthermore, while much of that legislation came from departments overseen by Labour ministers, many of the policies were also in keeping with longer-term Fine Gael initiatives and the aims of the Just Society.

Fine Gael and Labour came to power at a time of crisis internationally, when governments struggled to cope with rising inflation and public indebtedness in the aftermath of the first oil crisis. But as many of the contributors to *The Shock of the Global* – a study of the 1970s – have shown,[96] amidst the political, social and economic turmoil, there was also progress and transformation. It was a period of social change: of demands for divorce and abortion, and second wave feminism campaigned for greater rights for women. Ireland was not isolated from many of the trends that marked the 1970s (although abortion did not make it on the political agenda until the 1980s). Fine Gael and Labour had presented themselves at the 1973 election as the socially progressive parties in the political system, outflanking Fianna Fáil. Rather like the advent of New Labour in Britain in 1997, Roy Foster recalled that at the time the Coalition felt like a 'new start'.[97] However, the economic optimism that greeted the parties on their election was short-lived, and the promise of the 'government of all the talents' soon melted away as the coalition found itself grappling with fiscal expansion and the effects of stagflation. Fine Gael and Labour had pledged to transform Ireland into a 'modern progressive society based on social justice'.[98] Despite the economic difficulties, some important progress was made in the realm of social policy. Legislation affecting the status of women, offering support to families of physically and mentally disabled children and providing for greater and better housing were all indicators of change. These policies often reflected demands for change from certain sections of society, although the debate that surrounded them also revealed a continuing conservatism, indicating that the period of transition experienced in the 1960s was not complete.

Figure 1 Free State government meeting, January 1923. Reproduced by kind permission of UCD Archives

Figure 2 James Dillon addressing Fine Gael Ard Fheis. Reproduced with kind permission of Fine Gael

Figure 3 Declan Costello. Reproduced with kind permission of St Michael's House

Figure 4 Declan Costello and Patrick Hillery. Reproduced with kind permission of St Michael's House

Figure 5 Liam Cosgrave addressing Fine Gael Ard Fheis, c. 1969. Reproduced with kind permission of Fine Gael

Figure 6 Fine Gael Ard Fheis under Garret FitzGerald's leadership. Reproduced with kind permission of Fine Gael

Figure 7 Garret FitzGerald opening new party headquarters on Upper Mount Street. Reproduced with kind permission of Fine Gael

Figure 8 First national conference of Young Fine Gael, November 1977. Reproduced with kind permission of Fine Gael

Figure 9 Garret FitzGerald on the campaign trail with Tom Raftery for 1984 European Elections. Reproduced with kind permission of Fine Gael

Figure 10 Leaflet from the 1987 general election. Reproduced with kind permission of both Alan Kinsella and Fine Gael

6
National Coalition, 1973–77

1973 was the first time that Fine Gael found itself in government since the party adopted Declan Costello's Just Society proposals as official policy in the 1960s. Costello himself had reversed his decision to retire and had successfully re-entered politics. It has already been argued that Fine Gael's slight shift to the left as a result of his policies had contributed to the formation of the coalition, while elements of the fourteen-point plan reflected his thinking. In his first interview after being elected Taoiseach, Liam Cosgrave spoke to Rodney Rice for RTÉ Radio and outlined his principle priorities for government. He emphasised social welfare reform, an increase in pensions, the removal of VAT from food and the transfer of a portion of the health charges from rates to the central fund.[1] The government's social reform agenda gave Fine Gael an opportunity to satisfy many of the aims of the Just Society. But by the middle of the party's term in power, the editors of *The Vulcan* – the newsletter of the Trinity branch of Fine Gael – claimed that the Just Society had been abandoned.[2] It would be incorrect to suggest that that document was a guiding consideration in policy formulation for the party by the 1970s, however. Although the language of social reform was prominent in the election campaign, the Just Society was only discussed in profiles of Costello whose return to politics had piqued the interest of journalists.[3] *Towards a Just Society* was very much a document of its time, reflective of the emerging thinking in the 1960s. Elements of it certainly appeared on the National Coalition's agenda. The housing policy pursued by the Minister for Local Government sought to rectify problems that Costello had been active in highlighting in the 1960s. The provisions for home help for disabled children were similar to those he had advocated in his 1965 document. And the youth policy framed by John Bruton had much in common with the youth section of *Towards a Just Society*. But other aspects of Costello's proposals had become dated by the time Fine Gael took office. Economic planning based on the French model, for example, was as irrelevant to the 1970s as protectionism had been to the sixties. As Jim Dorgan put it, 'We were the party of the Just Society ... but it was a long way behind us by then'.[4] Furthermore, as Declan Costello was Attorney General in the National Coalition, and not a minister, he did not contribute to policy formulation. His most important contributions at this time came in the area of law, rather than social, reform: the establishment of the Law Reform Commission and of the office of DPP.

Towards a modern progressive society

The fourteen-point programme had stated that 'the elimination of poverty and the ending of social injustice will be a major priority in the next government's programme'. If the traditional one hundred day marker is used as an indicator of performance, the National Coalition had a positive start. Having taken office in March 1973, Richie Ryan delivered his first budget as Minister for Finance to the Dáil two months later. In particular, the fourteen-point programme pledged to introduce special legislation to relieve the plight of the aged, deprived children, the widowed, orphaned and deserted, and the physically and mentally handicapped. Ryan's budget began the process of delivering on that promise. In so doing, he built on the process of developing income maintenance services initiated under the Fianna Fáil governments. From the mid-1960s, that party had introduced, for example, an occupational insurance scheme, free travel for old-age pensioners, invalidity pensions for the long-term ill and deserted wives' allowance.[5]

An extra £30 million in spending was available to Ryan as a result of EEC membership. Ireland no longer had to pay agricultural subsidies, which had become substantial, and those savings were redirected into social improvement, with social welfare being the main beneficiary. In order to honour the National Coalition's social commitments, Ryan also took the same approach as his Fianna Fáil predecessor, George Colley, and planned for a current budget deficit. In doing so the previous year, Colley had broken with the tradition of balancing the budget that dated to the foundation of the State. The strategy was broadly in line with advice from the OECD and the NESC.[6] Ryan's money bill was described by *The Irish Times* as 'the greatest social welfare budget of all time',[7] while Liam Cosgrave declared at his party's Ard Fheis three days later:

> These measures collectively represent the most revolutionary and progressive single step towards a society of justice and compassion that has ever been taken in the history of this State; and it represents only the first such step which it is the intention of this government, with the people's support, to take in pursuit of a better Ireland.[8]

Although *The Irish Times* was a sympathetic newspaper and Cosgrave could be expected to give such a grandiose speech at the first gathering of his party since entering government, the thrust of both their analysis was fair. The qualifying age for the old-age pension (including access to free travel, electricity and television licence) was lowered from seventy to sixty-nine years and was incrementally reduced during the life of the twentieth Dáil. By the time the coalition left office in 1977, the retirement age was sixty-seven. The means test for disabled persons, as well as for old age and widow's non-contributory pensions, was relaxed. The budget also made provision for a new home-care allowance for physically and mentally disabled children under sixteen resident at home. Previously there had been no direct help available – a situation of which Declan Costello had been particularly critical in *Towards a Just Society*. Later in 1973, the Department of Social Welfare introduced a free travel scheme covering bus and rail services throughout the country for all blind persons over the age of twenty-one years, facilitating approximately 7,000 blind people. Free travel for the blind had previously been restricted to Dublin Bus services only.[9]

The content of the budget was shaped to an extent by public demands. The IWLM listed those areas in which reform was required: equal pay, equality before the law, equal education opportunities, contraception, and justice for deserted wives, widows and unmarried mothers.[10] The new coalition's first budget was being closely watched by various women's groups, concerned about the extent to which the government would deliver on the promise in the fourteen-point programme to end all existing forms of discrimination against women. Declaring that Irish women had the 'status of donkeys', Mrs E. Roche of Haddington Road in Dublin, in an open letter to the various groups, implored them to continue applying pressure.[11] Ryan's budget, however, contained several offerings that satisfied many of the demands raised during the 1973 campaign.

By providing for unmarried mothers and deserted wives, it recognised a changing society and redefined the traditional family household. It also brought Ireland closer to European norms. A means-tested deserted wives allowance had been introduced by the Fianna Fáil government in 1970. Conditions were stringent and an extensive application form had to be completed.[12] If a deserted wife was divorced abroad by her husband, she became ineligible for the allowance. The AIM Group had lobbied politicians during the election on this matter, calling on women to contact their local TDs asking them how they felt about the 'plight of the deprived and deserted wife' and what they intended to do about it.[13] Ryan's budget reversed the policy of disqualification, while also giving an extra pound per week in the payment. His move was not welcomed by all, however. The Single Women's Association, for example, demanded to know why such women were being given special treatment when they were effectively single, and concluded that 'as far as the Just Society government is concerned, the single woman doesn't exist'.[14]

The Commission on the Status of Women, which had been instituted in 1969 in response to pressure from women's groups, had issued its final report at the end of 1972. Following on from one of their recommendations, Ryan announced in his budget speech a plan to provide for the first time in the history of the State for unmarried mothers, giving them benefits similar to that of deserted wives. This represented progress in the area of family policy by broadening the definition of what constituted a family. The problems confronting unmarried mothers had been raised in a frank article in *Woman's Way* – then Ireland's leading magazine for women – at the start of 1973. As the magazine bluntly put it, 'The single pregnant woman is a reality. Her baby is a person. Why should either of them suffer so because we choose not to accept a fact of life?'[15] Maura O'Dea, herself a single mother, had founded the Cherish organisation in 1972 along with six other women. One of their aims was 'to make the single mother and child accepted members of society'. In the organisation's first newsletter, Cherish issued an appeal to parents of pregnant daughters to 'come to your senses'. It was lamented that some parents would 'accept abortion or the daughter that hides away and then has her child adopted', but they would not accept their daughter and grandchild as 'having the right to exist as a family' with full support.[16] One of Cherish's main priorities was to campaign for revision of the law in regard to maintenance, and the organisation played an important role in lobbying for the unmarried mother's allowance introduced by Ryan.

The reaction to that provision highlighted the persistence of traditional values and the extent of the stigma that Cherish sought to combat. The government was hit with a barrage of letters accusing it of condoning promiscuous behaviour by financially rewarding unmarried mothers – a woman 'who has sinned', as one critic put it.[17] Aside from the perceived moral implications, the reality of the changing family unit was not broadly welcomed. This reflected not only the continuing conservatism of the time, but also, perhaps subconsciously, contemporary thinking around the importance of the traditional family set-up. Angela Macnamara was the best-known agony aunt in Ireland in the 1960s and 1970s. She stressed the importance of the traditional family model in her popular (and conservative) advice column, published in the *Sunday Press*. Paul Ryan has found that in her seventeen years replying to letter-writers, Macnamara never once advised separation from a spouse, even in cases of domestic abuse.[18] In one instance that Ryan cites, she referred to the potential confusion of sexual identity for young boys in the absence of the father. This was a view supported by contemporary research. Throughout the 1960s, there was a growing literature that argued that the father's presence was crucial for a boy's sexual development.[19] A 1973 article in the *Journal of Consulting and Clinical Psychology* commented on the complex psychological factors involved in homosexuality, noting that the relationship between parent and child 'affects the child's sex-role identification'.[20] The provisions for single mothers and deserted wives represented an important state guarantee of support for motherhood outside of the nuclear family.[21] But although this legislation was essentially progressive, bringing Ireland into line with European norms, it was partially built on conservative views: it had been framed in the context of the legalisation of abortion in Britain in 1967. That legislation forced Irish policymakers to recognise an alternative family structure: an unmarried mother was morally less problematic than a woman who was seen as abdicating motherhood through abortion. Aside from social stigma, for many women who ended their pregnancy, financial considerations had played a role. This was also the case for single women who placed their children for adoption. It was suggested that seventy per cent of unmarried mothers who put their children up for adoption did so because they had no real alternative.[22]

There were developments also in the area of children's allowance. The 1973 budget provided for an increase in the monthly allowance of £1.50 per child, while the cut-off age was raised from sixteen to eighteen years for those continuing in full-time education or serving an apprenticeship. According to its June 1973 newsletter, AIM was 'pleased on the whole' with these changes. However, ADAPT continued the campaign to have children's allowance paid to wives.[23] Commenting on the Commission on the Status of Women report, Richie Ryan had described 'the old patriarchal society' as 'an anachronism'.[24] Legislation on children's allowance introduced by the coalition recognised equality between husband and wife. Since its introduction in 1944, the payment had been made to fathers. The committee that had considered the initiative had rejected arguments in favour of female recipients, stating that such an arrangement would 'run counter to the generally accepted principles concerning ... the father's position as head of the family'.[25] When the issue was raised in the Dáil at the time, Seán Lemass, who had conceived the policy, similarly argued, 'we should regard the father as the head of the family and responsible for the proper utilisation of the family income'.[26] Fathers were given the option to designate their wives as the recipient, but at the time that the legislation was being amended, it was estimated that only 300,000 fathers had done so.[27] The concern was that the money received by fathers was not being spent appropriately. Five days before the Labour Party met for is annual conference in Cork in 1973, members of the AIM group held a meeting with Frank Cluskey, Parliamentary Secretary to the Minister for Social Welfare, to impress on him the necessity of amending the system. He subsequently announced at his party's conference that the system would be changed. The Social Welfare Bill that followed in 1974 thus built on the 1973 budget provisions and made mothers the beneficiaries of the allowance. In introducing the Maintenance Orders Act, 1974, the coalition satisfied another demand of the AIM group, which had been consulted on the committee stage of the bill. This legislation, which came into force on 1 April 1975, provided for the reciprocal enforcement of maintenance orders with the UK. Problems persisted, but it was an important step forward.

Economic downturn

Shortly after Richie Ryan delivered his successful first budget, the Arab–Israeli, or Yom Kippur, war of October 1973 caused an international economic crisis. The oil embargo by Arab exporters, which resulted in a shortage, led to the quadrupling of crude oil prices from $3 to $12 a barrel. This was a worrying development for a country like Ireland that relied on the Middle East for ninety per cent of its oil needs.[28] The price of petrol at Irish garages more than doubled between 1973 and 1979.[29] Under the heading 'stopping the price rises', the fourteen-point programme had outlined stabilising prices, halting redundancies and reducing unemployment as the immediate economic aims of the government. This was to be achieved through a programme of planned economic development. However, the downturn in the global economy restricted the National Coalition's capacity to achieve its aims and limited its policymaking options. By the end of August 1973, Michael O'Leary, the Minister for Labour, had written to Cosgrave that the fourteen-point plan was 'pretty well exhausted' and advocated a new, comprehensive statement of the government's policy objectives.[30] Far from the programme of planned economic development promised in the statement of intent, the government's strategy, as a result of the economic crisis, was one of reaction to international events and the resulting problems. The closest the government came to a plan was a Green Paper, *Economic and Social Development 1976–1980*, in September 1976, which Jack Lynch dismissed as 'nothing new, nothing specific and nothing useful'.[31] These were not just the inevitable criticisms of the opposition. The document seemed to be little more than an extended argument in favour of pay restraint rather than an outline for a new programme for economic development.[32] That the content was limited in scope was hardly surprising, given the context in which it was published. It was prepared in advance of a Tripartite Conference, to be convened in October 1976 and with the intention of discussing pay developments in 1977 against the setting of economic performance.[33]

The government was unable to stabilise prices or curb unemployment; these were closely linked. The anti-inflation measures introduced by the National Price Commission did not work, and, in some cases, exacerbated the difficulties facing businesses. The effects of stagflation could be seen in the employment figures. The NESC's report for 1974 observed that year's outlook to be 'one of very weak growth and increasing unemployment'. The average unemployment rate stood at 6.3 per cent of the labour force, compared with 5.9 per cent in 1973. Consumer prices were eighteen per cent higher than a year earlier. And it was noted that, were in not for membership of the EEC, agricultural incomes would have been substantially lower.[34] The Council's report the following year predicted that 1975 prices, on average, were likely to be more than twenty per cent higher than in 1974, unemployment would continue to grow, and farm incomes, even if they achieved a thirty per cent increase, would still be about twenty per cent lower than in 1973.[35] By 1976, an EEC report estimated inflation to be at 18.9 per cent, the highest in the community.[36] By the time that the coalition left office, unemployment was up from 71,435 in 1973 to 115,942, representing an increase from 7.9 per cent of the insured labour force to 12.5 per cent.[37]

Public sector borrowing requirements had soared, from 8.6 per cent of GNP in 1972/73 to 12.9 per cent by 1976/77.[38] Cosgrave acknowledged that the county was living beyond its means as spending outstripped incoming revenue. 'If we are to ride out the storm … nothing less is needed than a united national response', he warned towards the end of 1974.[39] The global recession deepened the following year. The government had expected that the major countries, in particular the United States and Germany, would act to offset the inflationary impact of the increase in oil prices that had occurred at the end of 1973. However, concerted action was not taken speedily enough to avert a world recession.[40] Though acknowledging the effects of the distress of the global economy on Ireland, the NESC also identified domestic pay agreements as one of the factors contributing to the country's economic difficulties: 'the 1974 and 1975 agreements were negotiated and ratified by employers and unions, despite their clearly adverse implications for output, employment and foreign trade'.[41] The 1974 agreement had resulted in a staggering 29.4 per cent increase, although that was reduced to 16.6 per cent in 1975.[42] On 10 December 1975, Liam Cosgrave made a televised appeal for a pay pause in which he expressed the view that the recent levels of pay increase 'would have been grossly excessive even under the most favourable economic conditions'.[43] The burden of public service pay was placed at £441 million in 1975, an increase of forty-two per cent since 1974.[44] It was intended that the pause would take effect once the settlements under the 1975 agreement expired. Naturally, the Unions did not respond well and pointed out that the pay pause would apply unevenly. Not all workers would receive the final instalment of the rise at the same time, meaning the pause would last longer for some.[45] The NESC's report on the economy in 1975 argued that the size of the increases in pay had contributed to a lack of competitiveness by Irish products on the world markets, leading to a fall in output and an increase in unemployment. This worsened Ireland's economic woes.[46]

The level of unrest among workers was reflected in the amount of, often prolonged, industrial action in the 1970s. In May 1974, Dublin bus drivers initiated what would be a nine-week work stoppage, and workers at Guinness brewery went on strike for the first time in 215 years. The following month, talks began aimed at averting strike action at Dublin, Shannon and Cork airports. A national bank strike ran between June and September 1976, while a dispute involving thirty carpenters and painters at RTÉ, supported by the station's employees, resulted in a two-week blackout. In total, 770,000 working days were lost to strike action that year.[47] Worker unrest was not confined to the National Coalition's time in power, however. Both 1978 and 1979 were years of widespread industrial action, amidst which PAYE workers across the country marched demanding tax reform. When the National Coalition left office in 1977, gross expenditure on social welfare had increased from 6.5 per cent of GNP in 1972/73 to 10.5 per cent, and most benefits rose by 125 per cent, greatly exceeding the increase in both wages and prices.[48] Allowing for population change, there was an increase in real terms of aggregate social welfare spending between 1973 and 1977.[49] Despite these improvements, the National Coalition did not achieve its aim of eliminating poverty and ending social injustice. One example of this is the government's failure to deliver free universal hospital care. On 30 August 1973, Brendan Corish, Minister for Health and Social Welfare, announced that from April 1974, every citizen, regardless of income, would be entitled to free hospital in- and out-patient services, maternity services and welfare services, as well as assistance towards the cost of drugs and medicines.[50] Corish's plan was thwarted, however, when the Medical Union and the Irish Medical Association refused to implement the scheme. Discussions with the medical groups had not opened immediately after Corish announced the plan; the delay was caused by talks relating to junior doctors' strikes. However, once dialogue began, a deadlock on the costing of the scheme emerged. The arguments put forward by the doctors opposing implementation were reminiscent of those made by the dispensary doctors in response to the proposals outlined in *Towards a Just Society*. There were also parallels with the Irish Medical Association's opposition to Noel Browne's Mother and Child scheme in the early 1950s. The Health Services (Limited Eligibility) Regulations, 1974, which would have brought the scheme into existence, was not moved in the Dáil on 26 March 1974, as expected. 'All not well with Corish health plan', 'Health plan postponed?' and 'No free health package',[51] read the front-page headlines of the daily newspapers the following morning. That afternoon, Corish addressed the Dáil. He described the scheme as representing a significant step towards the creation of a socially just Ireland and towards the government's commitment to introducing a system of social services. He was extremely critical of those who opposed the policy, lamenting that it was to his 'intense regret' that he had received neither the understanding nor the co-operation that could be expected by a Minister for Health implementing such a scheme. Fianna Fáil had been opposed from the outset, and Corish, criticising the party's spokesperson on health, Desmond O'Malley, argued it was fortunate that a 'distinguished member' of the O'Malley family had believed in equality of education. His harshest criticism, however, was reserved for the medical groups, which he depicted as being unreasonable in their demands for compensation. He outlined several attempts at compromise, all of which had been rejected. Consequently, he explained, he had decided to postpone the introduction to 'avoid any danger to human life and to avoid confrontation with the consultants on this occasion in the hope that they will reconsider their general attitude'.[52] The scheme was never revisited publicly, but rather it was quietly abandoned, its failure another reminder of the power of the medical groups as a lobby.

One area in which the National Coalition achieved definite success, despite the economic climate, was in housing. In the 1970s, Ireland invested a higher proportion of its national wealth in housing than Britain.[53] This benefited lower-income families in particular. The fourteen-point programme had stated that the new government would immediately declare a housing emergency. A priority for Labour, the policy also reflected a commitment from Fine Gael. Declan Costello had been very concerned about the housing situation in Dublin in the 1950s and 1960s, and it was one of the major factors that influenced his Just Society proposals. Fianna Fáil's establishment of the National Building Agency in 1963 had resulted in the construction of 111,000 new dwellings by 1970. However, population shifts over the next decade led to an increased demand for housing as immigration began to outstrip emigration for the first time since records began.[54] Interviewed just after receiving his seal of office, James Tully, the new Minister for Local Government, confirmed that housing would be the main priority for his Department.[55] He initiated a crash-housing programme two months later. The coalition pledged to increase house building to 25,000 units per year. Quarterly bulletins released by the Government Information Bureau show that the target was repeatedly met, if not surpassed. Over 100,000 new houses – an average of more than 25,000 a year – were constructed during the coalition's time in power. The Fianna Fáil government had introduced the Housing Act in 1966, which extended the long-established practice of tenant purchase in rural areas to urban local authority housing.[56] The coalition expanded the provisions of that legislation to assist those wishing to purchase. On 24 May 1973, the cabinet approved an amendment to house purchase loans. This raised the upper limit on loans for local authority housing to £4,500 and broadened access to those loans by increasing the income qualification to £2,000 per annum.[57]

By April 1977, as Richie Ryan prepared to frame what would be his last budget, large-scale projects were being ruled out. A letter to the Department of the Taoiseach from Finance outlined how personal taxation, borrowing requirements and the level of Gross National Product were 'already at excessively high levels'.[58] Additionally, according to a memo from the Department, provisions for new services or for an expansion of existing services that involved further expenditure would not be considered.[59] John Bruton's 'Youth and Sport' proposal was initially ruled out on these grounds. Richard Burke, the Minister for Education, had sanctioned Bruton, his parliamentary secretary, to start work on a youth policy document in August 1973. Three months earlier, Bruton had attended a European Sports Conference to gather information on care of deprived children, youth work and physiological service in schools, amongst other topics.[60] The area of youth policy had been receiving greater attention as a result of Ireland's expanding young population in the 1960s. As discussed in Chapter 3, the National Federation of Youth Clubs and the National Youth Council of Ireland (NYCI) were set up during that period. By 1969, for the first time, a parliamentary secretary with special responsibility for youth and sport was assigned to the Minister for Education. Bruton's work thus built on that of his predecessor, Michael O'Kennedy. When Fianna Fáil moved to the opposition benches in 1973, Pearse Wyse was appointed party spokesperson on youth and community development. Recognising the growth of the youth sector, Bruton sought to bring various groups into the consultation process. Towards the end of 1973, he invited submissions 'to assist in the review of the long-term objectives of youth work'.[61] One of those received, *The Development of Youth Services* authored by the NYCI, proved to be particularly influential. Much of the content of Bruton's final report reflected the proposals outlined within it. Though acknowledging the important role of volunteers, the need for full-time workers who would liaise with, support and train volunteers in the community was emphasised. It was also argued that participation in local community would create more responsible members of society. These recommendations were reminiscent of those suggested in Declan Costello's *Towards a Just Society*; he, too, had recognised the importance of supplementing the work of voluntary workers with that of trained professionals.

Not only had Bruton to convince Finance to fund his project at a time when spending was being cut but he was also faced with speculation about the necessity for a youth and sport initiative at government level. In the margin of a copy of a letter from Cosgrave to Bruton, Dermot Nally, secretary at the Department of the Taoiseach, had commented 'where did all this come from? If people want it, why are they not encouraged to go away and do it themselves?'[62] But reports had shown that community action, though helpful, had its limits. And Bruton, having invited submissions and therefore indicating that a youth policy was being considered, was under pressure from various youth groups to deliver a national framework.[63] Pearse Wyse introduced a private member's motion in 1975 deploring the 'failure of the government to produce a comprehensive policy on youth development'.[64] Fianna Fáil was cleverly positioning itself as a party representative of the young voter. A series of regional conferences had been held throughout 1974, culminating in the first annual national youth conference in January 1975. The second such conference coincided with Fianna Fáil's fiftieth anniversary, and Seamus Brennan, the party's twenty-eight-year-old general secretary, called on the young members to assert themselves as Fianna Fáil's 'social conscience'.[65] Charles Haughey, reflecting on the anniversary, linked the party's traditional values to youth policy and spoke to one branch meeting of the party's youth group about the importance of cherishing all the children of the nation.[66] Opposition afforded Fianna Fáil the luxury of espousing the necessity of a youth policy, free from the economic considerations that constrained the government.

Behind the scenes, John Bruton was fighting a battle with the Department of Finance, and his sense of frustration can be clearly felt through his correspondence with various departmental officials but, most particularly, with Liam Cosgrave. His document was submitted to cabinet by Burke on 9 April 1976 and, subject to some revisions, it was approved for publication at a time to be decided by the Taoiseach. Bruton sent the amended document to Cosgrave on 15 November, requesting that a date for release be considered. He received a brief reply the following day from the Taoiseach's office, stating that the matter was being examined and that Cosgrave would revert back. The follow-up letter of 24 November dealt a severe blow to the progress of the proposal. Cosgrave explained that the budgetary position had 'deteriorated greatly' since the decision of 9 April and, consequently, 'a very restrictive attitude to the provision of additional funds for new services' had been adopted. He therefore recommended postponing any announcement until after the Estimates for 1977 had been determined.[67] The view of the Department of Finance was that Bruton had underestimated the cost of the programme, and Richie Ryan deemed the proposals 'entirely inappropriate at the present time of financial difficulty'. He recommended against publication of the document in a communication to the Department of the Taoiseach in April 1977.[68] Cosgrave agreed with Ryan that the policy could not be published in its existing form. Conscious, though, that there were expectations on the government to deliver a youth policy, he proposed that Finance consider the policy with a scaled-back budget.[69]

In a last effort, Bruton attempted to appeal to his colleagues on more personal grounds, arguing that there were obvious electoral advantages to such a policy and that it should also be considered in light of its appeal to young voters.[70] In what was publicly presented as a cost-saving measure, the coalition had taken the decision in 1976 to defer the census, and in so doing denied themselves an opportunity to take a snapshot of the population. When it was eventually ordered in 1979 by the then Fianna Fáil government, it revealed that Ireland had become the youngest and fastest growing population in Western Europe.[71] The findings of the census aside, however, there were 440,000 first-time voters on the register for the 1977 election. Fianna Fáil made a conscious effort to target the youth vote, yet to be committed to any party. Bruton's policy document would have been useful to the coalition partners as an example of their commitment to that demographic, particularly since it so closely reflected the requirements outlined by the NYCI. The report was eventually published in June 1977, but it was lost among the election coverage (polling day was 16 June). Furthermore, Fianna Fáil had launched an election manifesto with a specific section on youth policy, which bore a striking resemblance to Bruton's proposals. After the election, the new Fianna Fáil government refused to commit itself to Bruton's document and commissioned its own report. *The Development of Youth Work Services in Ireland*, published in 1980, essentially reiterated the central message of the Bruton report.[72] This minor episode offers a glimpse into the conditions under which the National Coalition framed legislation.

The challenge of social reform

One of the government's more controversial measures to promote social justice was the Wealth Tax. In their fourteen-point programme, the coalition partners had pledged to relieve the 'heavy and unjust burden on ordinary house purchasers and farmers' by abolishing estate duties and replacing them with 'taxation confined to the really wealthy and to property passing on death outside the immediate family'. The Wealth Tax was part of a new set of capital taxes introduced by the government, which also included a capital gains tax and a capital acquisitions tax on gifts and inheritance, designed to replace Estate Duties. The Wealth Tax component was identified, quite rightly, by Dick Walsh, political correspondent of *The Irish Times*, as the second most divisive decision by the government, after the contraception legislation.[73] The response received from conservative elements in society once more reflected the difficulty in formulating and implementing legislation that was perceived to challenge traditional Ireland. John Kelly wrote to Cosgrave in May 1974 that there was 'terrifically strong feeling against' the measure within the party, with some deputies threatening to vote against it because of its potential effects on the local elections. Kelly surmised that such was the strength of opposition to the measure that 'it will have to be pruned so radically as to be unrecognisable'.[74] The original proposals outlined in the 1974 White Paper were considerably scaled back due to the pressure of interest groups, and the final terms of the Wealth Tax bore little resemblance to them. The public opposition, discussed presently, was mostly a reaction to the White Paper proposals, and such was the strength of feeling that it continued unabated after the revised terms were published. Those 1974 proposals included a modest threshold of estates over £40,000 and few exemptions. The actual thresholds introduced were far higher: £70,000 for a single person, £90,000 for a widowed person and £200,000 for married persons.[75] With the modifications and extensive list of exemptions, the number of people liable was considerably reduced, with the consequence that the Wealth Tax, in the opinion of a 1985 ESRI paper, 'must be regarded as a costly failure'.[76]

When the Just Society document was being assembled in the mid-1960s, Cosgrave's policy committee had resisted the inclusion of a wealth tax on the grounds that it would prove unpopular – a view vindicated by the response received in the 1970s. Farmers and business owners were particularly vocal. Richard Bourke, a Kildare-based farmer, claimed the tax would put him out of business in three or four years,[77] while Anne Cassin, who had a 250-acre farm in Dublin, stated that there was 'no way' she would be able to pay.[78] Traditional Fine Gael voters – whom Cosgrave would have had in mind in 1964/65 – were particularly uneasy. Ned McGuire, the former co-owner of the upmarket department store Brown Thomas, argued that the rates were 'savagely high' and complained that the new tax 'could not be better designed to make life impossible in Ireland'.[79] He had been the party's main fundraiser in the 1960s.[80] Dr G. P. Crookes, a long-term supporter of the party who wrote to the Taoiseach in 1974 to register his disappointment, was not alone in questioning his continued allegiance to Fine Gael.[81] Party branches, such as those in Bradford and Monasteravin, mindful of the farmer vote, also passed resolutions registering their opposition to the measure.[82] It was hardly surprising, therefore, that John Bruton communicated to Cosgrave the feeling that the tax had 'fundamentally shaken the confidence of our supporters'.[83] As he recalled, during the election campaign, Fine Gael had emphasised replacing estate duties, which was a popular promise with farmers particularly, but did not clarify what would be substituted in their place. As Fine Gael's core vote had traditionally consisted of the farming community, particularly the larger farmers, the Wealth Tax put a lot of rural TDs in a difficult position.[84] Despite this, the only sign of opposition from the party in the Dáil came from the Dublin Central TD Maurice Dockrell. Declaring, 'I do not like this Bill',[85] he abstained from voting on the second stage. A three-line whip, which carried the threat of expulsion from the parliamentary party, was subsequently imposed for the report and final stages and Dockrell voted with his party.

The Wealth Tax was intended to promote horizontal equity by means of progressive taxation. It would supplement income tax by also targeting other forms of assets rather than income alone. A note from the Department of Finance pointed out that 'one of the criticisms levied against the estate duty system is that over the years, as a result of inflation and the general increase in values, the tax now catches persons who were never intended to be affected by it, or presses more heavily than intended on some categories'.[86] The notion of targeting the 'really wealthy' through a wealth tax was repeatedly emphasised. Speaking to the Junior Chamber Ireland luncheon, Ryan explained that 'only a relatively small number – about 500 quite wealthy people – will be financially disadvantaged, including those who have been successfully avoiding tax by means of legal loopholes'.[87] However, Senator Alexis Fitzgerald appeared to identify the root of the concern for many at the time: those objecting were either directly affected or were 'hoping one day to be rather better off than they are now'.[88] For farmers, in particular, this was a genuine worry. Between 1970 and 1974, the price of land significantly outstripped consumer prices: the consumer price index rose by 42 per cent compared to the 256 per cent increase in the index of land prices. If these increases persisted, it was feared that those below the threshold would be brought over it.[89]

As the tax was in line with Labour's traditional policies, critics of the day identified it as a Labour-inspired measure. Letters received at the Department of the Taoiseach urged Cosgrave not to 'sell out to Labour', while also suggesting that Fine Gael was being a 'slave to Labour just to stay in power' and that the legislation had been 'introduced under pressure from the Labour Party'.[90] While certainly a victory for Labour, the Wealth Tax had actually been introduced at the instigation of the Fine Gael Minister for Foreign Affairs, Garret FitzGerald (although many have argued that he would have been more suited to the Labour Party). It had been one of his long-term aims, but his attempts to have it incorporated into *Towards a Just Society* in 1965 had been 'shot down'.[91]

In his autobiography, FitzGerald contends that the measure was undermined by the Department of Finance, which he described as having been 'vehemently opposed'. He maintained that ten days after the National Coalition took office, a memorandum from the Department recommended abandoning the election promise.[92] These recollections are certainly in keeping with FitzGerald's own interpretation at the time. In 1974, he had circulated a report to his cabinet colleagues regarding the progress of a cabinet sub-committee in relation to its work on capital taxation. In it, he made reference to the Department of Finance's argument against the implementation of the government's election commitment.[93] However, the Minister's opposition might not have been quite as strenuous as FitzGerald suggests. His report earned him a strong rebuke from Richie Ryan, who considered it 'discourteous and disingenuous' that the Minister for Foreign Affairs would draft a report on the workings of a committee that fell under the remit of another department. More significantly, he denied FitzGerald's claims, and suggested that a 'readiness to suspect and to accuse' be 'replaced by a willingness to discuss'.[94] That there was some opposition, especially from the Finance civil servants, cannot be denied. This was based predominantly on the concern that revenue raised from the new tax would fall short of the existing yields. A briefing note for the cabinet sub-committee in mid-1973 pointed out that in countries operating a wealth tax, the proportion that it represented of total revenue was very small',[95] while a memo from late-1973 claimed that 'an annual wealth tax at the rates contemplated will not be a sufficient substitute' for death duties.[96] An OECD report from 1979 found that in 1976, Switzerland was the only one of the European countries with a wealth tax that raised more than one per cent of total tax revenue. For the other countries, including Ireland, the yield was below 0.5 per cent.[97] Annual Wealth Taxes generally did not raise revenue. But despite concerns behind the scenes, Ryan publicly endorsed the tax, and it seems more likely that if the measure was undermined and FitzGerald's own party wavered in its support, it was due to external pressures and electoral considerations.

The Wealth Tax was a blow, not just to Fine Gael but also to the government. As a result of the controversy, the coalition received little credit for abolishing death duties. Such was the opposition to the measure by the middle classes that by the time Fine Gael returned to power under Garret FitzGerald in 1981, it inhibited his party from 'responding to continuous pressure from Labour to restore the system'.[98] In addition to costing Fine Gael votes, there was a further downside to the new tax. The concerns of the Department of Finance were justified when it generated less money than the old death duties that it had replaced. It was subsequently abandoned in April 1978 by the new Fianna Fáil government. An ESRI study found that it was only in 1980 that the revenue from Capital Gains Tax and Capital Acquisitions Tax plus the Wealth Tax – although it had been abolished two years earlier, it still generated some revenue – exceeded in nominal terms the revenue generated by death duties alone in 1973–74. The revenue raised from the capital taxes package in 1980, in terms of 1973 prices, was £6.4 million, less than half the yield of death duties in 1973. Furthermore, it has been estimated that had the death duties not been abolished, they would have yielded £21.6 million in 1973 prices in 1980.[99]

Agents for change

Much of the legislation thus far discussed reflected changes in society and demands from various lobby groups to which the government chose to respond. However, the coalition also found itself presented with policy issues on which it was forced to legislate. During this time, women, through the courts system, acted as important agents for change, as did Europe. The fourteen-point programme, which made an express promise to introduce legislation to 'end all forms of existing discriminations against women', was framed at a time when there were certain expectations of policy on women's rights. The UN had designated 1975 the Year of the Woman, while equal pay had been one of the preconditions of Ireland's membership of the EEC. Such European directives on equality were the product of public policy worked out by member states as a collective response to domestic pressure for change.[100] In Ireland, the Commission on the Status of Women, which had been instituted in 1969, had presented its interim report in August 1971 and issued its final report in December 1972. As already seen, various women's groups and organisations had been active during the 1973 election. The combination of such reports and activities ensured that women's issues were a dominant theme on the political agenda. At legislative level, women's rights were significantly improved by the National Coalition. However, the government introduced legislation on female jurors, equal pay and contraception only because of outside directives or legal challenges.

The coalition was responsible for reversing legislation from the 1920s that excluded female jurors. This was one of the aims outlined in the IWLM's *Chains or Change* report, while the report by the Commission on the Status of Women also recommended that women be permitted to serve on juries. Although a positive step towards ending 'all forms of discrimination against women', the government had introduced the new legislation only because of a Supreme Court ruling after IWLM members Mary Anderson and Máirín de Búrca challenged the Juries Act, 1927. In 1924, Kevin O'Higgins, the Cumann na nGaedheal Minister for Justice, gave women the choice of opting-out of jury service. He subsequently sought to exclude women completely in his 1927 legislation, which also dispensed with female shorthand writers in court. He defended his decision on administrative grounds, arguing that there would be a massive undertaking involved in contacting all women, asking them if they wanted to serve, and then providing alternative accommodation in the courts for them. He was insistent that most women were unwilling or reluctant to serve. He also wanted to shelter women from potentially unsettling cases, matters 'one would not like to discuss with the feminine members of one's own family'.[101] There was a certain irony, as the *Irish Statesman* pointed out, that O'Higgins was a member of a government that had come to power on the back of a revolution in which 'women were in the fighting line from start to finish'.[102] The legislation was denounced by the Women's Independent Association as a 'retrograde step'.[103] It followed only six years after women were given the right to sit on juries for the first time in Britain.[104] Although, under pressure from the opposition, an amendment was included that allowed women to apply to serve, as Maryann Valiulis notes, it was 'merely the illusion of choice'.[105]

The 1927 Juries Act stood unamended until the *de Búrca vs the Attorney General* Supreme Court case caused the coalition to introduce the Juries Act, 1976. Anderson and de Búrca had been arrested outside the Dáil in August 1971 after a march against the Prohibition and Forcible Entry Bill organised by the Committee to Oppose Repressive Legislation. They were charged with using threatening and abusive language and with obstructing the Gardaí.[106] While awaiting trial, Anderson and de Búrca started proceedings in the High Court against the State. They argued that they could not receive a fair trial as their case would not be heard in front of a panel of their peers, due to the absence of female jurors. They also claimed that section three of the Juries Act, 1927, created a further imbalance as the jury would be composed only of men of a certain financial status. *De Búrca and Anderson vs the Attorney General* failed in June 1973 after Mr Justice Pringle J concluded that the constitution did not provide for wide representation on juries and that, historically, they had always been restricted to limited groups of persons.[107] However, the Supreme Court appeal, heard in November and December 1975, proved successful. It found both sections three and five to be unconstitutional. Thus, not only was the status of women upgraded, but service was also extended to men whose financial position vis-à-vis their land holdings had previously rendered them ineligible.

The position of women was further improved at this time in the area of equal pay. Commenting on the section in the report by the Commission on the Status of Women that enumerated the advantages to the State of equal pay, Richie Ryan remarked that 'the ending of any injustice is in itself a sufficient justification for doing what is right. When a Minister for Finance sees that the ending of injustice can give better value for money he has an added interest'.[108] Ultimately, though, in the short-term at least, Ryan would disagree about the financial benefit of implementing equal pay, despite his government's pledge to ending all forms of discrimination against women.

Various women's groups had been active in lobbying, though ultimately Europe was the agent for change. In preparing Ireland's application for EEC membership, policymakers would have been aware of the commitment to equal pay required under Article 119 of the Treaty of Rome. Britain had introduced equal pay for equal work in May 1970, but the legislation was not entirely effective as there was often difficulty in proving similarity of tasks.[109] The Equal Pay Act (Northern Ireland) was introduced the same year, although it had a limited impact.[110] As both pieces of legislation were imperfect, they were subject to later revisions. Following a meeting in Brussels in April 1973 to discuss the commitments of the new member states, the Irish government issued a statement confirming its commitment to Article 119, noting that significant steps had already been taken through the terms of the 1972 National Wage Agreement and the appointment of an Equal Pay Commissioner.[111] Similarly, later that month, the Minister for Labour, Michael O'Leary, sought to reassure a deputation from the executive council of the Irish Congress of Trade Unions (ICTU) following a meeting at which they urged the necessity for an early introduction of equal pay. O'Leary informed them that he hoped to have the legislation before the Dáil shortly.[112] In a case of bad timing, a letter appeared in the *Evening Press* at the end of April drawing attention to an advertisement for a vacancy at the Government Information Bureau, which offered different rates of pay depending on the successful candidate's gender.[113]

On 3 July 1973, Michael O'Leary introduced the Employment (Equal Pay) Bill, 1973 in the Dáil. Behind the scenes, as files within the National Archives clearly indicate, the government was less keen to uphold the commitment to equal pay than its public pronouncements suggested. Though the government was anxious to protect the less well-off from the unexpected downturn in the economy, the financial burden of implementing equal pay in the public sector was considered too great. Almost as soon as the preparatory documents crossed his desk, Richie Ryan had expressed concern about the cost implications.[114] In Britain, Roy Jenkins, Chancellor of the Exchequer, had also raised concerns about the cost of implementing equal pay during the cabinet's discussion of Barbara Castle's bill in early 1970.[115] Ryan reiterated his concerns in a circular to his cabinet colleagues in November 1973 in which he advocated delaying implementation until 1977.[116]

In May 1974, the Federated Union of Employers (FUE) had advocated delayed implementation of equal pay, arguing that it would safeguard jobs. Coverage of the FUE's opposition in the newspapers was accompanied by such headlines as 'Job position serious, says FUE' and 'Many firms unable to pay increases – FUE'.[117] The FUE linked government pay policy to the subject of equal pay, pointing out in one statement that before equal pay was even applied, some companies still had to contend with the wage increases due under the terms of the national agreement.[118] Patrick Hillery, however, rejected claims that implementation would lead to a loss of jobs. The former Fianna Fáil Minister had become the European Commissioner for Social Affairs after Ireland joined the EEC in 1973, and he played a prominent role in promoting equal pay at European level. Speaking at a press conference in Dublin, he questioned why women should be 'asked to accept the added sacrifice of waiting for equal pay in a period of recession'.[119]

A compromise was proposed by the government in the form of an amendment that would enable companies, which could certify by 1 January 1976 that the immediate introduction of equal pay would cause unemployment, to defer the measure. Women's groups and the Trade Unions responded with outrage. The Council for the Status of Women prepared to lodge a formal complaint to the President of the European Commission,[120] while Monica Barnes, who would later be elected as a Fine Gael TD, argued that 'every voter – man or woman – must now see why it is essential that more women are elected as TDs and Senators in the next general election'.[121] Gene FitzGerald, Fianna Fáil's spokesperson on labour, led the opposition's criticism of the amendment. He recommended to the parliamentary party that it should oppose any efforts to delay implementation.[122] The Labour Party was clearly struggling with the legislation. Members of the parliamentary party were under pressure from ICTU, which asked that Labour ministers demand at cabinet that the legislation be implemented with effect from 1 January 1976 without amendment.[123] The constituency council of the Dun Laoghaire branch of the Labour Party wrote to the *Irish Independent* on 6 January 1976 to record its 'total dissatisfaction' with the government's recent decisions; the signatories included Barry Desmond, the constituency's TD.[124] Later that month, Denise Rogers wrote to the paper on behalf of the Dublin South East constituency of the Labour Party calling on the parliamentary party to 'institute legislation guaranteeing full employment by the application of the Labour Party's socialist policies'.[125]

The government announced on 21 January 1976 that sex discrimination would be abolished, but this would not be extended to the gap between married and unmarried workers in the public service. Gene FitzGerald described it as a 'complete back-down', but still considered it far removed from the spirit of the 1974 legislation. Denis Coughlan's report from the Dáil noted how both Cosgrave and Paddy Cooney, Minister for Defence, had taken time to speak with Independent deputy Joseph Sheridan on their way into the chamber. It was speculated that he might be called upon if the Labour deputies revolted, which did not happen. That morning, though, Barry Desmond, Eileen Desmond, John O'Connell and David Thornley had met to discuss the government's announcement.[126] Barry Desmond's memoir, *Finally and in Conclusion*, is almost silent on the subject, noting only that legislation for equal pay was enacted.[127]

Pressure on the government increased. The European Trade Union Confederation had announced its support of ICTU.[128] Richie Ryan managed to convince the Fine Gael trade union conference not to force through an emergency motion calling on the government to implement equal pay: 'we cannot go begging and borrowing from the world to increase our own incomes'. But not all delegates were convinced by his speech, and Helen Burke, who had been due to propose the motion, told her colleagues: 'you have been fooled'.[129] A statement from the Institute of Professional Civil Servants described the government's actions as 'shabby and mean'. An equal pay petition, organised by trade unionists and women activists, was delivered to government buildings; it contained more than 35,000 signatures, including those of members of the opposition front bench.[130] Eleven thousand civil servants threatened strike action for 1 May 1976, which was later averted following a decision at a special conference of Civil and Public Service Staff Associations.[131]

As pressure mounted, the advice of Declan Costello was sought. The Attorney General advised the government that any measures to delay the introduction of equal pay would have no legal standing without a derogation from Brussels.[132] It was decided that he should travel to Brussels to make the request. On the day that he was there, the amendment legislation was circulated. O'Leary stressed that it would only be extended to those companies that could clearly link payment to a loss of jobs. Gene FitzGerald was scathing in the Dáil, describing the whole episode as a 'shabby, topsy-turvy, yo-yo area since last October'.[133] Before the official announcement was made, indicators suggested that the request would be rejected. The European Commission had only recently tightened its stance on equal pay. Although it had accepted the principle, it had shied away from enforcing the measure in practice. Patrick Hillery, in his capacity as European Commissioner for Social Affairs, sought to rectify this. He submitted a draft directive on equal pay in December 1973, and it was formally issued on 10 February 1975.[134] The European Commission rejected Ireland's request on 14 April 1976 and the Anti-Discrimination (Pay) Act, which had been passed in 1974, thus came into effect. Certain members of the cabinet were unable to disguise their displeasure, and Hillery bore the brunt. Michael O'Leary claimed that the Social Affairs Commissioner had 'belonged to a party that was no trailblazer for the rights of women'.[135] Richie Ryan was more severe in his criticism and called into question the independence of Hillery by accusing the Commissioner and the Fianna Fáil members of parliament of 'irresponsible antics ... and of abusing their position to damage Ireland's reputation'.[136] This earned him a strong rebuke. In an unusual move, the European Commission issued an official statement. It described the Commission as a collegiate body and said that, 'in accordance with the treaties and with the factual situation, its members exercise their duties in complete independence and in the general interests of the community'.[137] The irony, of course, was that the criticisms were based on dissatisfaction that Hillery had not supported his home country. To have done so, would have compromised the integrity and independence that Ryan and, to a lesser extent, O'Leary called into question.

An editorial in the *Irish Independent* lamented the timing, and essentially encapsulated the dilemma that the government had faced:

> The EEC decision on equal pay might be more acceptable generally in this country if we were experiencing normal economic conditions. We are not. Our unemployment figures are at an all-time high and the employment prospects for thousands of people coming out of school this year are bleak. Our commerce and industry is trying, with difficulty, to maintain a rate of business in the face of all kinds of trouble.[138]

But although the episode can be depicted as a battle between the realities of the economic climate versus a moral obligation, the deciding factor had been the Treaty of Rome, the European Community's foundation document. Before the official announcement was made, Garret FitzGerald conceded this fact: 'we cannot legislate in a matter subject to community law other than in accordance with community law'.[139] The government's handling of the situation – particularly by seeking the partial derogation – had damaged its credibility and compromised its record on women's rights. That record was further undermined by the debate on contraception.

During the 1973 election campaign, Labour's Ruairí Quinn had argued that 'an end to all forms of social and economic discrimination against women' would have to be coupled with 'change in the contraception, divorce and adoption laws'.[140] Although divorce law was not publicly addressed until the 1980s, the National Coalition did attempt to frame legislation that would legalise the sale of contraceptives to married couples. However, the decision to introduce the measure did not originate in cabinet, but rather it was a response to a legal action taken by an ordinary citizen. Though Quinn had spoken as a Labour candidate, his party was not fully united on the legalisation of the sale of contraceptives. The issue had proved bitterly divisive at the 1971 party conference, to the point that, as Ivana Bacik noted, 'delegates were literally spitting at each other'. When Noel Browne (by then a member) and John O'Connell introduced legislation in 1972, it was published as a private members' bill and three Labour TDs voted against it.[141] Indeed, some Labour members had wanted Browne expelled for initiating the debate within the party.[142]

On taking office, Liam Cosgrave informed one Dublin priest that the government had given the issue 'no consideration'.[143] The previous Lynch administration had also been reluctant to deal with the subject, and efforts by the Irish Family Planning Rights Association, set up in October 1970, to lobby for legalisation had been ignored.[144] The response to the coalition's Bill showed the difficulty facing an Irish government legislating on matters of moral concern. Public attitudes revealed anxieties over the family, sexuality and, arguably, shifting gender roles. We have already seen how financial support from the state for unmarried mothers and deserted wives recognised the changing family unit and the reality of a female head of household. The objections on moral grounds to those initiatives further expressed themselves in the debate surrounding the legalisation of the sale of contraceptives. The definition of Irish motherhood, as Tom Inglis has noted, was constructed in accordance with Catholic practices, which emphasised the responsibility of child-bearing.[145] By the middle of the twentieth century, Irish families tended to be twice as large as their European counterparts, a pattern that persisted until the mid-1960s.[146] In 1962, there were over 2,000 births to mothers with ten children or more.[147] Extracts published in *The Field Day Anthology of Irish Writing* from Dorine Rohan's 1969 book *Marriage Irish Style*, for which she had conducted individual interviews with both men and women, revealed the perfunctory nature of marital sex for many couples: a duty to be observed rather than enjoyed.[148] The expectation, rather than choice, of motherhood had also been expressed in Clarissa A Wood's 1949 *Woman Kneeling*. The focus of that essay was a woman – mother to a full age-range of children, from the youngest 'not creeping yet' to the eldest 'in and out of two jobs already' – praying that she was not pregnant again. 'Her children brought her no joy, nor could she see that they ever would'.[149]

Ireland was the only European economy to register a population decrease between the 1920s and 1960s.[150] Not until the 1970s was there an increase in birth rates.[151] The decline in population had placed a spotlight on the welfare of the child, which, in turn, placed an emphasis on the unborn, and artificial contraception came under scrutiny. A leaflet issued by Mna na hÉireann in 1976 claimed that Ireland was 'grossly under-populated', and, pointing to a proliferation of (unspecified) natural resources, made the ludicrous claim that the country could support a population of forty million.[152] The alleged characteristics of the only child were also cited as a counter argument to the availability of contraceptives. These children, according to one letter sent to the Taoiseach's office, were 'bored, pampered, unhappy, selfish and jealous'.[153] In particular, there was an anxiety that single people would have access to contraception, which would lead to promiscuity and possibly abortion, although abortion as an issue in itself did not make a significant impact until the 1980s.

If policymakers, politicians and certain sections of society were reluctant to confront the reality of a changing Ireland, it was not always possible to escape it. Television played an important role in this regard. As John Bowman explains, the medium introduced viewers to opinions contrary to their own, and they could find themselves obliged to confront controversial topics through such popular programmes as *The Riordans*.[154] A drama-serial set in rural Ireland, and it was broadcast by RTÉ between 1965 and 1978 and broached a number of topical issues, including sexuality and the use of contraceptives. One particular episode in which a priest advised the use of artificial contraception to a mother fearful of further pregnancy caused a public outcry.[155] Generally, though, actor Frank Kelly, who has had a long career in satire and comedy, found that there was a freedom to expand on humorous topics on radio and television as the 1970s progressed: 'it was easier to do things without giving offence ... People became more liberal'.[156] One particular sketch on *Hall's Pictorial Weekly* – RTÉ's satirical television programme on which he was one of the lead actors – showed Kelly and a number of other 'businessmen' gathered in a pub in the fictitious village of Ballymagash. One of the men was reading an advertisement from the *Irish Press* targeted at manufacturing entrepreneurs. In January 1978, the Industrial Development Authority (IDA) launched a new enterprise development programme, designed to make it easier for first-time entrepreneurs to raise working capital.[157] The 'businessmen' in the sketch were suspicious of the word 'entrepreneur'. 'There's a catch in it somewhere. What are they putting all them foreign words into it for?', Kelly's character pondered. The conversation soon moved on to 'them yokes' and 'women's lib', and it was suggested that the IDA was reluctant to say what they wanted people to manufacture, and that 'entrepreneur' was perhaps code for contraceptives (although the actual term was purposely never used). 'We couldn't have that. It'd be again our conscience', another member of the group concluded.[158] The sketch was revealing, and it reflected the contradiction in Ireland at the time. Irish society was becoming more open: the very fact that such a sketch could be broadcast was evidence of that. But it also pinpointed a continuing unease. Kelly's character joked about having no qualms in smuggling or submitting planning applications in Irish to confuse the locals but considered contraception morally wrong. Irish attitudes towards change reveal a certain awkwardness. As Paul Ryan put it, 'the transition provoked anxiety for conservative Catholics who struggled to see their bodies less as conduits of sin and more as instruments of pleasure'.[159]

The reality, though, was that despite the fact that the importation, display or sale of contraceptives was illegal under the Criminal Law Amendment Act, 1935, an increasing number of women were practising birth control each year. A total of 10,158 visits were made to the two family planning clinics in Dublin in 1972; the figure excludes those who privately consulted their GPs. The majority of these women requested prescriptions for the pill,[160] which could be prescribed as a cycle regulator for those women experiencing irregular periods. *Woman's Way* put the 'contraception controversy' on its front cover in June 1973. Irish feminists had attempted to force the issue on Saturday 22 May 1971. Forty-seven women travelled by train to Belfast with the intention of buying condoms and spermicides to bring back across the border. The aim, on returning to Dublin's Connolly Station, was to challenge customs officers to arrest them for flouting the law. However, no arrests were made. As Mary Kenny recalled, the customs men were 'mortified' but they 'quickly conceded they could not arrest all of us, and let us through'. They waved the banned items as they went.[161] The stunt naturally made the front page of the *Sunday Independent*, which declared that the IWLM had 'claimed its greatest victory'.[162] Though the event certainly publicised the contraceptives controversy, it also damaged the IWLM. There was a feeling among certain elements of the membership – in particular with Nuala Fennell, one of the more conservative members – that the movement should not become too associated in the public mind with ardent demonstrations on a few controversial issues. The group fragmented shortly afterwards.[163]

Front-page coverage in newspapers and women's magazines, satire or direct reference to contraceptives on television, stunts such as the 'condom train' and even the reality of the use of contraception by Irish couples were not enough, however, to convince a government to act. The National Coalition engaged with the reality of having to legislate for the sale of contraceptives only because of the Supreme Court ruling on the McGee case in December 1973. Twenty-nine-year-old Mary McGee had taken a challenge to the High Court after customs officers seized contraceptive jelly sent to her through the post from England. McGee, who already had four children, suffered from toxaemia, a condition that can affect the placenta and put the expectant mother at risk of stroke or even death. It had already caused serious complications during her previous pregnancies and her doctor advised that a further pregnancy placed her at serious risk of suffering a cerebral thrombosis (stroke). Her High Court case failed, prompting the challenge to the Supreme Court where the majority of judges ruled in her favour. Not only did this force the government to reconsider the matter, but the debate which followed also highlighted the differences between the liberals and conservatives in the coalition, which did not divide neatly on party lines. It also revealed similar tensions within society, which would become more pronounced with the abortion and divorce referenda of the 1980s.

The legislation prepared by the Minister for Justice was not progressive. It was not a question of making contraceptives available, but rather of limiting their sale. It thus reflected the continued reluctance by political parties to formulate progressive policy in the area of morality; the outgoing Fianna Fáil government had also been unwilling to legislate on the matter. The proposed legislation attracted the attention of the *New York Times*, which suggested that it would fail if Fianna Fáil opposed it because so many on the government benches were also critical.[164] Patrick Cooney's Importation, Sale and Manufacture of Contraceptive Bill, 1974, was never placed on the statute books due to a free vote on the government side during the second stage. It was the only occasion during the life of the twentieth Dáil that the government whip was not applied, and the result was a disaster for the coalition. Liam Cosgrave entered the *Níl* (no) lobby and voted with the opposition, helping to defeat the bill by seventy-five votes to sixty-one. He was joined by his party colleagues: the Minister for Education Richard Burke, Tom Enright, Martin Finn, Oliver Flanagan, Desmond Governey and Joseph McLoughlin. Labour's Dan Spring did not travel to Dublin for the vote. He was attending a civil court case in Cork that day, but, as Stephen Collins suggests, many of his colleagues interpreted his absence as a political statement. The rural TD was out of sympathy with the more socially liberal members of the party.[165] Cosgrave had presided at the cabinet meeting on 19 March when Cooney was authorised to move for leave to introduce the Bill in the Dáil and circulate the text to deputies.[166] He never discussed his intention to vote against the government, explaining that he acted on his own 'without trying to influence how others would vote'.[167] Naturally, this caused much anger. As John Bruton, normally a supporter of Cosgrave, put it, 'it was quite shocking ... It just wasn't good leadership'.[168] Barry Desmond maintained in his memoir that 'the government was never to recover its internal trust' after Cosgrave's vote, the impact of which on the coalition's unity was 'corrosive'.[169] Conor Cruise O'Brien was far less critical of the Fine Gael leader. Referring to Cosgrave's unwillingness to state his intention before the division was taken, Cruise O'Brien concluded, 'in these circumstances I cannot see how anyone has the right to claim to have been let down by what he did'.[170] Nonetheless, it was a blow to the government, and, though the issue of contraception was not specifically dealt with in the fourteen-point programme, the whole debacle called into question the coalition's commitment to creating a 'modern progressive society'. It was also an embarrassing occasion for Fine Gael. Jim Dorgan recalled that the issue was raised on doorsteps at the 1977 election, with voters querying how committed Fine Gael was to its policies, if the leader stood for something else.[171] The coalition was fortunate that it lacked a strong opposition. Frank Dunlop, who joined Fianna Fáil as head of research that year, recalled encountering a party 'suffering from what would now be seen as post-traumatic stress', adding that it was in a 'time warp'.[172] Jack Lynch's front bench had been depleted through the departure of Patrick Hillery to Europe as EEC Commissioner at the start of 1973; Brian Lenihan had lost his seat at the 1973 election; and Erskine Childers had moved to Áras an Uachtaráin to take up the presidency in June 1973. Commentators were in agreement that it was this lack of an alternative that held the coalition together.[173]

Cosgrave's actions were hardly surprising, nor were his views incompatible with his earlier support for creating a 'Just Society': Declan Costello's document had not dealt with moral issues. Indeed, Costello, as attorney general, took a cautious and conservative stance on the issue of contraceptives, often frustrating Cooney.[174] Additionally, through his willingness to support the Offences Against the State (Amendment) Bill in 1972, despite the views of his colleagues, Cosgrave had demonstrated that his own strongly-held values transcended party loyalty. Like his father, he too was a devout Catholic. Furthermore, as Henry Kelly once put it, 'His Pope was Pius not John'.[175] In an interview published at the start of 1974, Cosgrave had expressed the view that Irish people were 'opposed to any form of what one calls "permissive society"'.[176] The flood of letters that reached the Department of the Taoiseach in the months after appeared to confirm this. The correspondence was interspersed with communications from such groups as Irish Women United,[177] a group of 'women's liberationists' who came together in April 1975 and subsequently formally founded the organisation at a conference on 8 June. They proposed, as an amendment to Cooney's failed bill, free legal contraception in the belief that the 'women in Ireland should have the full right to control their fertility'.[178] However, the majority of those letters retained supported Cosgrave's decision, which many interpreted as a stand against the moral corruption of Irish society. Similar letters continued to reach his Department in the years that followed in response to a further attempt by Senator Mary Robinson's to introduce a private members' bill. One voter claimed that it would become the 'means of weakening the social, moral and physical structure of our society and would inevitably cause a serious upheaval in the whole fabric of society';[179] his was not a singular view. The divisiveness of the subject was such that it dealt Mary Robinson's general election bid a serious blow in 1977 when leaflets were distributed claiming that she made a penny on every pill sold due to her marriage to Robinson of Hayes, Conyngham and Robinson chemists. The 'Robinson' was not her husband, but, as she explained, 'a claim like that two days before an election is impossible to counter and I was therefore tarred with that brush'.[180] Conor Cruise O'Brien's speech to the Annual Conference of the Irish Humanist Association in March 1976 in which he criticised the defeat of the 1974 bill, as well as promoting a more liberal agenda, was also seen as a cause for concern. He had expressed the view that:

> [A]n electorate almost all of whose members have been brought up to believe that divorce and contraception are in all circumstances morally wrong, will have difficulty in seeing why these should not be legally prohibited, particularly if they are informed by their spiritual leaders that it is the duty of legislators to see to these.[181]

The government collectively distanced itself from his pronouncements. In response to a parliamentary question from Joe Dowling, Fianna Fáil TD for Dublin South-West, the Minister for Justice explained that the speech represented the personal view of Cruise O'Brien.[182]

Although, as discussed earlier, the National Coalition encountered opposition to the Wealth Tax, it was arguably more difficult for the government to tackle areas of moral concern. For social conservatives, fears about the availability of contraceptives were part of a broader anxiety. In Britain, access to the pill gave women control over their fertility, breaking the link between pleasure and procreation.[183] The availability of contraception was identified in British conservative circles as threatening to uproot sexuality from its grounding in marriage, and fears of promiscuity and a perceived increase in abortion had fuelled opposition to birth control.[184] There were similar concerns in Ireland. When Mary Robinson drafted her first Bill in 1971 to amend the 1935 Act, Desmond O'Malley, then Minister for Justice in a Fianna Fáil government, had argued that those who advocated change did not 'appreciate the practical difficulties in the way of permitting married couples access to contraceptives without at the same time making them readily available to single persons and even young adolescents'. His fear that there would be no way to prevent the single woman from accessing contraception was the main stumbling block to the drafting of legislation.[185] Similar concerns were expressed regarding the National Coalition's Bill. Furthermore, looking to international developments – the Abortion Act 1967 in England and the judgement in Roe versus Wade in America in 1973 – there was a concern that the liberal agenda would lead to the legalisation of abortion in Ireland. A leaflet produced by Catholic Family Life made a clear link between the two: 'Abortion cannot be divorced from contraception'.[186] Letters expressing similar sentiments were sent to the government from the League of Decency and the Council of Social Concern.[187] And when the Well Woman Centre opened on Dublin's Lower Leeson Street in January 1978, it was picketed by members of Mna na hÉireann and Parent Concern who carried posters that read 'Parents! Contraception means promiscuity and abortion!'[188] When the new Fianna Fáil government was preparing to frame its legislation, a request was transmitted from the Department of Foreign Affairs to the Irish Ambassadors to London, Luxembourg, Paris, Rome, Bonn, Brussels and Copenhagen asking for information on the legal position of these EEC member states on contraception. The letter included a question about the number of abortions carried out over the previous five-year period.[189] Although it was not until the 1980s that the bitterly divisive abortion debate, examined in Chapter 8, emerged, it quietly helped shape the response to the demand for change in the 1970s.

There was a glimpse at this time of the pluralist views of Garret FitzGerald and the need to reform the ethos of the Irish state to accommodate Northern Protestants that he would articulate more fully as government leader in the 1980s. In a 1973 memorandum to Agostino Casaroli, Secretary of the Council for the Public Affairs of the Church at Vatican City, he had identified certain legislation in the Republic as a barrier to better relations between the two parts of the island. Noting that the effect of the ban on the sale of contraceptives on Protestant opinion in Northern Ireland 'can be readily imagined', he had argued that there was a strong case for amending the law, either by a government initiative or by private members' bill, 'which the government would find it very difficult to resist, especially given the present situation in Northern Ireland'.[190] FitzGerald clearly overestimated the extent to which his pluralist outlook was shared by his colleagues, particularly Cosgrave. Such was the strength of the Taoiseach's conviction that he felt that changes could not be pursued 'even for the sake of Northern relations' – a view that reflected some of the correspondence which arrived at his Department. One woman, for example, wrote that the 'six counties' were 'less important than preserving our society from being debauched to pander to a minority'.[191] As the government's time in office was coming to a close, the Taoiseach was asked in an interview for the French newspaper *Le Monde* if he envisaged any contraception policy. 'No', was the simple reply.[192] The Fianna Fáil government eventually enacted legislation in 1979. The party pledged in its 1977 election manifesto to 'ensure the widest possible acceptance of positive policy for family planning and enact the necessary legislation'.[193] Given the response to the National Coalition's efforts, any proposal that would have 'the widest possible acceptance' would have to be limited in scope. Indeed, Fianna Fáil's legislation introduced by Charles Haughey was not designed to be a liberal measure. Rather, it was 'conceived in conservative and restrictive terms',[194] and contraception was to be made available only to married couples with a doctor's prescription.

Northern Ireland

The shadow of the North loomed over the National Coalition during its time in power, as it had done with the outgoing Fianna Fáil government. Declan Costello, delivering the oration at the annual Michael Collins commemoration at Béal na mBláth in 1973, observed, 'we are living in times of great national distress, where small groups of men, blinded by twisted ideologies, are committing hideous crimes against their fellowmen'.[195] The coalition partners had opened their statement of intent with a promise to protect the liberty and safety of the individual citizen and to uphold the democratic institutions of the state. The two parties also pledged themselves in that document to a policy that would endeavour to promote a peaceful solution to the Northern problem and to bring an end to bloodshed, injustice and sectarian division. It seemed initially that Liam Cosgrave secured a breakthrough on North-South relations.

The much-discussed British White Paper, *Northern Ireland Constitutional Proposals*, was finally published in March 1973. It made clear that any future settlement would have to be based on some form of a nationalist-unionist power-sharing executive, and that there would be an Irish dimension for consultation and co-operation. This, and subsequent Agreements, was interpreted by Unionists as a measure that would eventually facilitate the creation of a united Ireland. The emergence of Brian Faulkner provided a figure willing to compromise with reformist nationalism, albeit in an effort to preserve the Union. A reluctant convert to accommodation, he faced opposition from sections of the Ulster Unionist Party.[196] Prominent among the opponents was William Craig who had read the civil rights campaign as an IRA-plot to destroy Northern Ireland's place in the UK.[197] Evidence that Faulknerite Unionism was slipping was apparent when a resolution opposing power-sharing was almost passed by the Ulster Unionist Council in November 1973,[198] just one month before the Sunningdale conference was convened.

Representatives of the British and Irish governments met with future members of the power-sharing arrangement, elected at the Assembly elections in June 1973, at Sunningdale Civil Service College, Berkshire, in December 1973. There it was agreed that the 'Irish dimension' envisaged in the White Paper was to take the form of a two-tier Council of Ireland, drawn from both sides of the border. In exchange, the government of the Republic acknowledged that there could be no change to the status of Northern Ireland until a majority of the people of Northern Ireland desired such a change. The Council of Ireland was the major flaw of the Sunningdale Agreement. The parameters were not clearly defined, permitting the different groups to attach their own meaning and understanding of its functions to it. Bew *et al.* (2002) note that when the SDLP depicted it as a mechanism for easing the transition to a united Ireland, it was done to 'exultant choruses of the Unionist right'.[199] As the SDLP was committed to the 'fundamental and primary objective' of creating an all-Ireland Republic,[200] Unionists took the party's description of the Council as proof of the dangers of sharing power with the nationalist party. Those who participated in the Sunningdale conference seem to have underestimated the growing feeling on the part of the broader unionist community of frustration and fear that accommodating nationalists would eventually lead to a united Ireland. Opposition grew in 1974, led by the United Ulster Unionist Council. There was also opposition within the Republic. Kevin Boland, a former member of Fianna Fáil who had resigned over the arms crisis and went on to form the short-lived Aontacht Eireann, challenged the Agreement in the High Court, arguing that the recognition of the existence of the Northern Ireland state was unconstitutional. However, he lost his case (and the subsequent appeal in the Supreme Court) after the judges concluded that the Agreement amounted to only a *de facto* recognition, rather than *de jure* confirmation, of the formal existence of Northern Ireland.[201]

1974 proved an especially difficult year on the security front for the coalition. On 11 March, the Provisional IRA murdered Billy Fox, a Fine Gael senator and former TD for the border constituency of Monaghan. He was the first member of the Oireachtas to be murdered since the assassination of Kevin O'Higgins, Cumann na nGaedheal Minister for Justice, in July 1927. Fox had been visiting a farmhouse near Clones in Co Monaghan, which the IRA, believing it was being used to store weapons, raided. He was shot and fatally wounded. Two months later, on 17 May 1974, Dublin City was rocked as three car bombs went off in Talbot Street, Parnell Street and South Leinster Street around 5.30pm. A fourth bomb detonated at 7pm on North Road, Monaghan. They had been planted by the UVF – although the loyalist organisation did not claim responsibility until 1993 – in an effort to undermine the Sunningdale Agreement. Thirty-three people were killed on what was the single worst day of the Troubles. At the time of the bombings, the Ulster Workers' Council (UWC) was engaged in a far-reaching strike that greatly compromised the Northern economy in an act of solidarity with those Unionists within the Assembly opposed to power-sharing. Austin Currie, then a member of the SDLP, recalled that by 28 May:

> [A] minimal petrol and oil supply was being operated by the Army; the power stations were near to total shutdown and the Army was not capable of operating them; the water and sewage services were at grave risk, with the possibility of raw sewage polluting the streets and threatening the health of the population; the UWC had stopped supplies of foodstuffs to farmers and food distribution was in danger.[202]

Eleven days after the Dublin-Monaghan bombings, the Northern Ireland power-sharing experiment collapsed when Faulkner resigned as his position had become untenable. Direct rule was reinstated.

The following year, eight IRA prisoners in Portlaoise Prison initiated a hunger strike on 3 January in demand of special status. A threat to assassinate Ministers if any of the men died was issued. A second group began refusing food on 13 January. The prospect of creating a Republican martyr brought the situation to a head when Patrick Ward was admitted to the intensive care unit at Jervis Street hospital after refusing food for forty-five days. Ward was serving a three-year prison sentence for possession of firearms and membership of the IRA. A settlement was announced shortly after his admission to hospital on 16 February. The aftermath of Michael Gaughan's death in Britain's Pankhurst Prison following sixty-five days on hunger strike in 1974 would have been fresh in the government's mind. A member of the IRA, Gaughan had been demanding political status. In what was reported to be one of the biggest Republican gatherings in London in recent years, an estimated 5,000 people had accompanied his body to the church, led by a procession of men wearing black berets, dark jackets and sunglasses.[203] At the end of the Portlaoise hunger strike in 1975, a statement issued by Patrick Cooney, Minister for Justice, through the Government Information Service, explained that 'certain matters, which were not matters of principle as far as the government was concerned, were resolved satisfactorily'.[204] An unidentified intermediary was reported as having convinced the Republicans that the government would not concede issues of principle.[205] Later that year, in October, a Republican group kidnapped Dr Tiede Herrema, a Dutch industrialist who ran a large wire factory in Co Limerick, and demanded the release of the IRA prisoners in Portlaoise in exchange for Herrema's safe return. Conor Cruise O'Brien recalled in his memoirs how Cosgrave took a firm stand. When the government discussed the ultimatum, Cosgrave simply said, 'I take it we're all agreed we don't reply'. After a brief silence, he moved on to the next item of business. Herrema was subsequently rescued after the Gardaí discovered the location of where he was being held.[206]

July 1976 was particularly difficult. On the first Saturday of the month, bombs, planted by the Ulster Freedom Fighters, exploded in five hotels across the Republic: Gresham in Dublin, Royal St George in Limerick, Great Southern in Rosslare, Salthill Hotel in Galway and Great Southern in Killarney. This was damaging to tourism. Speaking at the Strawberry Fair in Enniscorthy, Co Wexford that afternoon, Liam Cosgrave had commented on how tourist trade from Britain was already down 500,000 compared with the mid-1960s.[207] On coming to office, and in keeping with its commitment in the fourteen-point plan to support tourism, the coalition had reversed the outgoing government's plan to purchase an executive jet for use by ministers. 'It would not be justifiable to add to the current financial difficulties of Aer Lingus attributable to the fall off in traffic due to the violence in the North, by siphoning away passengers and revenue from Aer Lingus'.[208] Despite the difficulties in the North, the Irish Tourist Board had worked hard to project an image of a peaceful Ireland in its promotions. As violence intruded on life in the South, that image would become more difficult to sustain. On 15 July, security at the Special Criminal Court was breached after three bombs that had been smuggled in exploded, allowing five prisoners attending trial to escape. Four were recaptured almost immediately. The following day the *Irish Press* carried pictures on the front page of the sizeable hole blown in the wall of the court by one of the blasts.[209] Less than a week later, on the morning of 21 July, Christopher Ewart Biggs, the new British Ambassador, and Judith Cooke, private secretary to the permanent under-secretary of the Northern Ireland Office, were killed after their car hit a landmine planted by the Provisional IRA in South County Dublin. Brian Cubbon, the permanent under-secretary, and Brian O'Driscoll, the driver, were also injured. Speaking in the British House of Commons and foreshadowing the views that she would express as Prime Minister, Margaret Thatcher, then leader of the opposition, remarked, 'We do not know what the terrorists hope ultimately to achieve by this senseless and brutal act, but may we make it quite clear that they will never weaken our resolve to root out terrorism by every possible means and to demonstrate to the law-abiding citizens of both our countries that the rule of law and civilised values must and will survive?'[210] Cosgrave's government naturally agreed that a strong and clear message needed to be sent. Consequently, it was proposed that, before the Ambassador's remains were flown home, he should lie in state in St Patrick's Cathedral, with a state removal to the airport the following day. 'All of this', it was suggested, 'would have the effect of emphasising in public, and especially in bringing it home to television viewers in Britain, that the State here and the general public should not be confused with the perpetrators of the outrage'.[211] Ultimately, though, his widow decided against a state funeral, but later wrote to Cosgrave that 'the feeling that Ireland is sharing our loss with us is a great comfort'.[212]

This catalogue of violence – in particular, the explosions at the Special Criminal Court and the murder of the British Ambassador – resulted in the introduction of new legislation at the end of August 1976. The Dáil was recalled for a special meeting to debate the Emergency Powers Bill and Criminal Law Bill, with Cosgrave moving that 'arising out of the armed conflict now taking place in Northern Ireland, a national emergency exists affecting the vital interests of the State'.[213] The former provided for the detention up to seven days of those suspected of crimes under the Offences Against the State Act. The latter imposed a ten-year prison sentence for inviting someone to join or support an unlawful organisation, and a ten-year penalty for helping a person to escape or remain at large. The package of legislation also provided for other wide-ranging powers that included life imprisonment for kidnapping and false imprisonment, designated as felonies, and granted power to Gardaí to stop and search people and vehicles.[214] The legislation was debated for two weeks, with Fianna Fáil offering vigorous opposition. Jack Lynch, responding to Cosgrave on the first day of debate, argued that the courthouse explosion and the murder of Ewart Biggs alone were not enough to justify declaring a state of emergency, adding that 'in the hands of the wrong government it could open the door to a police state'.[215] He also used his speech to broaden the scope of the discussion and to attack the coalition on its law and order record. Because of the disastrous handling of the economy and social issues, he claimed, the government had clung to the law and order image, but if a state of emergency were declared, it would be the final nail in the coffin for the coalition's record as a government. Moving beyond the Northern Ireland security question, he also spoke of increasing crime, vandalism and hooliganism: 'old people, indeed even young able-bodied people, are not only afraid to walk the streets at night. They are no longer secure from attack and robbery in their own homes'.[216] If the Northern Ireland security question mattered little to the ordinary voter, the issue of local crime certainly did. Over half of all national crime was concentrated in Dublin. Between 1972 and 1975, for example, the breaking and entering of houses and shops in the city increased by forty-seven per cent.[217] Lynch played a clever game in undermining a core value that Fine Gael in general and Cosgrave in particular held dearly.

Labour had great difficulty with the legislation, as evidenced by the reaction of its members. Noel Browne, Michael Mullen, Mary Robinson and David Thornley spoke and voted against the bills; John O'Connell, Michael D Higgins and John Horgan criticised the bills but abstained from the vote; while Barry

Desmond, Brendan Halligan and Ruairi Quinn expressed concerns but voted for the bills. Conor Cruise O'Brien was the only Labour member to speak in favour of the measures.[218] President Cearbhall Ó Dálaigh expressed concern about the Emergency Powers Bill and consulted with the Council of State. In accordance with his powers under article 26 of the Constitution, he subsequently referred the Bill to the Supreme Court to test its constitutionality. The Supreme Court found the legislation to be in accordance with the law, and Ó Dálaigh signed the bill on 16 October. The government's handling of the crises that culminated in the legislation showed a willingness to take a tough stand against paramilitary activity. However, an intemperate remark in the aftermath of Ó Dálaigh's referral, coupled with the Taoiseach's response, greatly undermined the coalition. Paddy Donegan described Ó Dálaigh as a 'thundering disgrace'. His criticism had important implications: Donegan was Minister for Defence and the president is the titular commander-in-chief of the defence forces. Donegan offered his resignation for what he later described as an 'unwarranted attack',[219] but Cosgrave declined to accept it (although six weeks after making the remark, Donegan was demoted to Minister for Lands). Ultimately, the resignation came from Ó Dálaigh, who stated that his decision had been motivated by the need to protect the integrity of the office. As Kevin Rafter points out, it seems that Cosgrave, who had had a poor relationship with the president,'saw a ministerial casualty as having greater party and governmental consequence than the fallout from presidential embarrassment'.[220]

The government suffered further negative publicity as a consequence of Cosgrave's Ard Fheis speech on the eve of the dissolution in May 1977. With the government's record on law and order questioned by Jack Lynch and criticisms in the media of the government's handling of the recent security crises, particularly the Portlaoise hunger strikes, Cosgrave sought to respond. During his leader's address he declared:

> Not for the first time has this party stood between the people of this country and anarchy. And remember, those people who comment so freely and write so freely – some of them aren't even Irish – no doubt many of you are familiar with an expression in some parts of the country where an outsider is described as a blow-in. Some of these are blow-ins. Now as far as we're concerned they can blow out or blow up.[221]

A report on the coalition by the ITGWU was not alone in describing the event as a 'Nuremberg-type Ard Fheis'.[222] The 'thunderous applause'[223] his speech received unnerved observers, already cautious of Cosgrave's unwillingness to countenance allegations of the 'heavy gang', an anti-IRA component of the Gardaí.

David Ervine, a former member of the UVF, recalled of the Dublin-Monaghan bombings, 'there was a sense that yes, somebody was hitting back: "Now you know how we feel'".[224] Perhaps surprisingly, public opinion in the Republic on the subject of unity hardened slightly between 1973 and 1978, rather than turning away from the prospect of closer involvement with the political problems of Northern Ireland.[225] But, much like the earlier bombings in Dublin in 1972, though the events of 17 May 1974 had horrified the Republic, they – and the larger security question – did not dominate the hustings at the 1977 election. Rather, like 1973, the main themes of the campaign focussed on bread and butter issues.

Exit the coalition

If the coalition had increased public expenditure and introduced a package of social reform in an effort to buy votes, its social policies proved to be of little electoral benefit as the two parties faced the electorate amidst high levels of unemployment and inflation. *Hall's Pictorial Weekly* had lampooned Richie Ryan, once praised for the first budget that he had delivered, as 'Richie Ruin', the Minister for Hardship. In a re-enactment of his 1976 budget speech, Ryan was seen to promise the provision of bowls of gruel to mothers and children, the reopening of work houses and the return of the ration book.[226] The programme, which was the creation of Frank Hall, was widely considered at the time to have contributed to the demise of the government at the 1977 election. Hall's treatment of the incoming Fianna Fáil government was nowhere near as severe, and opponents pointed to his alleged political leanings as an explanation for the contrast. In response, Hall emphasised the different composition of the two governments: Lynch's colleagues lacked the colour of those who had sat at the cabinet table between 1973 and 1977. Recalling one episode, he suggested that few observers realised that the figure being satirised was the Minister for Economic Planning and Development, Martin O'Donoghue.[227] Reflecting on the programme's impact, Frank Kelly, who acted several roles on the programme, suggested, 'I think that can happen, but it's an accident waiting to happen, but it doesn't mean that the agenda of the programme is to bring down the government. It means that it's in the right place, at the right time, to do it. It just takes something to tip everything over'.[228]

A memorandum sent to members of the cabinet in 1975 indicated a level of awareness of that tipping point. Though it is often repeated that there was widespread expectation that the coalition would be the first in the history of the state to be returned for a second term, the memorandum marked 'top secret' warned that it was 'self-deluding to pretend that the possibility of electoral defeat is not a real one'. Inflation, farmer incomes and unemployment were identified as the key areas most likely to cause defeat. The frank document pointed out that 'inflation continues to undermine [the government's] image of competence. Unemployment is at its highest peak in peacetime'.[229] Despite all this, there was a perception that the Cosgrave-Corish government would be re-elected. 'Coalition are favourites', the *Sunday Independent* reported.[230] The views of the media were shared by the British Embassy in Dublin, which felt that the coalition 'could well gain a slightly increased majority, even with a smaller share of first preference votes'. The scale of Fianna Fáil's possible defeat, compared to 1973, was also considered.[231] And at Fine Gael's Ard Fheis on the weekend of 21 and 22 May 1977, an external observer reported that 'despite warnings against over-confidence from several ministers, the delegates seemed generally to take it for granted that the coalition could win'.[232] Brian Farrell and Maurice Manning later commented on the 'embarrassment of virtually the entire corps of observers and commentators, academic and journalistic, all of whom had failed to predict the outcome'.[233] The exception was a young Indian-Irish girl who, in March 1976, used tarot cards for the *Sunday Independent* to predict Cosgrave's defeat![234]

Cosgrave requested an early dissolution of the Dáil. This was done at the behest of the Labour Party. The decision was discussed at a cabinet meeting and when a vote was put to the ministers, Cosgrave's casting vote was necessary. Though he wanted to wait a further six months before going to the country, he was afraid that the cabinet might break up and he agreed to call an election.[235] Only after this was announced was an opinion poll to judge the re-election potential of the coalition commissioned. The delay was peculiar, especially given that Irish Marketing Surveys had been conducting polls since 1974. Howard Penniman suggested that the action set Cosgrave apart from his counterparts in other parliamentary democracies – most notably Pierre Trudeau who postponed the Canadian elections the same year – who had begun using polling to inform the timing of their elections.[236] With hindsight, the order of events represented the last of the 'old style' politics in Ireland, soon to be replaced with a more professional, carefully-marketed approach. But political opinion polling had not yet become mainstream and there was much suspicion of the findings. After all, Fergus Pyle, editor of *The Irish Times*, had suppressed publication of a poll commissioned by his newspaper for that very reason. It had forecast a fifty-two per cent share of first preference votes for Fianna Fáil, which would have delivered a significant majority. Pyle, like his staff, disbelieved the findings.[237] Besides, Cosgrave had good reason to be confident as a result of James Tully's 1974 Electoral Amendment Act. A response to the gerrymandering of Fianna Fáil's Gerry Boland with the Electoral Amendment Act in 1969, the Minister for Local Government had redrawn the constituency boundaries to favour the coalition partners. It was expected that it would deliver a bonus of six extra seats.[238] In describing his readjustment project, Tully remarked, 'I cannot improve on it anyway. I think it is great, fantastic'.[239] Michael Mills, the political correspondent of the *Irish Press*, predicted that the outcome of the election would be decided 'not by manifestos or credibility, but by the redrawing of constituencies'.[240] The problem, of course, was that the now famous Tullymander was based on the votes cast in 1973, and in his calculations, the Minister had failed to make allowance for any swing in the vote. Behind the scenes, research conducted by MRBI revealed that the coalition was facing defeat. Jack Jones presented the findings to Garret FitzGerald, Richie Ryan, Michael O'Leary, Brendan Halligan, Jim Dooge, Conor Cruise O'Brien, Justin Keating and Alexis FitzGerald at government buildings on 4 June. He recalled that when the results first came in the previous evening, such was the implication that 'we thought it wise to recheck our figures'. The coalition partners were on just thirty-five per cent (Fine Gael, twenty-first per cent; Labour ten per cent), compared to Fianna Fáil's fifty-nine per cent share of the vote.[241] Dooge remembered how they were drinking tea and coffee when Jones informed them of the disappointing findings: 'there was a rattling of saucers'.[242] Someone wondered aloud if it was possible to uncall an election.[243] As Dooge was closest to Liam Cosgrave, he was nominated to inform the Taoiseach, whose absence from the briefing reflected his general demeanour in government. Revealing his distrust of polls, Cosgrave asked if they could be relied on and Dooge explained that they had a five per cent margin of error. 'He trusted me on this, that he wasn't going to win, but it didn't stop him fighting'.[244] Within the first week of the campaign, Fianna Fáil's projected share of the vote was reduced to fifty-two per cent, but, crucially, Fine Gael failed to close the gap any further in the second or third week.

The election

The contrast with 1973 was astounding. The roles were reversed as Fianna Fáil seized the initiative, while Fine Gael and Labour repeated many of the mistakes Lynch's party had made four years earlier. 'The election caught the government by surprise', was the view of one demoralised Fine Gael candidate.[245] The coalition partners were slow to respond, while, in contrast, Fianna Fáil ran a professional, well-organised campaign that had many of the trappings of American electioneering.

Guidelines for Fianna Fáil canvassers were laid out in *An Coras Bua* – 'the system of winning' – a handbook that reveals a close attention to detail, down to the instruction to organisers that 'reporters need light, please provide accordingly [at public meetings]'.[246] Seamus Brennan, the party's newly appointed general secretary, had spent four weeks in early 1976 following the presidential primaries in America and holding meetings with various Democrat and Republican representatives. It was there that he saw the future style of Irish electioneering, tailored for an age of television.[247] Fianna Fáil's campaign the following year was notably influenced by what he learned, to the extent that the *New York Times* commented on the similarities.[248] As Olivia O'Leary points out, in an age of consumerism, brand recognition was hugely important. Fianna Fáil thus marketed the leader.[249] T-shirts emblazoned with

'Bring Back Jack' were accompanied by other party merchandise, including badges and car stickers, carrying the same slogan. These were immediately available on the day the election was announced. Fianna Fáil campaigns had always been leader-focussed, but the level of attention in 1977 was unprecedented.[250] Jack Lynch undertook a presidential-style leader's tour of the country, organised by Eoin Kenny. His tour schedule was carefully co-ordinated with the media, and special treatment was given to photographers from *The Irish Times* and *Irish Independent*. Lynch's daily speeches were reinforced with corresponding announcements from his front-bench members.[251] In contrast, there was little prior-awareness of Cosgrave's movements as he visited the country. Such was the style of Fianna Fáil's campaign that, as David Farrell has noted, there is a general consensus that Ireland's entry into the 'modern' era of campaigning was marked dramatically by it.[252] Jack Lynch's description of the unveiling of his party's manifesto had a wider application to Fianna Fáil's campaign: it 'was not just the opening of a carefully prepared election campaign. It was the culmination of four years of research and political reappraisal'.[253] During its time on the opposition benches, a demoralised Fianna Fáil was rebuilt and restructured. Under the direction of an organisational committee consisting of George Colley, Seamus Brennan and Joe O'Neill, there was a drive to reinvigorate the organisation and to remove paper cumainn, while efforts were made to deal with incumbents who were resisting strong running mates.[254] The importance of appealing to the youth and female vote was emphasised, and polling was conducted in marginal constituencies from December 1976 to gauge public sentiment on key issues.[255]

For Fine Gael, in comparison, campaign organisation was something of a shambles. Richie Ryan was appointed Director of Elections, despite admitting to Cosgrave that the demands of his position as Minister for Finance had meant that he was out of touch even with his own constituency. In the absence of any press officer, the inexperienced Moore McDowell was drafted in on the day the election was called. Party headquarters at Hume Street was ill-equipped to run a campaign, and lacked such basic and necessary facilities as a photocopier.[256] Five days *after* the campaign started, J. W. Sanfey, the party's general secretary, wrote to constituency secretaries to enquire about their election literature requirements.[257] The Fine Gael campaign was slow to get under way due to the fact that Cosgrave had ordered that selection conventions were not to be held until after the Dáil was dissolved. As a result, his attention, and that of Richie Ryan's, was distracted for the first three days of the campaign. Problems arose in a number of constituencies, including Kildare, North Tipperary and Dublin-Clontarf, where Ted Nealon, the head of Government Information Services, was a last-minute addition to the ticket. Labour also had difficulties. Although delegates at the national conference in November 1976 had voted six to one in favour of remaining in the coalition,[258] it was also apparent that the anti-coalition element had not been sated by the experience of government. Four hours were set aside for discussion of the subject, and of the twenty-five motions relating to the topic, twenty-one opposed coalition.[259] The party also faced more immediate organisational problems, which, in part, related to the anti-coalitionists Noel Browne and Matt Merrigan. Browne was selected to stand in the newly created constituency of Dublin-Artane, but the party's Administrative Council refused to ratify his nomination because he had not taken the Labour whip in the Seanad. Merrigan, who had expressed the fear that Labour would degenerate into the 'liberal rump' of Fine Gael,[260] withdrew his candidacy ahead of the Dublin-Finglas selection convention. He claimed that party headquarters were attempting to rig the vote through the creation of paper branches.[261] Both men subsequently contested the election under the banner of Independent Labour. *The Irish Times* reported that the party was split down the middle in Limerick, where a 5,000-signature petition by supporters of Mick Lipper to have him added to the ticket was rejected. He subsequently entered the contest as a 'Democratic Labour' candidate, running against the official Labour candidate, Steve Coughlan.[262] In all three constituencies, Labour suffered, failing to win any seats.

Richie Ryan held daily strategy meetings at the Department of Finance. They were attended by FitzGerald, Dooge and McDowell. Flor O'Mahony, who had advised Corish at the Department of Health and was unofficial chief strategist for Labour, and Seamus Scally, temporary general secretary, represented Labour at the meetings.[263] The coalition partners agreed a co-ordinated campaign. However, when Fine Gael placed a newspaper advertisement with the slogan 'Now you've got a good government, keep it' and asked readers to 'Vote Fine Gael',[264] the *Irish Press* was quick to point to the absence of any reference to Labour. When contacted by the newspaper, a party spokesperson explained that it had simply been an oversight, and that the omission would be rectified.[265] Although the appeal to 'Vote Fine Gael' was retained, it was expanded to include, 'Support the National Coalition' in subsequent advertisements.[266] Another advertisement that appeared shortly afterwards was more explicit in calling for reciprocal support. Making reference to the flexibility that PR gives voters to cross party lines, it asked Fine Gael supporters to continue their preferences for Labour, and for Labour supporters to do likewise for Fine Gael candidates.[267] The omission of Labour from the earlier advertisement appears to have been a genuine mistake. A message had been immediately rushed out to all Fine Gael canvassers, reminding them to emphasise the importance of continuing preferences for the Labour Party. As Michael Mills pointed out, the haste with which the message was dispatched indicated a concern that the transfer patterns of 1973 might not be repeated.[268] Furthermore, the party's campaign handbook, *Get Full Value from Every Vote*, was concerned wholly with encouraging cross-party voting.[269] Despite the co-ordinated newspaper advertisements (similar to the 1973 campaign), there was no plan to release a 1977 version of the fourteen-point programme. Rather, the coalition partners decided to stand on their own record. This strategy was hastily changed after Fianna Fáil launched a glittering fort-seven-page manifesto on 26 May, the day after the Dáil was dissolved. Martin O'Donoghue had prepared a document in 1976, approved by the Fianna Fáil front bench, which was subsequently published. *The Economic Emergency* was essentially an early draft of the 1977 manifesto, but the Fine Gael–Labour government largely ignored it at the time. The document was updated once the election was announced, with input from George Colley. *Action Plan for National Reconstruction* can be classed as Ireland's first modern manifesto. Unlike *Towards a Just Society*, it made specific promises that canvassers could tailor to target different voters they encountered at doorsteps. Fianna Fáil built its document around unemployment, inflation and prices, and made specific problems to counter these problems. With the dynamic title, *Action Plan for National Reconstruction*, the Fianna Fáil manifesto promised to rectify 'coalition mismanagement' and to confront unemployment and rising prices. New jobs and opportunities were to be created, while security and stability would be provided for those who had suffered the effects of inflation, it claimed. These issues, outlined in the introduction, were among the main lines on which the campaign was fought. And although the content had a broad appeal, the party deliberately targeted key voting groups: the young, women and farmers. The manifesto also promised the abolition of rates on all dwellings from January 1978, the removal of annual road tax on all cars up to 16 horse power from August 1977, to subsidise telephone charges for old age pensioners living alone, to provide a grant of £1,000 to first-time house buyers, and to ensure provision for recreational and shopping facilities and community centres in the planning of all new housing developments.

By releasing its manifesto first, Fianna Fáil seized the initiative and set the agenda for the campaign. Moreover, it placed Fine Gael and Labour on the defensive. In response, the parties appointed a committee to draft a manifesto. Though it consisted of Garret FitzGerald, Richie Ryan, Mark Clinton, Jim Tully, Justin Keating, Michael O'Leary, Brendan Halligan and Alexis FitzGerald, the resulting document was mainly the work of Garret FitzGerald. The *Programme for Progress*, contrary to the document's name, was composed mostly of the party's achievements in power and criticisms of Fianna Fáil. For example, it reminded voters that:

> Honouring its commitment prior to the last election, the National Coalition has, during its first four years in office, built 100,000 new houses, half as many again as the 66,000 built in the last four years of the previous administration.[270]

Fresh policies to achieve progress were noticeably absent. In a manner reminiscent of the launch of *Towards a Just Society* in 1965, the coalition partners showed themselves to be unprepared. The document was not completed until hours before its release at a press conference on 28 May.[271] The performance of the Irish economy was being monitored in Britain. Interestingly, a report submitted to the Cabinet Office shortly before the election was called suggested that 'there is no real reason to believe that their [Fianna Fáil's] economic management would have markedly greater success than that of the present government'. The similarities in approach were highlighted: a commitment to creating additional jobs and reducing unemployment through dialogue with trade unions to limit pay rises, coupled with additional government expenditure to generate extra employment.[272] R. M. Harris at the British Embassy in Dublin had also noted these similarities.[273] What Bruce Arnold observed of the two manifestos was equally true of the wider approach: the content of the National Coalition's document was as unrealistic as Fianna Fáil's, but it was the style of presentation that made the impact. Fianna Fáil 'offered yesterday an economic programme which has not been costed. And they did it with a suave and smiling confidence which was staggering'.[274]

Public opinion surveys had identified unemployment, especially among young people, as the single greatest national problem.[275] The latest unemployment figures showed 111,049 people on the live register,[276] but the figure was contested by Fianna Fáil, which argued that the live register did not take youth unemployment into account. In its manifesto, the party placed the number at the much higher figure of 160,000. Fianna Fáil proposed spending £100 million to create 20,000 new jobs in twelve months. This was to be done through building and construction works, and by employing extra Gardaí and teachers. It was also envisaged that a 'buy Irish' campaign would result in 10,000 extra jobs. In contrast, the coalition partners proposed spending £55 million to create 13,000 jobs through a new Manpower Authority and Development Corporation. They also contested Fianna Fáil's interpretation of the unemployment levels. In a deliberate attempt to undermine vote transfers between the coalition partners, Fianna Fáil produced an advertisement targeted at Labour supporters disenchanted by their party's involvement in government. An image of an extensive queue outside the dole office on Dublin's Gardiner Street was captioned '160,000 workless'. Placing the blame with Fine Gael, it added, 'and they expect Labour to vote them back to power'.[277] The EEC published a report on unemployment in early June. Though based on research conducted in 1975, the findings still had relevance to the debate during the campaign. Both sides claimed that the report reinforced their argument. FitzGerald asserted that because the unemployment figures included school leavers and those completing studies, the figure of 160,000 suggested by Fianna Fáil was 'totally false'. However, Martin O'Donoghue pointed out that the population had increased since 1975 and the survey did not take into account housewives and others 'who would like a job'. The figure of 160,000 was, he claimed, plausible.[278] Regardless of the precise number of people without a job, the problem of unemployment was a very real one and it remained one of the key issues throughout the campaign. It was hardly surprising, therefore, that ninety-six per cent of those surveyed for an *Irish Times* opinion poll, published on 8 June, approved of Fianna Fáil's job creation plans.[279]

As part of Fianna Fáil's campaign to target the floating votes of those who had been enfranchised under the Fourth Amendment of the Constitution Act, 1972, the party also pledged that £20 million would be set aside for projects specifically designed to create 5,000 new jobs for young people. It was observed in the manifesto that there were 'no jobs for young people leaving schools and colleges', a problem reiterated in the party's election song, *Your Kind of Country*. Penned by the Des O'Meara and Partners advertising agency, the score was composed by Tommy Ellis and it was sung by the well-known performer Colm C. T. Wilkinson. With such lines as 'we're more than just statistics', it was directed specifically at the almost half-million first time young voters and it played on the problem of unemployment. Fianna Fáil's ability to harness that vote proved central to the party's success. The importance of the youth vote was stressed in an *Irish Independent* editorial early in the campaign.[280] John Bruton had demonstrated that he understood this when he attempted to convince his colleagues of the electoral benefits of publishing 'Youth and Sport'. Much of what Fianna Fáil outlined in the youth section of its manifesto had a lot in common with the Bruton report. It too proposed, for example, that the Department of Education would work alongside national organisations to guide youth development and that structures should be put in place for the training of full-time and voluntary youth leaders. Fianna Fáil was clever in how it targeted the youth vote. Conscious that the politically uninterested might not read policy documents or a manifesto, the catchy tune of its election pop song, together with T-shirts, hats, badges and key-rings, were all gimmicks guaranteed to attract attention. It worked: the party won almost sixty-two per cent of the under-twenty-six vote.[281]

If the youth vote played an important role in restoring Jack Lynch as Taoiseach, than part of Fianna Fáil's victory, the *Irish Farmers Journal* suggested, was 'certainly due to a switch in the farmer vote'.[282] That newspaper had run several articles outlining Fianna Fáil's agricultural policies. Although it did not specifically endorse Fianna Fáil, and sometimes pointed out that it was unclear how certain policies would be implemented, it was obvious which set of proposals were favoured. One article noted that 'the main difference between the coalition and Fianna Fáil manifestos in relation to agriculture is that the Fianna Fáil document makes a number of specific pledges whereas the coalition document outlines a statement of intent with no major concessions'.[283] One of the big appeals of the manifesto was the proposed abolition of rates. These were to be abolished from January 1978, with a Fianna Fáil government paying twenty-five per cent of the bill in 1977. This had a broad appeal, but was especially attractive to farmers. A letter to the editor of the *Irish Farmers Journal* from John Kilbracken of Co Cavan succinctly summed up why:

> It has long been recognised that rates paid by farmers constitute a highly illogical and unfair system of taxation, partly because the rate varies arbitrarily, and widely, from county to county, but mainly because the sum payable is based on the valuation placed on a property well over a century ago and very seldom revisited.[284]

The *Irish Farmers Journal* was not alone in commenting on the reserved nature of the coalition's offerings. An editorial, for example, in the *Irish Independent* commented on the lack of information available about such innovations as the National Development Corporation and the National Development Fund, concluding that such proposals carried much less conviction as a consequence. This was in contrast to, what that newspaper described as, 'the most attractive package of tax cuts which has ever been presented to the people in advance of any previous election'.[285]

The coalition repeatedly attacked Fianna Fáil on the costing of its proposals. There was an air of irony to this. At the launch of the coalition's own document, Richie Ryan had refused to speculate on the financial implications, claiming it would be 'impossible to cost a programme in the present uncertain situation'.[286] Nonetheless, Garret FitzGerald attempted a breakdown of the Fianna Fáil programme, and concluded that £369 million in borrowing would be required to cover the cost of implementation, substantially more than the figure of £250 million projected by Fianna Fáil. Speaking on the necessity to continue restraint, Cosgrave declared 'what our opponents offer cannot be implemented'.[287] In response to Fine Gael's attacks, Fianna Fáil placed newspaper advertisements with the headline, 'Yes, our proposals will work', which responded to criticisms of the programme's financing.[288] In addition to raising concerns over the level of financing needed, the coalition partners also criticised the manner in which that money would be raised. From 1976, the government had made a conscious effort to scale back borrowing. It was a decision taken in the context of breaking the link with Sterling, which, it was felt, could only be achieved if there was confidence in Ireland's finances. This would be undermined by borrowing.[289] In contrast, Fianna Fáil proposed that the £160 million in tax cuts outlined in the *Action Plan for National Reconstruction* would be offset by an increase in international borrowing at a rate of thirteen per cent of GNP in 1978. FitzGerald was heavily critical and argued that the rate of borrowing required to finance the tax cut would be fourteen per cent, a figure in breach of EEC loan conditions. However, in the middle of the campaign, the *Sunday Independent* carried a front-page story by Vincent Browne with the headline, 'We can borrow. Fianna Fáil plan is on says bankers'. According to the article, an unnamed EEC official stated that, if the borrowing rate were kept below the 1975 level of seventeen per cent, a temporary slight increase would be understood.[290] The EEC, however, later issued an official statement denying that any such advice was given.[291] Although the attempt at a costing breakdown drew into question the viability of Fianna Fáil's programme – to the extent that the party clearly felt the need to defend itself – the strategy only repeated the same tactical error that Fianna Fáil had made in 1973. By placing their energies on attacking the Fianna Fáil plan, the coalition partners ensured that the campaign focussed on Fianna Fáil's proposals, increasing publicity and voter awareness of the content. An opinion poll conducted for *The Irish Times* just over one week before polling day found that seventy per cent of those questioned said they were aware of Fianna Fáil's and the National Coalition's documents, but that one in three could not name any of the coalition's proposals. Yet when asked about the main points of the Fianna Fáil programme, interviewees demonstrated a familiarity with the content. The promise to abolish rates, unsurprisingly, topped the list of the best-known points; it was followed by the abolition of road tax, job creation and increased personal tax allowance.[292]

The headline of *The Irish Times* on 18 June reported, 'Fianna Fáil sweeps to biggest victory. Three Ministers defeated as seven per cent swing routs coalition'.[293] Lynch's party won a record 84 of the available 148 seats in the Dáil. The result was a catastrophe for Fine Gael, and the party was left without TDs in four constituencies: Dublin-Artane, Kerry North, Kildare and Tipperary North. Nineteen TDs lost their seats, including the Minister for Justice, Patrick Cooney, and long-serving deputies, Maurice Dockrell and Fintan Coogan, who had been first elected to the Dáil in 1943 and 1954 respectively. The defeat of Brigid Hogan-O'Higgins, a TD since 1957, meant that for the first time since the foundation of the state there would not be a member of the Hogan or O'Higgins dynasties in the Dáil.[294] Notable Labour losses included Justin Keating, Minister for Industry and Commerce, Conor Cruise-O'Brien, Minister for Posts and Telegraphs, David Thornley and Brendan Halligan, who had taken a leave of absence as the party's general secretary after successfully contesting the Dublin South-West by-election in June 1976. Transfers between the two parties were not as strong as in 1973. Though the percentage of transfers received by Labour was actually up slightly (70.9 per cent to 72.8 per cent), there was a significant decrease in votes that transferred to Fine Gael (down from 71.7 per cent in 1973 to 58.3 per cent),[295] demonstrating that the coalition experience had soured supporters on continuing in government with Fine Gael. In the aftermath of the election, the anti-coalitionists in Labour resumed their campaign. A motion from Dublin District Council at the ITGWU annual conference in 1978 calling on the ITGWU to suspend its Labour Party affiliation if the organisation went into coalition again was narrowly lost by a margin of only seven votes.[296]

Both Liam Cosgrave and Brendan Corish stepped down as leaders of their respective parties after the election, initiating a trend that equated electoral failure in government with resignation. The *Irish Press* speculated that Fine Gael would return to the right and choose a leader who would recapture the farmer and business vote.[297] However, Garret FitzGerald had really marked himself out as a leader at this time. He was almost alone in actually challenging Fianna Fáil. Although his one-to-one television debates with George Colley did not have the same impact as they had done in 1973, FitzGerald showed himself willing to take on the opposition and engage in informed debate rather than to just criticise. This, added to the statesman reputation that he had gained as Minister for Foreign Affairs, positioned him to succeed Liam Cosgrave. As party leader, he would be in a much stronger position than Declan Costello had been to initiate change.

7
1980s: New Leader, New Party

Garret FitzGerald and Charles Haughey were the defining political figures of the 1980s. There's was 'a titanic conflict that dominated the political landscape of late twentieth century Ireland, much as the struggle between Gladstone and Disraeli had dominated British politics a hundred years before'.[1] Their rivalry was consolidated by the new development of televised leaders' debates at election time. In contrast to Haughey, FitzGerald became 'Garret the Good'. Coined by his opponents and intended as a term of derision, the moniker stuck with him and was an important factor in his success. It became all the more fitting after Haughey's corruption was later investigated and exposed by the McCracken and Moriarty Tribunals.[2] When FitzGerald was asked if he was aware of the moment that he first had an ambition to become a politician, he replied that he was fifteen. Fr Roland Burke Savage, who ran the debating society at Belvedere College, had suggested that he should consider a career in politics. FitzGerald recalled being told to aim for the office of Taoiseach, though he admitted that in later life Burke Savage had no memory of that element of his advice: 'perhaps I invented that part'.[3] He joined Fine Gael, he claimed, to transform the party. 'You don't join a party because you agree with it ... You join it because, through the party, you can influence change'. Support for Declan Costello's efforts in 1964 had encouraged him that there was a window of opportunity to affect change in the party.[4] Unlike Costello, FitzGerald wanted to be leader, recognising that the only way to bring about change was to direct it from the top. And as Gene Kerrigan put it, the changes implemented by FitzGerald were 'designed to create Fine Gael as much as to reform it'.[5]

Garret FitzGerald

Garret FitzGerald was born on 9 February 1926, the youngest of four sons. He was educated at Belvedere College and subsequently UCD. He graduated with an Arts degree in French, Spanish and History in 1946, later returning to undertake a PhD in economics. The subject of his doctoral thesis, submitted in 1967, was economic planning in Ireland. It was a concept that was very much in vogue in the early 1960s and was central to Costello's Just Society proposals. While at UCD, he was active in a number of student societies, including the Law Society, the Commerce Society and the Literary and Historical Society (L&H), but his activities were focussed mostly on the latter. He also studied law at Kings Inns and was called to the bar in 1947.

'All roads lead to politics' is the title of the second chapter of his major autobiography, *All in a Life*. Like Costello, FitzGerald was arguably predestined for a career in politics. His father served in the Cumann na nGaedheal government with John A Costello, and also held the position – Minister for External Affairs, as Foreign Affairs was then termed – that FitzGerald would be elevated to in 1973. On his occasion of his appointment as Minister for Foreign Affairs by W. T. Cosgrave's son, Liam, in 1973, Garret FitzGerald admitted to reflecting on the parallel with his father, describing it as a 'pleasant coincidence'.[6] He was very close to his father, and was influenced by his views politically, historically and theologically. He shared Desmond's conservatism, he claimed, until he began teaching at UCD where the students challenged his views.[7] He attributed much of his thinking on the North to his mother, Mabel. She had been born in 1884 in Belfast to a Presbyterian Unionist family, the McConnells. Despite her background, she became an Irish-language enthusiast and convinced nationalist during her time at university.[8]

As had been the case with Declan Costello, politics was not FitzGerald's first career choice. Indeed, he recalled how his father had not wanted him to enter politics on the strength of his name: 'I had to wait until I made my own name to some degree'.[9] On completing his BA, FitzGerald took up a position with Aer Lingus, fulfilling a dream that he claimed he had held since he was twelve.[10] He also embarked on a part-time career in journalism. By the age of twenty-three, he was the Irish correspondent for fourteen newspapers, ten in the Commonwealth and four in provincial Britain.[11] He subsequently began writing for the *Irish Independent*, before joining *The Irish Times* as an economics correspondent in December 1954; he wrote for that paper on and off for a half-century. His myriad of other jobs included lecturing positions at Trinity College, Dublin and UCD, chairman of the Irish Council of the European Movement and economic consultant. He eventually entered politics in 1965, more than a decade after Declan Costello. Although he declined to stand in that year's general election, he was persuaded by Costello and Alexis FitzGerald to contest the Seanad election.

The timing of his decision to finally enter politics was largely influenced by his wife Joan, who had resisted the idea of a political life. As Joan O'Farrell, the daughter of a British army officer, she had met FitzGerald at a meeting of the French Society at UCD in November 1943. She was in her third year and he had just begun his studies: 'I took a dislike to him. I thought he was very brash'.[12] They were married in 1947! Despite her initial opposition to him embarking on a political career, she ultimately became one of the best-known supporting figures in Irish politics. One obituary after her death in 1999 described her as 'probably the most influential partner of a premier in modern Irish history', continuing 'she colluded so closely with her husband ... when he was twice Taoiseach in the 1980s that many found it hard to establish where the influence of one ended and the other began'.[13] This was reflected in the multiple daily phone calls FitzGerald made to her from government buildings. He considered her 'a good judge of people, much better than I was. That proved useful when I wanted advice on picking my cabinet'.[14]

New leader

When Liam Cosgrave announced his intention on 23 June 1977 to step down after twelve years at the helm and retire to the backbenches, FitzGerald was the obvious choice to succeed him. Cosgrave's departure was inevitable, and speculation had begun almost as soon as he conceded defeat on results night, 17 June. That weekend, Vincent Browne reported in the *Sunday Independent* that several TDs had contacted each other by telephone to discuss Cosgrave's future as leader. Though Browne noted that Cosgrave's 'durability should not be overlooked',[15] there appeared to be a general consensus that his tenure had come to an end. An article the following day in the *Irish Press* named Garret FitzGerald, Peter Barry and Tom Fitzpatrick as potential successors.[16] The list grew once the official announcement was made, but FitzGerald was repeatedly singled out as the favourite. Much like Dillon's resignation in 1965, Cosgrave's announcement was expected, though the timing – coming at the first meeting after the 1977 election – had surprised members. However, in contrast to the manner in which he had been elected in 1965, Cosgrave proposed that the party meet again in eight days, on 1 July, to select his successor. Though he did not name his choice – and, indeed, he did not cast a vote in the contest – it was widely speculated that Richie Ryan was his preferred option. Ryan, however, had been blindsided by the announcement, and was absent as he was attending a meeting with the International Monetary Fund in Washington. A postponement of any formal canvassing of colleagues until his return was agreed, but the wheels of FitzGerald's campaign were already in motion. He had been due to leave for an OECD meeting in Paris, but decided not to travel. Though he maintained in his memoirs that he did not canvass actively, his supporters were not as conscientious.[17] *The Irish Times* carried the leadership question on the front page on 24 June: FitzGerald was once again considered the popular choice, though other contenders, including Richie Ryan, Tom Fitzpatrick and Peter Barry, were still mentioned. So too was Patrick Cooney, although the loss of his seat in the election effectively ruled him out. The Attorney General John Kelly had also indicated his availability, but explained that he would not be canvassing votes.[18]

Ultimately Ryan decided not to enter the race. Though he had once harboured leadership ambitions, his reputation as 'Richie Ruin' was unlikely to endear him or the party with him at the helm to the electorate. Additionally, as director of elections for 1977, he was tainted by the party's failure. He later explained that he felt pressured to run, but considered it necessary to remove himself from the contest to help create a consensus about the leadership.[19] For age reasons, Mark Clinton and Tom Fitzpatrick – both in their sixties – also opted not to contest the leadership. This left a straight fight between FitzGerald and Peter Barry, the outgoing Minister for Education and TD for Cork City South-East who had the backing of a number of rural deputies. Head of Barry's Tea, a well-established and nationally recognised family-business based in Cork, Barry would certainly have appealed to the business community, while his conservative credentials were such that a profile in the *Sunday Independent* described him as a credible alternative for those suspicious of FitzGerald's liberalism.[20] Ultimately, though, as Stephen O'Byrnes observed, 'FitzGerald was already a darling with the media and a statesman with an international reputation'.[21] His time as Minister for Foreign Affairs was crucial in forging that identity. Ireland had held the presidency of the European Community between 1 January and 30 June 1975. FitzGerald's presidency was acknowledged abroad as a major success for the country.[22] Furthermore, the fact that he did not continue in the Finance portfolio after Fine Gael took power in 1973 also meant that he was not directly tainted by the tough decisions facing Richie Ryan during the oil crisis and its aftermath. Although it is difficult to draw exact comparisons with 1973 because of the subsequent re-drawing of the boundaries, FitzGerald was the only Fine Gael minister at the 1977 election whose personal vote increased. Barry later recalled his awareness that the ordinary members wanted FitzGerald. This, coupled with a feeling that the people who were encouraging him to stand at the time were doing it from an 'anti-Garret, rather than pro-Peter point of view', convinced him to withdraw.[23] He consequently proposed FitzGerald, seconded by Kieran Crotty of Carlow-Kilkenny, for the leadership on 1 July. The endorsement was unanimous and FitzGerald, fifty-one, became the new leader.

FitzGerald's selection was generally considered a positive step forward for Fine Gael. Justin Keating had predicted that 'for either Fine Gael or Labour, in a fit of post-election depression, to rule out further coalition would be to copperfasten a Fianna Fáil victory'.[24] FitzGerald was considered best placed to reach an arrangement. Changes were also happening in Labour. Two hours before the Fine Gael meeting that selected FitzGerald, Frank Cluskey became the new leader of the Labour Party on the second vote, beating Michael O'Leary. A trade union official with the Workers' Union of Ireland (WUI), Cluskey was steeped in that tradition. His father, a butcher, was an active trade unionist and secretary of the butchers' section of the WUI between 1924 and 1954.[25] Before entering the Dáil in 1965, Cluskey had served as a councillor on Dublin City Council and later as City Commissioner. He had been Brendan Corish's parliamentary secretary at the Department of Health and Social Welfare during the National Coalition, and he presided over many of the progressive measures, discussed in Chapter 6, that came from that department. On the issue of the North, he shared Conor Cruise O'Brien's view that the Irish government's immediate objective ought to be structural reform, rather than re-unification.[26] His leadership of Labour was to prove short-lived, however, especially in comparison to that of his Fine Gael counterpart. There was no effort to rejuvenate the party in the way that FitzGerald would do with Fine Gael. After their appointments, the two men spoke briefly at Leinster House. Though nothing definite was agreed, the possibility of a future coalition was left open.[27] The election of both men to the leadership of their respective parties was reportedly seen by the rank-and-file as presenting a more optimistic outlook for the future.[28]

New personnel

FitzGerald unveiled his front bench on 14 September 1977. Four newly elected TDs were included: John Boland was appointed spokesperson on Health and Social Welfare, Austin Deasy on Fisheries, Jim Mitchell on Labour and Jim O'Keeffe on Law Reform and Human Rights. Oliver Flanagan, Paddy Donegan and Mark Clinton, three former Ministers, two of whom were unreservedly conservative, retired to the backbenches. Clinton was offered the position of deputy leader, but declined for personal reasons. The departure of Flanagan and Donegan was essential for the new image that FitzGerald was attempting to create for the party. He did, however, strike a balance between the two wings. Richie Ryan was retained, returning to Foreign Affairs, the portfolio he had held before the party went into government in 1973, as was Peter Barry. Minister for Transport and Power and subsequently Education in the National Coalition, Barry became the party's spokesman on Economic Affairs and Public Services. Overall, FitzGerald's fifteen appointments reduced the collective age of his frontbench by ten years from fifty-three to forty-three. As he explained, he had purposely chosen a young team because an opposition party had to look ahead five years.[29] Clearly, FitzGerald was positioning the party as a government-in-waiting.

FitzGerald later reshuffled his team after Richie Ryan and Tom O'Donnell successfully contested the 1979 European elections. He also officially appointed Peter Barry as his deputy leader, a role that Barry had informally filled since 1977. Paddy O'Toole and Michael Keating, both new to the Dáil, were brought onto the front bench and were given responsibility for Industry and Commerce and Law Reform and Human Rights respectively. Keating was later described as being 'almost alone nowadays' in embodying the 'Just Society syndrome within the party'.[30] Much like Declan Costello had with the housing conditions in his constituency in the 1960s, he drew attention in the late 1970s to the squalor and privation of places like Seán McDermott Street and questioned the justification of a Dáil that permitted such conditions to exist.[31] As a teenager growing up on Dublin's North Circular Road, he had considered politics after becoming involved with voluntary groups: 'I felt there were things wrong with the city and some of its people. Going to school, I was conscious there were some children who were hungry and who had patches on their clothes'.[32] Although they were from different backgrounds, his sense of social-consciousness mirrored Costello's. Keating joined the party because of the Just Society, becoming secretary of the organisation in Costello's constituency of Dublin North-West.

In order to achieve the party's transition from the opposition to the government benches, FitzGerald recognised the need to radically overhaul the party structure. He signalled that his first priority would be to revitalise and modernise Fine Gael. Already he had confirmed that there would not be a return to a time when Fine Gael had a part-time leader: in his acceptance address he stressed that the days of his multiple jobs were over.[33] Speaking at a party function in Donegal in July 1977, he explained that his aim was to recreate Fine Gael as 'the party of government of the 1980s'.[34] Declan Costello had previously attempted to modernise the party in the late 1950s and 1960s with the establishment of the Research Unit and to give it a sense of purpose by carving out a policy that allowed Fine Gael define itself as something other than Fianna Fáil's opposition. FitzGerald went even further. He undertook the herculean task of over-hauling the party's problematic organisation. He also shaped his strategy around the trends that had emerged from the 1977 election, that is, the important youth and women's vote.

The necessity for change had not only been reflected in the results of the election – which left some commentators, yet again, wondering about the future of Fine Gael's survival – but had also been observed in a report by the party's general secretaries, Gerry L'Estrange and Eddie Collins. Their findings were outlined at the 1978 Ard Fheis and revealed the poor state of the party. Only one-third of constituency executives had responded to a request for names of branches, membership numbers and financial state. This was hardly surprising given that many of the branches were found to be either non-existent or had been inactive for several years. Only two-thirds of those branches in good standing had affiliated for the Ard Fheis.[35] Much of the reorganisation that occurred within Fine Gael at this time mirrored the changes implemented by Fianna Fáil during its spell on the opposition benches between 1973 and 1977. Those behind-the-scenes changes, which contributed to Fianna Fáil's spectacular twenty-seat majority in 1977, did not escape FitzGerald, nor did the role of Seamus Brennan as general secretary in coordinating that campaign.

FitzGerald's first appointment as party leader was Peter Prendergast to the position of General Secretary. Just as Brennan had been brought in as a fresh, new face to replace Tommy Mullins who had served Fianna Fáil for more than thirty years, Prendergast succeeded Commandant Jim Sanfey. Sanfey had served in the Irish army with Liam Cosgrave during the Emergency and they retained a close friendship. Cosgrave hired him as general secretary in 1968. From 1973, in addition to his responsibilities at party headquarters, he also served as a Senator, having been appointed as one of the Taoiseach's nominees, and was the party's chief-whip in the upper chamber. Sanfey retired following Cosgrave's resignation as leader. When the position was advertised, there were seventy responses. Prendergast was chosen from a short-list of twenty.[36] His selection ended the practice of former army officers filling the role of general secretary: Sanfey had succeeded Colonel P. F. Dineen who had served in the defence forces between 1922 and 1948 before taking up the position until his retirement in April 1968.[37] Thirty-eight-year-old Prendergast also became the party's first full-time national organiser since Gerry Sweetman, who had died in 1970. Prendergast had joined the party in the late 1960s because of Declan Costello and the Just Society and stood unsuccessfully on the Fine Gael ticket in FitzGerald's constituency of Dublin South-East in 1973 and 1977. He impressed FitzGerald at that time with his intimate knowledge of politics and his administrative capacities.[38] He was clear on why the party failed in 1977: the parliamentary party, and particularly the cabinet, had become detached from the organisation and those who could advise on what was needed during the campaign were never given the opportunity to do so. He favoured opening up and strengthening the lines of communication between the various levels of the party: 'we can never again allow the politicians to get away from the organisation, and we have got to develop the structure and the means of communication which will keep their feet firmly on the ground'.[39] With a background in marketing, he would draw on those skills to prepare a strategy for the next election. Prendergast was the most influential of those around FitzGerald.

A second key appointment was Ted Nealon. A former editor of the *Sunday Review* and presenter and political commentator for RTÉ's current affairs programme *7 Days* for ten years, he subsequently took up the position of head of Government Information Services in 1975. He unsuccessfully contested the 1977 election on the Fine Gael ticket in Dublin-Clontarf. Reflecting the position he held during the National Coalition's time in power, FitzGerald appointed him director of the party's press and information services. When Nealon's application for the position was received, all other applications were discarded. 'It was clear that he was the most qualified person and he had the experience', FitzGerald explained.[40] He held that position until 1981 when he successfully contested his native Sligo-Leitrim constituency at that year's general election.

By the mid-1980s, FitzGerald had built a formidable team around him that also included Enda Marren, Frank Flannery and Shane Molloy. They were credited in 1985 with transforming Fine Gael from 'the loosely organised groups of men who arrived at the Dáil at 3 pm from the High Courts to the dynamic party it is today'.[41] Marren had been involved with the party since the 1970s, serving on the national executive and he was also a trustee. Flannery was a skilled strategist; he would later be responsible for re-building a shattered Fine Gael after it took a severe drubbing at the 2002 general election. Molloy's skill was to detect trends before they emerged.

New party

The new leader undertook a tour of the forty-four constituencies over a six-month period, usually accompanied by Prendergast. While this primarily allowed him to examine the state of the party's branch structure, it also offered him an opportunity to re-acquaint himself with the views of the grassroots and the issues of importance in the constituencies. As a member of cabinet in the National Coalition, FitzGerald's focus would have been re-directed, while his position as Minister for Foreign Affairs meant that he spent much time out of the country. A common thread in the reports on his activity was the commentary on FitzGerald's remarkable energy and the enthusiasm that greeted him. Michael Finlan's description was laced with action-related language:

> Garret FitzGerald's full-throttle energy shows no sign of running down as it propels him through the length and breadth of the country imparting the kiss of life to his distempered party.[42]

Similarly Gene Kerrigan's report on the flurry of activity that marked the final weekend of the tour made for almost exhausting reading:

> FitzGerald made seven public appearances, met and spoke privately with nine separate groups or individuals, held two press conferences, was interviewed twice for RTÉ, attended a funeral and visited one convent, four hospitals and a bishop. The exercise covered three counties and lasted 54 hours, plus traveling from and to Dublin.[43]

Re-organisation of the constituencies, where local TDs exercised great power, was imperative if the party was to professionalise and modernise. John O'Reilly, a local activist, had written to Cosgrave in 1969 about the Cork City branch, arguing that unless restructuring occurred, the party organisation would never grow and develop: 'Meetings are held at times and places not known to many as if it was a secret society ... The majority of people here in Cork do not know where the local rooms are and if they want to join the party who do they contact?'[44] Jim O'Keeffe offered a similar insight into the state of his own branch in West Cork at the time. He recalled the difficulty of trying to join the party in the early 1970s: 'there was no process, no procedure. I wasn't told about any meetings, anything like that'. Moreover, the sitting TDs and the top County Councillors controlled everything. The chairman, secretary and treasurer of his branch were all councillors, who kept a tight grip. As he recalled, 'it was very hard to breakthrough'.[45] O'Keffee's recollections of West Cork reflected Jim Dooge's description of the constituencies being run by a 'cabal'.[46]

Given the political individualism encouraged by the intra-party competitive nature of PR, these incumbents carefully nurtured their position. They regularly resisted attempts from party headquarters to add a second candidate to the ticket, which would require them to share their voter base. The consequence of this self-interest and self-preservation was that the wider interests of the party were rarely considered. That policy issues did not take precedence over local interests was hardly surprising. An IMS poll in 1976, for example, found that forty per cent of those surveyed felt that their vote was cast to elect a TD to look after the interest of their constituency, as opposed to voting to elect a government or to endorse a set of policies.[47] However, the rejection of a running mate sometimes meant that in constituencies where Fine Gael had the potential to take an additional seat, the opportunity was sometimes missed because the outgoing deputy had refused to have a running mate to whom he could transfer votes. Fine Gael was thus more a network of local notables rather than a cohesive political party. As FitzGerald told a meeting of the Roscommon Constituency Executive, 'Fine Gael is not a political party. It will be, but it isn't yet'.[48] He sought to tackle this long-standing practice of domineering incumbents and the problem of inactive or paper branches, and his revisions stretched from the grassroots to the upper echelons of the parliamentary party. By the end of 1977, with half of the constituencies visited, a new structure was beginning to evolve. And at the 1978 Ard Fheis, he warned that those elected representatives not pulling their weight would be moved to the side-lines before the next election.[49]

FitzGerald introduced a new party constitution that shifted the balance of power towards the ordinary members. It sought to overhaul the manner in which people were elected to the National Council. Removing power from the parliamentary party – a coalition of conservatives and liberals – was essential for providing a space in which a framework for his new agenda could be approved. The new constitution also provided for a youth group. Shortly after becoming leader, he had spoken of the need to change how the party operated in order to encourage more young people to engage. New structures would have to be created to allow for greater participation at regional and national level.[50] He announced on 7 November 1977 that Fine Gael had decided to establish a youth movement with branches in every constituency. Speaking at Castlebellingham in Co Louth, he explained that if the party wanted to displace Fianna Fáil, it would have to increase its share of the vote among the younger portion of the electorate.[51] Young Fine Gael (YFG) was to be independent of the senior party, responsible for organising its own meetings and would have its own annual convention.

The first was held in November 1977, at which Roy Dooney was elected the first national chair.

At the time of Garret FitzGerald's death in May 2011, there was a debate about the most effective way to increase female participation in Irish politics. FitzGerald, in his *Irish Times* column in September the previous year, returned to his views of three decades earlier when he wrote that 'parties must address the lack of significant female representation in parliament'.[52] The outcome was a gender quota, incorporated in the Electoral (Amendment) (Political Funding) Act, 2011. FitzGerald had actively sought to encourage women into Fine Gael during his leadership, which coincided with a conversion to party politics by some of the politicised women. He was not a feminist, however, but could be more accurately described, as Mary Kenny put it, as 'a liberal with a sympathetic opening to feminism'.[53]

There had always been disagreement about aims between and within the various women's organisations, but these became more pronounced as the 1970s progressed. The letters' pages of *Banshee*, the journal of Irish Women United, provide an insight into these differences of opinion. The editors did not shy away from their critics, and they published letters from women who felt that the organisation had been too emotive or alienating or radical in its approach.[54] By the turn of the 1980s, the women's movement had fragmented. Furthermore, women's issues had been pushed off the political agenda as a result of the legacy of the oil crises of the 1970s. The attention of politicians was redirected towards solving the economic crisis facing the state. Consequently, women began to consider a more direct role in politics, feeling that they could better affect change from within the political system. The Women's Progressive Association, one of the groups affiliated to the Council for the Status of Women, was founded by Margaret Waugh in 1970 with the aim of alerting women to the gender imbalance in party politics. Waugh had been outraged at Haughey's and Blaney's acquittal at the Arms Trial, and she was keen to encourage women into both local and national politics so that they could play an equal role in decisions regarding society.[55] The Association later became the Women's Political Association (WPA), and founder members included Gemma Hussey, Nuala Fennell, Audrey Conlon, Hilary Pratt and Phil Moore. Because of the prominence of women's issues from the 1973 election onwards, the political parties had already begun paying closer attention to the women's vote. Jack Lynch added six women to the Fianna Fáil ticket in 1977, although, overall, of the 175 candidates selected by the various parties to contest the election, only twelve were women.[56] WPA members contested that election as Independents using the slogan 'Why not a woman?'

Gemma Hussey, writing for the *Irish Press* in July 1977, speculated that women would welcome FitzGerald as the new leader of Fine Gael:

> Women in Ireland … may well feel that they would have an ally who would not only be prepared to listen to them, but who has shown in the

past his readiness to take up and defend a new idea or a new way of looking at things – not because it is popular, but because he believes in it.[57]

Nuala Fennell was one such woman. She described in her memoirs how she joined the party in 1978 because of FitzGerald, 'his liberalism, his enthusiasm for change and the promise of a better Ireland'. Membership prior to that was not an option: 'I would not have been an easy fit with the Fine Gael Taoiseach, Liam Cosgrave'.[58] Phil Moore of the WPA wrote of the 'excitement and solidarity felt by the women members' at FitzGerald's first Ard Fheis as leader in 1978. Many women had been given the opportunity to chair sessions and, she felt that 'a lot of barriers to women's advancement were broken forever' that weekend: 'The party had the opportunity to see that there are splendid women ready and willing to run for Fine Gael and can win; an opportunity denied them before'.[59]

As Lynch had done in 1977, FitzGerald added three women – Monica Barnes, Fennell and Katharine Bulbulia – to the party ticket in 1981. All three had played a prominent role in the women's movement. The party also increased its percentage of female candidates significantly. Only four per cent of the party's candidates in 1977 had been women, but by 1981 that number had increased three-fold to twelve per cent, a figure that remained relatively stable under FitzGerald's leadership. However, as research by Claire McGing has shown, it would be a mistake to suggest that FitzGerald actively recruited women who were new to the world of party politics in the 1980s. Many of the women who stood on the party ticket had been active members of Fine Gael for years before selection, with several, including Eithne Loftus and Bernie Gannon, already serving as constituency secretaries. Others, such as Nora Owen and Avril Doyle, also had family connections. Overall, though, Fine Gael, in comparison to Fianna Fáil and Labour, was certainly more open to running female candidates. Fianna Fáil never ran more than eight per cent in this period, while Labour's figure slowly declined from an impressive fifteen per cent in 1981 to only nine per cent in 1987.[60]

When FitzGerald formed his second government after the November 1982 general election, he appointed Gemma Hussey Minister for Education, later moving her into Social Welfare following a cabinet re-shuffle at the start of 1986. One of the WPA founders, Hussey was a high-profile member of the women's movement and she had been elected to the Seanad as an Independent in 1977. Her husband, Derry Hussey, was one of the so-called 'Donnybrook set', a group very close to FitzGerald. FitzGerald also created a new position: Minister for State with responsibility for Women's Affairs at the Department of the Taoiseach. The portfolio was given to Nuala Fennell, making her one of only three ministers for women's affairs in the European Union at the time. Fennell was one of the first members of the IWLM and one of the founders of the WPA and ADAPT. She was particularly active in promoting the rights of abused women, setting up AIM and its offshoot,

Women's Aid, which opened its first home for battered wives in 1974. She had unsuccessfully contested the 1977 election as an Independent. FitzGerald's intention was that she would co-ordinate with several different departments. An editorial in *Women's Aim* magazine pondered, 'Is this Ministry the brand-new highway along which Irish women will travel towards justice and equality or is it a convenient cul-de-sac down which such aspirations can be conveniently side-tracked and forgotten?'[61] The logistics of co-ordinating with different departments proved problematic, and Fennell was often frustrated. She was also given the brief of family law reform at the Department of Justice. This allowed her to work for reform from the inside on those issues on which she had so vigorously campaigned during the 1970s. Her most important contribution was the legislation that abolished the term 'illegitimacy' as a description of children born outside marriage. Although initiated under the Fine Gael-Labour government, it was only passed after the parties left office.

Further signalling a break with his predecessors, FitzGerald also moved party headquarters from the poky offices at Hume Street to Upper Mount Street, the location also of the Fianna Fáil party. The purchase of the new premises was partially financed by the '£5 a brick' appeal to party members.[62] This innovative fundraising method gave members a sense of ownership, directly connecting the grassroots to headquarters. His inaugural Ard Fheis as leader was central to cementing the image of a new party. The 55th Fine Gael Ard Fheis was the first to be held at the RDS, moving away from the traditional and smaller location of the Mansion House. The choice of venue was symbolic: it signalled that the party had the strength to match Fianna Fáil, which held its Ard Fheiseanna at the same location. The staging of Fine Gael Ard Fheis also differed to that of previous gatherings. Where the party's name and logo, or pictures of past leaders, had usually provided the backdrop to the stage at previous conferences, an image of FitzGerald now dominated the centre of the stage as part of the broader strategy to market the leader. *The Irish Times*, though admittedly a biased source, suggested that 'Fianna Fáil must watch Garret FitzGerald carefully. For he is probably the next Taoiseach'.[63] The cult of FitzGerald was already apparent that weekend. At the conclusion of his leader's speech, his rehearsed departure from the stage, followed by the members of the parliamentary party, was hijacked as supporters raised him on their shoulders.[64] With a growing momentum behind the FitzGerald brand, membership records show a substantial increase between 1977 and 1982, from 20,000 to 34,000.[65]

Into power

The first major test for the new party was the European Parliamentary Elections held across all nine of the member states and the Local Elections in June 1979. Fine Gael performed well following a campaign designed to highlight the party's message and to make it as accessible as possible. It was observed that 'they were ... going out of their way to facilitate the media'.[66] In what the party described as 'Mount Street brought to the people', FitzGerald undertook a bus tour throughout the country, holding up to forty press conferences.[67] The party also recorded a strong performance at local level, regaining much of the ground lost at the 1977 general election. This was attributed to a stronger organisation and proper planning.[68] The results were expected to give an 'injection of new vitality' to the party.[69]

Charles Haughey had succeeded Jack Lynch as Fianna Fáil leader and Taoiseach on 11 December 1979. Almost three years earlier a straw poll conducted by Frank Dunlop, the then press secretary to Lynch, had found that Haughey had 'nothing like enough support' to become leader.[70] However, during his period of exile following his sacking over the arms crisis, he had carefully networked with *cumainn* (branches) across the country, building up support from the party's backbenches. This was a significant factor in his victory over rival George Colley, former Tánaiste and Minister for Finance, whom he defeated by forty-four votes to thirty-eight in the leadership contest. His first administration was a short-lived minority government, and he took the encouraging results from a by-election in Donegal on 6 November 1980 as the opportunity to call a general election with the aim of consolidating his position. He had intended to make the announcement at the Fianna Fáil Ard Fheis on the weekend of 14 February 1981, effectively turning his leader's speech into an election rally. However, the tragedy at the Stardust nightclub, in which forty-eight young people died after a fire engulfed the building, occurred that weekend. As a mark of respect, the party cancelled its annual gathering. The announcement was delayed by three months and polling day was eventually set for 11 June 1981.

With the emergence of a more professional Fine Gael party, there was a marked contrast between the FitzGerald era and that which had preceded it. The campaign for the 1981 general election challenged the perception of Fine Gael as an amateur party. Behind the scenes, preparations had been underway for more than a year. Once the 1979 Local and European elections were over, the party began to prepare for a general election. As David Farrell has detailed, Ted Nealon established a communications committee in January 1980, which was intended to act in conjunction with Prendergast's strategy committee. The specific aim of Nealon's committee was to draw up a plan to market the party, its manifesto and the leadership. Nealon's intention was to present Fine Gael as the alternative government. His committee focussed on five areas: advertising, party political broadcasts, the leader's tour, campaign gimmickry and election literature.[71] Political marketing was a major growth industry in the 1980s. In Britain, the idea of marketing the party as a product was initiated by the Conservative Party, which had hired Saatchi and Saatchi in 1978, leading to a growth in political marketing in the 1980s.[72] Fine Gael's strategy for the 1981 election clearly falls into a marketing framework.[73]

If Fianna Fáil had stolen the momentum within hours of the 1977 general election being announced, the roles were again reversed in 1981. Fine Gael set the agenda from the outset. Already influenced by Fianna Fáil's internal reorganisation, FitzGerald's party now borrowed from the 1977 campaign tactics. Fine Gael produced its own version of *Your Kind of Country*. Performed by Denis Allen, it included the lines, 'Fine Gael, Fine Gael/A bright new future we hail/Led by Garret the man you know/You won't be taking a chance'.[74] Drawing on the recommendations of Nealon and Prendergast, the party ran a presidential-style election, centred on presenting FitzGerald as the alternative Taoiseach. FitzGerald's chartered train tour was reminiscent of Jack Lynch's bus tour. Across the country, FitzGerald shook hands with voters, often attempting to project a relaxed image by dispensing with his suit jacket and rolling up his sleeves. Photographs of the campaign, however, reveal the unease that the somewhat shy FitzGerald felt in larger groups.

The election delivered Fine Gael's biggest electoral breakthrough since the 1920s, when it operated as Cumann na nGaedheal. Twenty-six new deputies entered the Dáil. FitzGerald formed a minority government with Frank Cluskey's Labour Party. However, it was to be short-lived, brought down over a tough budget framed in the context of a strained economic climate and overly stretched state finances. Although the election that followed returned Fianna Fáil to power, the early 1980s were a period of political instability, and a further election provided FitzGerald with a second opportunity to form a government. It was during that administration that the identity crisis in Fine Gael, initiated by Declan Costello, became more pronounced as FitzGerald attempted to implement his legislative agenda.

8
The Constitutional Crusade

'Will Garret FitzGerald radically alter the orientation of the party? While his reputation is liberal and progressive, an analysis of his political attitudes suggests that he is actually quite conservative'.[1] Such were the musings of Vincent Browne in a *Magill* profile of the new Fine Gael leader in early 1978. They seem peculiar, given the reputation that FitzGerald developed and the fact that he considered himself a social, rather than Christian, democrat. From his association with Declan Costello in the 1960s through to his efforts to reform Fine Gael in the late 1970s and 1980s, FitzGerald has always been identified with Fine Gael's progressive wing. But Browne had perceptively identified a conservative tinge to his liberal appearance. FitzGerald was certainly to the left of the party's traditionalists, but much of his agenda for change in the 1980s was framed in conservative terms.

Pluralism

At the encouragement of Roland Burke Savage, his mentor and the editor of *Studies*, Garret FitzGerald published his personal manifesto in the winter 1964 edition of that journal. In 'Seeking a national purpose' he proposed developing an agreed philosophy for social action; one that would not only combine the various strands of Irish society (peasant, republican, Christian), but which also drew on universal philosophies and wider traditions. He argued against a society that tolerated bigotry or advanced sectarian views, and for a society that would be 'neither exclusive nor sectional'.[2] Eight years later, he published *Towards a New Ireland*. In the epilogue to that book he made reference to his *Studies* article: 'I would place more stress on the need to eliminate sectarianism ... I believe that much of what I wrote on the eve of my entry into politics remains valid as an ideal for Irish society'.[3] In the preface, he had defined his understanding of pluralism:

> A society within which people of different religious, cultural or linguistic traditions would be treated as equal citizens, and would be subjected to

no disability because they did not share the tradition that happens to be that of a numerical majority of the population.[4]

In 1972, FitzGerald was on the cusp of becoming a government minister for the first time, and he was five years away from being elected Fine Gael leader. The ideals he had laid out in the 1960s and early 1970s guided him in those positions of power. He used a variety of opportunities to speak in favour of a pluralist society. Holding the opinion that the minority at times must have found Ireland 'somewhat suffocating' because of legislation influenced by the traditions of the majority,[5] FitzGerald wanted to create a pluralist society with the aim of reuniting Ireland during his time in power.

In his memoirs, FitzGerald recalled that, speaking to the press after his election, he reasserted the social-democratic principles of the Just Society.[6] Although FitzGerald attempted to replicate Declan Costello's efforts to reposition Fine Gael, what later transpired in his Constitutional Crusade should not be seen as an extension of the Just Society. Though FitzGerald supported Costello's initiative in the 1960s, as his wife Joan explained shortly after he became leader, 'the question of the North and re-unification I think has always been his first concern'.[7] Indeed, Alexis FitzGerald had expressed concern about FitzGerald's self-confessed loyalty to Northern Ireland, and warned him against too obsessive an involvement in Northern affairs.[8]

When asked about his priorities after being appointed Minister for Foreign Affairs in 1973, FitzGerald had explained that he was keen to be involved in the Northern question. Noting his own personal connection, he explained how he had made efforts to contact various groups in the North, 'off my own bat', to be sensitive to the feelings there.[9] Later, in the course of the interview with Gerald Barry in which he declared the constitutional crusade, FitzGerald repeatedly emphasised his northern links. He could speak confidently, it was implied, on the views of Northern Protestants because he 'belonged' to them and he was 'brought up with them'. His mother, Mabel, was, of course, a Belfast Presbyterian. His views on a united Ireland were guided by the principles of Tone and Davis. Tone's famous pamphlet *An Argument on Behalf of the Catholics of Ireland* had made a persuasive argument favouring religious unity and equality. FitzGerald felt that the Irish state that had emerged was one imbued by the ethos of the majority of the people who lived in the Republic. The word 'sectarian' was continuously repeated during the interview as he spoke of legislative and political development on that part of the island. A desire to change that had prompted his decision to enter politics in 1965. Now, as Taoiseach, he explained, he wanted to 'lead a crusade, a Republican crusade to make this a genuine republic on the principals of Tone and Davis'.[10]

A poll conducted for UTV in December 1981, asked Catholics and Protestants, 'which of the two leaders in Dublin is more likely to bring about understanding between North and South?' Sixty-six per cent of Protestants and seventy-one per cent of Catholics favoured FitzGerald, compared with the four per cent Protestants and seventeen per cent Catholics who believed Haughey could deliver this.[11] FitzGerald's government achieved some success in the area of Northern Ireland, although early hopes were dashed. The New Ireland Forum, promoted by FitzGerald, opened in Dublin Castle on 30 May 1983. Representation was confined to the nationalist parties of Fianna Fáil, Fine Gael, the Labour Party and the SDLP after Sinn Féin and members of the Unionist community declined to participate. Its remit was to identify possible new structures and processes through which lasting peace and stability could be achieved.[12] The report was published on 2 May 1984 and outlined three proposals: a unitary state, a federal state or joint authority between the Republic and Britain. British Prime Minister Margaret Thatcher famously ruled out these proposals in her 'out, out, out' speech at a press conference.

Thatcher's attitude towards compromise on the Northern question hardened in the aftermath of the Forum due to the bombing of the Grand Hotel in Brighton in October 1984. Patrick Magee of the Provisional IRA had planted a long-delay bomb with the intention of assassinating Thatcher and her cabinet colleagues who were staying at the hotel for the Conservative Party conference. Five people were killed, including Sir Anthony Berry, the Conservative MP for Enfield Southgate. The atrocity brought back memories of the murder of Airey Neave, Thatcher's friend and adviser, who was killed by a car bomb planted by the Irish National Liberation Army (INLA) in 1979. She initially declined to further negotiate with the Irish government on the question of Northern Ireland but was later prevailed upon by her advisers to reopen discussions – a strategy also advocated by US President Ronald Regan. This ultimately resulted in the Hillsborough, or Anglo-Irish, Agreement in 1985. The Agreement affirmed that any change in the status of Northern Ireland would have to be confirmed by the majority in Northern Ireland, noting also that the existing majority did not favour change.[13]

FitzGerald aimed to achieve reunification through domestic policy intended to promote a pluralist society, appealing to Northern Unionists. This objective was not fulfilled. In attempting to give Fine Gael a definite purpose and outlook, he was unable to bring the collective party with him. Shortly after FitzGerald assumed the leadership, an editorial in *The Irish Times* speculated that Fine Gael's survival was dependent on finding a 'distinct and recognisable philosophy'.[14] Although FitzGerald would provide that, it came with a price. In an article full of vitriol – which claimed that FitzGerald's communication skills were such that when he appeared on television, one did not want to 'spit at the screen' – Anthony Cronin nonetheless made a perceptive observation: 'Can anybody imagine him leading all those Donegans and Oliver Flanagans? And if they could, has anybody any idea where he might lead them?' Though he suspected it, Cronin could not have fully appreciated at the time the extent to which FitzGerald's efforts to shift Fine Gael to the left would accentuate an identity crisis as the more traditionally conservative members struggled to locate themselves in a changing party.

The pro-life amendment

FitzGerald's second administration was dealt a severe blow at the outset from which it struggled to recover. Abortion in Ireland is a criminal offence under the Offences Against the Person Act, 1861. Many unwanted pregnancies had resulted from a lack of proper sex education coupled with the ban on artificial contraceptives that remained in place until 1979, and even then, they were only available in restricted circumstances. There was a hidden history in this period, of which people could not or would not speak. The stigma of being a single mother and the lack of support, both financially and socially, drove Irish girls and women to desperate lengths to end their pregnancies. This was apparent from the number of cases of infanticide in the first half of Ireland's twentieth century, captured in the sinister children's song *Weila, Weila Waile*, popularised by the ballad group The Dubliners in the 1960s. Telling the story of a woman who lived by the River Sáile and who had a three-month-old baby, it included the line, 'she stuck that penknife in the baby's heart'. In her study of infanticide, Clíona Rattigan concluded from the cases that she examined that 'many Irish people considered the murder of illegitimate children a lesser crime than the murder of children born within wedlock'.[15]

Novelist John Banville recalled that when he decided to write noir fiction, 1950s Ireland offered the perfect setting and inspiration for a crime writer looking to paint a dark picture: 'all that furtiveness, that covert sinning; all that despair, all that guilt'.[16] Backstreet abortion had made sensational headlines when Mamie Cadden, a qualified midwife, was sentenced to death by hanging in 1956 for the death of Helen O'Reilly on whom she had performed an illegal abortion. Cadden had not been the only person offering such services. There had been a thriving backstreet abortion industry in Ireland from the 1930s, although it was virtually wiped out in the 1940s as a result of a major clampdown.[17] Its existence was very publicly exposed through Cadden's high-profile trial, which served as an uncomfortable reminder that, in a State where all forms of artificial contraception and abortion were illegal, Irish women who did not have the money to travel to England had few reasonable choices.

Although the Abortion Act 1967, which was passed by the British parliament and became law on 27 April 1968, made it easier to access the service abroad, Irish women who could afford the journey had already been travelling in their thousands – the country's 'hidden diaspora', as Ann Rossiter terms them.[18] Unmarried mother's allowance had been introduced in 1973, partially in the hope of discouraging women from travelling to Britain to procure an abortion. Despite this, there was a steady increase in the numbers travelling to England and Wales. In 1971, 578 abortions were carried out on Irish women, an average of one for every thousand women between the ages of fifteen and forty-four. By 1979, that number had increased to 2,804 or an average of 4.1, and by 1981 it was at 3,603, an average of 5.1.[19]

These figures record only those women who provided their actual home addresses; many more gave an English address for the purposes of confidentiality. When Socialist Party TD Clare Daly used private members' time in 2012 to introduce a bill to legalise abortion, she brought the subject back onto the political agenda. Her actions prompted a myriad of women to share their stories. Among them was 'Josie', who contributed to a feature on the Colm Hayes Show on RTÉ Radio 2. She explained how she had come to regret her abortion in later life: 'it comes back to haunt you'. But, as an unmarried nineteen-year-old, she felt that she had no choice when she went to London for an abortion in 1982. She also noted the lack of aftercare in Ireland, recalling, 'I got a very, what you would call, sinister approach back then'.[20] The secrecy that surrounded the act added a further dimension to the trauma suffered by many women. Her story was not unique.

The Abortion Act of 1967 had contributed to the momentum for reform of abortion law internationally. This varied between abortions for a particular reason in countries liked Finland (1970) and Italy (1978), and elective abortions in countries such as Austria (1974) and Sweden (1974). There had been whisperings of the issue in Ireland during the 1970s in the context of the debate surrounding the legalisation of the sale of contraceptives. Conservatives had linked the availability of artificial contraception to promiscuity and abortion, and in 1973/74, the Irish Family League produced a small leaflet advocating an amendment that would enshrine a ban on abortion in the constitution. Throughout the 1970s, governments tended to respond to demands for change from society only after external pressure had been applied. Both the EEC and the judiciary had acted as agents for change, and it was feared that this role would be repeated in relation to abortion. Following a debate in the European Parliament in 1981 on the position of women in the EEC, Dermot Ryan, the Archbishop of Dublin, broke the Church's silence on the matter of a referendum and spoke of the need for constitutional reform. He even suggested the possibility of leaving the EEC in the event that it issued a directive decriminalising abortion. Members of the Pro-Life campaign latter impressed on Garret FitzGerald that a pro-life amendment would restrict the capacity of the European Court of Human Rights to 'force' abortion on the state. The arguments in favour of withdrawing from the European Community were short-sighted and were made without reference to the economic and political implications of such a decision. But they also reflected the passion of the moral debate.

While it was felt that there was scope to contain any potential European threat to Irish moral values, the fear persisted that the Irish Supreme Court could play a reforming role that would lead to the introduction of legislation in the Dáil decriminalising abortion. Pro-life campaigners were convinced that the ruling in the McGee case could lead to a court challenge that would overturn the ban on abortion. William Binchy, a barrister, was at the forefront of the campaign for reform. In a 1977 *Studies* article, he warned that the concept of privacy espoused by the decision in the McGee case was a 'time bomb, which, with changing attitudes, may yet explode in a manner which most of our citizens ... would deeply regret'.[21] Parallels were drawn with Roe versus Wade in America, which found that, except in narrow circumstances, the Constitution of the United States did not permit the government to interfere with a woman's right to choose abortion. Griswold versus Connecticut, which recognised a zone of privacy, was widely seen as the progenitor of Roe versus Wade, prompting comparisons in Ireland between Griswold and McGee. Mr Justice Brian Walsh had expressed his support for the right to life. But, his statement in the McGee ruling that no interpretation of the Constitution was intended to be final, alarmed pro-life campaigners, despite the fact that the Supreme Court was adamant there would be no Irish Wade.[22]

The Pro-Life Amendment Campaign (PLAC) was officially launched at a press conference on 27 April 1981. It was chaired by Dr Julia Vaughan, a gynaecologist, former nun and one-time assistant master at Holles Street Maternity Hospital. Professor John Bonnar, who had organised a conference at Trinity College in September 1980 of the World Federation of Doctors Who Respect Human Life, welcomed her involvement. He was not in favour of the campaign being fronted by men, 'especially senior academic gynaecologists who looked like a stuffy old bunch'.[23] PLAC was composed of a myriad of Catholic and pro-life groups. One of the key figures was Nial Darragh, chairman of the Council of Social Concern and also of the Society to Outlaw Pornography. The most prominent among the groupings was the Society for the Protection of the Unborn Child (SPUC). SPUC had been set up in Britain in January 1967 in response to the second reading of the Medical Termination of Pregnancy Bill (which became the Abortion Act, 1967). Members of the organisation subsequently visited Ireland in September 1980 and held two public meetings, out of which the Irish organisation grew. Within two years of it coming into existence in Ireland, it had formed forty branches, had a membership of 4,000 people, given talks at 250 schools and had held hundreds of public meetings.[24]

However, SPUC was only invited to join the pro-life amendment movement just before the press conference. The organisation's approach, in particular, the use of slides in school talks that showed aborted foetuses at various stages of development, had unsettled members of the pro-life movement who feared that such emotive tactics might alienate support.[25] Patsy Buckley, public relations officer for SPUC, admitted that the slides, which included an image of a black plastic bag filled with foetuses, 'could be regarded as shocking'.[26] Such actions, in the words of Vaughan, were 'not helpful'.[27] Nonetheless, with a nationwide network, SPUC had an important role to play in spreading the PLAC message: it provided a ready-made body of campaigners. PLAC also had the support of the Irish Medical Association. The IMA opened its annual general meeting in Kerry in 1982 with a mass celebrated by Bishop Kevin

McNamara who spoke against abortion and in support of PLAC. Eighty-four of Kerry's one hundred doctors signed a PLAC petition; three doctors who were abroad on holiday even faxed their signatures.[28]

At the press conference on 27 April 1981 to launch PLAC, the organisation announced its intention to lobby the main political parties for a referendum to amend the constitution. If the government were not prepared to initiate the process, then the organisation would begin a nation-wide campaign to collect signatures to support their request.[29] As Gary Murphy notes, previous Irish referenda had seen some interest group involvement, but none on the scale of the 1980s'.[30] Within two weeks, the organisation had secured a commitment from the two main parties. Individual meetings were arranged with the Fianna Fáil, Fine Gael and Labour Party leaders. The approach was well timed as rumours of a general election abounded.

PLAC representatives, led by Julia Vaughan, met with Charles Haughey in government buildings three days after their press conference. Although he agreed in principle to the amendment, he requested more time to consider it. He later confirmed to Vaughan in a letter on 14 May 'the total opposition of FF to abortion', and he gave a 'solemn assurance' that an 'appropriate constitutional amendment' would be 'brought forward as soon as circumstances permit'.[31] The inclusion of the vague 'as soon as circumstances permit' promise provided Haughey with room to manoeuvre.

Professor Eamon de Valera of the Mater Hospital led the delegation that met with FitzGerald. With the possibility of a general election looming, FitzGerald was in a vulnerable position. Maria Stack, a member of YFG and the party's youngest vice-President, had said that she favoured abortion in certain medical circumstances. Her initial comments had drawn strong condemnation from Oliver J. Flanagan, reflecting the type of divisions that a liberal agenda could cause in Fine Gael. They also prompted FitzGerald to issue a public statement affirming that Fine Gael was unalterably opposed to abortion. He added that 'for my part, I have ... on every occasion when the issue has arisen defended the right to life of the unborn child'. He also pointed out that YFG had recognised the life of the foetus from the moment of conception at its 1980 conference.[32] Her comments were raised at a meeting between FitzGerald and the PLAC representatives.[33] Fianna Fáil seized on the controversy, emphasising the seeming divisions within Fine Gael. Stack quickly moved to clarify her position, reversing her earlier statement and communicating to the National Executive that she was totally opposed to abortion.[34] The PLAC approach tested FitzGerald's and Fine Gael's commitment. Gemma Hussey was present at the meeting in FitzGerald's office. She recalled listening quietly as they put forward their argument, thinking that they were not winning. 'Somewhat to my surprise, Garret announced that he was going to [hold a referendum, if in government], that he'd been persuaded by their arguments and that the country didn't want abortion anyway'.[35] FitzGerald was trying to hold his party together, by appeasing the conservative elements. Moreover, he was also attempting to outmanoeuvre his Fianna Fáil rival in what one angry letter to the *Irish Farmers Journal* described as an 'anything you can do, I can do better' attitude.[36] PLAC met with Frank Cluskey and Barry Desmond on 12 May. Labour was the least committal of the three parties, promising only to consider the need for a referendum. A statement issued two days later explained that Labour was 'unequivocally opposed to abortion'.[37] Michael O'Leary, the new party leader, later issued a public letter to the Irish Council of Churches. It again emphasised Labour's doubts about the necessity for a referendum. As he explained, 'one can uphold the law against abortion and yet reject a proposal to incorporate a similar amendment to the Constitution'.[38]

Conscious of alienating the conservative vote at a time of great political instability and when a change of government was possible, Fianna Fáil and Fine Gael acceded to PLAC's request. Such was the strength of the lobby that the possibility of it throwing its weight behind either of the main parties was enough to persuade both to sign up to a referendum.[39] The commitment to such a referendum appeared to contradict everything that Garret FitzGerald had said about the need to build a pluralist Ireland, although he was yet to announce his Constitutional Crusade. In an editorial for *Magill*, Vincent Browne argued that the constitutional amendment actually had very little to do with abortion, but was really about re-asserting the Catholic ethos of the Irish state and reversing the trend towards a pluralist society. FitzGerald's decision is best understood in the context of the election. As Gene Kerrigan suggested shortly after the referendum, 'FitzGerald knew that if he didn't agree to pressure from the Knights of Columbanus-sponsored campaign, he would be in danger of being daubed a baby murderer while trying to fight an election'.[40] Although the nature of the proposed amendment was difficult to reconcile with FitzGerald's pluralist ethos, the pledge to hold a referendum was not particularly controversial in the sense that it reflected the dominant view in society.

As the two main parties had consented to an amendment, the issue of abortion did not feature heavily on the campaign trail for the 1981 general election. That election replaced Haughey's government with a Fine Gael–Labour coalition. On 26 January 1982, Fianna Fáil's Michael Barrett and Bobby Molloy asked the new Taoiseach if he intended to introduce legislation to amend the constitution.[41] FitzGerald appeared to waver. He explained that his government would consider whether the question of a pro-life amendment should be dealt with separately or as part of a constitutional review, prompting Barrett to question if he was 'reneging on another election promise'.[42] From the files at the Department of the Taoiseach, it is evident that the government was attempting to pull back from the absolute guarantee that FitzGerald had initially given. FitzGerald had announced his constitutional crusade the previous September and it is conceivable that this declaration caused him to rethink the wisdom of such a referendum.

From FitzGerald's earlier writings, it is clear that he did not deem concessions on abortion (unlike divorce) necessary to entice Unionists into a united Ireland. *Towards a New Ireland* was FitzGerald's blueprint for the type of society he wanted to create. In the penultimate chapter of the book, he summarised the specific steps that could be taken to seek reunification of the country in terms that would be acceptable to Northern Protestants.[43] Abortion was not included. In fact, several pages earlier, he had argued that abortion 'is not an issue with the bulk of Northern Protestant opinion'.[44] He clearly did not consider legislating on the subject necessary for building a pluralist society. Nonetheless, aware that a connection would be made between the two and that criticism would inevitably follow, he dealt with the subject of pluralism in the context of the proposed amendment during his leader's address at the Fine Gael Ard Fheis in 1982:

> I know that there are those who see a problem in reconciling the objective of a pluralist society in this State, as a prelude to a pluralist Ireland, with the proposal to strengthen the projection of life in our Constitution. I believe that this is a false dilemma that we have created for ourselves, however.[45]

A portion of FitzGerald's speech was later reproduced in a full-page PLAC advertisement in *The Irish Times*. Asserting that 'this is not a sectarian or denominational question', it stressed that, from their perspective, the amendment campaign was only about the right to life of the unborn child.[46]

FitzGerald, however, clearly underestimated Protestant views on abortion, or, more specifically, on the state legislating for abortion. Even if the moral ethics surrounding the medical procedure were taken out of the equation, FitzGerald had still undermined his own message. Because, although he had claimed that abortion was not an issue for Northern Protestants, he had also written about the need to assure Unionists that the law-making process in the Irish state would not be subject to the demands of the Catholic lobby. The eighth amendment to the constitution was very clearly a product, and reflected the power, of that lobby.

The Protestant churches did oppose abortion, except in extenuating circumstances, although these were broader than the exceptions recognised by the Catholic Church. Despite opposing indiscriminate abortion, the Protestant churches did not welcome the amendment. From their perspective, governments should not legislate on areas of private morality.

If FitzGerald's government pulled back from its commitment – and there is clear evidence to show that it tried – it seems likely that this position was strongly influenced by the views of Peter Sutherland, the Attorney General. Sutherland was of the opinion that a constitutional amendment was unnecessary, as the right to life of the unborn was already protected under existing legislation. Moreover, he was uncomfortable with the wording. PLAC had proposed: 'The state recognises the absolute right to life of every unborn child from conception, and accordingly guarantees to respect and protect such a right by law'.[47] Sutherland felt that the wording of the amendment was 'ambiguous' and 'unsatisfactory', and that it would 'lead inevitably to confusion and uncertainty'. The result of this, he asserted, would be a dangerous situation in which a doctor faced with the dilemma of saving the life of the mother through a termination, having regard to the equal rights of the unborn and the mother, would conclude that he could do nothing. He strongly advised against putting such an amendment to the people.[48] In response to Sutherland's concerns, a reply to pro-life campaigners who wrote to the Department was drafted. The approved format of the answer included the lines, 'The Taoiseach has indicated that the government is unalterably opposed to the legalisation of abortion and is committed to taking whatever steps are necessary to ensure that the right to life is protected under the constitution'.[49] It was felt that this was justified in light of Sutherland's opinion. 'Whatever steps are necessary' did not necessarily mean a referendum, nor did the phrase preclude FitzGerald from incorporating the measure into a wider reform of the constitution, already under consideration by the Attorney General. The possibility of an overhaul of the constitution would have allowed for an indefinite postponement of any action on abortion. PLAC subsequently challenged FitzGerald on this, prompting his assurance that he was committed to bringing forward an immediate amendment of the constitution if, pending completion of the Attorney General's review, such a course was to become necessary as a result of a Supreme Court decision on the matter.[50]

FitzGerald's first minority coalition was to be short-lived, brought down by a budget, discussed below, that unwisely included a tax on children's shoes. The events that followed the government's defeat on the budget were intriguing. As a telephone log-book in Paddy Hillery's papers clearly show, several phones calls were placed to Áras an Uachtaráin by Fianna Fáil deputies. The first came from Charles Haughey, five minutes before FitzGerald telephoned President Hillery to inform him that he would visit the Áras at 10 pm to request that the Dáil be dissolved. Follow-up calls were made by Brian Lenihan, Sylvester Barrett and Haughey's secretary, Catherine Butler. Their aim was to convince Hillery to deny FitzGerald a dissolution, allowing Fianna Fáil to form a government without recourse to an election. Hillery was clearly anxious to protect the independence of the presidency, and his response to a call received in which it was indicated that Haughey intended to visit the Áras at 10.30 pm showed that he was tiring of the repeated efforts: 'tell him I do not think it appropriate to speak to him'.[51] FitzGerald arrived at the Áras shortly after the time he indicated and left just under forty minutes later; the date for the new election was set for 18 February 1982.

Fine Gael and Labour faced into the election on the back of Bruton's tough budget, with all of the government's harsh measures publicly laid out. Waterford TD Austin Deasy, commenting on FitzGerald's gamble that the country would back the tough budget, recalled, 'He totally screwed it up'.[52] The coalition partners initially stood over the budget, although the situation was not helped by FitzGerald's quip that children's shoes could not be exempt from VAT because women with small feet would be able to avoid the tax. The remark has since gone into Irish political folklore, and though intended in a joking manner at the time, it was particularly damaging. Labour sought concessions, and eventually FitzGerald agreed to remove children's clothing from the bracket. Had this reversal come earlier, it could have saved the government.

The composition of the Dáil changed little after the election, placing the balance of power within the hands of the 'others' once more. Tony Gregory, a former member of Sinn Féin and now an Independent TD for the constituency of Dublin Central, was courted by both Haughey and FitzGerald. Haughey appealed to Gregory on the grounds of their shared background. As Gregory once recalled, 'He was very down to earth. He kept telling us, "Lads, you know I'm just down the road from yiz! I'm from Marino. I'm a Northsider like youse!"'.[53] That link was important. As Maureen O'Sullivan, a close friend and central member of Gregory's campaign team, suggested, Gregory had some talks with FitzGerald but 'not very many because I think he felt that Charlie Haughey was the one who had the more working-class empathy'.[54] What became known as the Gregory Deal, returned Haughey – who had fought off a leadership challenge – to office in March 1982. Immediately, Haughey announced his government's intention to hold a referendum on the abortion question.

Memoranda on the implications of the referendum for North-South relations were prepared by staff at the Departments of the Taoiseach and Foreign Affairs. Given Fianna Fáil's traditional stance on partition, this was hardly surprising. Martin Mansergh warned that the pro-life amendment would be used by opponents in the North as an argument against reunification by claiming that Ireland was not a pluralist country.[55] What is more intriguing is that such a discussion does not appear to have taken place when FitzGerald was in government, despite his stated aim of improving the relationship. Such documents, however, may be contained in State papers yet to be released under the thirty-year rule. The reaction in the North was predictable: Ian Paisley denounced the amendment as the end of pluralism and the imposition of Catholic dogma, while his Democratic Unionist Party (DUP) colleague, Jim Allister, considered it a deterrent to Unionists from any involvement in a 'priest ridden' state. However, these views were not confined to extreme loyalists. David Cook, deputy leader of the Alliance Party, also said that the amendment would damage the development of a pluralist Ireland, while the SDLP's Bríd Rogers described it as 'very divisive and unnecessary'.[56] Rev Ernest Gallagher and Rev Eric Gallagher of the Methodist Church; Dean Victor Griffin of St Patrick's Cathedral, Dublin; and Rev Terence McCaughey, Rev Peter Tarleton and Stanely Worrall of the Methodist College, Belfast, all agreed to act as sponsors for the Anti-Amendment Campaign (AAC), chaired by Mary Holland.[57]

Peter Sutherland's memoranda on the referendum were not submitted to the incoming Attorney General, Patrick Connolly, when the change of government occurred in February 1982. Connolly also had his reservations, and the advice was presumably withheld to circumvent any further delay. The parliamentary draftsman produced a number of alternatives, of which Connolly recommended the following for approval.

The State acknowledges the right to life of the unborn. The State, therefore, condemns abortion and subject to the right to life of other persons, guarantees in its laws to respect, and as far as practicable by its law to defend, the right to life of the unborn.

Significantly, Connolly advised that rape and incest should not be exempt, nor should the mental state of the mother in cases where the foetus was so deformed that life outside the womb would not be possible.[58] These important extenuating circumstances were not catered for when tested. In 1992, the eighth amendment to the Constitution was invoked in what became the X Case, and was used by the High Court to prevent a fourteen-year-old girl, pregnant as a result of rape, from travelling to the UK for an abortion. The Supreme Court overturned the decision, although the girl at the centre of the case ultimately miscarried. When Connolly was forced to resign after a murderer was found at his home, he was succeeded by John L. Murray, who also produced a number of alternative amendments. The text of the eighth amendment was finally agreed on 2 November 1982 at a meeting of the Fianna Fáil government. However, the Eighth Amendment of the Constitution (Abortion) Bill, 1982 lapsed with the dissolution of the 23rd Dáil two days later after Haughey's government collapsed.

Haughey's administration had been short lived, characterised by the now famous GUBU – grotesque, unprecedented, bizarre, unbelievable – expression coined by Conor Cruise O'Brien. A series of peculiar events, which included a murderer being found in the home of Attorney General, plagued the Thirty-Third Dáil. Though FitzGerald and Fine Gael were waiting in the wings, Labour appeared to have reverted to its anti-coalition stance of the 1960s. Just as Declan Costello had been denied an opportunity to implement the Just Society then, so too it seemed that FitzGerald's constitutional crusade might remain a pipedream. Labour held its annual conference in Galway in October 1982 where familiar concerns about the implications of coalition were replayed once more. This resulted in the resignation of Michael O'Leary as party leader. He was replaced by Dick Spring, a former international rugby player who had entered politics only the previous year to defend his father's seat in Kerry North.

Though the economy featured in the three-week campaign that followed the dissolution of the Thirty-Third Dáil, there were other indications of the types of challenges facing the next government, the most notable, of course, being the question of abortion. Jim Kemmy, by then a member of the Democratic Socialist Party, and Labour's Michael D. Higgins had both spoken out against the amendment and faced campaigns directed against their liberal stance. Both lost their seats, a telling commentary on the sensitivity of abortion as an electoral issue. The election resulted in yet another change of government, returning Fine Gael and Labour to power. FitzGerald's new administration enjoyed more stability than either of the previous two governments.

When FitzGerald returned to the subject of a pro-life amendment, it was the Fianna Fáil wording that was ultimately chosen:

> The state acknowledges the right to life of the unborn and, with due regard to the equal right to life of the mother, guarantees in its laws to protect, and, as far as practicable, by its laws, to defend and vindicate that right.[59]

In addition to dissension within the parliamentary party, FitzGerald also faced opposition from Young Fine Gael. Members declared themselves overwhelmingly opposed to the amendment campaign at their annual conference in Galway, arguing that it was unnecessary. It was a bruising affair for Garret FitzGerald as the young members of the organisation that he had founded turned on him. They pleaded with him to remember the Just Society. This was a quintessential example of how the term had become a convenient slogan for the party, a symbol for change to be invoked where necessary. However, it was disingenuous to do so in this situation. As already established, the Just Society had not commented on matters of a moral nature and, given Costello's strong Catholic beliefs, he would have taken a conservative line on such subjects. Not all branches of YFG supported the national campaign, however. The constituency executive of the Longford-Westmeath branch held an emergency meeting on 26 August 1983 to disassociate themselves from the campaign launched by the YFG national executive. They considered the decision on the referendum to be a matter of conscience for the voter, not a political issue.[60]

The referendum campaign was bitter. With a subject as emotionally charged as abortion, it was hardly surprising that the atmosphere was tense. Stephen Collins, then reporting for the *Irish Press*, recalled 'the nastiness' of the campaign; Fine Gael's Gemma Hussey described it as 'vicious'; while Fianna Fáil's Mary O'Rourke remembered it as being 'brutal'.[61] The campaign was fought mostly between PLAC and the Anti-Amendment Campaign; the political parties had only a minimal role. The pro-life campaigners had the distinct advantage of being better organised and funded than their opposition. Although they refused to disclose the actual cost of their campaign, it was estimated that PLAC spent in the region of £100,000. They had undertaken a successful fund-raising drive, overseen by Senator

Des Hanafin, who had been an important fundraiser for Fianna Fáil. In comparison, the AAC is estimated to have spent the far smaller sum of £30,000.[62] The pro-life campaign also had the distinct advantage of being united behind one objective. Although the AAC was opposed to the amendment, there were differing reasons why. Some members wanted abortion legalised, while others were opposed to abortion but felt that a referendum was unnecessary because the existing law was sufficient and that international trends were unlikely to be repeated in Ireland. That the group was supported by the Women's Right to Choose Group, which advocated the decriminalisation of abortion, was used by the opposition in an effort to undermine the AAC: 'so much for the smoke-screen surrounding the notion that you do not have to be pro-abortion to vote No'.[63] And when AAC chair Mary Holland revealed that she had had an abortion, she was subsequently called a murderer at public meetings.[64] In the early stages of the campaign, the AAC had also argued that a referendum was a waste of money at a time of great economic difficulty – it is estimated that it cost the state £850,000[65] – an argument that initially found some sympathy.[66]

FitzGerald had ordered that the parliamentary party should not take an active public part in the campaign. However, the party's pro-life lobby, led by Oliver Flanagan, Tom O'Donnell, Michael Joe Cosgrave and Alice Glenn, campaigned actively in favour of the amendment. Flanagan, in particular, campaigned extensively in various constituencies outside his own of Laois-Offaly. Divisions within Fine Gael worsened as the campaign continued. Although FitzGerald appeared to be at variance with the party's youth group, some members of the parliamentary party later became suspicious that he was using YFG's anti-amendment campaign as a channel for the expression of a policy line he failed to impose on the party.[67]

The letters pages of various newspapers give an insight into the views of professional, religious and ordinary people alike. The letters generally reflected the nature of the campaign: those in favour of the amendment were clear-cut and they were opposed to abortion on moral and religious grounds. Those who opposed the amendment did so for a mix of reasons. Dr Simon O'Byrne of the Adam & Eve Counselling Centre in Dublin wrote that 'personal decisions and judgements on moral issues must take a subordinate place to the teaching of Jesus Christ and also to the explanation of that teaching by the Church authority'.[68] Similarly, Con Riordan of Leitrim wrote 'abortion and Christianity are irreconcilable',[69] while Patrick J. Hammell of Birr, Co Offaly, interpreted the meaning of a 'no' vote as: 'I do not want the constitution to protect the life of the unborn child'.[70] However, Edward MacKeever of Kilmessan in Co Meath, despite his beliefs in the Catholic Church's teachings, did not believe that there should be a referendum.[71] Dr Edward Hanlon, a consultant psychiatrist in Letterkenny, advanced a number of reasons as to why people should vote no. The amendment would 'not save any lives, neither foetal or maternal' and, he felt, the chances of the Supreme Court favouring the legalisation of abortion were 'extremely remote'. He also lamented the fact that the campaign had divided the Catholic and Protestant churches, which had had a much healthier working relationship in recent years.[72]

The referendum was carried on 7 September 1983 by a majority of two to one, with 841,233 people voting yes and 416,136 voting no. In addition to the constitutional amendment, there was a ban on providing information on obtaining abortions abroad. The pregnancy advisory sections of such imported publications as *Cosmopolitan* and *Elle* were blacked out,[73] while British telephone directories were withdrawn from Irish libraries because they listed the numbers of termination clinics in Britain.[74] In the years after the passage of the pro-life amendment, the Wexford branch of SPUC organised an annual pilgrimage on 8 September to the Marian shrine of Our Lady's Island 'in reparation for the continuing evil of abortion'.[75] Many of those who had played a prominent role in promoting the rights of the unborn child would later re-emerge to help defeat the divorce referendum in 1986.

The campaign revealed much about society. Ireland was still a country in transition, and, despite the progress and reform of the 1960s and 1970s, there was a continuing conservatism. For an older generation, there was clear anxiety, as they tried to locate their place in a changing Ireland where traditional values were no longer a certainty. This anxiety was perfectly captured by one mother:

> In my day we were told that all immodest actions, close dancing, immoral literature and passionate kissing were sins against the sixth commandment, but things seem to be changing. Has the moral law become a little lax since our day? I worry because I have four teenagers between the ages of eighteen and thirteen and would be afraid if they ever did anything wrong, even passionate kissing, that they might not confess it and so remain in a state of mortal sin. Is there a clear yes or no now any more?[76]

An editorial in the *Anglo-Celt* suggested that the referendum might have 'stirred the conscience of the nation', making people more charitable and more compassionate so that babies could be born outside marriage without stigma.[77] It was an optimistic hope: the letters pages of *Woman's Way* in the years after the referendum indicated that change was slow. One mother wrote about her daughter who was expecting a child for a married man who had offered to leave his wife: 'if she keeps the baby and sets up home with him everyone will know they're not married and that the child is illegitimate'. Far from the sympathetic response to the plight of her family's reputation that the concerned mother sought, Mary Dowling, author of the 'Get things straight' column, chided her from not putting the needs of her own daughter before the opinions of others.[78] Another woman was concerned that, in her family's keenness to mark her fiftieth wedding anniversary, they would discover that she and her husband were married only forty-nine years, and that their eldest child had been born two months after the wedding. Almost five decades later, there was still then a stigma, or at least fear of one, of conceiving outside of wedlock.[79] A young woman wrote of the fear of being told to leave the family home after she fell pregnant for a man who had no intentions of marriage.[80] The hypocrisy of collective society was summed up by a single-mother who noted of 'the Irish', 'they don't want you to have an abortion, but then they just talk about you and won't help'.[81]

This sample of letters reveals a number of things. They reflect the continuing rigidity of views on moral issues, as already demonstrated during the referendum campaign; there was still an urge to conform to society. But there was also what Paul Ryan terms 'fault lines of intergenerational conflict'.[82] As Brian Girvin suggested, a new type of Catholic was emerging. For those living in towns and particularly for those under thirty years of age, religion had ceased to be a guide to behaviour.[83] The 'yes' vote was strongest in rural Ireland: the further west one looked, the larger the 'yes' vote became.[84] Girvin's contention that individual conscience had become the main guide to action for a younger generation is borne out in the style of questions directed to advice columnists. Angela MacNamara recalled in her memoir how questions in the 1960s that asked, for example, if cheek-to-cheek dancing was a sin were replaced by queries about pre-marital sex by the late 1970s.[85] By the 1980s, women were asking for advice on the repercussions of one-night stands.[86] Of course, not all letters related to sex, but the gradual change in the nature of questions connected to such activity reflects a more relaxed attitude of a younger generation, less bound by Catholic teaching.

In some respects, the content, but more particularly the sub-text, of the debate in the 1980s harked back to the conservatism of the Victorian era. This was not confined to Ireland: British Prime Minister Margaret Thatcher made several references to Victorian values during her time in office. As Jane Juffer has noted, there was nostalgia in the 1980s for Victorian England and the sureties that its code of conduct offered.[87] However, the idea of a virtuous society was more apparent than real. Robert Louis Stevenson aptly captured the contradiction between private and public morality in his 1886 novella, *Strange Case of Dr Jekyll and Mr Hyde* which told the story of how one man's split personality allowed him to assume contrasting public and private personas. Despite the emphasis on sexual morality in the nineteenth century, there was a thriving abortion industry that contradicted the values preached. Unwittingly, perhaps, the pro-life campaign in Ireland in the 1980s reflected this type of hypocrisy. Women had been travelling to the UK in their thousands because abortion was illegal in Ireland. Enshrining the right to life of the unborn in the constitution was not going to stem the flow. In fact, this was a point made by civil servants on several occasions.[88] Moreover, Dr Michael Woods, Minister for Health in Haughey's government, made this point publicly: 'I believe that the process of amending our Constitution should mark the beginning of a sustained campaign to ensure that Irish women are not pressured to seek solutions to their problems in the abortion clinics of another country'. He referred to the need for greater support services for women facing difficulties in their pregnancy and assistance for single parents.[89] But the pro-life campaign was not distracted from their mission, and focussed almost entirely on ensuring that the procedure would never be available in the country. Though certainly not approving of abortions undertaken in England, exporting the problem at least preserved the appearance of Ireland's public morality.

This was a trend well established since the foundation of the state. In the early years of the Free State, there was a conscious effort by both the Cumann na nGaedheal and Fianna Fáil governments to project an image of independent Ireland as a moral, virtuous nation. This was reflected in the ban on divorce and on the sale and import of contraceptives and the legislation relating to censorship and liquor licensing laws. More significantly, the report of the Carrigan Committee was suppressed. The committee, chaired by William Carrigan, had been appointed by the Minister for Justice, James FitzGerald-Kenney, in 1930 to consider amendments to the 1880 and 1885 Criminal Law Amendment Acts. The report was influenced by Garda Commissioner Eoin O'Duffy, whose submission included cases of rape, incest, indecent assault and homosexuality. However, James Geoghegan, the Minister for Justice after the change of power in 1932, voicing similar concerns to his predecessor about publicising such activity in the public realm, recommended that the report should not be published.[90] This obsession with projecting the image of a virtuous Ireland was one that persisted, to the detriment of the country's development. As Diarmaid Ferriter observed, 'such focus on moral panic ... not only inhibited the development of a strong social and labour movement but also facilitated the continued hiding of many of Ireland's social problems'.[91]

The Magdalene Laundries, operated by four orders of nuns between 1922 and 1996, are a further example. Mostly commonly associated in the public mind with 'the fallen', the reality was far more complex. They housed women who had been referred by the Courts following criminal convictions, children formerly resident in industrial schools, girls rejected by foster families, young women over the age of sixteen who had been removed from abusive homes, women with mental or physical disabilities, and poor or homeless women and girls who were placed there by their parents.[92] On average, the women admitted to the laundries spent between six months and a year there, although others never left and were subsequently buried in unmarked graves following their death. This process could not have been overseen in isolation, and it required the cooperation of both society and the state.[93] The laundries were a 'mechanism that society, religious orders and the state came up with to try and get rid of people deemed not to be conforming to the so-called mythical, cultural purity that was suppose to be part of Irish identity'.[94] The first detailed report on the laundries, published in early 2013, provided clear evidence of direct state involvement. Complied by an inter-departmental committee chaired by Senator Martin McAleese, it revealed that the state's participation varied from providing funding and financial assistance to referring or facilitating 26.5 per cent of the cases of which routes of entry are known between 1922 and the closure of the institutions in 1996.[95] In his apology on behalf of the state, Taoiseach Enda Kenny commented on how he was struck by the fact that for generations Ireland had 'created a particular portrait of itself as a good-living, God-fearing nation. Through this and other reports we know this flattering self-portrait to be fictitious'. He acknowledged how 'scruples' were sacrificed for a 'public apparatus' constructed to ensure that society adhered to a particular moral code.[96] When viewed in the context of Irish identity, the debate in 1983 conforms to the desire to uphold that moral code. The pro-life lobby never really engaged with the reasons for unwanted pregnancies or why women felt it necessary to terminate their pregnancies. A discussion on alternative ways to support such women was neither engaged in nor actively promoted.

Divorce

The amendment campaign left many wondering about FitzGerald's abilities to lead a coalition effectively. He later admitted that he had regretted the referendum. The amendment, after all, had been proceeded with despite the cautionary advice of three Attorneys General. An editorial in the *Connacht Sentinel* remarked 'there is something pathetic about a head of government admitting he was wrong in his warm endorsement of the wording and his promise to put that wording to the people'.[97] Early on, Gemma Hussey had written in her diary that 'Garret has shown a lack of leadership',[98] and it was hardly surprising that whispers of potential alternative leaders waiting in the wings began to circulate. If the amendment campaign had derailed FitzGerald's constitutional crusade, the referendum on divorce offered him the chance to revive his pluralist agenda – and to prove his leadership. It was also an opportunity to frame legislation reflective of a changing Ireland. The 1970s saw new trends in marriage and family life. As previously outlined, the reality of the single mother was recognised through state financial assistance in 1973. For the first time, the 1979 census classified population by number and type of family. In her study of family change in Ireland, Finola Kennedy noted that marriage had 'fallen out of fashion' in that decade, and that from 1974 onwards the annual number of marriages continued to fall until the mid-1990s.[99] Attitudes changed towards marriage as a result of the raft of legislation affecting the status of women in the 1970s: the lifting of the marriage bar opened up employment opportunities, while access to contraception allowed women determine the timing of motherhood. In an interview for *Magill* on the new generation, Catriona Quigley explained why she married. Originally from Dundalk, she relocated to Dublin in 1977 to study science at Maynooth College and she moved in with her boyfriend mid-way through her studies. 'I didn't believe in marriage. I just thought it was a load of rubbish. However, I couldn't cope with the family pressure to "do the right thing". So, just before I was conferred in 1983 I got married'.[100] Her recollections point to the inter-generational differences of opinion that were becoming more pronounced.

By the 1980s, marriage had lost popularity, while the rate of births outside of marriage soared.[101] Between 1971 and 1981, the birth rate of non-married couples doubled, while in 1983, 'illegitimate births' (as they were then termed) accounted for 6.8 per cent of all births.[102] Marriage was no longer the exclusive model of family life. In addition to the emergence of liberal attitudes towards relationships, the reality of marital breakdown could not be ignored. There was a notable growth of single party households in all OECD countries, with marital breakdown in most countries replacing widowhood as the leading cause of single parenthood.[103] Divorce Law changed in nearly every Western country between 1969 and 1985;[104] Ireland was the exception. It was against this backdrop that the debate on legalising divorce took place. The Divorce Action Group (DAG), chaired by Jean Tansey, emerged in 1980. From 1981 onwards, along with AIM and the Council for Civil Liberties, it played an important role in convincing the government of the need for divorce legislation.

Prior to the birth of independence, divorce had been available in Ireland. This was achieved by seeking a private bill in the House of Lords once a decree of judicial separation had been passed by the High Courts in Dublin. The 1922 Constitution of the Irish Free State did not address the subject. When the attorney general Hugh Kennedy approached W. T. Cosgrave, President of the Executive Council (forerunner of the office of the Taoiseach), to clarify the new state's position, he expressed the view that, although personally strongly opposed, 'we should make provision for those who approve of that sort of thing'. A devout Catholic, Cosgrave consulted with the Archbishop of Dublin, Edward Byrne, who, unsurprisingly, advised against continuing the practice. The government subsequently moved to prevent applications for divorce in the Free State.[105] It was, FitzGerald suggested in *Towards a New Ireland*, 'one of the first indications of a growing Roman Catholic influence in the new state'.[106] Senator W. B. Yeats was the most outspoken critic. During the debate in the Senate, he had warned, 'If you show that this country, Southern Ireland, is going to be governed by Catholic ideas and by Catholic ideas alone, you will never get the North'.[107] His argument foreshadowed FitzGerald's line of reasoning.

In 1966, Seán Lemass ordered the formation of an Oireachtas Committee composed of a cross-section of Dáil deputies and Senators to conduct a general review of the Constitution, the first of its kind since Bunreacht na hÉireann was devised. In the report, issued the following year, the Committee considered such matters as emergency powers, the number of Dáil deputies and the composition of the Seanad, amongst others. It also considered the question of divorce, which was banned under article 41.3.2 of the 1937 constitution. The committee recommended that the article prohibiting divorce be amended to make the option to end marriage available in certain circumstances. Cardinal Conway rejected even this limited measure: 'everyone knows how these things spread once the gates are opened',[108] while Cathal Daly, Bishop of Ardagh and Clonmacnois, believed it would be a 'step towards de-Christianising our society'.[109]

At the 1978 Ard Fheis, Fine Gael delegates had voted in favour of removing the constitutional ban on divorce, and public opinion throughout the mid-eighties indicated growing support for restricted divorce. If FitzGerald's referendum on divorce could be labelled progressive in terms of an effort to improve North-South relations, in the moral sphere, it was framed in conservative terms. Addressing a meeting of the Law Students Debating Society of Ireland at Kings Inns in 1977, FitzGerald had rejected the notion that divorce was a civil right, arguing that it was far more complex and that a 'right' was difficult to define. He also rejected the argument that marriage should be terminated because of the effects on children living in a divided household. He saw this as an argument for legal separation, which was already in existence.[110] FitzGerald proposed the referendum to safeguard the institution of marriage. His discussion of the subject in *Towards a New Ireland* had been cautious. He had written of removing article 41.3.2 as a gesture, 'an indication of good will', and speculated that such constitutional change might satisfy Protestants, without actually having to introduce legislation permitting divorce. He also pondered a split approach, taking the case of the UK as an example where divorce law differed between England, Scotland and Wales.[111]

Speaking at the launch of the National Partnership through Equality policy document, he admitted that his party had no policy on divorce and that it was likely to be divided on the subject. Consequently, he wanted an all-party Oireachtas committee established to investigate the matter.[112] In July 1983, the Fine Gael–Labour government set up an all-party joint committee on marital breakdown. More than 700 written and twenty-four oral submissions were received from individuals and such groups as AIM, DAG, the Irish Council for Civil Liberties and the Catholic Marriage Advisory Council.[113] When the report was delivered, DAG dismissed it as 'a complete waste of time'.[114] The committee had recommended that the irretrievable breakdown of marriage should be grounds for a judicial separation but had stopped short of recommending divorce. Mary, one of the women who had made a submission, felt let down: 'it was a waste of time. They took advantage of my trust'.[115]

Fergus Finlay's autobiography portrays a lack of organisation and unpreparedness on the part of the government for the campaign. Despite announcing his intention to hold a referendum, FitzGerald delayed naming a date as he sought to persuade the Catholic Church that the time was appropriate to introduce a modest measure of reform. This also led to a delay in preparing the necessary background papers to aid the government with any issues that could arise during the campaign. As Finlay put it, when FitzGerald did eventually officially sanction the Referendum Bill, 'we were woefully unprepared'. He also recalled receiving a phone call after the campaign was over from Geraldine Kennedy, then of the *Sunday Tribune*, asking if any of the pro-amendment side had read William Binchy's *The Case Against Divorce*. The book set out all the main arguments that would be deployed by the anti-amendment campaign. 'As far as I could discover, nobody on our side had read it!'.[116]

The anti-divorce lobby stole the initiative. The speed at which the government had successfully pushed family planning legislation through the Dáil in 1985 – the debate took only five days – had alarmed 'family values' groups. The subject of divorce was already being discussed, and there was a fear that the government might attempt to move quickly again. Moreover, that the family planning legislation had passed, despite opposition from the Church, was interpreted as a defeat for the Church and there was a fear this could be repeated with the divorce referendum. Those who opposed the measure were united under the umbrella of the Anti-Divorce Campaign (ADC) organisation, chaired by Des Hanafin, who had been active in the pro-life campaign in 1983. The ADC came into existence only after the referendum was announced, but it derived strength from a pre-existing organisation, Family Solidarity, which had been set up in 1983.[117] By being better organised and more prepared than their opponents, they set the agenda for the campaign. Their message that the amendment would impoverish women and undermine their rights was so effective that it placed the pro-lobby on the back foot, forcing them to shape their campaign in response to such arguments. The Oireachtas Committee on Women's Rights, for example, felt compelled to stress on the eve of polling that succession rights of children from a first marriage would not change.[118]

Michele Dillon has noted that demand for reform of divorce law in western countries pre-dated the arrival of second wave feminism. The case was the reverse in Ireland, where demands in the 1980s followed twenty years of vigorous feminist organisation and activity in the West. Irish women could thus be expected to argue vigorously in favour of divorce, but this was not the case.[119] Divorce had not been on the agenda of the Irish Women's Liberation Movement in the 1970s and was not directly included in *Chains or Change?*, although that document did contain a 'five reasons to live in sin' section. Nell McCafferty later described the omission as an example of their innocence: 'It just did not occur to us that marriage could or should be legally terminated'. Abortion was not considered either. 'In truth, we hadn't a clue about these matters'.[120] This was despite the fact that June Levine was one of the twelve founding members of the IWLM. Levine, who had married at the age of nineteen, was scathing about attitudes towards marital breakdown in Ireland. In an article for *Women's Aim* in 1980, she described feeling alone, like a 'rare creature who had had everything and fluffed it'.[121] Dillon noted that 'the comments of the women columnists in the national press, Mary Holland and Nuala O'Faolain of *The Irish Times* and Nell McCafferty of the *Irish Press*, all well-known Irish feminists and advocates of women's rights, were distinctive for the paucity of remarks specifically discussing divorce and women'.[122]

The Council for the Status of Women welcomed the legislation and urged people to vote in favour of the referendum. However, it did not assume an activist role during the campaign, despite endorsing the referendum. This underscored its role as an administrative organisation for women's groups rather than as an active lobby.[123] There was strong opposition to divorce from women, particularly mothers, who feared the economic consequences of marital breakdown. The impoverishment of women was a central theme of the ADC's campaign strategy. William Binchy pointed out that divorced women would no longer have succession rights, protection under the Family Home Protection Act or an entitlement to maintenance under the Family Law (Maintenance of Spouses and Children) Act. He claimed that 'whatever statutory protection would replace them simply could not be as effective as they are now'.[124] Politicians opposing the amendment echoed his views. Oliver J. Flanagan was not alone in claiming that 'the divorced woman would never be far from poverty'.[125] It was a very real concern for women. Although the number of women in the workforce had grown exponentially, their earning power was not as great as men's. The general OECD experience was that about ten times as many women as men were heads of single families after marital breakdown, and that the outstanding feature of those families was low income and a very high risk of poverty.[126] A 1980 survey of single motherhood in Northern Ireland conducted by the Equal Opportunities Commission found that nine per cent of Northern Ireland's families were single-parent families, and, of that group, divorced and separated women were the largest sub-group. Of the entire grouping, which also included widows and unmarried mothers, sixty-eight per cent of the families recorded an income below the poverty line. Single male parents accounted for only eight per cent of the total, and few, due to the financial security of employment, fell below the poverty line.[127]

The experience of deserted wives in Ireland also served as a cautionary tale. A number of submissions to the working party on women's affairs and family law reform, which reported in February 1985, referred to the difficulty which many separated wives had in securing maintenance from their husbands.[128] Although opinion polls in the lead up to voting day suggested that the referendum would be carried, support for the measure was gendered. As Frances Gardiner has pointed out, while forty-six per cent of men intended to vote against the measure, the number of women voting the same way, at sixty-four per cent, was considerably higher, indicating an anxiety.[129] Mary Harney was not alone in lamenting Alice Glenn's likening of women voting for divorce to turkeys voting for Christmas.[130] However, the much-recited and often-criticised remark made during the debate on the second stage of the amendment in the Dáil did actually capture a genuine sense of fear.

The conservative lobby also linked a woman's identity to her marital status. Glenn spoke of how there could be no family home after the departure of the husband. As the Constitution protects the family, the divorced wife 'becomes a non-person', she argued.[131] The pro-lobby attempted to counter the ADC by stressing benefits to women. In an eve of voting address, FitzGerald told voters that they were being misled. He sought to assure them that voting yes would not be against their interest: 'If it were, I would never have been associated with this proposal'. The position of wives would be strengthened by the amendment, giving them property rights in the family home that they did not already have. He appealed to voters to 'think of those women and children who are presently trapped in unhappy situations' and to give them a choice by voting yes.[132] His appeal was reproduced as a message to voters on the front-page of the *Irish Independent* on polling day.[133] However, Fergus Finlay 'came to believe ... that a great many women, who had been prepared to vote for divorce before it started, began to see divorce as a reward for philandering husbands'.[134]

Although the referendum split society, it was far less divisive than the abortion campaign had been. For Fine Gael, however, it contributed further to the divisions within the party. The liberal-conservative divide in the party was almost immediately apparent after FitzGerald announced that he favoured a referendum, in response to which Paddy Cooney publicly declared that the majority of Fine Gael was opposed. During the campaign, Cooney continued to stress his opposition to divorce, and his stance influenced many of the rural deputies. The majority of Fine Gael deputies did not participate in the campaign, although Charlie Flanagan recalled one surreal moment that aptly captured the divisions in Fine Gael. While addressing a pro-divorce meeting, his father, Oliver J., was addressing an anti-divorce meeting in the next room.[135] One figure who kept a low-profile was John Burton. He recalled making only one speech on the subject. Though he publicly supported the government, privately, as a conventional Catholic, he was opposed to divorce. Bruton would go on to become Fine Gael leader in 1990 and Taoiseach between 1994 and 1997. During his time in power, divorce was eventually legalised, albeit by a slender majority. By then, Bruton had revised his views on divorce, but they were still framed in conservative terms. Acknowledging that marriages were breaking down anyway, he came to see divorce as offering individuals a chance to remarry. Divorce, as he explained, was not primarily about separating couples, but rather it could preserve the institution of marriage by giving people a second chance.[136] Throughout the 1986 campaign, the notion of protecting the institution of marriage by allowing divorce in restrictive circumstances was emphasised. Echoing the views of his party leader at a meeting in Donegal, Paddy O'Toole, Fine Gael TD for Mayo East and Minister for the Gaeltacht and Defence, affirmed that the 'purpose of introducing divorce legislation was ultimately to allow for the possibility of remarriage'.[137]

Magazines and letters' pages offer a flavour of the view of ordinary citizens on divorce. *Woman's Way* carried a feature on separation in its January 1986 edition. Mary, one of the women interviewed, maintained her opposition to divorce, despite the fact that she was separated. She felt that it was important psychologically for her children to know that their parents would always stay married, despite not living together.[138] Similarly, Mrs M. K. of Tipperary wrote to the editor of *Woman's Way* to express the view that 'one husband, one wife must be the rule', and she stressed the importance of both persons to child-rearing.[139] The experience of Jane, recorded in *Women's Aim*, contrasted with the views of Mary and Mrs M. K. She wrote of how her parents had separated when she was twelve: 'judging our lives before and after the split, I believe good one parent families are better for the children ... Living in a home where there is nothing but constant rows and unhappiness is bound to have an effect on anyone, but more so on young impressionable children. I found this myself'.[140] Similarly, Dick Keane of Dun Laoghaire in Co Dublin, drew a distinction between the trauma of marital breakdown and of divorce in a letter to the editor of the *Irish Independent*: 'the tragedy of marriage breakdown is a deep trauma for all concerned – husband, wife and children. Divorce is merely the legal ending of a marriage already irretrievably broken down'.[141] Far from being the easy option, John McGahern likened divorce to death, 'but instead of that inevitable end, the person that we have loved stands there as a living reproach of deep failure'.[142]

MRBI had been tracking public opinion on divorce since September 1983. Between then and February 1986, before the government issued its statement of intent, a total of seven national opinion polls were conducted for *The Irish Times*. A substantial majority, rising from sixty-five per cent in September 1983 to seventy-seven per cent in February 1986, responded favourably to the question, 'Do you feel that divorce should be permitted in certain circumstances, or do you feel that it should never be permitted here in Ireland?'[143] However, when an additional question was included that asked voters if they would vote to remove or retain the constitutional ban on divorce in a referendum, the reaction was less favourable. In general, there was a twenty-five per cent differential between those who felt divorce should be permitted in certain circumstances and those who would vote to remove the ban from the Constitution. Jack Jones, MRBI chairman, concluded that although the findings clearly showed sympathy towards marital breakdown, there was also a definite concern that divorce should not be a 'free for all' situation. It was thus apparent from January 1985 that the wording of the amendment would have to specifically address the circumstances voters had in mind. 'In my opinion, it would have been very difficult, if not impossible, to draft legislation to meet these perceived circumstances', he noted.[144]

To that point, those surveyed were being asked about a theoretical situation. However, once the government published its statement of intent on 24 April 1986, the referendum, and thus the possibility of divorce, became a reality. Naturally, MRBI revised the style of question to reflect this. Having provided the actual wording of the proposed amendment, the question asked if the individual would vote for or against the amendment that would permit divorce in certain circumstances. The first such poll, conducted on 24 April and published in *The Irish Times* on 5 May, found that fifty-seven per cent intended to vote yes, while thirty-six per cent would vote no and seven per cent were undecided.[145] Although the pro-lobby was still ahead, there appeared to be a twenty per cent drop in support since February of those who favoured the introduction of divorce in certain circumstances. This may well be explained by the shift from the theoretical to the real, or, as Pat Lyons discusses, a change from 'easy' to 'hard' questions. The polls taken in a non-campaign period did not necessitate that participants give any immediate consideration to the implications of public policy. In contrast, polls conducted during the referendum campaign involved consideration by participants of specific changes to the Constitution.[146]

On 15 June, with eleven days to polling, the *Sunday Independent* published the findings of an IMS poll with the summation: 'the pro-divorce lobby ... now seems set for victory'. Although support had fallen considerably from the twenty-one point lead recorded by *The Irish Times*/MRBI poll in April, the lobby was still ahead by twelve points or a fifty-six per cent to forty-four per cent majority in favour. The survey of voter opinion also revealed that, for the first time, with the exception of Fianna Fáil, the other political parties had a pro-divorce majority among their supporters.[147] The *Sunday Independent*'s prediction seemed premature, however, when, five days later, an MRBI poll published in *The Irish Times* showed the no-lobby in the lead with fifty-five per cent intending to vote against the amendment. The swing was confirmed in an MRBI poll conducted for one of the parties on 23 June – three days before polling – that found sixty per cent of voters intended to reject the amendment.[148] The failure of the divorce referendum marked the end of the constitutional crusade. The voters had clearly rejected FitzGerald's agenda to transform Ireland into a pluralist society. The episode further added to the sense of disillusion with those who had supported his attempts to transform Fine Gael. Alan Shatter recalled, 'It was Garret's influence that brought me into Fine Gael. It was nearly Garret's influence that drove me out of Fine Gael'.[149]

The economy

As FitzGerald's government considered socio-moral questions, they also grappled with the ever-struggling economy and the challenge of how to solve the growing national debt. After taking office, the coalition partners announced that the outgoing government had concealed the critical state of the public finances. In an interview with Gerald Barry reviewing the first three months in power, FitzGerald commented that he had 'inherited [a] country facing national bankruptcy'.[150] In his State of the Nation address on 9 January 1980, then Taoiseach Charles Haughey had declared that the country was living beyond its means. Income from taxes in 1979 had fallen short of what was required to run the state, necessitating borrowing at a level that could not be sustained. 'There are many things which will just have to be curtailed or postponed until such time as we can get the financial situation right', he declared.[151] Haughey's address had been prompted by the second oil crisis of the 1970s. However, in contrast to the strategy Haughey outlined, public spending actually increased to the point that Michael O'Kennedy, in a memorandum to his cabinet colleagues later that year, expressed concern about the state of the country's finances. The Minister for Finance stressed the need to avoid excessive spending: 'Little or no effort has been made to stay within expenditure allowances'.[152] The problem persisted. It did not take the opening of the archives for the relevant years to uncover the mishandling of the state finances. 'How Haughey cooked the books in '81' made the front cover of *Magill* in February 1982.[153] What the release of the State papers in 2011 for 1981 did do, however, was to reveal the extent to which a cavalier attitude had prevailed, particularly in relation to entertainment expenses. One submission to the Department of Finance contained a receipt for a 'working dinner' for cabinet members at Johnny's Restaurant, Malahide for £659.96, which surpassed the limit for expenses by £524.96. In addition to the actual dinner, Haughey had also ordered fourteen bottles of wine, a bottle of port and a bottle of brandy, as well as cigars and cigarettes to the value of £34.46. Although the total significantly exceeded the guidelines, it was approved by the Department of Finance.[154] According to another invoice, £280.21 was spent on wine and spirits used for official entertainment by the Taoiseach in his office.[155] Other entertainment receipts included a dinner at Le Coq Hardi Restaurant hosted by Frank Dunlop for selected political correspondents; the bill of £330.71 also exceeded the limit but was passed by the Department of Finance.[156] There are numerous other receipts of a similar nature within the files. Despite often-repeated limitations on expenditure from the Department of Finance, that Department continued to waive the excess spend. Clearly Haughey, contrary to the advice he gave the country, was not tightening the belt of government spending on entertainment, nor was Finance willing to challenge him on it.

John Bruton, who had questioned the state of the country's finance in his reply to the budget the previous year, recalled having suspicions but was, nonetheless, 'shocked that things were that bad'.[157] Nuala Fennell likened it to 'four years spending like drunken sailors'.[158] After naming his cabinet, FitzGerald told the Dáil that 'the scale of the mess is beyond anything that had to be faced previously'.[159] He later explained that while pre-election speeches had made reference to a possible deficit of £800 million, the reality was closer to £950 million and the following year would be worse again.[160] The budget provisions for the year had already been spent, but Haughey's government adjusted the figures to indicate a healthier balance. This was done without making cuts in other areas to provide a cash injection to the state's finances. As the new Taoiseach put it, 'we had not appreciated nor had any idea of [the depth of the problem]'.[161] Earlier that year, *Magill* had run an interview with five leading economists, all of whom were in agreement that if the situation continued there would be major financial collapse, massive unemployment and an erosion of the standard of living.[162] FitzGerald's first administration thus inherited an extraordinarily difficult financial situation.

Such was the scale of the crisis that John Bruton, the new Minister for Finance in the three-week-old coalition, introduced a mini-budget on 21 July 1981. Introducing it, Bruton spoke of how his prime concern was to ensure that Ireland remained an independent economy. He argued that the use of foreign borrowing to finance daily expenses negated the Sinn Féin principle of self-reliance upon which the state was founded.[163] There was something odd about Bruton referring to Sinn Féin principles, given his preference for the Irish Parliamentary Party (IPP). When it came to Fine Gael, he had always emphasised and valued the IPP tradition over the Cumann na nGaedheal, descendants of Michael Collins, element.[164] And later, when he became Taoiseach, a painting of the IPP leader John Redmond famously adorned his office wall rather than the image of Collins usually favoured by Fine Gael Taoisigh. Fianna Fáil's George Colley was responsible for the first budget deficit in 1972, an approach generally replicated by each subsequent Minister for Finance. The cumulative effect was that exchequer-borrowing requirements had been growing to the point where they were no longer sustainable. In 1980, forty-seven per cent of all Irish borrowing was raised outside the country.[165] The government's plan to return the Irish economy to a sound footing was to be based on a dual strategy of revising and curtailing certain expenditure and taxation changes designed to increase the overall tax yield.[166] The *Irish Press* chose the headline 'The squeeze is on' to describe the budget's provisions, which included an increase in VAT from ten per cent to fifteen per cent, four pence on a packet of twenty cigarettes and the re-introduction of car tax.[167]

The government's margin was so tight that Oliver J. Flanagan, who had been admitted to St Vincent's Hospital the previous week with angina and was ordered to rest, was brought to the Dáil. A bed was supplied in the House for him to relax between votes.[168] The budget was carried, generally with the support of Independents Jim Kemmy (formerly of the Labour Party) and Sean Dublin Bay Loftus. Kemmy had contested the 1981 election on a platform advocating the deletion of articles 2 and 3 from the Constitution, describing Ireland's claim of jurisdiction over Northern Ireland as 'bogus'.[169] He strongly approved of the FitzGerald's aim to build a pluralist society and was a consistent supporter of the government until Bruton presented his full budget.

Bruton unveiled his major budget on 27 January 1982. It was his intention to remove the budget deficit, and he introduced a package of direct and indirect taxes. Social welfare increases were only barely mentioned, as commentators focussed on the tougher aspects, which had prompted some deputies to leave the chamber before the Minister finished his speech. The budget is perhaps best remembered for placing VAT on all footwear, including children's shoes. Crucially, Kemmy and Dublin Bay Loftus withdrew their support over the measures. As the division for the first vote was called, FitzGerald was seen kneeling by Kemmy's seat in an unsuccessful attempt to persuade him to support the budget. The government lost the first vote by a margin of one after Kemmy entered the *Níl* (no) lobby.

When FitzGerald returned to power after the November 1982 general election, he appointed Alan Dukes Minister for Finance. Dukes had been Minister for Agriculture in FitzGerald's first government, elevated to that position on his first day in the Dáil. Department officials urged the new Finance Minister to reduce the current budget deficit as quickly as possible and by the maximum possible amount. Labour did not approve of this strategy, and it created tensions between the coalition partners.[170]

The government published the policy document *Building on Reality, 1985–1987* in October 1984. It outlined four main objectives for economic development: increase employment, halt the rise in taxation, improve and develop social policy and reduce borrowing. In *The Way Forward*, the previous Fianna Fáil government had planned to phase out the current budget deficit by 1987. That strategy was replaced in *Building on Reality* with the aim of reducing the deficit to five per cent of GNP. Contemporary commentators were critical of much of the programme. Writing in *The Irish Banking Review*, Patrick Geary, professor of economics at Maynooth College, acknowledged that the government was limited in its scope for designing policy due to past misjudgements and the serious condition of the public finances. He also acknowledged that the plan contained a number of positive elements, such as the allocation of extra resources to road construction, which was expected to yield significant social benefits. However, the plan was not without its shortcomings. Because of Ireland's exposure to world economic conditions due to the importance of trade and the size of foreign debt, forecasts of those conditions would have to be factored into any serious plan. However, *Building on Reality* failed to give an indication of how its targets and policies would be effected if, for example, world interest rates declined. 'The plan should have stated the kind of revisions which would be made should there be a much more or less favourable world economic environment' than outlined in the document. Geary was also surprised that unemployment – considered the most important problem facing the country – was given such little attention. The proposals for profit sharing and work shareholding would have no impact in the short term. Of the decision to replace phasing out the budget deficit by 1987 with a more modest decrease, he observed that 'the government bought some room for manoeuvre in the short term ... [but] has raised the stakes for future years'. If the target were not reached, the government's reputation and credibility would be severely damaged.[171]

On the weekend of 5 October 1986, Bruton acknowledged the severity of the situation. The government had borrowed £4.5 billion since 1984, with interest repayments of £6 billion. Speaking on RTÉ's *This Week*, he said that it would take the country fifteen years to get out of the financial mess. As a step towards solving the financial problems, cuts in public spending would have to be implemented.[172] Depressing figures were released within the space of a week at the start of 1987. The publication on 2 January of the 1986 exchequer returns showed a deficit of £1,385 million, or £145 million more than was targeted in the previous budget. There was a mild reassurance for the government, as the spending over-run was not as high as predicted, although it was still three times the 1985 figure.[173] One week later, the Central Statistics Office released the latest unemployment figures, showing record levels of unemployment. The figure of 250,200 meant that one in five was out of work. The government attributed this to a traditional run-down in activity by many industries at the end of the year, as well as the effects of seasonal work, but the figures, according to Donal Nevin, General Secretary of ICTU, were 'a threat to the fabric of our society'. Haughey was even more damning, describing them, as well as the emigration levels, as 'a massive human disaster'.[174]

By the time that Fine Gael and Labour left office, the national debt had doubled. President Hillery dissolved the twenty-forth Dáil on 21 January 1987. The Labour Party had withdrawn from the coalition the previous day. According to Ruairí Quinn, the Labour Ministers knew from around October 1986 when the estimates started to come through that they would not be able to carry the party with them: 'We went right through Christmas knowing at a certain point that we would withdraw'.[175] The estimates, published on 16 October, included a drawing down of £600 million in foreign loans in an effort to inject some liquidity into the Dublin money markets and to ease pressure on interest rates.[176] More specifically, from the Labour perspective, they also included spending cuts of £250 million. 'Tremors beginning to be felt', Gemma Hussey noted in her diary after the estimates were released.[177] When Labour's formal withdrawal from government finally came in the New Year, Quinn recalled that there were handshakes and some tears in the cabinet room. 'It wasn't rancorous'.[178]

FitzGerald as leader

In reply to those who wondered if Garret FitzGerald was too nice for politics, for the leadership of the country, Conor Cruise O'Brien has remarked, 'He is about as nice as you can be and get ahead in politics, but no nicer. There is steel under all that pretty wool'.[179] Certainly, FitzGerald had risen through the ranks very quickly, his advancement in no way due to his family name. He had marked himself out as a man of ability, and within thirteen years of being elected to Leinster House, he had risen to the leadership – the target that he had set himself on entering politics. He was a man of ambition and determination, but, somewhat paradoxically, he also suffered indecisiveness – a trait that would become increasingly apparent during his second term as Taoiseach. There were other indications also that he sometimes lacked the ability to impose his authority. Vincent Browne reported in *Magill* how, in the aftermath of a by-election in Donegal in November 1980, some Fine Gael deputies, disappointed with the result, felt that inducements were needed and that FitzGerald's message that public expenditure should not be increased was a disincentive to voters. At a meeting of the party in December, John Bruton, then spokesman on Agriculture, announced that he was preparing a programme for farmers that would require substantial commitments on public expenditure. FitzGerald initially repeated the official line, but capitulated a few days later. The programme, costed at £80 million, was publicly unveiled.[180] It sent mixed messages to the public.

His cabinet meetings are legendary, aptly described as marathon sessions that went 'on and on'.[181] It seemed that an enquiring mind, coupled with his training to see debates from all sides, was a hindrance to an academic turned politician. Gemma Hussey's diaries from her time as Minister for Education, written without a view to publication,[182] offer a thorough account of cabinet life during FitzGerald's second government. Though her respect for FitzGerald is clear from her entries, there was a growing sense of frustration about his leadership. In the confines of those private pages, she freely admitted at the start of 1984 that 'the Coalition is proving not to be a great thing for the country' (though she added, 'but the Fianna Fáil alternative is worse').[183] There was a sense that the coalition partners, rather than governing, were actually just 'muddling along'.[184] By May 1986, she had observed, 'There is uncertainty about the life of this Dáil, a nervousness about, a real feeling of something unstable'.[185] The government faced a difficult challenge because of the financial situation it had inherited, although some of their own economic policy choices had exacerbated the situation.

The question of FitzGerald's leadership occurs frequently in Hussey's diaries. The steeliness of character that Cruise O'Brien identified when they served together as ministers in the National Coalition appeared to escape FitzGerald when he became government leader, and, at one point in 1984, Hussey considered him to be someone who lacked steel and could not be 'totally relied on'.[186] She made the observation in the aftermath of the abortion referendum, which FitzGerald himself admitted he did not handle well.[187] The whole episode questioned FitzGerald's strength as a leader. From as early as December 1984, she recorded that his position was 'under fire'. The situation only worsened as FitzGerald's policies continued to divide Fine Gael, so that by May 1986, she considered FitzGerald to no longer be in control of the party. Alan Dukes was mentioned as a possible successor in October.[188] Her suggestion that 'he found it difficult to bring people with him'[189] was certainly accurate. His policies widened the gulf between the party's two wings, and the failure to sell them to the electorate undermined his objective of creating a pluralist society. But although conservative Catholics considered FitzGerald a liberal, there were definite signs that conservative thinking, which Vincent Browne had identified, underpinned his policymaking decisions. This is difficult to reconcile with public and popular perceptions of FitzGerald.

FitzGerald is Fine Gael's most highly regarded leader – a position confirmed by Michael Gallagher's and Michael Marsh's autumn 1999 survey of party members and their views.[190] He redesigned Fine Gael, took the party into power twice and achieved, what was then, its highest point. Less commented on is the fact that he also brought the party to its lowest point and that his stated aim constitutional reform failed. As his coffin, draped in the flag of the Irish Republic, left the Church of the Sacred Heart in Donnybrook on 22 May 2011, it was greeted by spontaneous applause, a gesture repeated by those who lined the funeral cortege's route to the cemetery. But this was not simply a mark of respect for the deceased. The furore that surrounded remarks made by Leo Varadkar, then Fine Gael spokesperson on Enterprise, Trade and Employment in March 2010, revealed the measure of affection for FitzGerald.

Commenting on Fianna Fáil's handling of the country's finances in 2010, the Dublin West TD summoned the legacy of the 1980s to criticise then Taoiseach Brian Cowen. 'The Taoiseach is no Seán Lemass, Jack Lynch or John Bruton', he told the Dáil. 'He is a Garret FitzGerald. He has trebled the national debt and effectively destroyed the country'.[191] His comparison, but, more particularly, his criticism of his party's former leader caused consternation. The *Evening Herald* reported that a major row had erupted in Fine Gael.[192] Fergus O'Dowd, the party's TD for Louth, led the calls for Varadkar to retract his statement. Even Fianna Fáil's Pat Carey criticised the

Fine Gael TD on RTÉ's current affairs programme, *Prime Time*.[193] Varadkar later remarked that what he had said in the Dáil was over the top, but that he stood over his criticisms of FitzGerald's performance as Taoiseach in the realm of economics.[194] He had a valid point about that government's economic legacy. It was Eamonn Sweeney of the *Irish Independent* who best summed up the episode and what it revealed about Fine Gael attitudes: 'Garret FitzGerald is unique in Irish public life in that he is judged not by his achievements, but by his intentions'.[195]

9
A Liberal Ireland?

'The Irish today are torn. Of course, they want to enjoy the fruits of modern material progress. And many of them also want the full personal rights of a modern liberal society; but many others are still warily conservative'.[1] Such were the observations of John Ardagh, who travelled around Ireland between 1991 and 1993 researching his book, *Ireland and the Irish*. He was writing in the aftermath of a divorce and two abortion referenda, when the Irish electorate voted conclusively to maintain the conservative status quo. Since 1972, the Irish people have voted for change in the area of 'regime': adjusting the voting age and approving membership of the European Community, for example. However, on issues of a moral nature, there has not been the same willingness to embrace change.[2]

By the time that Garret Fitzgerald stepped down as leader of Fine Gael, he had taken the party to both its highest and lowest points, and when he left office, Fine Gael had ten seats less than when he had taken over. The party was also suffering an identity crisis. The divisions, which had emerged in the 1960s over Declan Costello's Just Society, became far more pronounced as FitzGerald took the party into government because, unlike Costello, he actually had the opportunity to implement his policies. As already discussed, he carried out a delicate balancing act as he attempted to keep together a party internally divided on all of the major socio-moral issues that faced his government.

Alan Dukes succeeded FitzGerald, becoming the party's youngest leader. What followed was a period of instability as the leadership became the target for members disgruntled with the party's problems. Dukes was considered aloof by some, and the advisability of his Tallaght Strategy – which was, in fact, first proposed by FitzGerald on results' night in 1987 – was questioned by some elements in the party. Although Fine Gael's share of the vote rose marginally in 1989, Dukes's leadership was not secure and it was fatally compromised by the 1990 presidential election. The failure to deliver a high-profile candidate, combined with a lacklustre campaign, resulted in a motion of no confidence, which Dukes pre-empted by resigning on

30 November 1990. The efforts by a section of the party to oust him ushered in a new phase in the party. Until that point, as John Bruton pointed out, Fine Gael had acted like a family.[3] Now, however, the party began to turn on its leader as frustrations grew. As Olivia O'Leary put it, 'it is a real sign of a party in free-fall when it becomes a serial leader killer'.[4]

During FitzGerald's second term in office, Dukes, Hussey and FitzGerald were closer to the Labour ministers than most of their colleagues. They represented the more social progressive elements of the party. When John Bruton succeeded Alan Dukes, the more conservative elements once again dominated the party. As Fine Gael struggled to locate its place in the party system, he spent ten uneasy years at the helm, surviving no less than three motions of no-confidence, before becoming the first Fine Gael leader to be voted out of that position. Despite ordering a review of the party's difficulties and taking Fine Gael into government in 1994, he was ousted by the self-styled 'dream team'[5] of Michael Noonan and Jim Mitchell. This latest leadership challenge unsettled the party on the eve of the 2002 election, and the campaign never really got off the ground. Fine Gael's 2002 contest was summed up in Geraldine Kennedy's observation that 'the crass non-professionalism' was astounding; by the image of a Roscommon voter shoving a pie in the face of Michael Noonan, who was haunted by the legacy of the Hepatitis C scandal from his time as Minister for Health; and of a visibly distraught Noonan conceding election as his party colleagues lost their seats in spectacular numbers. Fine Gael's vote collapsed, leaving it with its lowest ever share of Dáil seats. The in-fighting had almost destroyed the party, practically wiping out the frontbench, and, not for the first time, it left many wondering about the future. As Gay Mitchell remarked, 'the electorate was unsure what we stood for'.[6]

Aside from leadership disputes and internal arguments, Fine Gael's position in the party system was disrupted by the birth of the Progressive Democrats in 1985. There was growing discontent over the social-democratic complexion that FitzGerald had created for Fine Gael. There was no alternative for the discontented, however, until the arrival of the PDs in 1985. Although that party originated from a split from Fianna Fáil, it predominantly attracted Fine Gael voters. Its neoliberal outlook and message of tax reform were attractive to Fine Gael members, most notably Michael McDowell who had served as chairman of FitzGerald's Dublin South-East constituency and would eventually become leader of the new party. During their existence, the PDs continued to attract support away from Fine Gael, until that trend was eventually reversed at the 2007 general election. Eoin O'Malley and Mathew Kirby, in their perceptive study of Fine Gael's decline after the FitzGerald era, concluded that, while both Labour and the PDs attracted support from Fine Gael, the party's decline had been due to the loss of its *raison d'être*, that is, to provide the basis for alternative governments.[7] That loss was due to Fianna Fáil's 'coalitionability'. Fine Gael had always been an essential element in any effort to remove Fianna Fáil from power. But with Fianna Fáil more willing to consider alliances with other parties, it was possible for voters to influence the composition of government without including Fine Gael, with the result that the party became irrelevant to government formation.[8]

In the aftermath of 2002's historic low, Frank Flannery authored a major report. 'Forget about history, traditions, places in history, famous old faces, and political records', he advised. In some ways, his advice had much in common with Costello's Just Society, which also turned its back on the past, and encouraged Fine Gael to concern itself with the future. The process of re-building Fine Gael after 2002 culminated with the party finally returning to government in 2011 under Enda Kenny's leadership. It was not a simple process, however, and frustration once more manifested itself in a leadership challenge in February 2010 when Richard Bruton, unsuccessfully, attempted to displace Kenny.

After the 2011 general election, Fine Gael emerged as the largest party in the State, forming a coalition with the Labour Party. Tensions or disagreements in a party are always far more apparent in government, and Fine Gael has once more found its cohesiveness publicly challenged by the issue of abortion. Despite developments in society, abortion remains a divisive topic. On 28 October 2012, Savita Halappanavar, who was seventeen weeks pregnant, died at University Hospital Galway after suffering a miscarriage. Her husband maintained that she had requested an abortion, which had been denied as a foetal heartbeat was detectable. Although initially denying the remark, Ann Maria Burke, midwife manager at Galway University Hospital, admitted telling the Halappanavar family that Savita could not have an abortion because 'Ireland is a Catholic Country'.[9] The Dublin North TD Clare Daly had already attempted to force the issue of abortion back on to the political agenda earlier that year, on the twentieth anniversary of the X Case. Halappanavar's death brought the subject back onto the agenda in a far more dramatic way as reports made both domestic and international newspapers. Although *The Irish Times* noted that 'abortion views of some Fine Gael TDs have shifted',[10] it was still a case that Fine Gael was the 'most divided of the main parties on the issue of abortion'.[11] As a political party, Fine Gael has obviously modernised and strengthened its structures and organisations, but on socio-moral issues, there is a definite line of continuity with the party's conservative past. On 30 April 2013, after a marathon cabinet meeting, the Fine Gael-Labour coalition announced that the Protection of Life in Pregnancy Bill would be brought before the Oireachtas.

At a press conference the following morning, Taoiseach and Fine Gael leader Enda Kenny stressed that the Bill would only legislate for the decision resulting from the referendum that followed the X Case, and that it was not designed to introduce new terms. He also confirmed that the whip would be applied.[12] Lucinda Creighton, Minister of State for European Affairs, had already expressed deep personal reservations about the legislation and she became the most high-profile member of the government to defy the whip. This resulted in her automatic expulsion from the Fine Gael parliamentary party and her replacement as junior minister by the Dublin-Central TD Paschal Donohoe. She was one of only five government members to vote against the legislation as some TDs who had previously expressed doubts or concerns followed the official government line.

The Protection of Life During Pregnancy Bill was approved in the Dáil by 127 votes to 31 and subsequently by the Seanad in July 2013. Before signing it into law, President Michael D. Higgins exercised his right under Article 26 of the Constitution and convened the Council of State to discuss the content of the Bill. However, he ultimately decided not to refer the legislation to the Supreme Court to test its constitutionality. The legislation is a development in terms of abortion rights in Ireland and there has been a far wider debate in parliament than ever before, but the historical importance of the Bill should not be over-stated: it is a limited measure. Clare Daly had earlier accused the government of framing legislation 'so restrictive that most women who will be affected will not bother and, instead, they will continue to make the journey to Britain so that the Government can continue to pretend that there is no Irish abortion'.[13] The debate in 2012/13 is certainly no where near as divisive as it was in the 1980s, but much of the rhetoric, particularly on the pro-life side, strongly echoes that of the 1980s pointing to the persistence of conservatism on certain issues of morality in Irish politics and society.

Long before Declan Costello or Garret FitzGerald, Fine Gael had always been a coalition of interests. Its antecedents, Cumann na nGaedheal, were held together by support for the Anglo-Irish Treaty, while other important policy areas, in particular, the economic question of free trade versus protection, divided members. But what Costello and, more particularly, FitzGerald, did was to move to the party in a direction that did not sit comfortably with Fine Gael's traditional stance. The party has had to contend with this ever since.

Notes

Introduction

1. Interview with Jim O'Keeffe, 26 January 2010.
2. Interview with Garret FitzGerald, 8 September 2009.
3. *Irish Independent*, 7 June 2011.
4. G. FitzGerald (1964) 'Seeking a National Purpose', *Studies*; G. FitzGerald (1972) *Towards a New Ireland* (London: C. Knight).
5. See Hugh O'Connell's article for *The Journal*. *i.e.*: http://www.thejournal.ie/taoiseach-pays-tribute-to-former-high-court-president-declan-costello-149899-Jun2011/ [accessed 2 July 2011].
6. *The Irish Times*, 12 October 1981.
7. *FitzGerald at 80*, RTÉ1, first aired August 2006.
8. *Irish Independent*, 19 May 2011.
9. B. Girvin, B. (2008) 'Continuity, Change and Crisis in Ireland: New Perspectives, Research and Interpretation', *Irish Political Studies*, 23, 4, p. 457.
10. B. Maye (1993) *Fine Gael, 1923–1987: A General History with Biographical Sketches of Leading Members* (Dublin: Blackwater Press), p. ii.
11. T. Bartlett (2010) *Ireland: A History* (Cambridge: Cambridge University Press); D. Ferrier (2004) *The Transformation of Ireland 1900–2000* (London: Profile Books); D. Keogh (1994) *Twentieth Century Ireland: Nation and State* (Dublin: Gill and Macmillan). He does not feature in A. Jackson (1999) *Ireland 1798–1998: Politics and War* (Oxford: Blackwell Publishing) or J.J. Lee (1989) *Ireland, 1912–1985: Politics and Society* (Cambridge: Cambridge University Press).
12. *The Irish Times*, 8 June 2011.

1 A New Ireland?

1. J. McGahern (1991) *Amongst Women* (London: Faber), pp. 4–5.
2. This is the title given to a collection of essays edited by Dermot Keogh, Finbarr O'Shea and Carmel Quinlan (Cork, 2004).
3. E. Hobsbawm (1995) *Age of Extremes: The Short Twentieth Century, 1914–1991* (London: Michael Joseph), p. 288.
4. R. Burke Savage (1963) 'Ireland 1963–1973', *Studies*, p. 115.
5. D. Thornley (1964) 'Ireland: The End of an Era?', *Studies*, p. 53.
6. M. Laffan (1999) *The Resurrection of Ireland: The Sinn Féin Party, 1916–1923* (Cambridge: Cambridge University Press), p. 259.
7. J. A. Murphy (1975) *Ireland in the Twentieth Century* (Dublin: Gill and Macmillan), p. 10.
8. R. Fanning (1983) *Independent Ireland* (Dublin: Helicon) p. 39.
9. M. O'Callagan (1984) 'Language, Nationality and Cultural Identity in the Irish Free State, 1922–7: The *Irish Statesman* and the *Catholic Bulletin* Reappraised', *Irish Historical Studies*, 14, 94, p. 227.
10. C. Meehan (2010) *The Cosgrave Party: A History of Cumann na nGaedheal, 1923–1933* (Dublin: Royal Irish Academy), pp. 44–60.

11. Fanning, *Independent Ireland*, p. 59.
12. *Quadragesimo Anno: Encyclical of Pope Pius XI on Reconstruction of the Social Order* (1931).
13. L. Fuller (2002) *Irish Catholicism since 1950: The Undoing of a Culture* (Dublin: Gill and Macmillan), p. 69.
14. E. McKee (1986) 'Church-State Relations and the Development of Irish Health Policy: The Mother and Child Scheme, 1944–53', *Irish Historical Studies*, 25, 98, pp. 159–94.
15. M. Rogan (2011) *Prison Policy in Ireland: Politics, Penal-Welfarism and Political Imprisonment* (New York: Routledge), p. 86.
16. T. Judt (2005) *Postwar: A History of Europe since 1945* (London: Heinemann), p. 91. In the case of Britain, the money was needed to pay off the country's massive debt, and consequently had no impact on investment or modernisation of industry, p. 161.
17. Judt, *Postwar*, p. 97.
18. Cormac Ó Gráda, 'Five Crises', Central Bank of Ireland TK Whitaker Lecture, 29 June 2011. Available from http://www.centralbank.ie/press-area/speeches/Pages/AddressbyProfessorCormacO'Gráda,oftheSchoolofEconomics,UCD,totheCentralBankWhitakerLecture,29June,2011.aspx [accessed 10 July 2012].
19. T. Garvin (2010) *News from a New Republic: Ireland in the 1950s* (Dublin: Gill and Macmillan), p. 28.
20. G. Murphy (2004) 'From Economic Nationalism to European Union', in B. Girvin and G. Murphy (eds.), *The Lemass Era: Politics and Society in the Ireland of Seán Lemass* (Dublin: University College Dublin Press), p. 29.
21. *The Irish Times*, 27 February 1956, quoted in Garvin, *News from a New Republic*, p. 53.
22. J. K. Jacobsen (1994) *Chasing Progress in the Irish Republic: Ideology, Democracy and Dependent Development* (Cambridge: Cambridge University Press), p. 64.
23. C. Ó Gráda (1997) *A Rocky Road: The Irish Economy since the 1920s* (Manchester: Manchester University Press), p. 57.
24. Garvin, *News from a New Republic*, p. 53.
25. S. J. Lee (1996) *Aspects of British Political History, 1914–1995* (London, New York: Routledge), p. 199.
26. Murphy, 'From Economic Nationalism to European Union', p. 29.
27. Quoted in Ó Gráda, *A Rocky Road*, p. 74.
28. J. B. Keane (1999) *Many Young Men of Twenty: A Bar-Room Sketch* (Dublin: Mercier Press), p. 135.
29. J. A. O'Brien (ed.) (1954) *The Vanishing Irish: The Enigma of the Modern World* (London: W.H. Allen).
30. D. B. Rottman and P. J. O'Connell (1982) 'The Changing Social Structure', in F. Litton (ed.), *Unequal Achievement: The Irish Experience, 1957–1982* (Dublin: Institute of Public Administration), p. 79.
31. R. C. Geary (1951) 'Irish Economic Development since the Treaty', *Studies*, 40, p. 401.
32. E. Delaney (2004) 'The vanishing Irish? The Exodus from Ireland in the 1950s', in D. Keogh, F. O'Shea and C. Quinlan (eds.), *The Lost Decade: Ireland in the 1950s* (Cork: Mercier), p. 81.
33. Quoted in F. Tobin (1984) *The Best of Decades: Ireland in the Nineteen Sixties* (Dublin: Gill and Macmillan), p. 37.
34. See C. Meehan (2011) 'Michael Sweetman and the Just Society', in B. Sweetman-Fitzgerald (ed.), *Essays in Memory of Michael Sweetman* (Dublin: A&A Farmar).

35. Quoted in D. Ferriter (2007) *Judging Dev: A Reassessment of the Life and Legacy of Eamon de Valera* (Dublin: Royal Irish Academy), p. 285.
36. E. Delaney (1998) 'State, Politics and Demography: The Case of Irish Emigration, 1921–71', *Irish Political Studies*, 31, 1, p. 34.
37. Quoted in D. Ferriter (2004) *The Transformation of Ireland 1900–2000* (London: Profile Books), p. 478.
38. Garvin, *News from a New republic*, p. 60.
39. Quoted in J. Ardagh (1995) *Ireland and the Irish: Portrait of a Changing Society* (London: Penguin), p. 9.
40. B. Girvin and G. Murphy (2005) 'Whose Ireland? The Lemass Era', in B. Girvin and G. Murphy (eds.), *The Lemass Era: Politics and Society in the Ireland of Seán Lemass* (Dublin: University College Dublin Press), p. 7.
41. Address to the Irish Association, 19 March 1957, reproduced in *Studies* (1957) 46, 182 (summer 1957), pp. 137–49.
42. Fuller, *Irish Catholicism since 1950*, p. 80.
43. P. Fitzgerald and B. Lambkin (2008) *Migration in Irish history, 1607–2007* (Basingstoke: Palgrave Macmillan), p. 226.
44. A. Punch and C. Finneran (2000) 'Changing Population Structure', in A. Redmond (ed.), *That was Then, This is Now: Change in Ireland, 1949–1999* (Dublin: Central Statistics Office), p. 14.
45. P. Conroy (1999) 'From the Fifties to the Nineties: Social Policy Comes Out of the Shadows', in G. Kelly, A. O'Donnell, P. Kennedy and S. Quinn (eds.), *Irish Social Policy in Context* (Dublin: University College Dublin Press), pp. 34–5.
46. J. Lee (1982) 'Society and Culture', in F. Litton (ed.), *Unequal Achievement: The Irish Experience, 1957–1982* (Dublin: Institute of Public Administration), p. 3.
47. Rottman and O'Connell, 'The Changing Social Structure', p. 68.
48. T. Garvin (2004) *Preventing the Future. Why was Ireland so Poor for so Long?* (Dublin: Gill and Macmillan), pp. 33–4.
49. I am grateful to Dr Kevin Rafter of DCU for drawing my attention to this.
50. Garvin, *News from a New Republic*, p. 13.
51. D. Murphy (2000) 'Introduction', in A. Redmond (ed.), *That was Then, This is Now: Change in Ireland, 1949–1999* (Dublin: Central Statistics Office), p. 6.
52. A. Redmond and M. Heanne (2000) 'Aspects of Society', in A. Redmond (ed.), *That was Then, This is Now: Change in Ireland, 1949–1999* (Dublin: Central Statistics Office), p. 52.
53. A. Reynolds (2009) *My Autobiography* (London: Transworld Ireland), p. 29.
54. J. McGahern (2005) *Memoir* (London: Faber), p. 2.
55. Quoted in Fuller, *Irish Catholicism since 1950*, p. 123.
56. T. Farmar (2011) *Privileged Lives: A Social History of Middle-Class Ireland, 1882–1989* (Dublin: A&A Farmar), pp. 203 and 233.
57. McGahern, *Memoir*, p. 164.
58. G. Kerrigan (1998) *Another Country: Growing up in '50s Ireland* (Dublin: Gill and Macmillan), p. 161.
59. J. Bowman (2011) *Window and Mirror: RTÉ Television, 1961–2011* (Cork: Collins Press), p. 75.
60. *Woman's Way*, 3 May 1985.
61. D. Ferriter (2009) *Occasions of Sin: Sex and Society in Modern Ireland* (London: Profile Books), p. 374.
62. Quoted in Bowman, *Window and Mirror*, p. 20.
63. Quoted in *Nusight*, 13 October 1967.

64. P. Ryan (2012) *Asking Angela Macnamara: An Intimate History of Irish Lives* (Dublin: Irish Academic Press), p. 16.
65. Fuller, *Irish Catholicism since 1950*, p. 107.
66. Ian Linden (2000) quoted in 'The Priest in Politics', in J. Dunne, A. Ingram and F. Litton (eds.), *Questioning Ireland: Debates in Political Philosophy and Public Policy* (Dublin: Institute of Public Administration), p. 242.
67. P. Ginsborg (1990) *A History of Contemporary Italy: Society and Politics, 1943–1988* (London: Penguin), p. 260.
68. *Mater et Magistra: Encyclical of Pope John XXIII on Christianity and Social Progress* (1961).
69. Fuller, *Irish Catholicism since 1950*, p. 110.
70. *Towards a Just Society* (1965).
71. Tobin, *The Best of Decades*.
72. Quoted in Farmar, *Privileged Lives*, p. 240.
73. Quoted in D. Ferriter (2010) '"The Stupid Propaganda of the Calamity Mongers"?: The Middle Class and Irish Politics, 1945–97', in F. Lane (ed.), *Politics, Society and the Middle Class in Modern Ireland* (Basingstoke: Palgrave Macmillan, 2010), p. 273.
74. Rottman and O'Connell, 'The Changing Social Structure', p. 75.
75. Ginsborg, *A History of Contemporary Italy*, pp. 213 and 216.
76. N. Acheson, B. Harvey, J. Kearney and A. Williamson (2004) *Two Paths, One Purpose: Voluntary Action in Ireland, North and South* (Dublin: Institute of Public Affairs), p. 93.
77. Farmar, *Privileged Lives*, p. 200.
78. J. Downey (2009) *In My Own Time: Inside Irish Politics and Society* (Dublin: Gill and Macmillan), p. 50.
79. *The Irish Times*, 17 June 1963.
80. Returns had not been received from Limerick Corporation, Clonmel Borough Council, and the City Councils of Carlow, Cavan, Clare, Cork South, Donegal, Galway, Kilkenny, Laois, Limerick, Louth, Monaghan, Waterford and Wexford.
81. *Dáil debates*, vol. 203, cols. 997–1000, 18 June 1963 (Neil Blaney).
82. *Dáil debates*, vol. 203, col. 1177, 18 June 1963 (Declan Costello).
83. M. Considine and Fiona Dukelow (2009) *Irish Social Policy: A Critical Introduction* (Dublin: Gill and Macmillan), p. 347.
84. Transcript of *One-to-One* interview conducted by David McCullagh, first broadcast 14 September 2009, RTÉ1.
85. Correspondence with Declan Costello, 12 March 2009.
86. D. McCullagh (2010) *The Reluctant Taoiseach: A Biography of John A Costello* (Dublin, Gill and Macmillan), pp. 147 and 163.
87. *The Irish Times*, 9 March 1985.
88. Transcript of *One-to-One* interview conducted by David McCullagh, first broadcast 14 September 2009, RTÉ1.
89. Transcript of *One-to-One* interview conducted by David McCullagh, first broadcast 14 September 2009, RTÉ1.
90. Conversation with Declan Costello, 5 February 2009.
91. Extract from Declan Costello interview, reproduced on *Bowman: Sunday Morning*, RTÉ Radio 1, 12 June 2011.

2 Winning the Party

1. John A. Costello to James Dillon, 13 January 1960, P190/340, Costello Papers, University College Dublin Archives (hereafter UCDA).

2. Meeting of the parliamentary party, Fine Gael Minute Books, in possession of Maurice Manning.
3. *Irish Times*, 24 October 1964.
4. M. Gallagher and M. Marsh (2002) *Days of Blue Loyalty: The Politics of Membership of the Fine Gael Party* (Dublin: PSAI Press), p. 26.
5. John A. Costello to James Dillon, 13 January 1960, P190/340, Costello Papers, UCDA.
6. Circular to Fine Gael parliamentary party, 27 April 1964, in possession of the Costello family.
7. C. Meehan (2010) *The Cosgrave Party: A History of Cumann na nGaedheal, 1923–1933* (Dublin: Royal Irish Academy), pp. 215–24.
8. K. Rafter (2009) *Fine Gael: Party at the Crossroads* (Dublin: New Island), p. 102.
9. C. O'Leary (1979) *Irish Elections, 1918–1977: Parties, Voters and Proportional Representation* (Dublin: Gill and Macmillan), p. 38.
10. P. Lindsay (1992) *Memories* (Dublin: Blackwater Press), pp. 152–53.
11. Lindsay, *Memories*, p. 156.
12. F. Dunlop (2004) *Yes, Taoiseach: Irish Politics from Behind Closed Doors* (Dublin: Penguin Ireland), p. 11.
13. D. McCullagh (2010) *The Reluctant Taoiseach: A Biography of John A Costello* (Dublin, Gill and Macmillan), p. 372.
14. Meeting of the parliamentary party, 18 November 1959, Fine Gael minute books.
15. M. Gallagher and M. Marsh (2002) *Days of Blue Loyalty: The Politics of Membership of the Fine Gael Party* (Dublin: PSAI Press), p. 49.
16. John Bruton (1993) 'Foreword', in B. Maye (ed.), *Fine Gael, 1923–1987: A General History with Biographical Sketches of Leading Members* (Dublin: Blackwater Press), p. iii.
17. Costello was leader of the Opposition, while Richard Mulcahy was leader of Fine Gael. This peculiar dual role was a legacy of the arrangements for the first inter-party government, which were retained for the second also. Formed in 1948, almost the full spectrum of the Irish party system came together to bring to an end sixteen years of un-interrupted Fianna Fáil government. As Fine Gael was the largest of the parties, Mulcahy, as leader, should have become Taoiseach. However, he was unacceptable to Sean MacBride of the republican Clann na Poblachta because of the Civil War legacy. Consequently, a 'compromise Taoiseach' emerged in John A. Costello – who had no connection with the military aspect of the independence struggle – while Mulcahy remained leader of Fine Gael.
18. McCullagh, *Reluctant Taoiseach*, p. 379.
19. M. Manning (1999) *James Dillon: A Biography* (Dublin: Wolfhound Press), p. 327. The figures are doubtful, however, as they exceed the number of members of the parliamentary party.
20. Quoted in T. Garvin (2009) *Judging Lemass: the Measure of the Man* (Dublin: Royal Irish Academy), p. 207.
21. B. Evans (2011) *Seán Lemass: Democratic Dictator* (Cork: Collins Press), p. 213.
22. During the course of the debate, references were made to the Civil War, the 77 executions, the Blueshirts and to the Locke's Distillery case of 1948. Brian Lenihan told the opposition 'the gas chamber is the place for you ... you are good manure that is all you are'. See Farmar, *Privileged Lives*, p. 249.
23. *National Observer*, vol. 2, no. 5 (November 1959), P53/509, Hayes Papers, UCDA.
24. John Healy writing in *Irish Farmers Journal*, 8 May 1965.
25. Meeting of the parliamentary party, Fine Gael minute books.
26. Circular from Richard Mulcahy to all front bench members, 30 October 1957, P151/804, MacEoin Papers, UCDA.

27. Meeting of the parliamentary party, 26 February 1964, Fine Gael minute books.
28. *Irish Times*, 18 May 1964.
29. John A. Costello to Fine Gael North Cork Annual Constituency Convention, 6 December 1957, *Fine Gael Digest*, vol. 8, no. 1 (February 1958), pp. 4 and 18.
30. Ard Fheis speech, 5 February 1958, P190/315, Costello papers, UCDA.
31. Meeting of the parliamentary party, 9 July 1958, Fine Gael minute books.
32. J. H. Whyte (2003) 'Reconciliation, Rights and Protests, 1963–8', in J. R. Hill (ed.), *A New History of Ireland: Volume 7: Ireland, 1921–84* (Oxford: Oxford University Press), p. 622.
33. Speech by Dillon, *Fine Gael Digest*, Ard Fheis issue (1960), p. 8.
34. There had been a scarcity of initiatives to eradicate the disease in the 1950s, which threatened trade with Britain. See P. Rouse (2000) *Ireland's Own Soil: Government and Agriculture in Ireland, 1945–1965* (Dublin: Irish Farmers Journal), pp. 195–206.
35. Manning, *James Dillon*, p. 229.
36. Speech by Dillon, *Fine Gael Digest*, Ard Fheis issue (1960), p. 8.
37. Notes on minutes of meetings of the special committee on organisation held at Leinster House on 25 and 26 July 1960, 27 July 1960, P151/810, MacEoin Papers, UCDA.
38. James Dillon to each Fine Gael deputy, 27 July 1960, P151/810, MacEoin Papers, UCDA.
39. Minutes of the parliamentary party, 8 April 1959, Fine Gael minute books.
40. John A. Costello to James Dillon, 13 January 1960, P190/340, Costello Papers, UCDA.
41. *Irish Times*, 6 October 1961.
42. *Irish Times*, 7 October 1961.
43. Manning, *James Dillon*, p. 347.
44. D. McCullagh (1998) *A Makeshift Majority: The First Inter-Party Government, 1948–51* (Dublin: Institute of Public Administration), p. 2.
45. McCullagh, *A Makeshift Majority*, p. 7.
46. *National Observer*, vol. 2, no. 5 (November 1959).
47. Meeting of the parliamentary party, 26 February 1964, Fine Gael minute books.
48. John A. Costello to James Dillon, 13 January 1960, P190/340, Costello Papers, UCDA.
49. Quoted in B. Halligan (ed.) (2006) *The Brendan Corish Seminar Proceedings* (Dublin: Scáthán Publications), p. 13.
50. Quoted in I. McCabe (1991) *A Diplomatic History of Ireland, 1948–49: the Republic, the Commonwealth and NATO* (Dublin: Irish Academic Press), p. 22.
51. *Fine Gael Digest*, vol. 8, no. 1 (February 1958), p. 2.
52. John Grattan Esmonde, 'Should Fine Gael Go It Alone?', *National Observer*, vol. 2, no. 5 (November 1959).
53. J. Horgan (1997), *Seán Lemass: The Enigmatic Patriot* (Dublin: Gill and Macmillan), p. 231.
54. *Points for Speakers and Canvassers no. 1*, Cork City and Kildare by-elections, 1964, P 151/899, MacEoin Papers, UCDA.
55. Speech by James Dillon at National Council Meeting, Leinster House, 5 November 1963, P 151/899, MacEoin Papers, UCDA.
56. *Irish Independent*, 17 February 1964.
57. *Irish Times*, 21 February 1964.
58. Meeting of the parliamentary party, 26 February 1964, Fine Gael minute books.

59. J. Bowman (2011) *Window and Mirror: RTÉ Television, 1961–2011* (Cork: Collins Press), p. 23.
60. Meeting of the parliamentary party, 4 March 1964, Fine Gael minute books.
61. Interview with Garret FitzGerald, 8 September 2009.
62. B. Halligan, 'What if Declan Costello had Become Leader of Fine Gael?', *What if...?*, RTÉ Radio 1, first broadcast 17 September 2006.
63. M. Gallagher (1982) *The Irish Labour Party in Transition, 1957–82* (Manchester: Manchester University Press), p. 55.
64. Declan Costello in conversation with Elaine Byrne and Garret FitzGerald, *The Irish Times*, 15 November 2008.
65. Transcript of *One-to-One* interview conducted by David McCullagh, first broadcast 14 September 2009, RTÉ1.
66. Interview with Vincent Browne, 22 July 2010.
67. Halligan, 'What if Declan Costello had Become Leader of Fine Gael?'.
68. *Connacht Tribune*, 3 April 1965.
69. Meeting of the parliamentary party, 29 April 1964, Fine Gael minute books.
70. M. Manning, (2006) *The Blueshirts* (Dublin: Gill and Macmillan), pp. 181 and 191.
71. Meeting of the parliamentary party, 26 May 1964, Fine Gael minute books.
72. *Nusight*, April 1970.
73. G. FitzGerald (1992) *All in a Life: An Autobiography* (Dublin: Gill and Macmillan), pp. 76–7.
74. Meeting of the parliamentary party, 5 May 1964, Fine Gael minute books.
75. P. Lindsay (1992) *Memories* (Dublin: Blackwater Press), p. 167.
76. *Dáil debates*, vol. 9, col. 562, 30 October 1924 (Patrick McGilligan).
77. C. Meehan (2010) *The Cosgrave Party: A History of Cumann na nGaedheal, 1923–1933* (Dublin: Royal Irish Academy), pp. 59–60.
78. *Connaught Telegraph*, 6 June 1964.
79. Meeting of the parliamentary party, 26 May 1964, Fine Gael minute books.
80. Quoted in McCullagh, *The Reluctant Taoiseach*, p. 296.
81. Meeting of the parliamentary party, 26 May 1964, Fine Gael minute books.
82. Transcript of *One-to-One* interview conducted by David McCullagh, first broadcast 14 September 2009, RTÉ1.
83. *Nusight*, April 1970.
84. P. Harte (2005) *Young Tigers and Mongrel Foxes: A Life in Politics* (Dublin: O'Brien), p. 75.
85. Transcript of *One-to-One* interview conducted by David McCullagh, first broadcast 14 September 2009, RTÉ1.
86. *The Irish Times*, 18 May 1964.
87. See, for example, the editorial on 2 June 1964.
88. *Irish Independent*, 19 May 1964.
89. *The Irish Times*, 18 May 1964.
90. *The Irish Times*, 14 May 1964.
91. Transcript of *One-to-One* interview conducted by David McCullagh, first broadcast 14 September 2009, RTÉ1.
92. *Irish Independent*, 21 May 1964.
93. Interview with Jim Dorgan, 12 April 2012.
94. *Irish Independent*, 20 May 1964.
95. Circular from Garret Cooney, Honorary Secretary, to all members, 16 July 1964, Minutes of the Fine Gael Central Branch, P39/C/D/13, Fine Gael Constituency Papers, UCDA.

96. *Irish Independent*, 25 May 1964.
97. Quoted in *Irish Times*, 20 May 1964.
98. *The Irish Times*, 20 May 1964.
99. *The Irish Independent*, 19 May 1964.
100. *The Irish Times*, 20 May 1964.
101. Lindsay, *Memories*, p. 169.
102. Interview with Donal Flynn, 21 June 2011.
103. *The Irish Times*, 2 May 1964.
104. *Irish Independent*, 20 May 1964.
105. *Irish Independent*, 20 May 1964.
106. *The Irish Times*, 23 May 1964.
107. Meeting of the parliamentary party, 20 May 1964, Fine Gael minute books.
108. Meeting of the parliamentary party, 26 May 1964, Fine Gael minute books.
109. Conversation with David McCullagh, 2 February 2010.
110. Meeting of parliamentary party, 26 May 1964, Fine Gael minute books.
111. Nine-point plan, in possession of Costello family.
112. Manning, *James Dillon*, p. 366.
113. *The Kerryman*, 23 May 1964.
114. G. Murphy (2002) 'The Irish Government, the National Farmers Association, and the European Economic Community, 1955–1964', *New Hibernia Review*, 6, 4, p. 69.
115. See Chapter 3.
116. M. McWey, 'Personal Recollections', unpublished paper, Gerard Sweetman symposium, NUI Maynooth, 22 September 2012.
117. Interview with Mick Kilkenny, quoted in McCullagh, *The Reluctant Taoiseach*, p. 391.
118. FitzGerald, *All in a Life*, p. 63.
119. FitzGerald, *All in a life*, p. 68.
120. Correspondence with Liam Cosgrave, 19 February 2010.
121. Interview with Dónal Flynn, 21 June 2011.
122. Interview with Garret FitzGerald, 8 September 2009.
123. *One-to-one* interview with Richie Ryan conducted by David McCullagh, first broadcast 26 October 2009, RTÉ 1.
124. 'Introduction', *Towards a Just Society*, 1965 election manifesto in possession of Costello family.
125. *The Irish Times*, 2 December 1964.
126. M. Gallagher (2009) *Irish Elections, 1948–77: Results and Analysis* (London, New York: Routledge), p. 193.
127. Manning, *James Dillon*, p. 368.
128. *The Irish Times*, 2 January 1965.
129. Quoted in Manning, *James Dillon*, p. 369.
130. G. FitzGerald (2010) *Just Garret: Tales from the Political Front Line* (Dublin: Liberties Press), p. 94.

3 1965: The First Failure

1. G. FitzGerald (1992) *All in a Life: An Autobiography* (Dublin: Gill and Macmillan), p. 69.
2. Costello to meeting of Fine Gael election workers, Dublin, *Irish Press*, 22 March 1965.
3. *Tipperary Star*, 20 March 1965, *The Irish Times*, 21 February 1964.

4. *The Irish Times*, January 1965.
5. Interview with Garret FitzGerald, 8 September 2009.
6. *Towards a Just Society* (1965). All further unattributed quotes come from this document.
7. Conversation with Declan Costello, 5 February 2009.
8. M. Kenny and M. J. Smith (1997) 'Discourses of Modernization: Gaitskell, Blair and the Reform of Clause IV', *British Elections and Parties Review*, 7, 1, p. 114.
9. J. Charmley (2008) *A History of Conservative Politics since 1830* (Basingstoke: Palgrave Macmillan), p. 174.
10. *Hibernia*, July 1965, P35d/73, Patrick McGilligan Papers, UCDA.
11. J. Monnet, (1978) *Memoirs*, translation by Richard Mayne (London: Collins), p. 240.
12. M. Larkin (1997) *France since the Popular Front: Government and People, 1936–1996* (Oxford: Oxford University Press), p. 186.
13. Transcript of *One-to-One* interview conducted by David McCullagh, first broadcast 14 September 2009, RTÉ1.
14. C. Ó Gráda and K. O'Rourke (1996) 'Irish Economic Growth, 1945–88', in N. Cafts and G. Toniolo (eds.), *Economic Growth in Europe since 1945* (Cambridge: Cambridge University Press), p. 401.
15. Transcript of *One-to-One* interview conducted by David McCullagh, first broadcast 14 September 2009, RTÉ1.
16. Ó Gráda, 'Five Crises', Central Bank of Ireland TK Whitaker Lecture, 29 June 2011. Available from http://www.centralbank.ie/press-area/speeches/Pages/AddressbyProfessorCormacO'Gráda,oftheSchoolofEconomics,UCD,tothe CentralBankWhitakerLecture,29June,2011.aspx [accessed 10 July 2012].
17. *Points and Speakers for Canvassers*, March 1965, P39/GE/127, UCDA.
18. A. J. Matusow (2009) *The Unravelling of America: A History of Liberalism in the 1960s* (Athens: University of Georgia Press), p. 124.
19. Interview with Garret FitzGerald, 8 September 2009.
20. R. Barrington (2000) *Health, Medicine and Politics in Ireland, 1900–1970* (Dublin: Institute of Public Administration), p. 254.
21. *The Health Services and their Further Development*, 1966.
22. M. E. Daly (2012) 'The Curse of the Irish Hospitals' Sweepstake: A Hospital System, not a Health System', *Working Papers in History and Policy*, 2, p. 4.
23. Daly, 'The Curse of the Irish Hospitals' Sweepstake', p. 4.
24. T. Farmar (2011) *Privileged Lives: A Social History of Middle-Class Ireland, 1882–1989* (Dublin: A&A Farmar), p. 199.
25. *Dáil debates*, vol. 192, col. 721, 23 November 1961.
26. *Irish Press*, 27 April 1964.
27. *The Irish Times*, 21 May 1964.
28. D. McCullagh (2010) *The Reluctant Taoiseach: A Biography of John A Costello* (Dublin, Gill and Macmillan), pp. 45–6.
29. *The Irish Times*, 16 April 1957.
30. Quoted in letter to the editor from Maurice Bracken, Chairman, St Michael's House, *The Irish Times*, 10 June 2011.
31. *The Irish Times*, 10 June 2011.
32. Interview with Paddy Harte, 20 January 2010.
33. Quoted in A. Ryan (1999) *Walls of Silence: Ireland's Policy towards People with a Mental Disability* (Kilkenny: Red Lion Press), pp. 28–9.
34. A. Ryan (2003) 'The Health Service: One Mother's Story', in J. Scally (ed.), *A Just Society? Ethics and Values in Contemporary Ireland* (Dublin: Liffey Press), pp. 161–6.

35. D. Walsh and A. Daly (2004) *Mental Illness in Ireland, 1750–2002: Reflections on the Rise and Fall of Institutional Care* (Dublin: Health Research Board), p. 11.
36. *Report of Commission of Inquiry on Mental Illness*, 1966.
37. Noel Reilly to P.F. Dineen, 19 March 1965, P39/GE/132, UCDA.
38. Seaghán Ua Conchubhair to PF Dineen, 22 March 1965, and Dineen's reply, 31 March 1965, P39/GE/132, UCDA.
39. Seaghán Ua Conchubhair to PF Dineen, 3 April 1965, P39/GE/132, UCDA.
40. Noel Reilly to P.F. Dineen, 26 March 1965, and Dineen's reply, 31 March 1965, P39/GE/132, UCDA.
41. Summary Statistics. Available from http://www.dohc.ie/statistics/health_statistics/table_a1.html [accessed 14 February 2012].
42. E. Kiely and P. Kennedy (2005), 'Youth Policy', in S. Quinn, P. Kennedy, A. Matthews and G. Kiely (eds.), *Contemporary Irish Social Policy* (Dublin: University College Dublin Press), p. 195.
43. W. Forde (1995) *Growing up in Ireland: The Development of Irish Youth Services* (Wexford: CARA Publications), p. 6.
44. Forde, *Growing up in Ireland*, p. 23.
45. A. Redmond and M. Heanne (2000) 'Aspects of Society', in A. Redmond (ed.), *That was Then, This is Now: Change in Ireland, 1949–1999* (Dublin: Central Statistics Office), pp. 51–2.
46. M. Raftery and E. O'Sullivan (1999) *Suffer the Little Children: The Inside Story of Ireland's Industrial Schools* (Dublin: New Island), p. 12.
47. Raftery and O'Sullivan, *Suffer the Little Children*, p. 22.
48. Raftery and O'Sullivan, *Suffer the Little Children*, p. 12.
49. *Report of Commission of Inquiry on Mental Illness*, 1966.
50. M. Hederman, (2008) 'The Tuairim Phenomenon: A Forum for Challenge in 1950s Ireland', in Y. Thornley (ed.), *Unquiet Spirit: Essays in Memory of David Thornley* (Dublin: Liberties Press), p. 67.
51. R. Gilligan, (2009) 'The "Public Child" and the Reluctant State?', *Éire-Ireland*, 44: 1 and 2, pp. 273–4.
52. V. Richardson (2005) 'Children and Social Policy', in S. Quinn, P. Kennedy, A. Matthews and G. Kiely (eds.), *Contemporary Irish Social Policy* (Dublin: University College Dublin Press), p. 161.
53. D. Corless (2007) *Party Nation: Ireland's General Elections – the Strokes, Jokes, Spinners and Winners* (Dublin: Merlin Publishing), pp. 156–7.
54. J. Bowman (2011) *Window and Mirror: RTÉ Television, 1961–2011* (Cork: Collins Press), p. 200.
55. Circular to all candidates and key men, 18 March 1965, P39/GE/139, Fine Gael election papers, UCDA.
56. P. F. Dineen to Michael Sweetman, 20 April 1965, P39/GE/139, Fine Gael election papers, UCDA.
57. Conversation with Maurice Manning, 23 November 2009.
58. List of workers, n.d., P39/GE/139, Fine Gael election papers, UCDA.
59. Meeting of the parliamentary party, 16 July 1963, Fine Gael minute books.
60. Garret Cooney to all members, 17 January and 24 February 1964, P39/C/D/13, Fine Gael constituency papers, UCDA.
61. Notes for National Council Meeting, 4 May 1965, P39/GE/125, Fine Gael election papers, UCDA.
62. P. F. Dineen to Michael K. O'Driscoll, mid-Cork constituency secretary, 1 June 1965, P39/C/C/49, Fine Gael constituency papers, UCDA.

63. Notice of Central Branch seminar training, 1969, P39/C/D/18, UCDA.
64. *Sunday Independent*, 17 May 1964.
65. See for example, *Irish Independent*, 14 May 1964, *The Irish Times*, 21 and 23 May 1964.
66. Fianna Fáil handbill, 1965 election, P39/GE/141, Fine Gael Election papers, UCDA.
67. Article for inclusion in *The Kerryman*, March 1965, P39/GE/143, Fine Gael Election papers, UCDA.
68. Notes for National Council Meeting, 4 May 1965, P39/GE/125, Fine Gael Election papers, UCDA.
69. *The Irish Times*, 20 March 1965.
70. Distribution of policy document, n.d., P39/GE/128, Fine Gael election papers, UCDA.
71. 'Our plans are working', *Offaly Independent*, *Roscommon Champion*, 3 April 1965.
72. *The Irish Times*, 23 March 1965.
73. *Tipperary Star*, 27 March 1965.
74. Notes on the result of the general election, n.d., P39/GE/125, Fine Gael general election papers, UCDA.
75. B. Chubb (1959), 'Ireland 1957', in D.E. Butler (ed.), *Elections Abroad* (New York: St Martin's Press), p. 198.
76. See Chapter 2.
77. Interview with Donal Flynn, 21 June 2011 and Jim Dorgan, 26 January 2012.
78. *Action Plan for National Reconstruction*, Fianna Fáil election manifesto, 1977.
79. Interview with Jim O'Keeffe, 26 January 2010.
80. Notes on the result of the general election, 22 April 1965, P39/GE/125, Fine Gael election papers, UCDA.
81. Transcript of *One-to-One* interview conducted by David McCullagh, first broadcast 14 September 2009, RTÉ1.
82. *Roscommon Champion*, 3 April 1965.
83. *Tipperary Star*, 3 April 1965.
84. T. Däubler (2012) 'The Preparation and Use of Election Manifestos: Learning from the Irish Case', *Irish Political Studies*, 27, 1, p. 67.
85. Interview with Jim Dooge, 12 November 2009.
86. Sean McKenna to P.F. Dineen, 6 February 1965, and Dineen reply, 10 February 1965, P39/C/KK/12, Fine Gael Constituency Papers, UCDA.
87. *Longford Leader*, 3 April 1965.
88. See, for example, *Donegal Democrat*, 26 March 1965; *Offaly Independent*, 27 March 1965; *Leitrim Observer*, 3 April 1965; *Anglo-Celt*, 3 April 1965.
89. *Longford Leader*, 27 March 1965.
90. D. M. Farrell (2004) 'Before Campaigns were "Modern": Irish Electioneering in Times Past', in T. Garvin, M. Manning and R. Sinnott (eds.), *Dissecting Irish Politics: Essays in Honour of Brian Farrell* (Dublin: University College Dublin Press), p. 179.
91. C. Ó Gráda (1997) *A Rocky Road: the Irish Economy since the 1920s* (Manchester: Manchester University Press), p. 57.
92. Quoted in McCullagh, *The Reluctant Taoiseach*, pp. 347–8.
93. Address to the electors of Louth, P176/840, Fianna Fáil papers, UCDA.
94. Handbill, P176/840, Fianna Fáil papers, UCDA.
95. *Roscommon Champion*, 27 March 1965.
96. Mid-campaign survey, sent by Don O'Higgins to Michael O'Higgins, 29 March 1965, P39/GE/129, Fine Gael general election papers, UCDA.
97. *Leitrim Observer*, 3 April 1965.

98. Patrick Lindsay, Radio Éireann, 26 March 1965, P39/GE/135, Fine Gael election papers, UCDA.
99. *Offaly Independent*, 3 April 1965.
100. M. Gallagher (1985) *Political Parties in the Republic of Ireland* (Manchester: Manchester University Press), p. 77.
101. *Irish Farmers Journal*, 10 April 1965.
102. Mid-campaign survey sent by Don O'Higgins to Michael O'Higgins, 29 March 1965, P39/GE/129, Fine Gael general election papers, UCDA.
103. M. Gallagher (1982) *The Irish Labour Party in Transition, 1957–82* (Manchester: Manchester University Press), p. 59.
104. J. H. Whyte (2003) 'Reconciliation, Rights and Protests, 1963–8', in J. R. Hill (ed.), *A New History of Ireland: Volume 7: Ireland, 1921–84* (Oxford: Oxford University Press), p. 314.
105. Reply to enquiries, 1965, P39/GE/133, Fine Gael Election Papers, UCDA.
106. R. A. Butler quoted in S. J. Lee (1996) *Aspects of British Political History, 1914–1995* (London, New York: Routledge), p. 197.
107. *The Irish Times*, 27 May 1964.
108. See, for example, Conn Sheehan to Liam Cosgrave, 13 March 1965, P39/GE/133, UCDA.
109. R. Sinnott (1995) *Irish Voters Decide: Voting Behaviour and Referendums since 1918* (Manchester: Manchester University Press), p. 71.
110. Sean McKenna to Dineen, 23 May 1964, P39/C/KK/11, Fine Gael constituency papers, UCDA.
111. M. Gallagher (2009) *Irish Elections, 1948–77: Results and Analysis* (London, New York: Routledge), p. 234.
112. Notes on the result of the general election, 22 April 1965, P39/GE/125, Fine Gael election papers, UCDA.
113. *Roscommon Champion*, 3 April 1965.
114. Gallagher, *Political Parties in the Republic of Ireland*, p. 106.
115. T. Varley (2010) 'On the Road to Extinction: Agrarian Parties in Twentieth-Century Ireland', *Irish Political Studies*, 25, 4, p. 595.
116. Notes on the result of the general election, n.d., P39/GE/125, Fine Gael election papers, UCDA.
117. M. Gallagher (1976) 'Electoral Support for Irish Political Parties, 1927–73', *Sage Professional Papers in Contemporary Political Sociology*, 2, 17, p. 38.
118. B. Evans (2011) *Seán Lemass: Democratic Dictator* (Cork: Collins Press), p. 218.
119. Dick Walsh interview with Paddy Smith, *The Irish Times*, 21 May 1977.
120. Quoted in G. Murphy (2002) 'The Irish Government, the National Farmers Association, and the European Economic Community, 1955–1964', *New Hibernia Review*, 6, 4, p. 68.
121. J. Horgan (1997) *Seán Lemass: The Enigmatic Patriot* (Dublin: Gill and Macmillan), p. 208.

4 1969: The Second Failure

1. P. Harte (2005) *Young Tigers and Mongrel Foxes: A Life in Politics* (Dublin: O'Brien), p. 78.
2. Interview with Jim Dooge, 12 November 2009.
3. S. Collins (1996) *The Cosgrave Legacy* (Dublin: Blackwater Press), p. 84.

4. Conversation with Liam Cosgrave, 22 April 2013.
5. *The Irish Times*, 22 April 1965.
6. M. Manning (1999) *James Dillon: A Biography* (Dublin: Wolfhound Press), p. 375.
7. Manning, *James Dillon*, p. 375.
8. Interview with Jim Dooge, 12 November 2009 and conversation with Liam Cosgrave 22 April 2013.
9. Meeting of the parliamentary party, 21 April 1965, Fine Gael minute books.
10. *The Irish Times*, 25 February 1973.
11. Interview with Vincent Browne, 22 July 2010.
12. V. Browne, 'Costello's vision was of equality and justice', *The Irish Times*, 8 June 2011.
13. Manning, *James Dillon*, p. 375.
14. Interviews with Barbara Sweetman-FitzGerald, 10 February 2010; Donal Flynn, 21 June 2011; Jim Dorgan, 26 January 2012.
15. Interview with Jim O'Keeffe, 26 January 2010.
16. *The Irish Times*, 27 March 1965.
17. Quoted in *Irish Independent*, 31 March 1967.
18. Collins, *The Cosgrave Legacy*, p. 85.
19. Correspondence with Liam Cosgrave, 19 February 2010.
20. Interview with Donal Flynn, 21 June 2011.
21. Interview with John Bruton, 28 September 2012.
22. R. Fanning, 'Alexis FitzGerald and the Traffic in Power', *Magill*, 1 September 1985.
23. R. Fanning, 'Garret FitzGerald and the Quest for a New Ireland', *Inaugural Garret FitzGerald Memorial Lecture*, National University of Ireland, 2011, p. 13.
24. Correspondence with Liam Cosgrave, 19 February 2010.
25. P. Lindsay (1992) *Memories* (Dublin: Blackwater Press), p. 158.
26. *Irish Independent*, 30 April 1965.
27. T. F. O'Higgins (1996) *A Double Life* (Dublin: Town House), p. 191.
28. *Irish Farmers Journal*, 8 May 1965.
29. Observations on Cosgrave's frontbench, unsigned, n.d. [1965?], Michael Sweetman papers, in possession of Barbara Sweetman-FitzGerald.
30. *The Irish Times*, 26 May 1972.
31. J. Bruton (2011) 'Young Fine Gaelers', in B. Sweetman-FitzGerald (ed.), *The Widest Circle: Remembering Michael Sweetman* (Dublin: A&A Farmar), p. 49.
32. G. FitzGerald (2010) *Just Garret: Tales from the Political Front Line* (Dublin: Liberties Press), p. 105.
33. O'Higgins, *A Double Life*, p. 193.
34. C. Meehan (2012) 'Constructing the Irish Presidency: The Early Incumbents, 1938–1973', *Irish Political Studies*, 27, 4 (2012), pp. 559–60.
35. Meeting of the parliamentary party, 2 February 1966, Fine Gael minute books.
36. See, for example, the speech by Tom O'Donnell at Clare convention, 6 March 1966, Fine Gael Presidential Election Papers, P39/PR/90, UCDA.
37. Election Leaflet, 1966. Available from http://irishelectionliterature.wordpress.com/2011/10/20/tom-ohiggins-fine-gael-1966-presidential-election/ [accessed 10 June 2012].
38. FitzGerald, *Just Garret*, p. 104.
39. *The Irish Times*, 27 April 1966.
40. Draft speech on Northern Ireland, n.d., Michael Sweetman papers, in possession of Barbara Sweetman-FitzGerald.

41. Meehan, 'Constructing the Irish presidency', p. 571.
42. O'Higgins, *A Double Life*, p. 204.
43. Circular of congratulations from Colonel Dineen, 3 June 1966, P39/PR/121, Fine Gael presidential papers, UCDA.
44. *The Citizen*, February 1967.
45. *Dáil debates*, vol. 215, col. 988, 11 May 1965.
46. *Dáil debates*, vol. 215, col. 1003, 11 May 1965.
47. FitzGerald, *Just Garret*, p. 100.
48. *The Irish Times*, 10 June 1966.
49. G. Ó Tuataigh (1979) 'Language, Literature and Culture in Ireland since the War', in J. J. Lee (ed.) *Ireland 1945–70* (Dublin: Gill and Macmillan), p. 116.
50. *The Irish Times*, 22 October 1959.
51. Quoted in D. Keogh (1994) *Twentieth Century Ireland: Nation and State* (Dublin: Gill and Macmillan), p. 248.
52. *The Irish Times*, 11 November 1961.
53. *The Irish Times*, 6 June 1966.
54. *Fine Gael Policy for a Just Society: Irish Language* (1966).
55. *Fine Gael Policy for a Just Society: Irish Language* (1966).
56. Ó Tuataigh, 'Language, literature and culture in Ireland since the War', p. 112.
57. *Fine Gael Policy for a Just Society: Irish Language* (1966).
58. M. O'Laoire (2008) 'The Language Situation in Ireland', in R. B. Kaplan and R. B. Baldauf (eds.), *Language Planning and Policy. Europe, Volume 3: the Baltic States, Ireland and Italy* (Clevedon: Multilingual Matters), p. 207.
59. *The Irish Times*, 6 July 1966.
60. *The Irish Times*, 13 July 1966.
61. J. Sheridan (1979) 'Education and Society in Ireland, 1945–70', in J. J. Lee (ed.), *Ireland 1945–70* (Dublin: Gill and Macmillan), p. 61.
62. T. Garvin (2004) *Preventing the Future. Why was Ireland so Poor for so Long?* (Dublin: Gill and Macmillan), p. 87.
63. T. O'Connor and A. O'Halloran (2008) *Politics in a Changing Ireland, 1960–2007: A Tribute to Seamus Pattison* (Dublin: Institute of Public Administration), pp. 72–3.
64. Quoted in Garvin, *Preventing the Future*, p. 87.
65. J. Walsh (2005) *The Politics of Expansion: The Transformation of Educational Policy in the Republic of Ireland, 1957–72* (Manchester: Manchester University Press), p. 150.
66. J. Bruton (1993) 'Foreword', in B. Maye (ed.),*Fine Gael, 1923–1987: A General History with Biographical Sketches of Leading Members* (Dublin: Blackwater Press), p. v.
67. *The Irish Times*, 26 June 1967.
68. Walsh, *The Politics of Expansion*, pp. 182–4.
69. *The Irish Times*, 11 May 1967.
70. Statement, 8 February 1967, reproduced in *Irish Independent*, 9 January 1969.
71. *Irish Independent*, 10 February 1967.
72. *Irish Press*, 9 February 1967.
73. *The Irish Times*, 4 January 1969.
74. *The Citizen*, February 1967.
75. Letter to Liam Cosgrave, 7 January 1969, reproduced in *Irish Independent*, 9 January 1969.
76. Quoted in *Nusight*, June 1969.
77. *Irish Press*, 14 January 1969.
78. John Healy, *The Irish Times*, 4 January 1969.

79. *Irish Independent*, 8 January 1969.
80. Harte, *Young Tigers*, p. 81.
81. Interview with Jim Dooge, 12 November 2009.
82. Declan Costello to John Kelly, 29 April 1969, P147/25, Kelly Papers, UCDA.
83. Tom O'Higgins quoted in C. Meehan (2011) 'Michael Sweetman and the Just Society', in B. Sweetman-Fitzgerald (ed.), *Essays in Memory of Michael Sweetman* (Dublin: A&A Farmar), p. 64
84. Correspondence between Declan Costello and John Kelly, n.d, P147/25, Kelly Papers, UCDA.
85. Costello to Kelly, 29 April 1969, P147/25, Kelly Papers, UCDA.
86. *The Irish Times*, 14 May 1968.
87. Interview with Jim Dooge, 12 November 2009.
88. *The Irish Times*, 15 May 1968.
89. *The Irish Times*, 15 May 1968.
90. Quoted in *Nusight*, April 1970.
91. Records of the Clare constituency, 19 February 1969, P39/C/CE/16, UCDA.
92. Records of Cork City North-West, 1 March 1969, P39/C/C/17, UCDA.
93. M. Manning (1979) 'The Farmers', in J. J. Lee (ed.), *Ireland 1945–70* (Dublin: Gill and Macmillan), pp. 54–5.
94. Liam Cosgrave speech, GPO, 17 June 1969, Fine Gael election papers, P39/GE/159, UCDA.
95. Meehan, 'Michael Sweetman and the Just Society', pp. 70–1.
96. Liam Cosgrave speech, Dun Laoghaire, 9 June 1969, Fine Gael election papers, P39/GE/159, UCDA.
97. *The Time for Change Has Come*, P147/28, Kelly Papers, UCDA.
98. Transcript of *Seven Days* programme, 4 June 1968, Fine Gael Election Papers, P39/GE/151, UCDA.
99. J. W. Sanfey to Donal Flynn, 28 June 1968, P39/C/D/17, UCDA.
100. Interview with Donal Flynn, 21 June 2011.
101. Circular from Elizabeth McNamara, Central Branch Honorary Secretary, to each member, 9 September 1968, P39/C/D/17, UCDA.
102. P. Daly (2012) 'Labour and the Pursuit of Power', in P. Daly, R. O'Brien and P. Rouse (eds.), *Making the Difference? The Irish Labour Party, 1912–2012* (Cork: Collins Press), p. 90.
103. *Irish Press*, 21 June 1969.

5 From Leader in Crisis to Leader in Government

1. *Nusight*, December 1969.
2. *Magill*, 7 June 1981.
3. Interview with Jim Dooge, 12 November 2009.
4. Liam Cosgrave speech, GPO, 17 June 1969, Fine Gael election papers, P39/GE/159, UCDA.
5. *Irish Press*, 14 September 1968.
6. Resolution from Carlow Organising Committee, 8 February 1968, P39/C/CW/15, Fine Gael Constituency Papers, UCDA.
7. *The Irish Times*, 22 June 1968.
8. Quoted in *The Irish Times*, 23 February 1971.
9. *Nusight*, November 1968.

10. See, for example, R. F. Foster (2008) *Luck and the Irish: A Brief History of Change, 1970–2000* (London: Penguin), pp. 69–71.
11. R. Fanning, 'Alexis FitzGerald and the Traffic in Power', *Magill*, 1 September 1985.
12. Interview with Vincent Browne, 22 July 2010.
13. Interview with Vincent Browne, 22 July 2010.
14. G. FitzGerald (1992) *All in a Life: An Autobiography* (Dublin: Gill and Macmillan), p. 78.
15. FitzGerald, *All in a Life*, p. 79.
16. Fine Gael newsletter, October 1969, P39/C/CN/16, Fine Gael Constituency Papers, UCDA.
17. *Nusight*, December 1969.
18. Brian Lenihan speech, Roscommon, 27 February 1973, P176/842, Fianna Fáil Papers, UCDA.
19. *Dáil debates*, vol. 264, col. 275, 29 November 1972 (Patrick Cooney).
20. *Dáil debates*, vol. 264, cols. 291 and 299, 29 November 1972 (Liam Cosgrave).
21. P. Harte (2005) *Young Tigers and Mongrel Foxes: A Life in Politics* (Dublin: O'Brien), p. 100.
22. *The Irish Times*, 9 December 1972.
23. *Dáil debates*, vol. 264, col. 300, 29 November 1972 (Frank Cluskey).
24. *Irish Press*, 1 December 1972.
25. *The Irish Times*, 29 November 1972.
26. *Irish Press*, 1 December 1972.
27. *The Irish Times*, 29 November 1972.
28. T. F. O'Higgins (1996) *A Double Life* (Dublin: Town House), p. 246.
29. *Irish Press*, 2 December 1972.
30. *Dáil debates*, vol. 264, col. 829, 1 December 1972 (Tom O'Higgins).
31. O'Higgins, *A Double Life*, pp. 250–1.
32. *Irish Press*, 1 December 1972.
33. E. Moloney (2010) *Voices from the Grave: Two Men's War in Ireland* (London: Faber), p. 340.
34. *Dáil debates*, vol. 264, col. 831, 1 December 1972 (Tom O'Higgins).
35. O'Higgins, *A Double Life*, pp. 252–3.
36. S. Collins (1996) *The Cosgrave Legacy* (Dublin: Blackwater Press), p. 115.
37. *Sunday Independent*, 3 December 1972.
38. *Dáil debates*, vol. 264, col. 865, 1 December 1972 (Brendan Corish).
39. *Irish Press*, 2 December 1972.
40. *Irish Times*, 2 December 1972.
41. *Dáil debates*, vol. 264, col. 924, 1 December 1972 (Seán Sherwin).
42. http://www.finegael.ie/your-fine-gael/values/ [accessed 20 August 2012].
43. O'Higgins, *A Double Life*, p. 241.
44. N. Puirséil (2007) *The Irish Labour Party, 1922–73* (Dublin: University College Dublin), pp. 264 and 270.
45. Puirséil, *The Irish Labour Party*, pp. 264 and 285.
46. Quoted in P. Daly 'Labour and the Pursuit of Power', in P. Daly, R. O'Brien and P. Rouse (eds.), *Making the Difference? The Irish Labour Party, 1912–2012* (Cork: Collins Press), p. 90.
47. Collins, *The Cosgrave Legacy*, pp. 103–6.
48. B. Desmond (2000) *Finally and in Conclusion: A Political Memoir* (Dublin: New Island), p. 55.
49. Desmond, *Finally and in Conclusion*, p. 56.

50. *The Irish Times*, 29 January 1970.
51. Puirséil, *The Irish Labour Party*, p. 203.
52. Brendan Halligan speaking on 'What if Declan Costello had become leader of Fine Gael?', *What if...?*, RTÉ Radio 1, first broadcast 17 September 2006.
53. Plan of action for forthcoming general election, 1 December 1972, unsorted Brendan Corish Papers, Irish Labour History Museum & Archive (hereafter ILHM & A).
54. Statement of intent, unsorted Brendan Corish papers (ILHM & A).
55. *The Irish Times*, 27 February 1973.
56. *Fortnight*, 57, 2 March 1973.
57. Quoted in *The Irish Times*, 16 February 1973.
58. *Irish Press*, 12 February 1973.
59. *The Irish Times*, 8 and 12 February 1973.
60. *The Irish Times*, 16 February 1973.
61. *Irish Independent*, 26 February 1973.
62. N. Baxter-Moore (1973) 'The Election Campaign, February 1973', in J. Knight and N. Baxter-Moore (eds.), *Republic of Ireland: The General Elections of 1969 and 1973* (London: Arthur McDougal Fund), p. 20.
63. C. O'Leary (1979) *Irish Elections, 1918–1977: Parties, Voters and Proportional Representation* (Dublin: Gill and Macmillan), p. 79.
64. *The Irish Times*, 27 February 1973.
65. *Bread and Roses*, no. 2 (n.d., mid-1970s).
66. M. McNamara and P. Mooney (2000) *Women in Parliament: Ireland, 19182000* (Dublin: Wolfhound Press), p. 17.
67. F. Buckley and C. McGing (2011) 'Women and the Election', in M. Gallagher and M. Marsh (eds.), *How Ireland Voted 2011: The Full Story of Ireland's Earthquake Election* (Basingstoke: Palgrave Macmillan), pp. 223–4.
68. *The Irish Times*, 2 April 1971.
69. A. Stopper (2006) *Mondays at Gaj's: The Story of the Irish Women's Liberation Movement* (Dublin: Liffey Press), p. 2.
70. *Banshee: Journal of Irish Women United*, 1, 1 (1975).
71. Interview with Jim Dooge, 12 November 2009.
72. *Seanad Debates*, vol. 164, col. 4, 11 October 2000 (Maurice Manning).
73. *Fortnight*, 29, 26 (1971), p. 8.
74. *Dáil debates*, vol. 246, col. 870, 8 May 1970 (Neil Blaney).
75. M. Manning (1978) 'The Political Parties', in H. R. Penniman (ed.), *Ireland at the Polls: the Dáil Elections of 1977* (Washington: American Enterprise Institute for Public Policy Research), p. 81.
76. Figures from M. Gallagher (2009) *Irish Elections, 1948–77: Results and Analysis* (London, New York: Routledge), p. 315.
77. Figures from Gallagher, *Irish Elections, 1948–77*, p. 277.
78. James Knight (1973) 'The Results of the 1973 Election', in J. Knight and N. Baxter-Moore (eds.), *Republic of Ireland: The General Elections of 1969 and 1973* (London: Arthur McDougal Fund), p. 25.
79. Brendan Halligan to Brendan Corish, 28 June 1972, Brendan Corish Papers, ILHM & A.
80. Collins, *The Cosgrave Legacy*, p. 136.
81. *Dáil debates*, vol. 265, col. 38, 14 March 1973 (Liam Cosgrave).
82. FitzGerald, *All in a Life*, p. 293.
83. *The Irish Times*, 21 and 27 February 1973.
84. Interview with Donal Flynn, 21 June 2011.

85. 'Documentary on One: The Twentieth Dáil'. Available from http://www.rte.ie/ radio1/doconone/radio-documentary-20th-dail.html [accessed 20 June 2012].
86. Correspondence with Liam Cosgrave, 19 February 2010.
87. Launch of McCullagh's *The Reluctant Taoiseach* at the Mansion House, Dublin, 13 October 2010.
88. 'Documentary on One: The Twentieth Dáil'. Available from http://www.rte.ie/ radio1/doconone/radio-documentary-20th-dail.html [accessed 20 June 2012].
89. J. J. Lee (1990) *Ireland 1912–1985: Politics and Society* (Cambridge: Cambridge University Press), p. 475.
90. C. Nic Dháibhéid (2011) *Seán MacBride: A Republican Life, 1904–1946* (Liverpool: Liverpool University Press), p. 201.
91. FitzGerald, *All in a Life*, pp. 293–4.
92. Maye, *Fine Gael*, p. 140.
93. Quoted in Collins, *The Cosgrave Legacy*, p. 205.
94. Correspondence with Liam Cosgrave, 19 February 2010.
95. *One-to-One* interview with Richie Ryan conducted by David McCullagh, first broadcast 26 October 2009, RTÉ1.
96. N. Ferguson, C. S. Maier, E. Manela and D. J. Sargent (eds.) (2010) *The Shock of the Global: the 1970s in Perspective* (London: Belknap).
97. R. F. Foster (2008) *Luck and the Irish: A Brief History of Change, 1970–2000* (London: Penguin), p. 72.
98. Statement of intent, unsorted Brendan Corish papers, ILHM & A.

6 National Coalition, 1973–77

1. 'Documentary on One: The Twentieth Dáil'. Available from http://www.rte.ie/ radio1/doconone/radio-documentary-20th-dail.html [accessed 20 June 2012].
2. *The Vulcan*, 1975.
3. See, for example, *Irish Press*, 22 February 1973, *The Irish Times*, 25 February 1973.
4. Interview with Jim Dorgan, 12 April 2012.
5. T. McCashin (1982) 'Social Policy: 1957–82', in F. Litton (ed.), *Unequal Achievement: The Irish Experience, 1957–1982* (Dublin: Institute of Public Administration), p. 206.
6. C. Ó Gráda, (1997) *A Rocky Road: The Irish Economy since the 1920s* (Manchester: Manchester University Press), p. 69.
7. *The Irish Times*, 12 March 1973.
8. Speech to Fine Gael Ard Fheis, The Mansion House, 19 May 1973, 2004/22/37, Department of Taoiseach, National Archives of Ireland (hereafter NAI).
9. Statement issued on behalf of the Department of Social Welfare, GIS 2/88, NAI.
10. Irish Women's Liberation Movement, *Irishwomen: Chains or Change?* (1972).
11. Mrs E Roche to the Irish Countrywomen's Association, Irish Housewives Association, Women's Progressive Movement, Federation of Ladies Clubs, Cork Federation of Women's Organisations, Irish Widows Association, Women's Liberation Movement, n.d, 2004/21/54, Department of Taoiseach, NAI.
12. *Women's Aim*, 4 (January–March 1980).
13. Nuala Fennell on AIM for *Woman's Way*, 9 March 1973.
14. Eibhlin Ní Threunmhoir, Secretary, Single Women's Association, to Liam Cosgrave, 31 May 1973, 2004/21/54, Department of Taoiseach, NAI.

15. *Woman's Way*, 19 January 1973.
16. *Cherish News*, January 1974.
17. Eibhlin Ní Threunmhoir, Secretary, Single Women's Association, to Liam Cosgrave, 31 May 1973, 2004/21/54, Department of Taoiseach, NAI.
18. P. Ryan (2012) *Asking Angela Macnamara: An Intimate History of Irish Lives* (Dublin: Irish Academic Press), p. 96.
19. These pioneering works are outlined by H. B. Biller (1970) 'Father Absence and the Personality Development of the Male Child', *Developmental Psychology*, 2, 2, pp. 181–201.
20. N. L. Thompson Jr., D. M. Schwartz, B. R. McCandless and D. A. Edwards (1973) 'Parent-Child Relationships and Sexual Identity in Male and Female Homosexuals and Heterosexuals', *Journal of Consulting and Clinical Psychology*, 43, 1, p. 120.
21. E. Connolly (1999) 'The Republic of Ireland's Equality Contract: Women and Public policy', in Y. Galligan, E. Ward and R. Wilford (eds.), *Contesting Politics: Women in Ireland, North and South* (Oxford: Westview Press), p. 85.
22. *Banshee: Journal of Irish Women United*, 1, 2 (1975).
23. AIM Group newsletter, no. 3, June 1973.
24. Statement issued on behalf of Richie Ryan regarding publication of Commission on the Status of Women report, 8 May 1973, GIS 2/85, NAI.
25. Quoted in M. Cousins (1999) 'The Introduction of Children's Allowances in Ireland, 1939–1944', *Irish Economic and Social History*, 26, p. 41.
26. Quoted in Cousins, 'The Introduction of Children's Allowances in Ireland', p. 47.
27. Statement issued on behalf of the Department of Social Welfare, 21 May 1974, GIS 2/91, NAI.
28. Interview by Kingsbury Smith, *Boston Herald American*, 2 September 1974, 2004/22/36, Department of Taoiseach, NAI.
29. K. McCormack and P. Meany (2000) 'Consumer Prices and Expenditure', in A. Redmond (ed.), *That was Then, This is Now: Change in Ireland, 1949–1999* (Dublin: Central Statistics Office), p. 74.
30. Michael O'Leary to Liam Cosgrave, 31 August 1973, 2004/21/338, Department of Taoiseach, NAI.
31. *Irish Press*, 18 October 1976.
32. M. Gallagher (1982) *The Irish Labour Party in Transition, 1957–82* (Manchester: Manchester University Press), p. 199.
33. N. Hardiman (1988) *Pay, Politics and Economic Performance in Ireland 1970–1987* (Oxford: Clarendon), p. 66.
34. National Economic and Social Council (NESC) (1974) *Economy in 1974 and Prospects for 1975*, p. 7.
35. National Economic and Social Council (NESC) (1975) *Economy in 1975 and Prospects for 1976*, p. 17.
36. D. Ferriter (2012) *Ambiguous Republic: Ireland in the 1970s* (London: Profile Books), p. 480.
37. Gallagher, *The Irish Labour Party*, p. 198.
38. C. Ó Gráda and K. O'Rourke (1996) 'Irish Economic Growth, 1945–88', in N. Cafts and G. Toniolo (eds.), *Economic Growth in Europe since 1945* (Cambridge: Cambridge University Press), p. 402.
39. Statement issued 26 September 1974, GIS 2/92, NAI.
40. National Economic and Social Council (NESC) (1975) *Economy in 1975 and Prospects for 1976*, pp. 5 and 23.

41. NESC, *Economy in 1975 and Prospects for 1976*, p. 25.
42. J. J. Lee (1990) *Ireland 1912–1985: Politics and Society* (Cambridge: Cambridge University Press), p. 471.
43. Speech to the annual dinner of the Dun Laoghaire Chamber of Commerce, 24 Jan. 1976, 2004/22/59, Department of Taoiseach, NAI.
44. *The Irish Times*, 31 December 1975.
45. *The Irish Times*, 31 December 1975.
46. NESC, *Economy in 1975 and Prospects for 1976*, p. 29.
47. E. Sweeney (2010) *Down, Down, Deeper and Down: Ireland in the 70s & 80s* (Dublin: Gill and Macmillan), p. 51, 109.
48. Collins, *The Cosgrave Legacy*, p. 158.
49. McCashin, 'Social Policy', p. 209.
50. Statement issued on behalf of the Department of Health and Social Welfare, 30 August 1973, GIS 2/87, NAI.
51. *The Irish Times, Irish Press, Irish Independent*, 27 March 1974.
52. *Dáil debates*, vol. 271, cols. 909–914, 27 March 1974 (Brendan Corish).
53. A. Power (1993) *Hovels to High Rise: State Housing in Europe since 1850* (London, New York: Routledge), p. 349.
54. Power, *Hovels to High Rise*, p. 339.
55. 'Documentary on One: The Twentieth Dáil'. Available from http://www.rte.ie/radio1/doconone/radio-documentary-20th-dail.html [accessed 20 June 2012].
56. C. O'Connell (2007) *The State and Housing in Ireland: Ideology, Policy and Practice* (New York: Nova Science Publishing), p. 106.
57. Cabinet minutes, 24 May 1973, 2004/20/1, NAI.
58. Department of Finance to Department of Taoiseach, 14 April 1977, 2007/116/434, Department of Taoiseach, NAI.
59. Department of Finance memo, April 1977, 2007/116/434, Department of Taoiseach, NAI.
60. P. Ó Dubhláin, private secretary to John Bruton, to Department of Foreign Affairs, 3 May 1973, P215/508, Garret FitzGerald Papers, UCDA.
61. Statement issued on behalf of John Bruton, 10 December 1973, GIS 2/88, NAI.
62. Liam Cosgrave to John Bruton, 16 November 1976, 2006/133/463, Department of Taoiseach, NAI.
63. Interview with John Bruton, 28 September 2012.
64. *Dáil debates*, vol. 281, col. 903, 27 May 1975 (Pearse Wyse).
65. *Irish Press*, 12 January 1976.
66. *Irish Press*, 8 December 1975.
67. Correspondence between John Bruton and Liam Cosgrave, 15, 16 and 24 November 1976, 2007/133/463, Department of Taoiseach, NAI.
68. Secretary of Department of Finance to Secretary of Department of Taoiseach, 13 April 1977, 2007/116/434, Department of Taoiseach, NAI.
69. Liam Cosgrave to Richie Ryan, 4 February 1977, 2007/116/434, Department of Taoiseach, NAI.
70. John Bruton to Liam Cosgrave, 19 January 1977, 2007/116/434, Department of Taoiseach, NAI.
71. B. Farrell (1987) 'The Context of Three Elections', in H. R. Penniman and B. Farrell (eds.), *Ireland at the Polls, 1981, 1982 and 1987: A Study of Four General Elections* (Durham: Duke University Press), p. 4.
72. M. O'hAodain (2010) 'The Contemporary Relevance of Historical Trends on Youth Work in Ireland', in P. Burgess and P Hermann (eds.), *Highways, Crossroads*

and *Cul de Sacs: Journeys into Irish Youth and Community Work* (Europäischer Hochschulverlag GmbH & Co.), p. 56.
73. *The Irish Times*, 13 July 1974.
74. John Kelly to Liam Cosgrave, 3 May 1974, P147/44, Kelly Papers, UCDA.
75. C. Sandford and O. Morrissey (1985) *The Irish Wealth Tax: A Case Study in Economics and Politics. Economic and Social Research Institute Paper 123* (Dublin: Economic and Social Research Institute), p. 21.
76. Sandford and Morrissey, *The Irish Wealth Tax*, p. 5.
77. Richard Bourke to Liam Cosgrave, 4 May 1974, 2005/7/293, Department of Taoiseach, NAI.
78. Anne Cassin to Liam Cosgrave, 1 May 1974, 2005/7/294, Department of Taoiseach, NAI.
79. Ned McGuire to Liam Cosgrave, 19 March 1974, 2005/7/292, Department of Taoiseach, NAI.
80. *FitzGerald at 80*, RTÉ1, first aired August 2006.
81. GP Crookes to Liam Cosgrave, 20 June 1974 2005/7/294, Department of Taoiseach, NAI.
82. Branch resolutions, 5 and 10 May 1974, 2005/7/293, Department of Taoiseach, NAI.
83. Quoted in D. Ferriter (2010) '"The Stupid Propaganda of the Calamity Mongers"?: The Middle Class and Irish Politics, 1945–97', in F. Lane (ed.), *Politics, Society and the Middle Class in Modern Ireland* (Basingstoke: Palgrave Macmillan), p. 281.
84. Interview with John Bruton, 28 September 2012.
85. *Dáil debates*, vol. 278, col. 1523, 5 March 1975 (Maurice Dockrell).
86. Note on contribution of an annual wealth tax and a gifts tax to curbing wealth concentration prepared for meeting of cabinet sub-committee, 20 November 1973, 2005/9/166, Department of Finance, NAI.
87. Address by Richie Ryan to Junior Chamber Ireland luncheon, 28 April 1974, 2005/7/292, Department of Taoiseach, NAI.
88. Alexis Fitzgerald to Liam Cosgrave, 8 March 1974, 2005/7/292, Department of Taoiseach, NAI.
89. Sandford and Morrissey, *The Irish Wealth Tax*, p. 31.
90. Anne Ahearne to Liam Cosgrave, 20 March 1974; Anne Ahearne to Percy Dockrell, 19 March 1974; Peter Roper to Percy Dockrell, 21 March 1974, 2005/7/292, Department of Taoiseach, NAI. The file contains various other letters expressing similar views.
91. Interview with Garret FitzGerald, 8 September 2009.
92. FitzGerald, *All in a Life*, pp. 298–302.
93. Draft report on progress of economic sub-committee of cabinet in relation to work on capital taxation, 2 January 1974, 2005/9/166, Department of Finance, NAI.
94. Richie Ryan to Garret FitzGerald, 7 January 1974, 2005/9/166, Department of Finance, NAI.
95. Brief for meeting of cabinet sub-committee, 17 July 1973, 2005/9/166, Department of Finance, NAI.
96. Memorandum on alternative system of capital taxation, [November 1973], 2005/9/166, Department of Finance, NAI.
97. Quoted in Sandford and Morrissey, *The Irish Wealth Tax*, p. 13.
98. FitzGerald, *All in a Life*, p. 300.
99. Quoted in Sandford and Morrissey, *The Irish Wealth Tax*, p. 37.

100. E. Connolly (1999) 'The Republic of Ireland's Equality Contract: Women and Public policy', in Y. Galligan, E. Ward and R. Wilford (eds.), *Contesting Politics: Women in Ireland, North and South* (Oxford: Westview Press), p. 85.
101. J. P. McCarthy (2006) *Kevin O'Higgins: Builder of the Irish State* (Dublin: Irish Academic Press), p. 265–75.
102. Quoted in *Irish Independent*, 26 February 1927.
103. Quoted in M. G. Valiulis (1992) 'Defining their Role in the New State: Irishwomen's Protest Against the Juries Act of 1927', *Canadian Journal of Irish Studies*, 18, 1, p. 44.
104. S. J. Lee (1996) *Aspects of British Political History, 1914–1995* (London, New York: Routledge), p. 341.
105. Valiulis, 'Defining their Role in the New State', p. 52.
106. *Irish Independent*, 6 August 1971.
107. *Jury Service Consultation Paper* (Law Reform Commission, March 2010), p. 22.
108. Statement issued on behalf of Richie Ryan regarding publication of Commission on the Status of Women report, 8 May 1973, GIS 2/85, NAI.
109. Lee, *Aspects of British Political History*, p. 346.
110. E. Mahon and V. Morgan (1999) 'State Feminism in Ireland', in Y. Galligan, E. Ward and R. Wilford (eds.), *Contesting Politics: Women in Ireland, North and South* (Oxford: Westview Press), p. 61.
111. Report on Article 119 Special Group meeting, 2 and 3 April 1973, 2005/14/01, Department of Justice, NAI.
112. Statement issued on behalf of the Minister for Labour, 18 April 1973, GIS 2/85, NAI.
113. Letter to the *Evening Press*, 30 April 1973, 2004/21/54, Department of Taoiseach, NAI.
114. Minutes of government meeting, 21 June 1973, 2004/21/611, Department of Taoiseach, NAI.
115. R. Crossman (1977) *The Diaries of a Cabinet Minister, Volume Three: Secretary of State for Social Services, 1968–1970* (London: Hamilton), p. 627.
116. Memorandum for government, 29 November 1973, 2004/21/611, Department of Taoiseach, NAI.
117. *The Irish Times*, 17 and 25 October 1974.
118. *The Irish Times*, 25 October 1974.
119. *Irish Independent*, 9 March 1975.
120. *The Irish Times*, 7 January 1976.
121. Letter to the editor, *The Irish Times*, 10 January 1976.
122. *The Irish Times*, 8 January 1976.
123. *The Irish Times*, 13 January 1976.
124. *Irish Independent*, 6 January 1976.
125. *Irish Independent*, 27 January 1976.
126. *The Irish Times*, 22 January 1976.
127. B. Desmond (2000) *Finally and in Conclusion: A Political Memoir* (Dublin: New Island), p. 59.
128. *The Irish Times*, 17 January 1976.
129. *The Irish Times*, 19 January 1976.
130. *Irish Independent*, 28 January 1976.
131. *The Irish Times*, 31 January 1976; *Irish Independent*, 22 February 1976.
132. Minutes of government meeting, 20 January 1976, 2005/133/396, Department of Taoiseach, NAI.

133. *The Irish Times*, 12 February 1976.
134. J. Walsh (2008) *Patrick Hillery: The Official Biography* (Dublin: New Island), pp. 381–2.
135. *The Irish Times*, 12 February 1976.
136. *The Irish Times*, 16 February 1976.
137. *The Irish Times*, 19 February 1976.
138. *Irish Independent*, 13 February 1976.
139. *The Irish Times*, 9 February 1976.
140. *The Irish Times*, 13 February 1973.
141. I. Bacik (2012) 'Labour and the Liberal Agenda', in P. Daly, R. O'Brien and P. Rouse (eds.), *Making the Difference? The Irish Labour Party, 1912–2012* (Cork: Collins Press), p. 179.
142. D. Ferriter (2009) *Occasions of Sin: Sex and Society in Modern Ireland* (London: Profile Books), p. 418.
143. Quoted in Ferriter, *Occasions of Sin*, p. 419.
144. Ferriter, *Occasions of Sin*, p. 410.
145. See T. Inglis (1987) *Moral Monopoly: The Catholic Church in Modern Irish Society* (Dublin: University College Dublin Press).
146. D. B. and P. J. O'Connell (1982) 'The Changing Social Structure', in F. Litton (ed.), *Unequal Achievement: The Irish Experience, 1957–1982* (Dublin: Institute of Public Administration), p. 77.
147. M. Heanne (2000) 'Matters of Life and Death', in A. Redmond (ed.), *That was Then, This is Now: Change in Ireland, 1949–1999* (Dublin: Central Statistics Office), p. 32.
148. Extract from D. Rohan (2002) 'Marriage Irish Style', in A. Bourke, S. Kilfeather, M. Luddy, M. MacCurtain, G. Meaney, M. Ní Dhonnchadha, M. O'Dowd and C. Wills (eds.), *The Field Day Anthology of Irish Writing*, vol. 4 (Cork: Cork University Press), p. 586.
149. Extract from C. A. Woods (2002) 'Woman Kneeling', in A. Bourke, S. Kilfeather, M. Luddy, M. MacCurtain, G. Meaney, M. Ní Dhonnchadha, M. O'Dowd and C. Wills (eds.), *The Field Day Anthology of Irish Writing*, vol. 4 (Cork: Cork University Press).p. 586.
150. Ó Gráda, *A Rocky Road*, p. 41.
151. A. Punch and C. Finneran (2000) 'Changing Population Structure', in A. Redmond (ed.), *That was Then, This is Now: Change in Ireland, 1949–1999* (Dublin: Central Statistics Office), p. 14.
152. Mna nah Éireann leaflet, 1976, 2006/133/215, Department of the Taoiseach, NAI.
153. Quoted in Ferriter, *Occasions of Sin*, p. 413.
154. Bowman, *Window and Mirror*, pp. 223–4.
155. Bowman, *Window and Mirror*, p. 159.
156. Interview with Frank Kelly, 22 July 2011.
157. *Irish Press*, 12 January 1978.
158. *The Very Best of Hall's Pictorial Weekly*, vol. 2 (1970–1982).
159. P. Ryan (2012) *Asking Angela Macnamara: An Intimate History of Irish Lives* (Dublin: Irish Academic Press), p. 3.
160. Feature on contraception, *Woman's Way*, 1 June 1973.
161. Mary Kenny for the *Irish Independent*, 13 May 2001.
162. *Sunday Independent*, 23 May 1971.
163. N. Fennell (2009) *Political Woman: A Memoir* (Dublin: Currach Press), pp. 62–3.

164. *New York Times*, 22 March 1974.
165. S. Collins (1993) *Spring and the Labour story* (Dublin: O'Brien Press), pp. 45–6.
166. Meeting of the cabinet, 19 March 1974, 2005/6/1, Cabinet Minutes, NAI.
167. Correspondence with Liam Cosgrave, 19 February 2010.
168. Interview with John Bruton, 28 September 2012.
169. Desmond, *Finally and in Conclusion*, p. 232.
170. Quoted in B. Girvin (2008) 'Contraception, Moral Panic and Social Change in Ireland, 1969–79', *Irish Political Studies*, 32, 4, p. 571.
171. Interview with Jim Dorgan, 12 April 2012.
172. F. Dunlop (2004) *Yes, Taoiseach: Irish Politics from Behind Closed Doors* (Dublin: Penguin Ireland), p. 9.
173. See, for example, Dennis Kennedy (1974) for *Fortnight*, 87, 9.
174. Ferriter, *Occasions of Sin*, p. 421.
175. Henry Kelly for *Nusight*, June 1969.
176. Interview with Cosgrave by Philippe Heymann, *Vision*, 30 January 1974, 2004/22/36, Department of Taoiseach, NAI.
177. Irish Women United to Liam Cosgrave, 2 December 1975, 2006/133/215, Department of Taoiseach, NAI.
178. *Banshee: Journal of Irish Women United*, 1, 1 (1975).
179. Patrick Curran to Liam Cosgrave, 23 November 1975, 2006/133/215, Department of Taoiseach, NAI.
180. *Hot Press* interview, 1990, reproduced 17 September 1997.
181. Address by Conor Cruise O'Brien to Annual Conference of the Irish Humanist Association, Co Down, 27 March 1976, 2006/133/215, Department of Taoiseach, NAI.
182. *Dáil debates*, vol. 289, col. 899, 6 April 1976.
183. Girvin, 'Contraception, Moral Panic and Social Change in Ireland, 1969–79', p. 557.
184. B. Brooks (1983) *Abortion in England, 1900–1967* (London: Croom Helm), p. 12.
185. Quoted in Girvin, 'Contraception, Moral Panic and Social Change in Ireland, 1969–79', p. 567.
186. *Who Killed Junior?* booklet, issued by Catholic Family Life, n.d., 2010/53/241, Department of Taoiseach, NAI.
187. Marion Kennedy, Parents' Committee, League of Decency, to Gerald Collins, Minister for Justice, 3 February 1978; Nial Darragh, Chair of Council of Social Concern, to Jack Lynch [1979?], 2010/53/241, Department of Taoiseach, NAI.
188. *The Irish Times*, 18 January 1978.
189. Letter from Damien Boyle, Rúnaí, Department of Foreign Affairs, to Ambassadors, 12 May 1978, 2009/111/49, Department of Taoiseach, NAI.
190. Garret FitzGerald to Agostino Casaroli, Secretary of the Council for the Public Affairs of the Church, Vatican City, Italy, 14 August 1973, Department of Taoiseach, 2004/27/12, NAI.
191. Máire Inion Uí Bhreathnach to Liam Cosgrave, 11 October 1973, 2004/21/460, Department of Taoiseach, NAI.
192. Transcript of *Le Monde* interview, 13 May 1977, 2007/116/337, Department of Taoiseach, NAI.
193. *Action Plan for National Reconstruction*, 1977.
194. Girvin, 'Contraception, Moral Panic and Social Change in Ireland, 1969–79', p. 555.
195. Oration at annual Michael Collins commemoration, *The Irish Times*, 20 August 1973.

196. P. Bew, P. Gibbon and H. Patterson (2002) *Northern Ireland, 1921–2001: Political Forces and Social Classes* (London: Serif), p. 185.
197. T. Hennessey (1996) 'Ulster Unionism and Loyalty to the Crown of the United Kingdom, 1912–74', in R. English and G. Walker (eds.), *Unionism in Modern Ireland: New Perspectives on Politics and Culture* (Hampshire: Macmillan Press), p. 121.
198. Bew, Gibbon and Patterson, *Northern Ireland*, p. 189.
199. Bew, Gibbon and Patterson, *Northern Ireland*, p. 189.
200. Quoted in Hennessey, 'Ulster Unionism and Loyalty to the Crown of the United Kingdom', p. 122.
201. J. Tonge (2002) *Northern Ireland: Conflict and Change* (Harlow: Longman), p. 118.
202. A. Currie (2004) *All Hell will Break Loose* (Dublin: O'Brien Press), p. 276.
203. *The Irish Times*, 8 June 1974.
204. Statement issued on behalf of Patrick Cooney, 16 February 1975, GIS 2/95, NAI.
205. *Irish Press*, 17 February 1975.
206. C. Cruise O'Brien (1998) *Memoir: Life and Times* (Dublin: Poolbeg Press), pp. 354–5.
207. *Sunday Independent*, 4 July 1976.
208. Statement issued on behalf of Richie Ryan, 31 March 1973, GIS 2/85, NAI.
209. *Irish Press*, 16 July 1976.
210. *Hansard*, vol. 915, col. 1800, 21 July 1976 (Margaret Thatcher).
211. 2006/133/708, Department of Taoiseach, NAI.
212. Jane Ewart Biggs to Liam Cosgrave, 10 August 1976, 2006/133/708, Department of Taoiseach, NAI.
213. *Dáil debates*, vol. 292, col. 3, 31 August 1976 (Liam Cosgrave).
214. *The Irish Times*, 25 August 1976.
215. *Dáil debates*, vol. 292, cols. 18 and 20, 31 August 1976 (Jack Lynch).
216. *Dáil debates*, vol. 292, cols. 23 and 27, 31 August 1976 (Jack Lynch).
217. *Sunday Independent*, 5 June 1977.
218. Gallagher, *The Irish Labour Party*, p. 206.
219. Quoted in Desmond, *Finally and in Conclusion*, p. 196.
220. K. Rafter (2012) 'Redefining the Irish Presidency: The Politics of a "Non-Political" Office, 1973–90', *Irish Political Studies*, 27, 4, p. 588.
221. *The Irish Times*, 28 May 1977.
222. *Irish Independent*, 6 May 1978.
223. Collins, *The Cosgrave Legacy*, p. 194.
224. Quoted in Moloney, *Voices from the Grave*, p. 348.
225. T. Garvin (1982) 'Change and the Political System', in F. Litton (ed.), *Unequal Achievement: The Irish Experience, 1957–1982* (Dublin: Institute of Public Administration), p. 33.
226. Excerpt from *Hall's Pictorial Weekly*. Available from http://www.rte.ie/laweb/ll/ll_t10b.html [accessed 15 November 2010].
227. *Magill*, 28 February 1980.
228. Interview with Frank Kelly, 22 July 2011.
229. Memorandum to the cabinet, 1975, Brendan Corish unsorted papers, ILHM & A.
230. *Sunday Independent*, 29 May 1977.
231. R. M. Harris, British Embassy Dublin, to P.G. Wallis, 31 March 1977, FCO 87/599, Kew.
232. Report on Fine Gael conference, unsigned, FCO 87/599, Kew.
233. B. Farrell and M. Manning (1978) 'The Election', in H. R. Penniman (ed.), *Ireland at the Polls: The Dáil Elections of 1977* (Washington: American Enterprise Institute for Public Policy Research), p. 133.

234. *Sunday Independent*, 19 June 1977.
235. Interview with Jim Dooge, 12 November 2009.
236. Howard R. Penniman (1978) 'Preface', in H. R. Penniman (ed.) *Ireland at the Polls: The Dáil Elections of 1977* (Washington: American Enterprise Institute for Public Policy Research), p. ii.
237. J. Downey (2009) *In My Own Time: Inside Irish Politics and Society* (Dublin: Gill and Macmillan), p. 173.
238. B. Farrell (1987) 'The Context of Three Elections', in H. R. Penniman and B. Farrell (eds.), *Ireland at the Polls, 1981, 1982 and 1987: A Study of Four General Elections* (Durham: Duke University Press), p. 3.
239. *The Irish Times*, 25 February 1974.
240. *Irish Press*, 1977.
241. J. Jones (2001) *In Your Opinion: Political and Social Trends through the Eyes of the Electorate* (Dublin: Town House and Country House), pp. 15–16.
242. Interview with Jim Dooge, 12 November 2009.
243. Episode one, *Fine Gael: A Family at War*, RTÉ 1, first aired 2003.
244. Interview with Jim Dooge, 12 November 2009.
245. *Sunday Independent*, 12 June 1977.
246. *An Coras Bua*, P176/940, Fianna Fáil election papers, UCDA.
247. O. O'Leary (2006) *Party Animals* (Dublin: O'Brien Press), p. 10.
248. *New York Times*, 19 June 1977.
249. O'Leary, *Party Animals*, p.10.
250. N. Whelan (2011) *Fianna Fáil: A Biography of the Party* (Dublin: Gill and Macmillan), p. 192.
251. Dunlop, *Yes, Taoiseach*, pp. 69–71.
252. D. M. Farrell (2004) 'Before Campaigns were "Modern": Irish Electioneering in Times Past', in T. Garvin, M. Manning and R. Sinnott (eds.), *Dissecting Irish Politics: Essays in Honour of Brian Farrell* (Dublin: University College Dublin Press), p. 178.
253. Quoted in Whelan, *Fianna Fáil*, p. 191.
254. Confidential report on the state of the organisation in Dublin, January 1975, P176/942, Fianna Fáil papers, UCDA.
255. *Irish Independent*, 17 June 1977.
256. S. O'Byrnes (1986) *Hiding Behind a Face: Fine Gael under FitzGerald* (Dublin: Gill and Macmillan).
257. Farrell, 'Before Campaigns were "modern"', p. 185.
258. *Irish Times*, 22 November 1976.
259. *Irish Independent*, 19 November 1976.
260. *Irish Times*, 9 December 1976.
261. *Fortnight*, 27 May 1977.
262. *The Irish Times*, 4 June 1977.
263. *Sunday Independent*, 12 June 1977.
264. *Irish Independent*, 30 May 1977.
265. *Irish Press*, 1 June 1977.
266. *Irish Independent*, 8 June 1977; *Sunday Independent*, 12 June 1977; *Irish Press*, 15 June 1977.
267. *Irish Press*, 15 June 1977.
268. *Irish Press*, 2 June 1977.
269. *Get Full Value from Every Vote*, P147/32, Kelly Papers, UCDA.
270. *Programme for Progress* (1977).
271. *Sunday Independent*, 12 June 1977.

272. Report on Economic Prospects of Republic of Ireland by J Plant, sent to Cabinet Office, 16 February 1977, FCO 87/598, Kew.
273. R. M. Harris to A. F. Goulty, 2 February 1977, FCO 87/598, Kew.
274. *Irish Independent*, 28 May 1977.
275. Farrell and Manning, 'The Election', p. 135.
276. *Sunday Independent*, 5 June 1977.
277. *Irish Press*, 7 June 1977.
278. *Irish Independent*, 9 June 1977.
279. *The Irish Times*, 8 June 1977.
280. *Irish Independent*, 31 May 1977.
281. *Magill*, May 1978.
282. *Irish Farmers Journal*, 25 June 1977.
283. *Irish Farmers Journal*, 4 June 1977.
284. *Irish Farmers Journal*, 25 June 1977.
285. *Irish Independent*, 30 May 1977.
286. *Sunday Independent*, 12 June 1977.
287. *Sunday Independent*, 29 May 1977.
288. *Irish Independent*, 9 June 1977.
289. *Sunday Independent*, 12 June 1977.
290. *Sunday Independent*, 5 June 1977.
291. *The Irish Times*, 7 June 1977.
292. *The Irish Times*, 8 June 1977.
293. *The Irish Times*, 18 June 1977.
294. Farrell and Manning, 'The Election', p. 154.
295. Figures from Gallagher, *Irish Elections 1948–77*, pp. 315 and 353.
296. *Irish Independent*, 6 May 1978.
297. *Irish Press*, 20 June 1977.

7 1980s: New Leader, New Party

1. R. Fanning, 'Garret FitzGerald and the Quest for a New Ireland', *Inaugural Garret FitzGerald Memorial Lecture*, National University of Ireland, 2011, p. 13.
2. For a discussion of Haughey and the tribunals, see E. Byrne (2012), *Political Corruption in Ireland, 1922–2010: A Crooked Harp?* (Manchester: Manchester University Press), pp. 145–59.
3. *FitzGerald at 80*, RTÉ1, first aired August 2006.
4. *FitzGerald at 80*, RTÉ1, first aired August 2006.
5. *Magill*, 2 April 1978.
6. 'Documentary on One: The Twentieth Dáil'. Available from http://www.rte.ie/radio1/doconone/radio-documentary-20th-dail.html [accessed 20 June 2012].
7. G. FitzGerald (2010) *Just Garret: Tales from the Political Front Line* (Dublin: Liberties Press), pp. 76–7.
8. D. Ferriter and C. J. Woods, 'Desmond FitzGerald', *Dictionary of Irish Biography*.
9. Interview with Garret FitzGerald, 8 September 2009.
10. *FitzGerald at 80*, RTÉ1, first aired August 2006.
11. *FitzGerald at 80*, RTÉ1, first aired August 2006.
12. Interview with Joan FitzGerald, *Garret FitzGerald: A Profile*, Channel 4, first aired 18 August 1991.
13. *The Independent*, 15 June 1999.

14. Interview with Garret FitzGerald, *RTÉ Guide*, April 2010, reproduced on RTÉ website, May 2011. Available from http://www.rte.ie/news/2011/0519/fitzgeraldg_interview.html [accessed 24 May 2011].
15. *Sunday Independent*, 19 June 1973.
16. *Irish Press*, 20 June 1977.
17. G. FitzGerald (1992) *All in a Life: An Autobiography* (Dublin: Gill and Macmillan), p. 323.
18. *The Irish Times*, 24 June 1977.
19. *The Irish Times*, 23 May 1978.
20. *Sunday Independent*, 26 June 1977.
21. S. O'Byrnes (1986) *Hiding Behind a Face: Fine Gael under FitzGerald* (Dublin: Gill and Macmillan), p. 14.
22. D. Keogh (1990) *Ireland and Europe 1919–1989: A Diplomatic and Political History* (Dublin: Gill and Macmillan), p. 258.
23. Miriam Meets ... Peter Barry and Deirdre Clune, RTÉ Radio 1, 7 August 2011.
24. *The Irish Times*, 24 June 1977.
25. P. J. Dempsey and L. W. White, 'Frank Cluskey', *Dictionary of Irish Biography*.
26. Dempsey and White, 'Frank Cluskey', *Dictionary of Irish Biography*.
27. *Irish Independent*, 2 July 1977.
28. *Irish Press*, 2 July 1977.
29. *The Irish Times*, 15 September 1977.
30. *Magill*, 7 June 1981.
31. *The Irish Times*, 4 April 1979.
32. *The Irish Times*, 3 December 1983.
33. *Irish Press*, 2 July 1977.
34. *The Irish Times*, 18 July 1977.
35. *The Irish Times*, 20 May 1978.
36. *The Irish Times*, 6 August 1977.
37. *The Irish Times*, 3 April 1968.
38. *Magill*, January 1978.
39. *The Irish Times*, 5 November 1977.
40. *The Irish Times*, 6 August 1977.
41. *The Irish Times*, 17 May 1985.
42. *The Irish Times*, 6 February 1978.
43. *Magill*, 2 April 1978.
44. John O'Reilly to Liam Cosgrave, 26 February 1969, P39/C/C/16, Fine Gael Constituency Papers, UCDA.
45. Interview with Jim O'Keeffe, 26 January 2010.
46. See Chapter 3.
47. T. Garvin (1982) 'Change and the Political System', in F. Litton (ed.), *Unequal Achievement: The Irish Experience, 1957–1982* (Dublin: Institute of Public Administration), p. 33.
48. Quoted in *Magill*, 2 April 1978.
49. *The Irish Times*, 22 May 1978.
50. *The Irish Times*, 22 July 1977.
51. *The Irish Times*, 8 November 1977.
52. *The Irish Times*, 11 September 2010.
53. *Irish Independent*, 20 May 2011.
54. See, for example, Geraldine Moane's letter in 1976. She was critical of an article praising those who had rejected marriage and the norms of a male dominated

society. 'For the majority of women, for whom marriage is a very important part of their lives, this kind of article is not going to have any effect'. *Banshee*, 1, 7 (1976).
55. M. E. Daly (2010). 'The "Women Element in Politics": Irish Women and the Vote, 1918–2008', in P. Thane and E. Breitenbach (eds.), *Women and Citizenship in Britain and Ireland in the 20th Century: What Difference did the Vote Make?* (London: Continuum), p. 86.
56. N. Fennell (2009) *Political Woman: A Memoir* (Dublin: Currach Press), p. 96.
57. *Irish Press*, 1 July 1977.
58. Fennell, *Political woman*, p. 108.
59. Letter to the editor, *The Irish Times*, 26 May 1978.
60. C. McGing and C. Meehan, 'Women in 1970s and '80s Ireland: Activists, Lobbyists and Politicians', unpublished seminar paper, National Library of Ireland, 21 November 2012. Research on candidate profiles and selection data by C. McGing.
61. *Women's Aim*, 12 (spring 1983).
62. *Magill*, 2 April 1978.
63. *The Irish Times*, 20 May 1978.
64. O. O'Leary (2004) *Politicians and Other Animals* (Dublin: O'Brien), p. 5.
65. M. Gallagher and M. Marsh (2002) *Days of Blue Loyalty: The Politics of Membership of the Fine Gael Party* (Dublin: PSAI Press), p. 52.
66. *Irish Independent*, 9 June 1979.
67. D. M. Farrell (1986) 'The Strategy to Market Fine Gael in 1981', *Irish Political Studies*, 1, p. 4.
68. *Irish Press*, 14 June 1979.
69. *Irish Independent*, 11 June 1979.
70. Report by P. J. Goulden on meeting with Frank Dunlop, 20 January 1977, FCO 87/598, Kew.
71. Farrell, 'The Strategy to Market Fine Gael in 1981', p. 4.
72. For a discussion of the development of political marketing in Britain, see (1990) 'Political Marketing', *Parliamentary Affairs*, 43, 2, pp. 284–88.
73. Farrell, 'The Strategy to Market Fine Gael in 1981', p. 3.
74. G. Hussey (1993) *Ireland Today: Anatomy of a Changing State* (Dublin: Townhouse), p. 167

8 The Constitutional Crusade

1. *Magill*, January 1978.
2. G. FitzGerald (1964) 'Seeking a National Purpose', *Studies*, pp. 337–51.
3. G. FitzGerald (1972) *Towards a New Ireland* (London: C. Knight), p. 179.
4. FitzGerald, *Towards a New Ireland*, p. viii.
5. *The Irish Times*, 28 June 1971.
6. G. FitzGerald (1992) *All in a Life: An Autobiography* (Dublin: Gill and Macmillan), p. 325.
7. Interview by Mary Maher with Joan FitzGerald, *The Irish Times*, 22 May 1978.
8. R. Fanning, 'Alexis FitzGerald and the Traffic in Power', *Magill*, 1 September 1985.
9. 'Documentary on One: The Twentieth Dáil'. Available from http://www.rte.ie/radio1/doconone/radio-documentary-20th-dail.html [accessed 20 June 2012].

10. That crusade involved removing articles 2 and 3 of the constitution. He was accused by Síle de Valera of displaying a 'Free State mentality', while Haughey argued that the government was seeking to give legal validity to partition. *The Irish Times*, 12 October 1981.
11. Document on Fianna Fáil election strategy, 3 February 1982, P147/36, Kelly Papers, UCDA.
12. *Report of the New Ireland Forum* (1984), p. 1.
13. Agreement between the Government of the United Kingdom of Great Britain and Northern Ireland and the Government of the Republic of Ireland (1985).
14. *The Irish Times*, 24 June 1977.
15. C. Rattigan (2012) *What Else Could I do? Single-Mothers and Infanticide, Ireland 1900–1950* (Dublin: Irish Academic Press), p. 2.
16. John Banville on 1950s Ireland. Available from http://www.benjaminblackbooks.com/1950sIreland.htm [accessed 13 May 2012].
17. R. Kavanagh (2005) *Mamie Cadden: Backstreet Abortionist* (Dublin: Mercier Press), p. 71.
18. In her book *Ireland's Hidden Diaspora*, Ann Rossiter details the abortion trail between 1980 and 2000.
19. Green Paper on Abortion, 1992, Appendix 2.
20. The Colm Hayes Show, RTÉ Radio 2, 17 April 2012. This was just one of the many radio and television programmes that covered the issue.
21. W. Binchy (1977) 'Marital Privacy and Family Law: A Reply to Mr O'Reilly', *Studies*, 66, 264, p. 333.
22. J. E. Spreng (2004) *Abortion and Divorce Law in Ireland* (Jefferson: McFarland), pp. 77–8.
23. Quoted in *Magill*, July 1982.
24. *Magill*, July 1982.
25. *Magill*, July 1982.
26. *The Irish Times*, 2 April 1982.
27. *Magill*, July 1982.
28. N. McCafferty (2004) *Nell* (Dublin, London: Penguin Ireland), p. 357.
29. *Irish Independent*, 28 April 1981.
30. G. Murphy (2010) 'Influencing Political Decision-Making: Interest Groups and Elections in Independent Ireland', *Irish Political Studies*, 25, 4, p. 575.
31. Charles Haughey to Julia Vaughan, 14 May 1981, S 22271A, Department of Taoiseach, NAI
32. *The Irish Times*, 8 April 1981.
33. Meeting of members of Pro-Life Movement, 30 April 1981, 2012/90/667, Department of Taoiseach, NAI.
34. *The Irish Times*, 9 April 1981.
35. Interview with Gemma Hussey, 27 July 2011.
36. *Irish Farmers Journal*, 3 September 1983.
37. *Irish Independent*, 15 May 1981.
38. Public Reply by Michael O'Leary, Leader of the Labour Party, to the Irish Council of Churches on the proposed constitutional amendment on abortion, 26 July 1982, 2012/90/668, Department of Taoiseach, NAI.
39. Murphy, 'Influencing Political Decision-making', p. 578.
40. *Magill*, March 1983.
41. *Dáil debates*, vol. 332, col. 1, 26 January 1982 (Michael Barrett and Bobby Molloy).

42. *Dáil debates*, vol. 332, cols. 2–3, 26 January 1982 (Garret FitzGerald and Michael Barrett).
43. FitzGerald, *Towards a New Ireland*, pp. 149–57.
44. FitzGerald, *Towards a New Ireland*, p. 152.
45. *The Irish Times*, 1982.
46. *The Irish Times*, 9 February 1983.
47. *Irish Independent*, 28 April 1981.
48. Memorandum from Peter Sutherland, 8 February 1982, 2012/90/667, Department of Taoiseach, NAI.
49. Sean O'Riordan to Taoiseach's office, 9 October 1981, 2011/127/817, Department of Taoiseach, NAI.
50. Draft reply to Pro-Life Campaign, 9 November 1981, 2012/90/667, Department of Taoiseach, NAI.
51. Telephone log, 27 January 1982, P205/145, Hillery Papers, UCDA.
52. Interview with Austin Deasy, *Fine Gael: A Family at War*, RTÉ 1, first aired 2003.
53. *Hot Press*, 23 January 2009.
54. Interview with Maureen O'Sullivan, 8 October 2011.
55. Memorandum by Martin Mansergh on pro-life amendment, 6 July 1982, 2012/90/667, Department of Taoiseach, NAI.
56. *Ulster Herald*, 17 September 1983.
57. *Sunday Independent*, 21 August 1983.
58. Memorandum by Patrick Connolly, 14 June 1982, 2012/90/667, Department of Taoiseach, NAI.
59. *Irish Press*, 3 November 1982.
60. Statement printed in *Westmeath Examiner*, 3 September 1983.
61. Interview with Mary O'Rourke, 21 September 2011.
62. *Sunday Independent*, 11 September 1983.
63. *Southern Star*, 3 September 1983.
64. McCafferty, *Nell*, p. 357.
65. *Sunday Independent*, 11 September 1983.
66. *Sunday Independent*, 21 August 1983.
67. *The Irish Times*, 2 September 1983.
68. Letter to the editor, *Connacht Sentinel*, 30 August 1983.
69. Letter to the editor, *Kerryman*, 12 August 1983.
70. Letter to the editor, *Nenagh Guardian*, 27 August 1983.
71. Letter to the editor, *Meath Chronicle*, 27 August 1983.
72. Letter to the editor, *Donegal News*, 3 September 1983.
73. J. Ardagh (1995) *Ireland and the Irish: Portrait of a Changing Society* (London: Penguin), p. 189.
74. McCafferty, *Nell*, p. 364.
75. Quoted in J. S. Donnelly (2005) 'Opposing the "Modern World": The Cult of the Virgin Mary in Ireland, 1965–85', *Éire-Ireland*, 40: 1 and 2, p. 238.
76. *Woman's Way*, 2 February 1973.
77. *Anglo-Celt*, 2 September 1983.
78. *Woman's Way*, 14 June 1985.
79. *Woman's Way*, 31 May 1985.
80. *Woman's Way*, 18 October 1985.
81. *Woman's Way*, 12 April 1985.
82. P. Ryan (2012) *Asking Angela Macnamara: An Intimate History of Irish Lives* (Dublin: Irish Academic Press), p. 11.

83. Girvin, 'Social Change and Moral Politics', p. 66.
84. Girvin, 'Social Change and Moral Politics', p. 66.
85. A. MacNamara (2003) *Yours Sincerely* (Dublin: Veritas), pp. 63 and 96.
86. See, for example, *Woman's Way*, 5 April 1985. One young woman wrote, 'After a disco I let a fellow I didn't know take me home and we made love in the car as I had too much to drink. It was the last I saw of him and I don't even know his surname or where he lives. I'm not pregnant, but I think I have VD and it must be him, because it couldn't be my boyfriend. Please tell me it's not that easy to catch VD and that I'm worrying about nothing'.
87. J. Juffer (1998) *At Home with Pornography: Women, Sex and Everyday Life* (New York: NYU Press), p. 145.
88. See, for example, Seán O'Riordan to Charles Haughey, 21 September 1982, 2012/90/668, Department of Taoiseach, NAI.
89. Address by Michael Woods to dinner of Fianna Fáil Cork North-East ward, 1 October 1982, 2012/90/669, Department of Taoiseach, NAI.
90. C. Meehan (2010) *The Cosgrave Party: A History of Cumann na nGaedheal, 1923–33* (Dublin: Royal Irish Academy), pp. 34–5.
91. D. Ferriter (2004) *The Transformation of Ireland 1900–2000* (London: Profile Books), p. 324.
92. Report of the Inter-Departmental Committee to establish the facts of State involvement with the Magdalen Laundries (2013), p. iii.
93. Ferriter, *Transformation*, p. 12.
94. D. Ferriter commenting on the publication of the Report, *Time*, February 2013.
95. Report of the Inter-Departmental Committee to establish the facts of State involvement with the Magdalen Laundries (2013), pp. i and v.
96. *Dáil debates*, 19 February 2013 (Enda Kenny).
97. *Connacht Sentinel*, 6 September 1983.
98. G. Hussey (1990) *At the Cutting Edge: Cabinet Diaries, 1982–1987* (Dublin: Gill and Macmillan), p. 37.
99. F. Kennedy (2001) *Cottage to Crèche: Family Change in Ireland* (Dublin: Institute of Public Administration), pp. 21–2.
100. Interview for 'The Class of "77" Feature', *Magill*, 1 January 1985.
101. Kennedy, *Cottage to Crèche*, p. 24.
102. *Irish Women: Agenda for Practical Action. Working Party on Women's Affairs and Family Law Reform*, February 1985, p. 253.
103. *Irish Women*, p. 251.
104. M. A. Glendon (1987) *Abortion and Divorce in Western Law* (London: Harvard University Press), p. 66.
105. Meehan, *The Cosgrave Party*, pp. 32–3.
106. FitzGerald, *Towards a New Ireland*, p. 22.
107. Meehan, *The Cosgrave Party*, p. 33.
108. *The Catholic Standard*, 22 December 1967, newspaper clippings on divorce, 2008/81/4, Department of Taoiseach, NAI.
109. *The Irish Times*, 21 December 1967, newspaper clippings on divorce, 2008/81/4, Department of Taoiseach, NAI.
110. *The Irish Times*, 9 November 1977.
111. FitzGerald, *Towards a New Ireland*, p. 151.
112. *Irish Press*, 7 April 1981.
113. Y. Galligan (1998) *Women and Politics in Contemporary Ireland: From the Margins to the Mainstream* (London: Pinter), p. 102.

114. *The Irish Times*, 3 April 1985.
115. *The Irish Times*, 3 April 1985.
116. F. Finlay (1998) *Snakes and Ladders* (Dublin: New Island Books) p. 33.
117. J. S. Donnelly (2005) 'Opposing the "Modern World": The Cult of the Virgin Mary in Ireland, 1965–85', *Éire-Ireland*, 40: 1 and 2, p. 242.
118. *The Irish Times*, 26 June 1986.
119. M. Dillon, (1993) *Debating Divorce: Moral Conflict in Ireland* (Lexington: University Press of Kentucky), pp. 71–2.
120. McCafferty, *Nell*, pp. 201–2.
121. *Women's Aim*, no. 6, September–December 1980.
122. Dillon, *Debating Divorce*, p. 86.
123. Dillon, *Debating Divorce*, p. 74.
124. *Irish Independent*, 16 June 1986.
125. *Irish Independent*, 17 June 1986.
126. *Irish Women*, p. 251.
127. *Irish Women*, p. 254.
128. *Irish Women*, p. 259.
129. F. Gardiner (2002) 'The women's movement and women politicians in the Republic of Ireland, 1980–2000', in Angela Bourke *et al* (eds.), *The Field Day Anthology of Irish Writing Volume 5: Irish Women's Writing and Traditions* (Cork: Cork University Press), p. 233.
130. Interview with Mary Harney, *Hot Press*, 2 July 1986.
131. *Dáil debates*, vol. 366, col. 843, 14 May 1986 (Alice Glenn).
132. *The Irish Times*, 26 June 1986.
133. *Irish Independent*, 26 June 1986.
134. Finlay, *Snakes and Ladders*, p. 33.
135. Interview with Charlie Flanagan, *Fine Gael: A Family at War*, RTÉ 1, first aired 2003.
136. Interview with John Bruton, 28 September 2012.
137. *Sunday Independent*, 15 June 1986.
138. *Woman's Way*, 24 January 1986.
139. *Woman's Way*, 29 November 1985.
140. *Women's Aim*, 1 (January–March 1979).
141. Letter to the editor, *Irish Independent*, 16 June 1986.
142. J. McGahern (2005) *Memoir* (London: Faber), p. 255.
143. J. Jones (2001) *In Your Opinion: Political and Social Trends through the Eyes of the Electorate* (Dublin: Town House and Country House), pp. 75–6.
144. Jones, *In Your Opinion*, pp. 76–7.
145. Jones, *In Your Opinion*, p. 78.
146. P. Lyons (2008) *Public Opinion, Politics and Society in Contemporary Ireland* (Dublin: Irish Academic Press), p. 130.
147. *Sunday Independent*, 15 June 1986.
148. Jones, *In Your Opinion*, pp. 78–9.
149. Interview with Alan Shatter, *Fine Gael: A Family at War*, RTÉ 1, first aired 2003.
150. *This Week*, RTÉ1, 27 September 1981, S 19336E, Department of Taoiseach, NAI.
151. *Irish Press*, 10 January 1980.
152. Review of 1980 budget outrun and prospects for 1981, 25 September 1980, S 21492, Department of Taoiseach, NAI.
153. *Magill*, 1 February 1982.
154. Submission to and reply from Department of Finance, February 1981, S 21131B, Department of Taoiseach, NAI.

155. Memo from the Department of the Taoiseach, February 1981, S 21131B, Department of Taoiseach, NAI.
156. Memo from the Department of the Taoiseach, 9 February 1981, S 21131B, Department of Taoiseach, NAI.
157. Interview with John Bruton, 28 September 2012.
158. *Dáil debates*, vol. 338, col. 748, 3 November 1982 (Nuala Fennell).
159. *Dáil debates*, vol. 329, col. 46, 30 June 1981 (Garret FitzGerald).
160. *This Week*, RTÉ1, 27 September 1981, S 19336E, Department of Taoiseach, NAI.
161. *This Week*, RTÉ1, 27 September 1981, S 19336E, Department of Taoiseach, NAI.
162. *Magill*, May 1981.
163. *Dáil debates*, vol. 329, col. 565, 21 July 1981 (John Bruton).
164. See C. Meehan (2008) 'Fine Gael's Uncomfortable History: The Legacy of Cumann na nGaedheal', *Éire-Ireland*, 43, 3 and 4, pp. 256–7.
165. *Dáil debates*, vol. 329, cols. 568, 21 July 1981 (John Bruton).
166. *Dáil debates*, vol. 329, cols. 571, 21 July 1981 (John Bruton).
167. *Irish Press*, 22 July 1981.
168. *Irish Press*, 22 July 1981.
169. *The Irish Times*, 15 June 1981.
170. B. Maye (1993) *Fine Gael, 1923–1987: A General History with Biographical Sketches of Leading Members* (Dublin: Blackwater Press), pp. 364–5.
171. P. T. Geary (1984) '"Building on Reality 1985–1987": An Appraisal of the Government's Plan', *The Irish Banking Review*, pp. 1–8.
172. S. Kenny and F. Keane (1987) *Irish Politics Now: 'This Week' Guide to the 25th Dáil* (Kerry: Brandon), p. 12.
173. *Irish Independent*, 3 January 1987.
174. *Irish Independent*, 10 January 1987.
175. Interview with Ruairí Quinn, 14 September 2011.
176. *Irish Independent*, 17 October 1986.
177. Hussey, *At the Cutting Edge*, p. 236.
178. Interview with Ruairí Quinn, 14 September 2011.
179. *Magill*, 7 June 1981.
180. *Magill*, 7 June 1981.
181. Hussey, *At the Cutting Edge*, p. 24.
182. Interview with Gemma Hussey, 27 July 2011.
183. Hussey, *At the Cutting Edge*, p. 90.
184. Hussey, *At the Cutting Edge*, p. 99.
185. Hussey, *At the Cutting Edge*, p. 213.
186. Hussey, *At the Cutting Edge*, p. 124.
187. *FitzGerald at 80*, RTÉ1, first aired August 2006.
188. Hussey, *At the Cutting Edge*, pp. 133, 206 and 235.
189. Interview with Gemma Hussey, 27 July 2011.
190. A survey, conducted in autumn 1999, of Fine Gael members' evaluations of past Taoisigh (including those from Fianna Fáil) found that FitzGerald ranked first, followed by W. T. Cosgrave. M. Gallagher and M. Marsh (2002) *Days of Blue Loyalty: The Politics of Membership of the Fine Gael Party* (Dublin: PSAI Press), p. 200.
191. *Dáil debates*, vol. 705, col. 36, 23 March 2010 (Leo Varadkar).
192. *Evening Herald*, 24 March 2010.
193. *Irish Independent*, 28 March 2010.
194. *Irish Examiner*, 27 March 2010.
195. *Irish Independent*, 28 March 2010.

9 A Liberal Ireland?

1. J. Ardagh (1995) *Ireland and the Irish: Portrait of a Changing Society* (London: Penguin), p. 3.
2. R. Sinnott (1995) *Irish Voters Decide: Voting Behaviour and Referendums since 1918* (Manchester: Manchester University Press), p. 230.
3. Interview with John Bruton, 28 September 2012.
4. O. O'Leary (2004) *Politicians and Other Animals* (Dublin: O'Brien Press) p. 22.
5. *The Irish Times*, 3 February 2001.
6. Quoted in E. O'Malley and M. Kerby (2004) 'Chronicle of a Death Foretold? Understanding the Decline of Fine Gael', *Irish Political Studies*, 19, 1, p. 41.
7. O'Malley and Kerby, 'Chronicle of a Death Foretold?', p. 41.
8. O'Malley and Kerby, 'Chronicle of a Death Foretold?', p. 41.
9. *The Irish Times*, 10 April 2013.
10. *The Irish Times*, 16 November 2012.
11. *The Irish Times*, 21 November 2012.
12. *The Irish Times*, 1 May 2013.
13. *The Irish Times*, 2 May 2013.

Bibliography

Primary sources

Archives

University College Dublin Archives
John A. Costello Papers
Fianna Fáil Papers
Fine Gael Constituency Papers
Fine Gael Election Papers
Garret FitzGerald Papers
Michael Hayes Papers
John Kelly Papers
Literary and Historical Society (L&H) Papers
Seán MacEntee Papers
Seán MacEoin Papers
Patrick McGillian Papers

Labour History Museum and Archive
Brendan Corish Papers

National Archives of Ireland
Department of Finance
Department of Justice
Department of the Taoiseach
Government Information Services
Liam Cosgrave Papers

Private Collections
Michael Sweetman Papers, in possession of Barbara Sweetman-FitzGerald.
Minute books of the Fine Gael parliamentary party, in possession of Maurice Manning.

Trinity Manuscripts
Erskine Hamilton Childers Papers

Magazines, newsletters, newspapers and periodicals
Aim News
Anglo-Celt
Banshee: Journal of Irish Women United
Bread and Roses
Catholic Herald
Cherish News
Connacht Sentinel
Connacht Tribune

Connaught Telegraph
Donegal Democrat
Donegal News
Evening Herald
Fortnight
Hot Press
Irish Examiner
Irish Farmers Journal
Irish Independent
Irish Press
Kerryman
Leitrim Observer
Longford Leader
Magill
Meath Chronicle
Nenagh Guardian
New York Times
Nusight
Offaly Independent
Roscommon Champion
Southern Star
Sunday Independent
The Irish Times
The Vulcan
Tipperary Star
Woman's Way
Women's Aim
Ulster Herald

Official publications

Dáil debates
Hansard
Seanad debates

Interviews and correspondence

Vincent Browne
John Bruton
Stephen Collins
Liam Cosgrave
Declan Costello
Eamon Delaney
Jim Dooge
Jim Dorgan
Alan Dukes
Garret FitzGerald
Donal Flynn
Paddy Harte
Gemma Hussey
Frank Kelly
Cormac Lucey

Maurice Manning
Gay Mitchell
Jim O'Keeffe
Mary O'Rourke
Maureen O'Sullivan
Ruairi Quinn
Barbara Sweetman-FitzGerald
Michael van Turnhout

Radio programmes
Bowman: Sunday Morning
Documentary on One: the Twentieth Dáil
Miriam Meets ... Peter Barry and Deirdre Clune
The Colm Hayes Show

Television programmes
Fine Gael: A Family at War
FitzGerald at 80
Garret FitzGerald: A Profile
Hall's Pictorial Weekly
State Funeral of Dr Garret FitzGerald

Secondary sources

Book chapters and journal articles

Bacik, I. (2012) 'Labour and the Liberal Agenda', in P. Daly, R. O'Brien and P. Rouse (eds.), *Making the Difference? The Irish Labour Party, 1912–2012* (Cork: Collins Press).
Biller, H. B. (1970) 'Father Absence and the Personality Development of the Male Child', *Developmental Psychology*, 2, 2.
Binchy, W. (1977) 'Marital Privacy and Family Law: A Reply to Mr O'Reilly', *Studies*, 66, 264.
Bruton, J. (2011) 'Young Fine Gaelers', in B. Sweetman-FitzGerald (ed.), *The Widest Circle: Remembering Michael Sweetman* (Dublin: A&A Farmar).
Buckley, F. and C. McGing (2011) 'Women and the Election', in M. Gallagher and M. Marsh (eds.), *How Ireland Voted 2011: The Full Story of Ireland's Earthquake Election* (Basingstoke: Palgrave Macmillan).
Burke Savage, R. (1963) 'Ireland 1963–1973', *Studies*.
Chubb, B. 'Ireland 1957' (1959), in D.E. Butler (ed.), *Elections Abroad* (New York: St Martin's Press).
Connolly, E. (1999) 'The Republic of Ireland's Equality Contract: Women and Public policy', in Y. Galligan, E. Ward and R. Wilford (eds.), *Contesting Politics: Women in Ireland, North and South* (Oxford: Westview Press).
Conroy, P. (1999) 'From the Fifties to the Nineties: Social Policy Comes Out of the Shadows', in G. Kelly, A. O'Donnell, P. Kennedy and S. Quinn (eds.), *Irish Social Policy in Context* (Dublin: University College Dublin Press).
Cousins, M. (1999) 'The Introduction of Children's Allowances in Ireland, 1939–1944', *Irish Economic and Social History*, 26.
Daly, M. E. (2010) 'The "Women Element in Politics": Irish Women and the Vote, 1918–2008', in P. Thane and E. Breitenbach (eds.), *Women and Citizenship in Britain and Ireland in the 20th Century: What Difference did the Vote Make?* (London: Continuum).

Daly, M. E. (2012) 'The Curse of the Irish Hospitals' Sweepstake: A Hospital System, not a Health System', *Working Papers in History and Policy*, 2.

Daly, P. (2012) 'Labour and the Pursuit of Power', in P. Daly, R. O'Brien and P. Rouse (eds.), *Making the Difference? The Irish Labour Party, 1912–2012* (Cork: Collins Press).

Däubler, T. (2012) 'The Preparation and Use of Election Manifestos: Learning from the Irish Case', *Irish Political Studies*, 27, 1.

Delaney, E. (1998) 'State, Politics and Demography: The Case of Irish Emigration, 1921–71', *Irish Political Studies*, 31, 1.

Delaney, E. (2004) 'The Vanishing Irish? The Exodus from Ireland in the 1950s', in D. Keogh, F. O'Shea and C. Quinlan (eds.), *The Lost Decade: Ireland in the 1950s* (Cork: Mercier).

Donnelly, J. S. (2005) 'Opposing the "Modern World": The Cult of the Virgin Mary in Ireland, 1965–85', *Éire-Ireland*, 40, 1 and 2.

Farrell, B. (1987) 'The Context of Three Elections', in H. R. Penniman and B. Farrell (eds.), *Ireland at the Polls, 1981, 1982 and 1987: A Study of Four General Elections* (Durham: Duke University Press).

Farrell, D. M. (2004) 'Before Campaigns were "Modern": Irish Electioneering in Times Past', in T. Garvin, M. Manning and R. Sinnott (eds.), *Dissecting Irish Politics: Essays in Honour of Brian Farrell* (Dublin: University College Dublin Press).

Farrell, David M. (1986) 'The Strategy to Market Fine Gael in 1981', *Irish Political Studies*, 1.

Ferriter, D. (2010) '"The Stupid Propaganda of the Calamity Mongers"?: The Middle Class and Irish Politics, 1945–97', in F. Lane (ed.), *Politics, Society and the Middle Class in Modern Ireland* (Basingstoke: Palgrave Macmillan).

FitzGerald, G. (1964) 'Seeking a National Purpose', *Studies*, 53.

Gallagher, M. (1976) 'Electoral Support for Irish Political Parties, 1927–73', *Sage Professional Papers in Contemporary Political Sociology*, 2, 17.

Garvin, T. (1982) 'Change and the Political System', in F. Litton (ed.), *Unequal Achievement: The Irish Experience, 1957–1982* (Dublin: Institute of Public Administration).

Ó Tuataigh, G. (1979) 'Language, Literature and Culture in Ireland since the War', in J. J. Lee (ed.), *Ireland 1945–70* (Dublin: Gill and Macmillan).

Geary, P. T. (1984) '"Building on Reality 1985–1987": An Appraisal of the Government's Plan', *The Irish Banking Review*.

Geary, R. C. (1951) 'Irish Economic Development since the Treaty', *Studies*, 40.

Gilligan, R. (2009) 'The "Public Child" and the Reluctant State?', *Éire-Ireland*, 44, 1 and 2.

Girvin, B. (1986) 'Social Change and Moral Politics: The Irish Constitutional Referendum 1983', *Political Studies*, 34, 1.

Girvin, B. (2008) 'Contraception, Moral Panic and Social Change in Ireland, 1969–79', *Irish Political Studies*, 32, 4.

Girvin, B. and G. Murphy (2005) 'Whose Ireland? The Lemass Era', in B. Girvin and G. Murphy (eds.), *The Lemass Era: Politics and Society in the Ireland of Seán Lemass* (Dublin: University College Dublin Press).

Harrop, M. (1990) 'Political Marketing', *Parliamentary Affairs*, 43, 2.

Heanne, M. (2000) 'Matters of Life and Death', in A. Redmond (ed.), *That was Then, This is Now: Change in Ireland, 1949–1999* (Dublin: Central Statistics Office).

Hederman, M. (2008) 'The Tuairim Phenomenon: A Forum for Challenge in 1950s Ireland', in Y. Thornley (ed.), *Unquiet Spirit: Essays in Memory of David Thornley* (Dublin: Liberties Press).

Hennessey, T. (1996) 'Ulster Unionism and Loyalty to the Crown of the United Kingdom, 1912–74', in R. English and G. Walker (eds.), *Unionism in Modern Ireland: New Perspectives on Politics and Culture* (Hampshire: Macmillan Press).

Kenny, M. and M. J. Smith (1997) 'Discourses of Modernization: Gaitskell, Blair and the Reform of Clause IV', *British Elections and Parties Review*, 7, 1.
Kiely, E. and P. Kennedy (2005) 'Youth Policy', in S. Quinn, P. Kennedy, A. Matthews and G. Kiely (eds.), *Contemporary Irish Social Policy* (Dublin: University College Dublin Press).
Knight, J. (1973) 'The results of the 1973 election', in J. Knight and N. Baxter-Moore (eds.), *Republic of Ireland: The General Elections of 1969 and 1973* (London: Arthur McDougal Fund).
Lee, J. (1982) 'Society and Culture', in F. Litton (ed.), *Unequal Achievement: The Irish Experience, 1957–1982* (Dublin: Institute of Public Administration).
Mahon, E. and V. Morgan (1999) 'State Feminism in Ireland', in Y. Galligan, E. Ward and R. Wilford (eds.), *Contesting Politics: Women in Ireland, North and South* (Oxford: Westview Press).
Manning, M. (1978) 'The Political Parties', in H. R. Penniman (ed.), *Ireland at the Polls: The Dáil Elections of 1977* (Washington: American Enterprise Institute for Public Policy Research).
Manning, M. (1979) 'The Farmers', in J. J. Lee (ed.), *Ireland 1945–70* (Dublin: Gill and Macmillan).
McCashin, T. (1982) 'Social Policy: 1957–82', in F. Litton (ed.), *Unequal Achievement: The Irish Experience, 1957–1982* (Dublin: Institute of Public Administration).
McCormack, K. and P. Meany (2000) 'Consumer Prices and Expenditure', in A. Redmond (ed.), *That was Then, This is Now: Change in Ireland, 1949–1999* (Dublin: Central Statistics Office).
McKee, E. (1986) 'Church-State Relations and the Development of Irish Health Policy: The Mother and Child Scheme, 1944–53', *Irish Historical Studies*, 25, 98.
Meehan, C. (2008) 'Fine Gael's Uncomfortable History: The Legacy of Cumann na nGaedheal', *Éire-Ireland*, 43, 3 and 4.
Meehan, C. (2011) 'Michael Sweetman and the Just Society' in B. Sweetman-Fitzgerald (ed.), *Essays in Memory of Michael Sweetman* (Dublin: A&A Farmar).
Meehan, C. (2012) 'Constructing the Irish Presidency: The Early Incumbents, 1938–1973', *Irish Political Studies*, 27, 4.
Murphy, D. (2000) 'Introduction', in A. Redmond (ed.), *That was Then, This is Now: Change in Ireland, 1949–1999* (Dublin: Central Statistics Office).
Murphy, G (2005) 'From Economic Nationalism to European Union', in B. Girvin and G. Murphy (eds.), *The Lemass Era: Politics and Society in the Ireland of Seán Lemass* (Dublin: University College Dublin Press).
Murphy, G. (2002) 'The Irish Government, the National Farmers Association, and the European Economic Community, 1955–1964', *New Hibernia Review*, 6, 4.
Murphy, G. (2010) 'Influencing Political Decision-Making: Interest Groups and Elections in Independent Ireland', *Irish Political Studies*, 25, 4.
Ó Gráda, C. and K. O'Rourke (1996) 'Irish Economic Growth, 1945–88', in N. Cafts and G. Toniolo (eds.), *Economic Growth in Europe since 1945* (Cambridge: Cambridge University Press).
O'Callagan, M. (1984) 'Language, Nationality and Cultural Identity in the Irish Free State, 1922–7: The *Irish Statesman* and the *Catholic Bulletin* Reappraised', *Irish Historical Studies*, 14, 94.
O'hAodain, M. (2010) 'The Contemporary Relevance of Historical Trends on Youth Work in Ireland', in P. Burgess and P Hermann (eds.), *Highways, Crossroads and Cul de Sacs: Journeys into Irish Youth and Community Work* (Bremen: Europäischer Hochschulverlag GmbH & Co.).

O'Laoire, M. (2008) 'The Language Situation in Ireland', in R. B. Kaplan and R. B. Baldauf (eds.), *Language Planning and Policy. Europe, Volume 3: The Baltic States, Ireland and Italy* (Clevedon: Multilingual Matters).

O'Malley, E. and M. Kerby (2004) 'Chronicle of a Death Foretold? Understanding the Decline of Fine Gael', *Irish Political Studies*, 19, 1.

Punch, A. and C. Finneran (2000) 'Changing Population Structure', in A. Redmond (ed.), *That was Then, This is Now: Change in Ireland, 1949–1999* (Dublin: Central Statistics Office).

Punch, A. and C. Finneran (2000) 'Changing Population Structure', in A. Redmond (ed.), *That was Then, This is Now: Change in Ireland, 1949–1999* (Dublin: Central Statistics Office).

Rafter, K. (2012) 'Redefining the Irish Presidency: The Politics of a "Non-Political" Office, 1973–90', *Irish Political Studies*, 27, 4.

Redmond, A. and M. Heanne (2000) 'Aspects of Society', in A. Redmond (ed.), *That was Then, This is Now: Change in Ireland, 1949–1999* (Dublin: Central Statistics Office).

Richardson, V. (2005) 'Children and Social Policy', in S. Quinn, P. Kennedy, A. Matthews and G. Kiely (eds.), *Contemporary Irish Social Policy* (Dublin: University College Dublin Press).

Rohan, D. (2002) 'Marriage Irish Style', in A. Bourke, S. Kilfeather, M. Luddy, M. MacCurtain, G. Meaney, M. NíDhonnchadha, M. O'Dowd and C. Wills (eds.), *The Field Day Anthology of Irish Writing*, vol. 4 (Cork: Cork University Press).

Rottman, D. B. and P. J. O'Connell (1982) 'The Changing Social Structure', in F. Litton (ed.), *Unequal Achievement: The Irish Experience, 1957–1982* (Dublin: Institute of Public Administration).

Ryan, A. (2003) 'The Health Service: One Mother's Story', in J. Scally (ed.), *A Just Society? Ethics and Values in Contemporary Ireland* (Dublin: Liffey Press).

Sheridan, J. (1979) 'Education and Society in Ireland, 1945–70', in J. J. Lee (ed.), *Ireland 1945–70* (Dublin: Gill and Macmillan).

Thompson Jr., N. L., D. M. Schwartz, B. R. McCandless and D. A. Edwards (1973) 'Parent-Child Relationships and Sexual Identity in Male and Female Homosexuals and Heterosexuals', *Journal of Consulting and Clinical Psychology*, 43, 1.

Thornley, D. (1964) 'Ireland: The End of an Era?', *Studies*, 53.

Valiulis, M. G. (1992) 'Defining their Role in the New State: Irishwomen's Protest against the Juries Act of 1927', *Canadian Journal of Irish Studies*, 18, 1.

Varley, T. (2010) 'On the Road to Extinction: Agrarian Parties in Twentieth-Century Ireland', *Irish Political Studies*, 25, 4.

Walsh, J. (2005) 'The Politics of Educational Expansion', in B. Girvin and G. Murphy (eds.), *The Lemass Era: Politics and Society in the Ireland of Seán Lemass* (Dublin: University College Dublin Press).

Whyte, J. H. (1974) 'Ireland: Politics Without Social Bases', in R. Rose (ed.), *Electoral Behaviour: A Comparative Handbook* (New York: Free Press).

Whyte, J. H. (2003) 'Reconciliation, Rights and Protests, 1963–8', in J. R. Hill (ed.), *A New History of Ireland: Volume 7: Ireland, 1921–84* (Oxford: Oxford University Press).

Woods, C. A. (2002) 'Woman Kneeling', in A. Bourke, S. Kilfeather, M. Luddy, M. MacCurtain, G. Meaney, M. NíDhonnchadha, M. O'Dowd and C. Wills (eds.), *The Field Day Anthology of Irish Writing*, vol. 4 (Cork: Cork University Press).

Books

Acheson, N., B. Harvey, J. Kearney and A. Williamson (2004) *Two Paths, One Purpose: Voluntary Action in Ireland, North and South* (Dublin: Institute of Public Affairs).

Ardagh, J. (1995) *Ireland and the Irish: Portrait of a Changing Society* (London: Penguin).
Barrington, R. (2000) *Health, Medicine and Politics in Ireland, 1900–1970* (Dublin: Institute of Public Administration).
Bew, P., P. Gibbon and H. Patterson (2002) *Northern Ireland, 1921–2001: Political Forces and Social Classes* (London: Serif).
Bourke, A., S. Kilfeather, M. Luddy, M. MacCurtain, G. Meaney, M. NíDhonnchadha, M. O'Dowd and C. Wills (eds.) (2002) *The Field Day Anthology of Irish Writing*, vol. 4 (Cork: Cork University Press).
Bowman, J. (2011) *Window and Mirror: RTÉ Television, 1961–2011* (Cork: Collins Press).
Brooks, B. (1983) *Abortion in England, 1900–1967* (London: Croom Helm).
Burgess, P. and P Hermann (eds.) (2010) *Highways, Crossroads and Cul de Sacs: Journeys into Irish Youth and Community Work* (Bremen: Europäischer Hochschulverlag GmbH & Co.).
Butler, D. E. (ed.) (1959) *Elections Abroad* (New York: St Martin's Press).
Byrne, E. (2012), *Political Corruption in Ireland, 1922–2010: A Crooked Harp?* (Manchester: Manchester University Press).
Cafts, N. and G. Toniolo (1996) *Economic Growth in Europe since 1945* (Cambridge: Cambridge University Press).
Charmley, J. (2008) *A History of Conservative Politics Since 1830* (Basingstoke: Palgrave Macmillan).
Collins, S. (1993) *Spring and the Labour Story* (Dublin: O'Brien Press).
Collins, S. (1996) *The Cosgrave Legacy* (Dublin: Blackwater Press).
Considine, M. and Fiona Dukelow (2009), *Irish Social Policy: A Critical Introduction* (Dublin: Gill and Macmillan).
Corless, D. (2007) *Party Nation: Ireland's General Elections – The Strokes, Jokes, Spinners and Winners* (Dublin: Merlin Publishing).
Crossman, R. (1977) *The Diaries of a Cabinet Minister, Volume Three: Secretary of State for Social Services, 1968–1970* (London: Hamilton).
Cruise O'Brien, C. (1998) *Memoir: Life and Times* (Dublin: Poolbeg Press).
Currie, A. (2004) *All Hell will Break Loose* (Dublin: O'Brien Press).
Daly, P., R. O'Brien and P. Rouse (eds.) (2012) *Making the Difference? The Irish Labour Party, 1912–2012* (Cork: Collins Press).
Desmond, B. (2000) *Finally and in Conclusion: A Political Memoir* (Dublin: New Island).
Dillon, M. (1993) *Debating Divorce: Moral Conflict in Ireland* (Lexington: University Press of Kentucky).
Downey, J. (2009) *In My Own Time: Inside Irish Politics and Society* (Dublin: Gill and Macmillan).
Dunlop, F. (2004) *Yes, Taoiseach: Irish Politics from Behind Closed Doors* (Dublin: Penguin Ireland).
Dunne, J., A. Ingram and F. Litton (eds.) (2000) *Questioning Ireland: Debates in Political Philosophy and Public Policy* (Dublin: Institute of Public Administration).
English, R. and G. Walker (eds.) (1996) *Unionism in Modern Ireland: New Perspectives on Politics and Culture* (Hampshire: Macmillan Press).
Evans, B. (2011) *Seán Lemass: Democratic Dictator* (Cork: Collins Press).
Fanning, R. (1983) *Independent Ireland* (Dublin: Helicon).
Farmar, T. (2011) *Privileged Lives: A Social History of Middle-Class Ireland, 1882–1989* (Dublin: A&A Farmar).
Fennell, N. (2009) *Political Woman: A Memoir* (Dublin: Currach Press).
Ferguson, N., C. S. Maier, E. Manela and D. J. Sargent (eds.) (2010) *The Shock of the Global: The 1970s in Perspective* (London: Belknap).

Ferriter, D. (2004) *The Transformation of Ireland 1900–2000* (London: Profile Books).
Ferriter, D. (2007) *Judging Dev: A Reassessment of the Life and Legacy of Eamon de Valera* (Dublin: Royal Irish Academy).
Ferriter, D. (2009) *Occasions of Sin: Sex and Society in Modern Ireland* (London: Profile Books).
Ferriter, D. (2012) *Ambiguous Republic: Ireland in the 1970s* (London: Profile Books).
Finlay, F. (1998) *Snakes and Ladders* (Dublin: New Island Books).
FitzGerald, G. (1972) *Towards a New Ireland* (London: C. Knight).
FitzGerald, G. (1992) *All in a Life: An Autobiography* (Dublin: Gill and Macmillan).
FitzGerald, G. (2010) *Just Garret: Tales from the Political Front Line* (Dublin: Liberties Press).
Fitzgerald, P. and B. Lambkin (2008) *Migration in Irish History, 1607–2007* (Basingstoke: Palgrave Macmillan).
Forde, W. (1995) *Growing up in Ireland: The Development of Irish Youth Services* (Wexford: CARA Publications).
Foster, R. F. (2008) *Luck and the Irish: A Brief History of Change, 1970–2000* (London: Penguin).
Fuller, L. (2002) *Irish Catholicism since 1950: The Undoing of a Culture* (Dublin: Gill and Macmillan).
Gallagher, M. (1982) *The Irish Labour Party in Transition, 1957–82* (Manchester: Manchester University Press).
Gallagher, M. (1985) *Political Parties in the Republic of Ireland* (Manchester: Manchester University Press).
Gallagher, M. (2009) *Irish Elections, 1948–77: Results and Analysis* (London, New York: Routledge).
Gallagher, M. and M. Marsh (2002) *Days of Blue Loyalty: The Politics of Membership of the Fine Gael Party* (Dublin: PSAI Press).
Gallagher, M. and M. Marsh (eds.) (2011) *How Ireland Voted 2011: The Full Story of Ireland's Earthquake Election* (Basingstoke: Palgrave Macmillan).
Galligan, Y. (1998) *Women and Politics in Contemporary Ireland: From the Margins to the Mainstream* (London: Pinter).
Galligan, Y., E. Ward and R. Wilford (eds.) (1999) *Contesting Politics: Women in Ireland, North and South* (Oxford: Westview Press).
Garvin, T., M. Manning and R. Sinnott (eds.) (2004) *Dissecting Irish Politics: Essays in Honour of Brian Farrell* (Dublin: University College Dublin Press).
Garvin, T. (2004) *Preventing the Future. Why was Ireland so Poor for so Long?* (Dublin: Gill and Macmillan).
Garvin, T. (2009) *Judging Lemass: The Measure of the Man* (Dublin: Royal Irish Academy).
Garvin, T. (2010), *News from a New Republic: Ireland in the 1950s* (Dublin: Gill and Macmillan).
Ginsborg, P. (1990) *A History of Contemporary Italy: Society and Politics, 1943–1988* (London: Penguin).
Girvin, B. and G. Murphy (eds.) (2005) *The Lemass Era: Politics and Society in the Ireland of Seán Lemass* (Dublin: University College Dublin Press).
Glendon, M. A. (1987) *Abortion and Divorce in Western Law* (London: Harvard University Press).
Halligan, B. (ed.) (2006) *The Brendan Corish Seminar Proceedings* (Dublin: Scáthán Publications).
Hardiman, N. (1988) *Pay, Politics and Economic Performance in Ireland 1970–1987* (Oxford: Clarendon).
Harte, P. (2005) *Young Tigers and Mongrel Foxes: A Life in Politics* (Dublin: O'Brien).

Hill, J. R. (ed.) (2003) *A New History of Ireland: Volume 7: Ireland, 1921–84* (Oxford: Oxford University Press).
Hobsbawm, E. (1995) *Age of Extremes: The Short Twentieth Century, 1914–1991* (London: Michael Joseph).
Horgan, J. (1997) *Seán Lemass: The Enigmatic Patriot* (Dublin: Gill and Macmillan).
Hussey, G. (1990) *At the Cutting Edge: Cabinet Diaries, 1982–1987* (Dublin: Gill and Macmillan).
Hussey, G. (1993) *Ireland Today: Anatomy of a Changing State* (Dublin: Townhouse).
Inglis, T. (1987) *Moral Monopoly: The Catholic Church in Modern Irish Society* (Dublin: University College Dublin Press).
Jacobsen, K. J. (1994) *Chasing Progress in the Irish Republic: Ideology, Democracy and Dependent Development* (Cambridge: Cambridge University Press).
Jones, J. (2001) *In Your Opinion: Political and Social Trends through the Eyes of the Electorate* (Dublin: Town House and Country House).
Judt, T. (2005) *Postwar: A History of Europe since 1945* (London: Heinemann).
Juffer, J. (1998) *At Home with Pornography: Women, Sex and Everyday Life* (New York: NYU Press).
Kaplan, R. B. and R. B. Baldauf (eds.) (2008) *Language Planning and Policy. Europe, Volume 3: The Baltic States, Ireland and Italy* (Clevedon: Multilingual Matters).
Kavanagh, R. (2005) *Mamie Cadden: Backstreet Abortionist* (Dublin: Mercier Press).
Keane, J. B. (1999), *Many Young Men of Twenty: A Bar-Room Sketch* (Dublin: Mercier Press).
Kelly, G., A. O'Donnell, P. Kennedy and S. Quinn (eds.) (1999) *Irish Social Policy in Context* (Dublin: University College Dublin Press).
Kennedy, F. (2001) *Cottage to Crèche: Family Change in Ireland* (Dublin: Institute of Public Administration).
Kenny, S. and F. Keane (1987) *Irish Politics Now: 'This Week' Guide to the 25th Dáil* (Kerry: Brandon).
Keogh, D. (1990) *Ireland and Europe 1919–1989: A Diplomatic and Political History* (Dublin: Gill and Macmillan).
Keogh, D. (1994), *Twentieth Century Ireland: Nation and State* (Dublin: Gill and Macmillan).
Keogh, D., F. O'Shea and C. Quinlan (eds.) (2004) *The Lost Decade: Ireland in the 1950s* (Cork: Mercier).
Kerrigan, G. (1998) *Another Country: Growing up in '50s Ireland* (Dublin: Gill and Macmillan).
Knight, J. and N. Baxter-Moore (eds.) (1973) *Republic of Ireland: The General Elections of 1969 and 1973* (London: Arthur McDougal Fund).
Laffan, M. (1999) *The Resurrection of Ireland: The Sinn Féin Party, 1916–1923* (Cambridge: Cambridge University Press).
Lane, F. (ed.) (2010) *Politics, Society and the Middle Class in Modern Ireland* (Basingstoke: Palgrave Macmillan, 2010).
Larkin, M. (1997) *France since the Popular Front: Government and People, 1936–1996* (Oxford: Oxford University Press).
Lee, J. J. (ed.) (1979) *Ireland 1945–70* (Dublin: Gill and Macmillan).
Lee, J. J. (1990) *Ireland 1912–1985: Politics and Society* (Cambridge: Cambridge University Press).
Lee, S. J. (1996) *Aspects of British Political History, 1914–1995* (London, New York: Routledge).
Lindsay, P. (1992) *Memories* (Dublin: Blackwater Press).
Litton, F. (ed.) (1982) *Unequal Achievement: The Irish Experience, 1957–1982* (Dublin: Institute of Public Administration).

Lyons, P. (2008) *Public Opinion, Politics and Society in Contemporary Ireland* (Dublin: Irish Academic Press).
Macnamara, A. (2003) *Yours Sincerely* (Dublin: Veritas).
McCabe, I. (1991) *A Diplomatic History of Ireland, 1948–49: The Republic, the Commonwealth and NATO* (Dublin: Irish Academic Press).
McCafferty, N. (2004) *Nell* (Dublin, London: Penguin Ireland).
McCarthy, J. P. (2006) *Kevin O'Higgins: Builder of the Irish State* (Dublin: Irish Academic Press).
McCullagh, D. (1998) *A Makeshift Majority: The First Inter-Party Government, 1948–51* (Dublin: Institute of Public Administration).
McCullagh, D. (2010) *The Reluctant Taoiseach: A Biography of John A Costello* (Dublin, Gill and Macmillan).
McGahern, J. (1991) *Amongst Women* (London: Faber).
McGahern, J. (2005) *Memoir* (London: Faber).
McNamara, M. and P. Mooney (2000) *Women in Parliament: Ireland, 1918–2000* (Dublin: Wolfhound Press).
Manning, M. (1999) *James Dillon: A Biography* (Dublin: Wolfhound Press).
Manning, M. (2006) *The Blueshirts* (Dublin: Gill and Macmillan).
Matusow, A. J. (2009) *The Unravelling of America: A History of Liberalism in the 1960s* (Athens: University of Georgia Press).
Maye, B. (1993) *Fine Gael, 1923–1987: A General History with Biographical Sketches of Leading Members* (Dublin: Blackwater Press).
Meehan, C. (2010) *The Cosgrave Party: A History of Cumann na nGaedheal, 1923–1933* (Dublin: Royal Irish Academy).
Moloney, E. (2010) *Voices from the Grave: Two Men's War in Ireland* (London: Faber).
Monnet, J. (1978) *Memoirs*, translation by Richard Mayne (London: Collins).
Murphy, J. A. (1975) *Ireland in the Twentieth Century* (Dublin: Gill and Macmillan).
NicDháibhéid, C. (2011) *Seán MacBride: A Republican Life, 1904–1946* (Liverpool: Liverpool University Press).
O'Brien, J. A. (ed.) (1954) *The Vanishing Irish: The Enigma of the Modern World* (London: W.H. Allen).
O'Byrnes, S. (1986) *Hiding behind a Face: Fine Gael under FitzGerald* (Dublin: Gill and Macmillan).
O'Connell, C. (2007) *The State and Housing in Ireland: Ideology, Policy and Practice* (New York: Nova Science Publishing).
O'Connor, T. and A. O'Halloran (2008) *Politics in a Changing Ireland, 1960–2007: A Tribute to Seamus Pattison* (Dublin: Institute of Public Administration).
Ó Gráda, C. (1997) *A Rocky Road: The Irish Economy since the 1920s* (Manchester: Manchester University Press).
O'Higgins, T. F. (1996) *A Double Life* (Dublin: Town House).
O'Leary, C. (1979) *Irish Elections, 1918–1977: Parties, Voters and Proportional Representation* (Dublin: Gill and Macmillan).
O'Leary, O. (2004) *Politicians and Other Animals* (Dublin: O'Brien Press).
O'Leary, O. (2006) *Party Animals* (Dublin: O'Brien Press).
O'Reilly, E. (1992) *Masterminds of the Right* (Dublin: Attic Press).
Penniman, H. R. (1978) *Ireland at the Polls: The Dáil Elections of 1977* (Washington: American Enterprise Institute for Public Policy Research).
Penniman, H. R. and B. Farrell (eds.) (1987), *Ireland at the Polls, 1981, 1982 and 1987: A Study of Four General Elections* (Durham: Duke University Press).
Power, A. (1993) *Hovels to High Rise: State Housing in Europe since 1850* (London, New York: Routledge).

Puirséil, N. (2007) *The Irish Labour Party, 1922–73* (Dublin: University College Dublin).
Raftery, M. and E. O'Sullivan (1999) *Suffer the Little Children: The Inside Story of Ireland's Industrial Schools* (Dublin: New Island).
Rafter, K. (2009) *Fine Gael: Party at the Crossroads* (Dublin: New Island).
Rattigan, C. (2012) *What Else Could I do? Single-Mothers and Infanticide, Ireland 1900–1950* (Dublin: Irish Academic Press).
Redmond, A. (ed.) (2000) *That was Then, This is Now: Change in Ireland, 1949–1999* (Dublin: Central Statistics Office).
Reynolds, A. (2009) *My Autobiography* (London: Transworld Ireland).
Rogan, M. (2011) *Prison Policy in Ireland: Politics, Penal-Welfarism and Political Imprisonment* (New York: Routledge).
Rose, R. (ed.) (1974) *Electoral Behaviour: A Comparative Handbook* (New York: Free Press).
Rossiter, A. (2009) *Ireland's Hidden Diaspora: The 'Abortion Trail' and the Making of a London-Irish Underground, 1980–2000* (London: IASC).
Rouse, P. (2000) *Ireland's Own Soil: Government and Agriculture in Ireland, 1945–1965* (Dublin: Irish Farmers Journal).
Quinn, S., P. Kennedy, A. Matthews and G. Kiely (eds.) (2005) *Contemporary Irish Social Policy* (Dublin: University College Dublin Press).
Ryan, A. (1999) *Walls of Silence: Ireland's Policy towards People with a Mental Disability* (Kilkenny: Red Lion Press).
Ryan, P. (2012) *Asking Angela Macnamara: An Intimate History of Irish Lives* (Dublin: Irish Academic Press).
Sandford, C. and O. Morrissey (1985) *The Irish Wealth Tax: A Case Study in Economics and Politics. Economic and Social Research Institute Paper 123* (Dublin: Economic and Social Research Institute).
Scally J. (ed.) (2003) *A Just Society? Ethics and Values in Contemporary Ireland* (Dublin: Liffey Press).
Sinnott, R. (1995) *Irish Voters Decide: Voting Behaviour and Referendums since 1918* (Manchester: Manchester University Press).
Spreng, J. E. (2004) *Abortion and Divorce Law in Ireland* (Jefferson: McFarland).
Stopper, A. (2006) *Mondays at Gaj's: The Story of the Irish Women's Liberation Movement* (Dublin: Liffey Press).
Sweeney, E. (2010) *Down, Down, Deeper and Down: Ireland in the 70s & 80s* (Dublin: Gill and Macmillan).
Sweetman-FitzGerald, B. (2011) *The Widest Circle: Remembering Michael Sweetman* (Dublin: A&A Farmar).
Thane, P. and E. Breitenbach (eds.) (2010) *Women and Citizenship in Britain and Ireland in the 20th Century: What Difference did the Vote Make?* (London: Continuum).
Thornley, Y. (ed.) (2008) *Unquiet Spirit: Essays in Memory of David Thornley* (Dublin: Liberties Press).
Tobin, F. (1984) *The Best of Decades: Ireland in the Nineteen Sixties* (Dublin: Gill and Macmillan).
Tonge, J. (2002) *Northern Ireland: Conflict and Change* (Harlow: Longman).
Walsh, D. and A. Daly (2004) *Mental Illness in Ireland, 1750–2002: Reflections on the Rise and Fall of Institutional Care* (Dublin: Health Research Board).
Walsh, J. (2005) *The Politics of Expansion: The Transformation of Educational Policy in the Republic of Ireland, 1957–72* (Manchester: Manchester University Press).
Walsh, J. (2008) *Patrick Hillery: The Official Biography* (Dublin: New Island).
Whelan, N. (2011) *Fianna Fáil: A Biography of the Party* (Dublin: Gill and Macmillan).

Index

7 Days 81, 84, 154
Abortion 99, 108, 125, 183, 192
Anti-Amendment Campaign
   (AAC) 172, 175
Backstreet Abortion 165, 177
Britain 19, 109, 130, 165–66, 167, 178
Catholic Church 14
Eighth Amendment of the
   Constitution, 1983 3, 127, 165–71, 172–73, 174–76, 184
Fine Gael Divisions 98, 168, 175, 196–97
Halappanavar, Savita 196
Northern Ireland 172
Pro-Life Amendment Campaign
   (PLAC) 167–69, 170–71, 174
Protection of Life During Pregnancy
   Act, 2013 196–97
Protestant Churches 170
Roe versus Wade 130, 167
Society for the Protection of Unborn
   Children (SPUC) 167, 176
Society's values 176–79, 194
X Case 19, 173, 196
See also: McGee Case
ADAPT 109, 158
Aer Lingus 24, 61, 65, 134, 149
Agriculture 9, 12, 24, 31, 36, 37, 55, 60, 61, 66, 78, 79, 98, 106, 110, 144, 189, 191
Agriculture, Department of 61, 78, 98, 189
Aiken, Frank 56
AIM Group 94, 107, 109, 159, 180, 181, 183, 185
Albermale Report 49
Alliance Party 172
Anderson, Mary 120
Andrews, Todd 22
Anglo-Irish Agreement, 1985 2, 164
Aontacht Eireann 132
Arab-Israeli War 110
Áras an Uachtaráin 39, 68, 128, 171

Arms crisis 2, 88, 89, 90, 95, 97, 132, 157, 160
Arnold, Bruce 143
Attlee, Clement 43

Backbencher (*See*: John Healy)
Banville, John 165
Barnes, Monica 122, 158
Barry, Gerald 3, 163, 187
Barry, Peter 98, 150, 151, 152
Belton, Paddy 27, 30, 38
Berry, Peter 89
Bevan, Aneurin 43
Blaney, Neil 17, 89, 95, 157
Blowick, Joseph 21, 60, 61
Blueshirts 21, 77
Boland, Gerry 138
Boland, Kevin 16, 132
Bourke, Richard 116
Bowman, John 3, 28, 98
Bracken, Maurice 46, 206
Brady, John 46
Brady, Seamus 33
Breen, Dan 58
Brennan, Seamus 114, 139, 140, 153
Briscoe, Robert 58
Browne, Noel 8, 112, 124, 135, 141
Browne, Vincent 29, 65, 77, 84, 145, 150, 162, 169, 191, 192
Bruton, John
   on Declan Costello as leader 65
   and Costello's retirement 76
   on Divorce 184–85
   Fine Gael leadership 22, 184, 195
   Fine Gael membership 22, 67
   on Free Education 73, 74
   on Liam Cosgrave 128
   Minister for Finance 171, 188–89
   Spokesman on Agriculture 191
   Taoiseach 22, 184, 192
   and Wealth Tax 117
   Youth Policy 49, 105, 113–16, 144
Bruton, Richard 196
Buckley, Fiona 93

Burke, Ann Maria 196
Burke Savage, Roland 6, 148, 162
Burke, James 33, 38
Burke, Joan 93
Burke, Richard 113, 115, 123, 128
By-elections
 Cork Borough, 1964 26–27
 Donegal, 1980 160, 191
 Dublin North-East, 1963 27
 Dublin South-West, 1976 146
 Galway East, 1964 39, 42, 60
 Kildare, 1964 26–27
 Mayo North, 1952 21
 Roscommon, 1964 37, 38
Byrne, Edward 180
Byrne, Gay 14
Byrne, Harry 57
Byrne, Hugh 80
Byrne, Paddy 27

Cadden, Mamie 165
Carter, Charles 11
Cassin, Anne 116
Castle, Barbara 121
Catholic Church 7, 8, 11, 14, 15, 45, 73, 93, 130, 166, 170, 175, 176, 182
Catholic Family Life 130
Central Bank 36
Cherish 94, 108
Childers, Erskine 128
Chubb, Basil 28, 51
Clann na Poblachta 21, 59, 202
Clann na Talmhan 21, 29, 59, 60, 61
Clinton, Mark 67, 84, 97, 98, 142, 151, 152
Cluskey, Frank 81, 86, 109, 151, 161, 169
Colley, George 73, 84, 92, 106, 140, 142, 147, 160, 188
Collins, Eddie 153
Collins, Michael 78, 131, 188
Collins, Stephen 65, 87, 89, 128, 174
Comhairle le Leas Oige 49
Commission of Inquiry on Mental Handicap 51
Commission of Inquiry on Mental Illness 47, 50, 51
Commission on Emigration and Other Population Problems 10
Commission on the Status of Women 107, 109, 119, 120
Commission to Inquire into Child Abuse 50
Common Agricultural Policy (CAP) 61
Conservative Party (Britain) 43, 59, 160, 164
Constitutional Crusade (*See*: Garret FitzGerald)
Constitution of Ireland
 Articles 2 and 3 189
 Article 41.2 93
 Article 41.3.2 181
 Article 26 136, 197
 PR 26, 83, 84
 Eighth Amendment 170–72, 173, 176
 Review 171, 181
Contraception 2, 14, 93, 94, 107, 116, 119, 124–27, 130, 131, 165, 166, 178, 180
 Importation, Sale and Manufacture of Contraceptives Bill, 1974 116, 127–29
Coogan, Fintan 146
Cooke, Judith 134
Cooney, Paddy
 Divorce 184
 Fine Gael leadership 150
 Importation, Sale and Manufacture of Contraceptives Bill, 1974 127–29
 Loss of seat 146, 150
 Minister for Defence 122
 Minister for Justice 98, 133
 Offences Against the State Act, 1972 85–87
Cooper, Ivan 88
Corish, Brendan
 on Coalition 57–58, 62, 81, 84–85, 90
 Coalition Negotiations 96–97
 and Liam Cosgrave 98–99
 and Declan Costello 28
 Minister for Health and Social Welfare 98, 112–13
 on Offences Against the State Bill, 1972 87
 Resignation as leader 146–47
 Tánaiste 98
Cosgrave, Liam 68, 73, 79, 80, 81, 92, 95, 106, 137, 155
 Army 66, 154
 and W.T. Cosgrave's legacy 66, 83, 86, 88

Cosgrave, Liam – *continued*
  Personality 66, 97
  POLITICAL CAREER
    Arms Crisis 89–90
    Chief Whip 31, 66
    and Declan Costello 65, 75, 76, 97
    First Elected, 1943 66
    and Just Society 28, 35–56, 38, 69, 70, 79
    Leadership contests 22, 63, 147, 150
    Leadership criticisms 82, 83, 84, 85, 86–87
    Minister for External Affairs 66
    'Mongrel Foxes' 67, 84
    Offences Against the State Bill, 1972 85–87, 88, 128
    Parliamentary Secretary 66
    Party Unity 66–67, 81, 84, 97
    Photo 102
    Proportional Representation 83–84
    and Gerry Sweetman 63–64, 66, 84
  TAOISEACH, 1973–77
    1977 General Election 138–39, 140
    and Coalition Negotiations 96–97
    Contraception 124, 128, 129, 131
    and Brendan Corish 96–97, 98–99
    on Economic Restraint 111, 114, 115–16, 145
    Heavy gang 136
    on Law and Order 66, 83, 87, 88, 134, 135, 136
    and Cearbhall Ó Dálaigh 136
    Resignation 146
    Sunningdale Agreement 132
    Taoiseach 82, 94, 96, 105, 110, 116, 117, 118, 122, 158
Cosgrave, W.T. 18, 63, 64, 66, 83, 86, 88, 96, 97, 100, 129, 149, 180
Costello, Declan
  LEGAL CAREER
    Attorney General 2, 18, 97, 106, 123, 128
    Called to the bar 18, 65
    Director of Public Prosecutions Office 18, 106
    Eileen Flynn Case 19
    Equal Pay 123
    High Court 18, 19
    Law Reform Commission 18, 106
    Whiddy Island Disaster 18
  X Case 19, 173
  PERSONAL LIFE
    Childhood 18
    Children 46
    and John A Costello 18, 19, 26, 29
    and Cumann na nGaedheal legacy 18
    Death ix, 4
    Education 18
    Health ix, 74, 75
    Personality 65, 74
    St Michael's House 46
    Tributes 4, 74
    and Wilfrid Costello (Brother) 46
  POLITICAL CAREER
    Beál na mBláth Oration 131
    Contraception 128
    Dublin North-West constituency 19, 31, 51, 79–80, 153
    Dublin South-West constituency 97
    Economic policies 15, 19, 30, 34, 38, 41, 42–44, 51, 54, 70, 74, 79, 80, 97, 153
    Eight-point plan 2, 7, 19, 20–21, 29–30, 34, 42
    Elected, 1951 18
    Fine Gael leadership 29, 64–65, 97
    Fine Gael membership 28–29
    on Handicap rights 46–47
    on Housing 17, 19, 31, 56, 105, 113
    Influence on Garret FitzGerald 1, 2–3, 28, 29
    National Observer 23, 25–26, 28
    Passed over for ministerial office 2, 19, 97
    Photographs 101
    Retirement 2, 51, 65, 74–76
    and Gerry Sweetman compromise 36–37
    Spokesman on Health and Social Welfare 66–67
    Research and Information Centre 28, 153
    and Transformation of Fine Gael 2, 20–21, 26, 28, 38
    Towards a Just Society content 42–51
Costello, John A. 20, 26, 35, 68, 84

Index

Attorney General 18, 149
and Declan Costello 18, 19, 29, 37
Part-time Leader 22
Taoiseach 18, 32, 56
Council for the Status of Women 122, 183
Council of Social Concern 130, 167
Cowen, Bernard 95
Cowen, Brian 192
Craig, William 91, 132
Crookes, G. P. 117
Cruise O'Brien, Conor 83, 97, 98, 128, 129, 134, 136, 139, 152, 173, 191, 192, 221
Cubbon, Brian 134
Cumann na nGaedheal 7, 8, 18, 21, 66, 74, 83, 100, 120, 132, 161, 178, 188, 197
Currie, Austin 133

Dalgan Lyons, Michael 61
Daly, Clare 166, 196, 197
de Bréadún, Deaglán 4
de Búrca, Máirín 120
De Gaulle, Charles 43, 61
De Valera, Eamon 8, 10, 12, 13, 22, 25, 39, 41, 67–69
Deasy, Austin 152, 171, 228
Deasy, Rickard 78
Democratic Unionist Party 172
Deserted wives 93, 94, 106, 107, 108, 125, 183
Desmond, Barry 73, 90, 122, 128, 135–36, 169
Desmond, Dan 73
Desmond, Eileen 39
Dillon-Malone, Patrick 68
Dillon, James 68
 Agriculture 24, 37
 and John A Costello 20, 25, 26
 and Just Society 30, 35, 36, 37, 39, 40, 52
 Irish language 71
 Leadership 22, 23
 and Patrick McGilligan 33
 Photo 100
 Resignation as leader 63–64, 150
 Turnover Tax 27
Dineen, P. F. 48, 51, 52, 55, 59, 69, 154

Director of Public Prosecutions (DPP) 18, 106
Disabilities (*see* Handicap)
Divorce 98, 99, 124, 129, 170, 194
 Anti-Divorce Campaign (ADC) 182
 Ban 178, 180, 181
 Deserted Wives 107, 183
 Divorce Action Group (DAG) 180
 Legalised 184
 Opinion Polls 185–86
 Referendum 3, 126, 176, 179, 182, 183, 184–85
 Wives' fears 182, 183–84
Dockrell, Maurice 30, 31, 67, 85, 96, 117, 146
Donegan, Paddy 32, 67, 87, 98, 136, 152, 164
Donohoe, Paschal 197
Donnellan, John 39, 64
Donnellan, Michael 39, 60
Dorgan, Jim 34, 54, 76, 105, 128
Douglas-Home, Alec 59
Doyle, Avril 158
Doyle, John 55
Dublin Bombings, 1972 87–88
Dublin-Monaghan Bombings 133, 136
Dukes, Alan 66, 189, 192, 194, 195
Dunlop, Frank 22, 128, 160, 187
Dunne, Tom 55

Emigration 6, 10, 11, 16, 42, 49, 56, 79, 113, 190
Enright, Tom 95, 128
Equal pay 16, 42, 94, 107, 119, 120–24
Ervine, David 136
Esmonde, Anthony 36, 63
Esmonde, John Grattan 25, 26, 203
ESRI 12, 116, 119
European Economic Community 1, 11, 15, 16, 106, 110, 111, 119, 121, 122, 124 128, 130, 143, 145–46, 166
European Elections 159–60
Ewart Biggs, Christopher 134–35

Farrell, Patricia 46, 47
Faulkner, Brian 132–33
Faulkner, Padraig 56

Ferriter, Diarmaid   4, 64, 178
Fianna Fáil
  Abortion   3, 168–69, 172–73, 174, 178
  Agricultural Policies   37, 60, 61
  Ard Fheis   159, 160
  Arms crisis   89–90, 132
  and Clann na Poblachta   21
  and Clann na Talmhan   60
  and Coalition   89, 195–96
  Contraception   127, 129, 130, 131
  Divorce   186
  Economic policies   11, 36, 44, 188, 189, 192
  Education policies   73–74
  Emergency legislation, 1976   135
  and Fine Gael challenge   28, 35, 38, 40, 55, 75
  Fine Gael criticisms   52, 56–57
  General Election, 1965   56–57, 58, 62
  General Election, 1969   80–81
  General Election, 1973   91–92, 95–96, 99
  General Election, 1977   41, 54, 137, 138, 139–47, 151
  Health policies   8, 45, 112
  Housing policies   8, 17–18, 113
  Irish language policies   70, 71
  Leadership   12, 13, 22, 23, 25, 160, 172
  New Ireland Forum   164
  Offences Against the State Act, 1972   83, 85–86, 87, 88
  Opposition benches   22, 24, 90, 114, 128
  Presidential Election, 1966   68–69
  and Progressive Democrats   195–96
  Proportional Representation   26, 83–84
  Social Welfare policies   16, 57, 106, 107
  and Women   157, 158
  Youth policies   114, 115–16
Fine Gael
  Central branch   34, 52, 54, 81
  Identity crisis   1, 65, 161, 164, 194, 197
  Law and order   23, 25, 26, 28, 66, 83, 85, 87, 88, 91, 135, 136
  Support base   32, 35, 37, 40, 43, 59, 60, 61, 117
1930s–50s
  Ard Fheis   20
  Attendance problems   20, 21–22
  Birth of Fine Gael   21
  and Clann na Poblachta   21
  and Clann na Talmhan   39, 60, 61
  Fine Gael Digest   26
  First Inter-Party government   18, 21, 25 , 32, 66
  National Observer   23, 25, 26
  Research and Information Centre   28, 153
  Second Inter-Party government   9, 18, 19, 22, 25, 31, 56–57, 63, 68, 90
1960s: OPPOSITION
  1961 General Election   24–25, 33, 45, 61
  1965 General Election   1, 2, 10, 29, 37, 38, 39, 40, 41–42, 51–62, 63, 67, 70, 78, 80, 81, 142, 144
  1969 General Election   29, 37, 51, 60, 62, 70, 75, 76, 78–82, 83, 85, 88–89, 95–96, 97
  Ard Fheis   23, 33–35, 46, 52, 59, 67, 69, 74, 76, 77–78, 100, 102
  Just Society Agricultural Policies   36–37, 60, 78–79
  Just Society Economic Policies   15, 1, 30, 34, 38, 41, 42–44, 54, 70, 78
  Just Society Education Policies   39, 48, 72–74, 78
  Just Society Health policies   45–58
  Just Society Housing policies   17, 19, 39, 56, 105, 113
  Just Society internal debate   2, 29–37
  Just Society Irish language policies   24, 70–72, 78
  Just Society Youth policies   48–51, 105, 114
  Leadership contest, 1965   63–66
  Leadership doubts   82, 83–84, 85, 86, 87
  Name change defeated   76–78
  Offences Against the State Act, 1972   83–88, 91, 128, 135
  Organisation and Propaganda Committee   28
  Policy Committee   10, 28, 30, 38, 39, 40
  Presidential election, 1966   67–69, 70

Index 249

PR referendum 1968 83–84
The Time for a Change has Come 80
Winning Through to a Just Society 60, 62, 78–79
1973–77: NATIONAL COALITION
  1977 General Election campaign 140–42, 145, 146–47
  1977 General Election predictions 137–38, 139
  Ard Fheis 106, 136, 138
  Budget, 1973 106–07
  Children's allowance 109
  Coalition negotiations 96–97
  Contraception 124–29
  Deserted wives allowance 107
  Dissolution of the Dáil 138
  Economic restraint 110–12
  Equal pay 120–24
  Female jurors 119–20
  Hall's Pictorial Weekly 137
  Health care 112–13
  Housing 113
  Oil crisis 110–11
  Security 131–37
  Strikes 111–12
  Sunningdale Agreement 132, 133
  The Vulcan 105
  Unmarried mothers allowance 107–09
  Wealth tax 116–19
  Youth policies 105, 113–16
1977–81: OPPOSITION
  Leadership contest 151–52
  New headquarters 103, 159
  Reorganisation 152, 153–57, 159
  Recruitment of women 157–58
  Young Fine Gael established 103, 156–57
1981–87: FINE GAEL-LABOUR COALITIONS
  Budget Defeat, 1981 171–72
  Building on Reality 189–90
  Divorce Referendum 179–87
  Economy 187–90
  Eighth Amendment of the Constitution 165–76
  Leadership doubts 191–92
1987–2011
  Divorce Referendum, 1995 184–85
  Garret FitzGerald criticism controversy 192–93
  Leadership heaves 194–95
  Presidential Election, 1990 194
  and Progressive Democrats 195–96
  Tallaght strategy 194
2011–13: FINE GAEL-LABOUR COALITION
  Abortion 196–97
  Electoral (Amendment) (Political Funding) Act, 2011 157
  Magdalene Laundries Report 178–79
  Protection of Life During Pregnancy Act, 2013 197
Finn, Martin 128
FitzGerald, Alexis 25, 68, 84, 117, 139, 142, 149, 163
FitzGerald, Garret 5
  PERSONAL LIFE
    Aer Lingus 65, 149
    Childhood 148
    Death 157, 192
    Education 148–49
    and Desmond FitzGerald 149
    and Joan FitzGerald (nee O'Farrell) 149–50
    and Mabel FitzGerald 2, 149, 163
    Journalism 51, 59, 149, 157
    Obituaries 2, 3, 192
    Personality 161, 191
    UCD lecturer 65, 149
  POLITICAL LIFE
    1965 General Election 51
    1966 Presidential Election 68
    1973 General Election 92, 94
    1977 General Election 139, 141, 142–43, 145, 147
    and Liam Cosgrave relationship 65, 97
    and Declan Costello 1, 2, 28, 76, 77
    on Equal pay 124
    Fine Gael identity crisis 1, 65, 160, 194–95, 197
    Fine Gael reorganisation 148, 152, 153–57, 159
    and Just Society 2, 38, 40, 41–42, 44–45, 59, 67, 75, 163
    Leadership contest 150–51
    Leadership potential 82, 84, 147, 148, 191
    Minister for Foreign Affairs 97–98, 155, 163

FitzGerald, Garret – *continued*
  'Mongrel Foxes' 84–85
  Photos 102–04
  Pluralism 2, 15, 67, 79, 130–31, 162–64, 186, 189
  Programme for Progress 142
  Senator 70
  Studies 2–3, 162
  and Gerry Sweetman 31
  Towards a New Ireland 3, 162, 180
  Wealth tax 38, 118–19
  and Women in politics 157–59
  Young Fine Gael 156–57, 174, 175
  TAOISEACH
  1981 General Election 160–61
  1982 General Election (February) 171–72
  Abortion 165, 166, 168–71, 174, 175, 192
  Anglo-Irish Agreement, 1985 164
  Budget defeat 171, 172, 189
  Constitutional Crusade 1, 2, 3, 5, 162–93
  Divorce 3, 179, 180, 181, 182, 184, 186
  and Tony Gregory 172
  Leadership questioned 179, 187, 191–93
  New Ireland Forum 164
  Resignation 194
  on State finances 187–88
FitzGerald, Joan 149–50, 163
FitzPatrick, Tom 98, 150, 151
Flanagan, Charlie 184
Flanagan, Oliver J 31, 84, 95, 128, 152, 164, 168, 175, 183, 189
Flannery, Frank 154, 155, 196
Fanning, Ronan 8, 65, 66
Flynn, Donal 38, 54, 65, 76, 81, 97
Flynn, Eileen 19
Fox, Billy 132
Foyle, Joseph 42

Gaitskell, Hugh 43
Gallagher, Michael 28–29, 57, 61, 192
Galvin, John 26
Garvin, Tom 9, 12
Gaughan, Michael 133
General Elections
  1918 7
  1943 60, 66
  1948 8, 21, 24, 25, 31, 57, 66
  1951 18, 24, 95
  1954 25, 57
  1957 24
  1961 24–25, 33, 45, 58, 60, 61, 95
  1965 1, 2, 10, 29, 37, 38, 39, 40, 41–42, 51–62, 63, 69, 70, 78, 80, 81, 142, 144
  1969 29, 37, 51, 60, 62, 70, 75, 76, 78–82, 83, 85, 88–89, 95–96, 97
  1973 2, 26, 38, 80, 82, 85, 90–96, 99, 107, 118, 124, 128, 138, 139, 141, 146, 154, 157
  1977 41, 54, 56, 66, 115, 126, 129, 131, 137, 138–47, 150, 151, 153, 154, 157, 158, 159, 160, 161
  1981 119, 154, 158, 160–61, 169, 189
  1982 (February) 171–72
  1982 (November) 158, 189
  1987 104, 158, 194
Girvin, Brian 4, 177
Gogan, Conal 51
Governey, Desmond 128
Government Information Service 113, 121, 133, 140, 154
Great Society 44

Hall, Frank 137
Hall's Pictorial Weekly 126, 137
Halligan, Brendan 28, 29, 64, 84, 90, 96, 136, 139, 142, 146
Handicap 8, 45, 46–47, 51, 70, 99, 105, 106, 107, 178
Harte, Paddy 33, 46, 63, 67, 76, 86
Haughey, Charles 114, 164, 169, 190
  Arms Crisis 89, 157
  Contraception 131
  Corruption 80, 148
  and Efforts to form government without an election 171
  Fine Gael criticism 74, 80
  Gregory Deal 172
  GUBU 173
  Leadership 84, 160
  PR 83
  Pro-Life Amendment 168, 178
  State finances 187–88
  Taoiseach 3, 168, 187

Index   251

Hayes, Michael   36
Healy, John   22, 51, 52, 53, 65, 67, 74, 86
Heavy Gang   136
Herrema, Tiede   133
Higgins, Michael D.   135, 174, 197
Hillery, Patrick   73, 84, 86, 100, 101, 122, 123, 124, 128, 171, 190
Hilliard, Michael   71
Hogan-O'Higgins, Bridget   146
Hogan, Surgeon   55
Housing   59
  Break-ins   13
  Cumann na nGaedheal policies   8
  Declan Costello   17, 19, 39
  Dangerous Housing   17
  Dublin Housing Action Committee   16–17
  Fianna Fail policies   8, 17–18, 56, 142
  National Coalition policies   91, 99, 105, 113, 142
  First-time buyers   12, 54
Hunger strike (*see*: strikes)

ICTU   121, 122, 123, 190
IDA   126
Illegitimacy   159, 165, 180
Industrial Schools   47, 49–50, 51, 178
Infanticide   165
IRA   58, 85, 87, 132, 133, 134, 136, 164
Irish Family Planning Rights Association   125
Irish Medical Association (IMA)   8, 46, 48, 112, 167
Irish Parliamentary Party (IPP)   188
Irish Women United   93–94, 129, 157
Irish Women's Liberation Movement (IWLM)   93–94, 107, 119, 120, 127, 158, 182–83
Irishwomen: chains or change?   94, 119, 182
ITGWU   86, 136, 146

Jenkins, Roy   121
Jennings, Joe   44
John XXIII, Pope   14, 15, 129
Johnson, Lyndon   44
Johnson, Thomas   7
Jones, Jack   139
Juries Service   119–20
Just Society *See*: Declan Costello

Keane, John B.   10
Keating, Justin   98, 139, 142, 146, 151
Keating, Michael   152, 153
Kelly, Frank   126, 137
Kelly, Henry   129
Kelly, John   76, 116, 150
Kennedy, Eileen   51
Kennedy, Finola   179
Kennedy, Geraldine   182, 195
Kennedy, Hugh   180
Kennedy Report (*see* Reformatory and Industrial Schools Systems Report)
Kenny, Enda   179, 196
Kerrigan, Gene   13, 148, 155, 169
Kenny, Mary   127, 157
Kirby, Matthew   195

Labour Party (Britain)   19, 43, 99
Labour Party (Ireland)
  1965 General Election   56, 57
  1973 General Election   90–91 94–96
  1977 General Election   143, 146
  Abortion   168, 169, 174
  Anti-coalition   25, 26, 57–58, 62, 66, 81, 84, 140, 141, 146, 173
  Coalition negotiations, 1973   96, 98
  Coalition re-considered, 1973   88–90
  and Declan Costello   28, 29, 74
  Democratic Programme   7
  Divorce   181
  Education policies   73
  Galway East by-election   39
  Government, 1981–82   161, 171, 172, 189
  Government, 1982–87   3, 190–91
  Government, 2011   196
  Leadership changes   151–52, 173
  National Coalition   2, 18, 38, 80, 99, 109, 110, 113, 117–19, 121–22, 124, 128, 135, 136, 142, 159
  New Ireland Forum   164
  Offences Against the State Act, 1972   85, 86, 87
Larkin, Denis   73
Law Reform Commission   18, 106
League of Decency   130, 221
Leneghan, Joe   21
Lenihan, Brian   23, 60, 85, 128, 171
Lindsay, Patrick   21, 35, 57, 67, 74
Lipper, Mick   141

Local Elections, 1979 159–60
Lynch, Jack 69, 70, 83, 84, 88, 89, 90, 91, 92, 95, 96, 110, 124, 128, 135, 136, 137, 138, 139, 140, 144, 146, 157, 158, 160, 161, 192

MacBride, Seán 98, 202
MacEntee, Seán 45
MacEoin, Seán 58
Macmillan, Harold 9
Macnamara, Angela 108, 177
Macra na Tuaithe 49
Magdalene Laundries 178–79
Maguire, John 76
Manning, Maurice 25, 52, 64, 65, 78, 95, 138
Mansion House 34, 77, 92, 159, 215
Marlborough House 37
Marren, Enda 76, 154, 155
Marriage, changing attitudes towards (*See also*: divorce) 179–80
Marshall Plan 9
Maye, Brian 4
Mater et Magistra 15
McAleese, Martin 179
McAleese, Mary 3
McAuliffe, Tim 73
McCafferty, Nell 97, 183
McCullagh, David 22, 25, 29, 97
McDonald, Charles 95, 96
McDowell, Moore 140, 141
McGahern, John 6, 13, 185
McGee case 127, 166–67
McGilligan, Patrick 30, 32, 33, 35, 58
McGing, Claire 93, 158
McGuinness, Catherine 73
McGuire, Ned 117
McInerney, Michael 65, 84
McKenna, Sean 55, 59
McLoughlin, Joseph 128
McQuaid, John Charles 12, 15
McWey, Michael 37
Marsh, Michael 192
Merrigan, Matt 141
Mills, Michael 26, 86, 138, 141
Mna na hÉireann 125, 130
Monnet, Jean 43
Moran, Michael 89
Mother and Child Scheme 8, 14, 45, 112
Mulcahy, Richard 22, 23, 202

Mullen, Michael 135
Murphy, Gary 168
Murphy, William 25

Nally, Dermot 114
National Centre Party 21
National Farmers Association (NFA) 37, 61, 78
National Federation of Youth Clubs 48, 114
National Observer 23, 25, 26, 28
National Youth Council of Ireland (NYCI) 48, 114
Nealon, Ted 140, 154, 160, 161
National and Economic Social Council (NESC) 12, 106, 110, 111
Nevin, Donal 73
Northern Ireland Constitutional Proposals (White Paper), 1973 91, 131, 132
Norton, William 26

O'Byrnes, Stephen 151
O'Callaghan, Margaret 7
O'Casey, Seán 17
O'Connell, Hugh 3
O'Connell, John 122, 124, 135
O'Connell, Maurice 74, 75, 76, 77, 84
Ó Dálaigh, Cearbhall 136
O'Dea, Maura 108
O'Donnell, Tom 98
O'Donoghue, John 51
O'Donoghue, Martin 137, 142, 143
O'Donovan, John 33
Ó Faoláin, Seán 11
O'Hara, Thomas 60
O'Higgins, Kevin 100, 120, 132
O'Higgins, Michael 25, 29, 30, 63, 64, 66, 81
O'Higgins, Tom 24, 36, 45, 67, 68–69, 70, 71, 76, 77, 84, 86, 87, 88
O'Keeffe, Jim 2, 54, 65, 152, 155
O'Kelly, Seán T. 67, 68
O'Leary, Michael 74, 98, 110, 121, 123, 124, 139, 142, 151, 169, 173
O'Leary, Olivia 195
O'Mahony, Flor 141
O'Malley, Des 83, 85, 86, 112, 130
O'Malley, Donogh 51, 73, 74, 112
O'Malley, Eoin 195

O'Neill, Joe 140
O'Sullivan, Eoin 50
O'Sullivan, John 51
OECD 72, 73, 106, 118, 150, 180, 183
Offences Against the State (Amendment) Act, 1972 83, 85–88
Oil Crisis 98, 99, 110, 111, 151, 157, 187

Pacem in Terris 15
Padbury Advertising 53, 55
Parent Concern 130
Pattison, Seamus 73
Paul VI, Pope 14
Pearse, Pádraig 8
Pius XI, Pope 8, 15, 129
Pluralism 2–3, 15, 67, 68, 71, 79, 80, 130, 131, 152–63, 164, 169, 170, 172, 179, 186, 189, 192
Political marketing 51, 53, 55, 154, 160–61
Prendergast, Peter 68, 153, 154, 160–61
Presidential Election, 1966 67–69
Prime Time 193
Pro-Life Amendment Campaign (*see*: abortion)
Progressive Democrats 59, 195
Proportional Representation (PR) 26, 83, 84

Quadragesimo Anno 8
Quinn, Ruairí 124, 136, 190, 191

Radio 3, 13, 51, 57, 64, 76, 98, 105, 126, 166
Rafter, Kevin 136
Raftery, Mary 50
Raftery, Tom 104
Royal Dublin Society (RDS) 159
Redmond, John 33
Reformatory and Industrial Schools Systems Report 50, 51
Reynolds, Albert 13, 89
Reynolds, David 88
Reynolds, Patrick J. 74
Rice, Rodney 105
Robinson, Mary 88, 129, 130, 135
Roe versus Wade (*see*: abortion)
Rogers, Denise 122
RTÉ 3, 12, 29, 51, 64, 81, 98, 105, 111, 126, 154, 155, 166, 190, 193

Ryan, Annie 47
Ryan, James 8, 16, 58
Ryan, Jim 59
Ryan, Paul 108, 126, 177
Ryan, Richie 30, 38, 84, 19, 98, 99, 106, 107, 108, 109, 110, 113, 115, 117, 118, 120, 121, 123, 124, 137, 139, 140, 141, 142, 145, 150, 151, 152

Saatchi and Saatchi 160
Sanfey, J. W. 81, 140, 154
SDLP 64, 86, 132, 133, 164, 172
Second Vatican Council (*See*: Vatican II)
Shannon electrification scheme 32–33
Sheridan, Joseph 95, 122
Showbands 13
Single mothers (*See*: unmarried mothers)
Single Women's Association 107
Sinn Féin 7, 11, 164, 172, 188
Sinnott, Richard 59
Smith, Paddy 61
Spring, Dan 128, 173
Spring, Dick 173
St Michael's House 46, 101
St Patrick's Institution 50
Strikes 11, 17, 111–12, 123, 133, 136
Studies 2, 6, 10, 11, 162, 166
Sunningdale Agreement 132, 133
Sweeney, Eamonn 193
Sweetman, Gerry 27–28, 54
  Blocked Fine Gael name change 77–78
  Blueshirts 31
  and Liam Cosgrave 63–64, 66, 84
  and Declan Costello compromise 36–37
  Death 80, 90, 154
  First elected 31
  Galway East by-election 39
  and Just Society 23–24, 29, 30, 31–32, 33, 35, 36, 37, 43, 60, 61, 77, 85
  Minister for Finance 9, 11, 31, 56
  National organiser 31, 154
  Presidential Election, 1966 68
  and TK Whitaker 31
Sweetman, Michael 10, 51, 67, 76, 80

Television 1, 13, 14, 15, 23, 28, 29, 51, 71, 91, 107, 125, 126, 127, 135, 139, 147, 164
Thatcher, Margaret 134, 164, 177
The Late Late Show 14
The Riordans 126
Thornley, David 6, 81, 122, 135, 146
Tobin, Fergal 16
Towards a Just Society, 1965 (*See also:* Eight-point plan, *Winning Through to a Just Society*) 7, 38, 44, 78, 80, 142
  Adopted as election manifesto 41, 42
  Agricultural policies 60
  Drafting 2, 28, 38–39, 41, 76
  Economic policies 42–44
  Education policies 72–73
  Expanding the content 70–74
  Fianna Fáil criticism 53, 56
  Fine Gael concerns 24, 58–59
  Health policies 42, 44–48, 107, 112
  Irish language policies 24
  Influences 15, 44–45
  Labour Party criticism 28–29
  Leadership attitudes 37, 40, 52–53
  Publication 38–39, 52–54
  Wealth Tax 38, 118
  Voter impact 41, 54–56, 60–62
  Youth policies 42, 48–51, 105, 114
Treacy, Seán 73
Tuairim 51

Ua Conchubhair, Seaghán 48
Ulster Freedom Fighters 134
Ulster Unionist Party 132
Ulster Workers' Council 133
United Loyalist Council 91
United Ulster Unionist Council 132
Unmarried mothers 93, 94, 107, 108, 109, 125, 165, 177, 179, 180, 183
UVF 87, 88, 133, 136

Varadkar, Leo 192, 193
Vatican II 1, 7, 8, 14, 15
Victorian Values 177
Viney, Michael 51

Ward, Patrick 133
Wealth Tax 38, 116–19, 129
Well Woman Centre 130
Whitaker, T.K. 11, 31
Winning Through to a Just Society (*See also: Towards a Just Society*) 62
  Agricultural Policies 60, 78–79
  Drafting 78
  Education Policies 72–74
  Irish Language Policies 70–72
  Leadership Attitudes 79
Woman's Way 14, 108, 126, 176, 185
Women's Independent Association 120
Wyse, Pearse 114

X Case 19, 173, 196

Printed and bound in the United States of America